Crime and Deviance

Legacies of Social Thought
Series Editor: Charles Lemert

Roads from Past to Future (1997)
by Charles Tilly

The Voice of Anna Julia Cooper (1998), including "A Voice from the South" and other essays, papers, and letters edited by Charles Lemert and Esme Bhan

Crime and Deviance: Essays and Innovations of Edwin M. Lemert (2000) edited by Charles C. Lemert and Michael F. Winter

Crime and Deviance

Essays and Innovations of Edwin M. Lemert

Edited and with Essays by
CHARLES C. LEMERT
and
MICHAEL F. WINTER

ROWMAN & LITTLEFIELD PUBLISHERS, INC.
Lanham • Boulder • New York • Oxford

ROWMAN & LITTLEFIELD PUBLISHERS, INC.

Published in the United States of America
by Rowman & Littlefield Publishers, Inc.
4720 Boston Way, Lanham, Maryland 20706
http://www.rowmanlittlefield.com

12 Hid's Copse Road
Cumnor Hill, Oxford OX2 9JJ, England

British Library Cataloguing in Publication Information Available

Library of Congress Cataloging-in-Publication Data
Lemert, Edwin McCarty, 1912-
Crime and deviance : essays and innovations of Edwin M. Lemert / edited and with essays by Charles C. Lemert and Michael F. Winter.
p. cm.
Includes bibliographical references and index.
ISBN 0-8476-9816-5 (alk. paper) — ISBN 0-8476-9817-3 (pbk. : alk. paper)
1. Crime—Sociological aspects. 2. Deviant behavior. 3. Sociological jurisprudence. 4. Lemert, Edwin McCarty, 1912- I. Lemert, Charles C., 1937- II. Winter, Michael Frederick, 1948- III. Title.

HV6028 .L45 2000
364.3—dc21

00-035295

Printed in the United States of America

∞ ™ The paper used in this publication meets the minimum requirements of American National Standard for Information Sciences—Permanence of Paper for Printed Library Materials, ANSI/NISO Z39.48–1992.

In memory of
Edwin M. Lemert—uncle, friend, pioneer;
And, on his behalf, for his children
James Lemert,
Blaine Lemert,
Sean Elizabeth Lemert,
Deborah Lemert Hudson,
Teri Lemert Moore;

And in memory of
Deirdre Lemert (1945–1999).

Contents

Acknowledgments

Our first and most pressing debt is to Edwin M. Lemert himself, who provided the material here assembled and who taught us much about the history of social problems, the study of social control in American sociology, and much more. This book would not have been possible without his legacy to choose from. It would have been much more difficult without frequent contact with him and many conversations about the development of his thought. We should also acknowledge his kind invitations to participate in seminars and give occasional lectures in his classes, and his willingness to provide opportunities to see how societal reaction theory as he formulated it came of age in his own teaching and research.

Thanks are due to a number of people who expressed interest and encouragement, and who also volunteered information. Among these are Lemert's former students, particularly Sheldon Messinger, who studied with Lemert at UCLA in the late 1940s and early 1950s, and many students from his later years at the University of California, Davis: Karen Joe Laidler, for example, helped sift through some of the papers Lemert had presented at conferences. Thanks are due also to Patrick Jackson, Jean Boettcher, and a number of others for sharing insights at various times.

A number of scholars Lemert knew as colleagues were also helpful: John Clausen, a social psychologist who taught at the University of California, Berkeley, and Henry Pontell and Gilbert Geis, both of the University of California, Irvine. Michael Petrunik of the University of Ottowa, who has written several important articles about Lemert's work, was invariably helpful in understanding the evolution of Lemert's thought. We owe special thanks to one of Lemert's Davis colleagues, Floyd Feeney, professor of law, University of California, Davis Law School. (Feeney served as an assistant director on President Johnson's Commission on Law Enforcement and the Administration of Justice, and was instrumental in securing Lemert's involvement in the Task Force on Juvenile Justice in the mid-1960s). Professor Feeney helped in formulating the criteria for making selections and urged their use in the arrangement of the contents.

We have benefited from much assistance in production. Angela Haren found time in a demanding schedule of classes to perform heroically in preparing the manuscript for submission. We also benefited from timely assistance from Miriam Hull, who clearly has a knack for layout and production. A very generous grant from the Research Committee of the Librarians Association of the University of California, Davis, enabled us to offset expenses of production, for which we are grateful; Nancy Kushigian, the chairman of that committee, was extremely helpful in preparing the request. Clinton Howard, Associate University Librarian for Collections and Technical Services at the University of California, Davis, provided encouragement and essential support from the beginning.

Introduction

Whatever Happened to the Criminal? Edwin Lemert's Societal Reaction

Charles Lemert

The end of the twentieth century was widely thought to have been the beginning of various new world orders. It was, if we allow ourselves to think back in time, one of those strange periods when it was impossible to tell what time it was—whether past or present, perhaps even some weird future. One can only look back in wonder at how people then understood their world and its problems. In those days, some talked about postmodernisms of various kinds. Others, more cautiously, spoke of global transformations. Everyone had some theory or another about what the world was coming to. Strange thing, this human need to account for change.

Strange, especially, because it is clear that some things never change. Crime, for example, and certainly rule breaking do not change, except perhaps in minor degrees of frequency and style. Edwin M. Lemert apparently came to this conclusion. No matter where one looks, evil is always to be found. This at least is an inference to be taken from Lemert's last book, *The Trouble with Evil* (from which chapter 10 here is drawn). If evil, then crime; or, if not crime, then surely some lesser violation of the rules of local life. For myself, I cannot think of a culture that lacks a creation myth or some other central theme that does not turn on punishment or, at least, the threat of dire consequences for social territories wrongly invaded. From Yahweh's expulsion of Adam and Eve to the accidental fate of Gilgamesh's companion, to Prometheus's theft of fire, to the evil spirits of the Mandan and the terrifying Vedic chaos, to the witches of Salem, and on and on—no culture of notable influence has been free of evil and its consequences for those who break the rules. Even where a high concept of crime may be absent, it is difficult to imagine how society might be properly ordered without the moral weight lent by the specific gravity of rule breaking.

If crime and its consequences are among those things that never change, why is it that *explanations* for rule breaking (as distinct from the deviations themselves) change so wildly out of apparent proportion to the fixity of the thing explained? Thus, we look back in wonderment at the muddled thinking of those who lived at the end of the twentieth century. In those days, especially in the 1990s, crime may well have been *the* single most talked about subject in the public sphere. Yet, almost no one then knew exactly what the expert criminologists thought. Public thinking about crime was willy-nilly. This was remarkable because, not so long before then, criminology had been a very public field of expertise. From about 1968, when Richard Nixon (no minor crook himself) seized the law-and-order theme that led to his election to the presidency of the United States, crime became that subject about which everyone just had to have an opinion, even a policy, if possible. In those days, criminologists ranked high among public experts, up the scale near economists. But, by the end of the century, this was no longer true. Perhaps the public was simply worn down by three trying decades of cumulative worry about crime and its cures.

It was as though the criminologists had been swallowed up by a huge bureaucratic whale in whose belly they continued their work, waiting, hoping for the moment when they would be thrown up to pronounce their wisdom. But in and about 1999, just more than thirty years after Nixon inaugurated his law-and-order regime, the public space once occupied by the criminologist was a weedy field. It was impossible to know what good could grow in so choked a terrain. Still, it grew to the point of being, some said, a leading nutrient of the growing economy. This field of uncertain good came to be called "the criminal justice system"—an oxymoron fit only to deepen the mystery of its purposes. No one knew who, exactly, was the client of such a system's justice. Surely, it was not the criminal as grammar would allow. Still, in the name of "criminal justice," jobs in prison construction and administration were plowed back into the American economy, then the driving force of the economic globalization.

Benedict Anderson once argued in *Imagined Communities* (1983) that modern, industrial capitalism began in earnest with the printing of books. If this sounds right, then it might be that postindustrial, global capitalism began with the efficient production of crime and its countermeasures. This point, at least, was the implication of Manuel Castells, whose book *End of the Millennium* (1998) listed the particular enterprises of the global criminal economy: illegal weapons sales, traffic in nuclear waste and materials, smuggling of illegal immigrants, abuse of women and children in the global sex industry, trafficking in body parts, money laundering. Each of these was a profit center for one or more of the many divisions of the global criminal justice operation.

In those days just before 2000, many speculated on the political economy of crime. The numbers surely would have been staggering had it been possible to calculate the true gross global economic product of the capital value of the visible criminal justice economy (prisons, policing, the courts—and their apparatuses) *added to* the black market profits of the global crimes on Castells's list. Even this would not count the incalculable costs of state-sponsored crimes—a prospect charmingly conveyed in Saskia Sassen's *Globalization and Its Discontents* (1998), in which she so delicately proposes the expression "informal economy" to describe the deviations that thrive, in her phrase, "between new developments and old regulations." When worlds change, the old rules are broken in sweatshops, *maquilladoras,* and bond markets—to mention but the more notorious.

Though its reach and forms of expression may change, crime is always with us. Yet, most strikingly, those theories of crime and rule breaking that, at the previous century's end, managed to find their way into the public controversies had about them a very bad smell. On the one hand, so far as innocent third-party watchers of the news were able to determine, whatever expert theories of crime there may have been, few of them succeeded in bracing public thinking.

Against all reasonable warnings, for example, capital punishment was inflicted without any detectable effect on the rate of violent crime. When, however, these rates declined, they did, so far as anyone could tell, according to causes hard to determine. In those days, not even the Europeans, having been puzzled by the idea of capital punishment (and outright disagreeable in regard to the alleged right to bear arms), could explain the fact that *their* crimes ran along much the same course as the American ones. Where there were fewer guns and executions, the violence tended toward political bombings. Still, violence thrived. And, more confusing still, when the rates of violent crime in many American cities began to decline in the 1990s, the rush to easy answers quickened apace. Just as no one could quite explain why, in the era of law and order, criminal activity seemed to grow, no one could explain why it abruptly began to decline. Some said the answer was more cops on the street. But this did not account for the countervailing evidence in places like Columbia and Mexico that had long been targets of massive international police and military wars on criminals trading in drugs. There violence continued without meaningful interruption.

The widespread confusion about crime—its causes and cures—reached its *reductio ad absurdum* in the summer of 1999 when a now (and, for his sake, mercifully) long-forgotten expert broke into the daily news. His proposition was that the decline in violent crimes was a manifest result of legalized abortion. He had a point fit for the flabby tenor of the times. Those with an eye for these things understood immediately that, whatever that expert might have meant, his proposal was well suited to a carceral society in which criminal justice was dispensed with efficient disregard for justifying reason. There had been, to that point, few more perfect expressions of efficient irrationality. Kill the criminals, or prevent their birth, and you kill the crimes. It is all in controlling the numbers.

This adventure back to the present, cast from a perspective somewhere in the past tense of an imaginary intelligent public opinion, tells us no more than two things: (1) that, at the end of the twentieth century, crime was still in evidence, as always, if in oddly fluctuating rates; and (2) that crime had become a subject of acute public irrationality. So much for modernity, in contrast to which the ancients were, if a bit vicious, at least clear about what was a crime and what was not. Long ago, everyone knew what was to be done about rule breaking —especially Oedipus, who, having violated the two most universal social rules, moved without prompting to inflict retribution on himself: blindness added to the limp, and excommunication. This kind of practical criminological certitude among the ancients is one of the uncontestable propositions in Emile Durkheim's theory of premodern crime. It was strict, unforgiving, repressive, but precise and coherent.

What the ancients knew, the moderns had forgotten. Even when there was uncertainty as to crime, everyone from Oedipus to Jeremy Bentham knew who the criminals were and could call them by name as they were expelled by the city gates. But somewhere in the last quarter of the twentieth century, the criminal became an empty object of administration with little or no human content.

What happened to the criminal? Edwin M. Lemert was among those who knew who the criminal was, and knew very well. Though he was not alone in this regard, Lemert was one of the twentieth century's most original and influential writers on crime and social rule breaking precisely because he took the criminal into his account of crime and deviance. And he did so with such a subtle regard for the play of society in the personal experience of the criminal that the very idea of a criminal justice system is shown up for what it is. In a time when public thinking on crime has the odor of vacuous rot, one could hardly do better than to read or reread a writer who developed his ideas at a time when, we now know, the problems that beset those living at the end of the twentieth century were just beginning.

Lemert's first book, *Social Pathology,* appeared in 1951. While popular culture may tidy up the 1950s as a time of affluence and mindless good pleasures, in the United States they were anything but. These were the days of cold war abroad and Red Scare at home. They were, in brief, a moment when at the very height of the American Century the world's leader was caught in the cross fires of its own moral contradictions. In the world, the United States was faced with the peripheral challenge of a Soviet regime whose appetite was always bigger than its stomach. Nonetheless, from the soul of guilt, America chose to respond by demonizing its lesser rival. In a habit of thought that endured down to the last days of the cold war in 1991, the Soviets were "the evil empire." At home, in odd disproportion to the slim evidence of communist influence, those suspected of the least, however adolescent, association with this evil empire were criminalized. In short, the world at large, like the domestic household, was thought to be one undifferentiated mass of deviations from the norms of the American century.

Then, in that collective rapture of shallow thinking, America revealed itself as morally insufficient to its own high values. No wonder that people of the African diaspora, in the United States and abroad, not to mention Africans themselves and others under American colonial reach, chose just then to assert themselves. The world's emperor was preoccupied with the communists, a preoccupation that was, in deeper aspect, a preoccupation with its own complicated lack of self-confidence. America was the World Ruler whose amplitude of economic dominance ought to have assured its confidence. But its nasty record of moral duplicity, most nasty on the record of racial injustice, soon ran up the flag of patriotic excess turned on its own. America thus allowed itself to be drawn into a global struggle that, by the time the twentieth century ended, was revealed for what it truly was—not a cosmic struggle of Manichean proportions so much as a diplomatic dilemma of ultimately economic resolution. By thus exposing its moral loin, the United States left a flank open to the decolonizing new nations and their kin of long remove at home. It was into this moral space that the communists could project themselves, nearly free of charge. The anticommunists lent them all the credence they needed.

Though Lemert considered these questions of his day in a long chapter on radicals and radicalism in *Social Pathology,* which appeared at the height of the Red Scare—and again, later, in scientific code, in "Paranoia and the Dynamics of Exclusion" (chapter 9 here, "You Are Not One of Us: Paranoia and Exclusion")—he refused to present his scientific work in political terms. But this does not mean that his sociology was not forged by the events of his time. What is instructive for us today is how Lemert, from the earliest of his works, kept his eye on two things at once. His most famous idea was that crime and deviance are products of a societal reaction (a phrase that bore the hints of the witch-hunts of that day). He meant to say that when people break rules, they do so as (in his phrase) "dynamic agents" whose autonomy is always hedged by the wider society's mechanisms of social control. Lemert meant precisely to say that when people go wrong and do wrong, they are still human beings, while at the same time they are beings subjected to structural forces beyond their control. The essence of the idea is thus the notion of secondary deviation, by which concept Lemert proposed, more clearly than anyone in that day, that criminal deviation, and other forms of rule breaking, are never simply "behaviors." Criminal careers are fashioned in the time of personal identity. To deviate over time is to assume a self-understanding consistent with the behavior. The criminal, like others who deviate from the rules in numerous ways, does so in dynamic, ongoing intimacy with the structures of social life, an intimacy that gives birth to the criminal—a very real, human being.

Lemert's idea of the criminal as a real, breathing individual was never more compellingly and humanely presented than in his touching empathy for the plight of the systematic check forger (in respect to which one of his three important essays on forgers appears as chapter 8 here). The check forger, much like the alleged communist conspirator, is the odd man out among criminals. He fits none of the profiles of the so-called criminal population. He is usually well educated, of middle-class culture, and when caught and judged, he becomes a model prisoner.

How does Lemert account for this? By a most beautiful display of empirical sensibility. He tells the stories convicted forgers told him—of how they came to think of themselves as artful deviants whose masterful work went unrecognized. People who pass bad paper must work alone, must be on the move, must assume a false name. They do a kind of brilliant work forever sealed, by its very nature, from the applause it merits. They commit crimes, to be sure; but in so doing, they do not cease to be needful, proud human beings. They may stumble into passing bad paper for the same reasons we all do when we float a check on Thursday in expectation of Friday's paycheck. They have needs they cannot cover. But they become "forgers" by the structural conditions of the criminal work itself that press against the specific social and economic limits of their lives. Yet, they also become criminals of a specialized kind in the sense of thinking of themselves in a way consistent with their behavior. But no one cares about those who pass bad paper because no one *can* care. All that is left to the "criminal," the artful passer of false identities, is to relax into the relief of being found out. They do not rejoice in their capture, but they do recognize the personal benefits gained when their good work is at long last discovered. Today, passing bad paper is fast fading from the scene as electronic banking complicates the game, making it less personal and hence less artful in human terms. Still, Lemert's idea applies, with only minor translation, to the plight of those around the world who do what work they can, whether legal or illegal, and do it because that is all that can be done and do it in the dark where no one notices.

Most especially, Lemert's picture of the criminal as a person of ordinary human qualities was entirely suited to the issue that prevailed over the course of his career and into our time. Just the year before, Lemert's *Social Pathology,* the first great book of a new and popular sociology, appeared. It was then that David Riesman gave us the expression "lonely crowd" and taught us to think of ourselves as having lost the original moral pulse of the Puritan fathers—as having become other-directed conformists instead of inner-directed entrepreneurs. Riesman was the first of many to find fame by calling the new men of the 1950s conformists. From that moment on, a whole new vocabulary, from high and low sources, descended on an unsuspecting public still weary of war—the man in the gray flannel suit, the impression manager, the status seeker. These were the men and women who lived in ticky-tacky little boxes with cracks in their picture windows and whose kids suffered identity crises. Everyone, it seemed—from Erik Erikson and Erving Goffman, through Vance Packard, to Bud Schulberg and Arthur Miller—had something to say about the evils of conformism, whether imposed by the fears of witch-hunts or, as Riesman thought, by some terrible interior loss of the old values.

Fifty years after, at century's end, when the original vocabulary of conformism had faded into a misty past along with communists and picture windows, the problem remained, as it does in our time.

It would be a short skip in time from the anxieties of social critics in the 1950s to the contradictory thinking of the 1960s. Those were the days when personal politics became the byword of social protest. Student radicals, feminists, black power advocates, gays, and lesbians cast off the old thinking to affirm their personal presence in the sphere of public life. They meant precisely to judge the social evils by which they were excluded and to invent a new politics of personal (as distinct from private) authority.

Yet, in a contradiction often noted, at the same time there arose, first in France, then in the United States and Europe at large, a new kind of thinking that dismissed the ideals of bourgeois subjecthood. Preoccupation with the refinements of the subject, the thinking went, deepens ignorance of the evil structures of the modern world. The American new social movements and the French structuralisms seemed to have been at complete odds with each other. But, it turned out, both claimed to be radical social critics. They were, in fact, joined in subterranean alliances, most notably in the influential ideas of C. Wright Mills, who taught that without an imaginative grasp of the power of structures, the individual was left to blame him- or herself.

Edwin Lemert expressed little sympathy for these new movements—anything but. Still, and remarkably so, he appreciated the point Mills made. The human subject, whether criminal or not, was always, necessarily situated between the limiting conditions of (in his words) his or her own well-structured personality and the cultural clashes than came down from the controlling social structures. What distinguished Lemert's thinking in the 1960s and 1970s was just how steadfast he remained to his own vision of the precarious balance of social forces in the experience of the individual. Lemert could not have joined the social movements of those days. But, just as firmly, he withheld enthusiasm for the sociological orthodoxy that arose from a terrible misreading of thinkers like Mills or of the events of the day. To my knowledge, Lemert never commented on the sociological infatuation with the now notorious agency–structure dichotomy. Somehow the idea of analyzing in abstract terms the individual as "merely an agent" or of collapsing the complex play of the controlling forces as "merely structures" was, to him, both unnecessary and a bit tasteless. Just the same, he took a stand on this issue, though in his own way, in "Beyond Mead," his presidential address to the Society for the Study of Social Problems in 1973 (chapter 3 here, "The Paradigm Reaches Its Limits"). When he saw that the sociology of deviance he had helped found was slipping into a kind of local social psychology, he called it back to the importance of structural forces.

That Lemert did not choose to engage the more popular dialogues of those years does not mean that he had nothing to contribute to the situation as it developed late in the twentieth century and early in the twenty-first. Without judging the merits of those controversies or taking a stand on the situation as it lay when the centuries turned, one can observe that the problem of the last half of the twentieth century persists. Somehow in the movement of thought and the latter-day enthusiasms for theories of change, it came to be that the delicate balance between the breathing individual and the varieties of social force was lost. This was no more the fault of the structuralists (who by the end of the century came to be thought of as postmodernists) than it was of the feminisms and other new social movements that engaged the doctrine of personal politics (and thereby came to stand in the right corners of the public eye as the cause of all social degradations). Nor are the social theorists, with their silly preoccupation with micro/macro game, to blame. They were just outside the game and, in any case, they made very much more sense than the desperate nonsense of the rational-choice theorists who, by making the individual's rationality the sum and substance of social action, dreamed of a return of an early nineteenth-century golden age.

Without pressing the point further, it is right to say that, when the new century came into its own, the world was left with the remnants of a problem that was first identified in the 1950s. The answer to questions of the individual's loss of inner purpose, of the decline into social conformism, is not, obviously, an overblown structuralism anymore than it is nostalgic individualism.

Edwin Lemert was not the only one to have recognized in the first instance that the answer somehow lay with a delicate respect for both—a respect in the form of a refusal to overplay the analytic hand in order to guard the social scientist's ultimate hole card: intellectual judgment derived from empirical description. It was precisely his high literary sensibility and his nose-to-the-ground sociology that allowed Lemert to set forth, in his relative youth, the principles of his sociology of deviance. Most particularly, Lemert was never astonished by deviant social behavior. In this, he enjoyed a kind of unacknowledged alliance with the new social movements he could not join. He was never surprised by the behavior of those effectively disapproved of because he, having been disapproved of in his youth, understood very well that individuals are individuals because they all live on that ground where unexpected remarks bear the heavy structuring weight of social events. If so, the criminal and the deviant were, at worse, prodigals to the normal of allegedly clean record.

Nor was Lemert the only one to have understood that the problem of the criminal was also the problem of all men and women. If he was less concerned with social criticism, he was more concerned to account for the human aspect of the lives of men and women who lived in the far deviant places. Check forgers and stutterers, alcoholics among the Northwest Indians and in the Pacific islands, prostitutes and radicals, the mentally ill and the blind—these who suffered various pathologies of a social origin were, in his view of their plight, not different in kind from all the rest. This he understood very well because he understood his own reactions to the societal effects of his family life, effects that, for better or worse, I too understand exceptionally well.

Before Edwin M. Lemert became the notable California sociologist, he was a prodigal son of the Ohio Lemerts. He was my father's brother, notorious in the clan as the one who was always away in strange places. I grew up hearing stories of his exploits—as a boxer in college, as an exile of some sort or another in Mexico, as a relation with a vague sort of fame I was too young to understand, of wild adventures (or so the stories went) in the Pacific islands and Alaska, of his asparagus farm in Michigan (which I once visited when I was just four and remember well), and of boat building (which the children of his second marriage remember for a summer's adventure amid the islands and native grounds of the Northwest).

Those who read this book through, thereby joining those already and long familiar with Lemert's work, will not be surprised to learn that he was both an adventurer and a prodigal of sorts. As a child, I knew him first by the family stories that were secondarily confirmed on any occasional, usually unannounced visit. From within the circle of stay-at-home Lemerts, Edwin was thought to be enchantingly odd. By more objective standards, his prodigality was an effect of the family reaction—though one, true to the theory of his adult life, he seemed to enjoy.

Whenever Uncle Ed blew into town, everything stopped. The fatted lamb was slaughtered, and a prim, southwestern Ohio version of a feast was called. This greatly annoyed my father, the "good" son to the one who flew the coop. While Ed boated amid the Northwest Pacific islands and lived among the island peoples of the far Pacific, my father stayed home. Their father, as Michael Winter reports in his excellent essay at the end of this book, wanted one to be the doctor, the other the lawyer. My father obeyed strictly. Ed obeyed obliquely by becoming one of his field's most original experts on what he describes, in the four last (previously unpublished) essays of the book, as "the school that never was: sociological jurisprudence."

Within the unsettled bosom of the family, my father attended local schools and colleges to become a working doctor to the working-class folk in the Fairmont flats of Cincinnati. He and his patients maintained a most delicate social contract. He cared for them (as often as not in their homes or shops). They quite simply called him "the doctor" and paid their bills when they could. Such were the social rewards granted those who stayed put. Uncle Ed clearly wanted none of this. Thus it was that this appreciably more deviant son of conservative midwestern people, schooled like his brother in the tried and true doctrines of Ohio's public schools and universities, became a California man for life.

Little of what Ed was or did made coherent sense to his brother and their parents—and "California" was as good a name for it as any my family could imagine. We Ohio Lemerts were not in those days readers. *Social Pathology* stood upright amid various Book of the Month Club selections in the same reproduction breakfront that stands today in the home of my brother (he, too, a doctor). It was, we realized, a sign of significant accomplishment that somehow all the adventures issued in a thick book without pictures of any kind. So far as I know, no one even tried to read the thing.

It was only much, much later in life when, by some mystery of avuncular effect, I began to read sociology, which led me soon enough to that big book. From it, I learned that its author was, indeed, a founder of one of the century's most sensibly liberal, and humane, theories of crime. This was one of the many reasons Edwin Lemert was so well regarded as to have served in 1967 on President Lyndon Johnson's presidential commission on Law Enforcement and the Administration of Justice. I recall the astonishment this service inspired even among the conservative Ohio Lemerts. Edwin had made no bones about his vote for Senator Barry Goldwater in 1964. He was a man who could very well keep his scientific attitudes in a different moral compartment from his private political sympathies.

Years later, after I had become a sociologist myself, I happily fell into the habit of driving to Davis to visit my uncle whenever some meeting brought me to California. Then I began to patch together the complicated nature of this man of embracing human compassion in his writing and trickster conservatism in private opinion. The former inspired a worldwide readership of sociologists who, to this day, write to tell me of some memorable meeting they had with my uncle years ago in Scotland or Italy or Hawaii. The latter, by contrast, drove colleagues in the department he founded in Davis to such distraction that eventually they voted to exclude him (late in his retirement) from participation in its meetings. He took both kinds of gesture in equal measure.

Political differences between us were considerable—so much so that, on one occasion, I embarrassed myself. I had driven up to Davis one night during a seminar at Berkeley. Upon returning to the next day's meetings of the group, comprising many of sociology's most distinguished feminists, I felt the contradiction of the two settings, which I explained to one among the group who knew both Ed and me, "Well, we don't agree on anything much, but we are drawn together at least by both having been beaten up by the same guy [my father, his brother]." The latter remark on the bond between us was true enough but spoiled my affirmation of the bond itself. Whoever heard me say this gently excused my apology for the visit, saying, "Look, he's family. That's enough reason." I needed the comfort to cover the rebuke I deserved.

Still, in that one moment, I believe I may have experienced the contradictions that both plagued and enriched Edwin Lemert's life. Perhaps his private political remarks were a kind of secondary embellishment on the primary theme of his life's work—his own way of remaining a dynamic agent in a field to which he had delivered so strong a liberal statement over many years. He was, as anyone who has read his work knows, a most humane scholar. But, as I say, outside the writing he did like to drive some people (and not just his father and my father) a little bit nuts. When he died, one of his children found among his papers a few pages of composition under the title "White Like Me." How could a man who was welcome without invitation in any number of Native American communities up and down the Pacific Northwest (and who would visit until the very last years) have such thoughts as must have been behind the title? Whatever it may have been, it was probably also a bit of the literary and personal flare that found its way into the life of the Ohio prodigal who liked to cut against the grain. Lemert could hardly be blamed for reacting over his life to the expectations held up for him by his conservative parents and his bitter, stay-at-home brother. From the point of view of the individual, the societal reaction has the effect of a sustained career of many individual reactions to, as he put it, the "*effective* disapproval" of those whose approval mattered. His reaction, like most human reactions to disapproval, was not pathological. But the habit of going against the grain of those near at hand is a comparable, if lesser, social effect of the societal reaction.

In this respect, Edwin Lemert set himself against the prevailing sentiments even in his scientific work. Lemert's very first publication in 1948, "Some Aspects of a General Theory of Sociopathic Behavior" (chapter 1 in this book, "From Social Pathology to Deviance"), began in the spirit that infused his writings over the years until his last publication, weeks after his death in 1996. Ed always came to bat square on the grain of scientific sociology. Hence among the first published words of his career: "The most important requirements of any social theory are that it delimit the field of study and detail the process of effective causation." Pretty straightforward stuff. But then he continued, in much the same elevated style, to undercut this sober protocol. "It occurred to the writer that the delimitation of the field by social pathologists might be studied in something like operational terms." He meant to introduce his scientific theory of sociopathy by, as he put it in feigned innocence, briefly reviewing statistical estimates of probable members of the then-accepted categories of sociopathic behavior as they appeared in the standard textbooks in the field. His conclusion? Not less than ten out of twelve Americans (83 percent) were sociopaths! Remember this was 1951.

His idea, we now know in retrospect, was that sociopathic behavior was in effect a nearly normal occurrence in the best of societies. Thereafter, without so much as a wink, Lemert proceeded to that first essay that led to *Social Pathology* three years later, which led in turn over four decades of work to his important contributions to a modern understanding of crime and social deviation. Perhaps we Ohio Lemerts, with all our native cautions, were not entirely wrong about our prodigal. It is possible, at least in the 1950s, when Edwin was formulating his most enduring ideas, that what he came to accomplish could only have begun in California. Back in Ohio we were worrying about the communists, which is different from worrying about those who worried about the communists. The balance was, perhaps, tipped toward the latter, more enlightened attitude in California. And even if it was not in those days, California, the home of the uprooted (even more then than today), was a more hospitable land in which to plant the idea that deviant behavior is as American as apple pie.

No one today should underestimate the extent to which Lemert invented his societal reaction theory of social deviance virtually *ex nihilo*. As he reflects in a previously unpublished essay, "How We Got Where We Are" (chapter 6), in his first years at UCLA when the department had a scant three sociologists, there were no adequate texts for public instruction on crime and deviance. He had to write his own—*Social Pathology: Systematic Approaches to the Study of Sociopathic Behavior* (1951) (of which important passages are found in chapter 2). True to the principles he enunciated in the shorter essay three years earlier, Lemert began by delimiting the field and establishing the seven principles of "effective causation." Those principles are worth listing in full to reveal the subtlety of his own social theory, which produced so many, varied empirical effects. He called them postulates. I quote, with minor editing:

1. There are modalities in human behavior . . . which can be identified and described for situations specified in time and space.
2. Behavioral deviations are a function of cultural conflict which is expressed through social organization.
3. There are societal reactions to deviations ranging from strong approval through indifference to strong disapproval.
4. Sociopathic behavior is deviation which is *effectively* disapproved.
5. The deviant person is one whose role, status, function, and self-definition are importantly shaped by how much deviation he engages in, by the degree of its social visibility, by the *particular* exposure he has to the societal reaction, and by the nature and strength of the societal reaction.
6. There are patterns of restriction and freedom in the social participation of deviants which are related directly to their status, role, and self-definitions. . . . .
7. Deviants are individuated with respect to their vulnerability to the societal reaction because: (a) the person is a dynamic agent, (b) there is a structuring to each personality which acts as a set of limits within which the societal reaction operates.

Lemert wrote out these postulates when he was just beginning. He was at the time barely thirty years old and not yet in a secure position in his university or his field. Yet, already it is plain that he was a man of considered judgment. One reads these principles with a sense of being in the presence of an author who says what he means.

But, beyond the writing—and Lemert was a most literary man—it is the ideas themselves. For here, in these postulates, lie the elements that made his ideas on crime and social deviance unusual in his time and still in ours.

Perhaps in those days more than now, a man with ideas that could change modern thinking about crime and deviance could only do so in a place like California. But Ed's California was not really that of Los Angeles, where he got his start. Over the long haul, it was the California of the great, northern agricultural valley settled on the plain watered, in good times, by Mount Shasta. His California was not the cool of Berkeley, or the movie-set pretty of Mendicino, or the mountain-fresh of the Sierras. It was the hot, low farming valleys all around Sacramento. Unlike many in his department over the years who commuted from Berkeley, Ed would not even settle for the lesser but evident cosmopolitan virtues of Davis. He chose instead to live in Winters, a small farming community some fifteen miles west. There he lived on and worked a ranch of some fifty acres. As he had grown asparagus in Kalamazoo, in the longer northern California years, Ed worked the land, kept some cattle, and lived as a rancher, without air conditioning. He moved to town (Winters still) when he was approaching eighty years of age. There he took his meals with other regulars at the Buckhorn Café. I always supposed that he removed himself to town only partly because the ranch had become too much. The other reason was that as the years slowed him down, he wanted to conserve energy for the daily trips to his office at the university in Davis. There he worked on various projects, including one last book, *The Trouble with Evil,* which appeared just months after his death in his eighty-fourth year.

Evil was Ed's game. He meant to explain it—not as a philosopher would, but as a hard-bitten old rancher would. When he presented his scientific work in public, he often wore boots and always wore a bolo tie. He wanted people to know that his science had roots in the ground. Thus, Edwin Lemert had little patience for theory, and even the last book, a kind of extended review of the research, was empirical in the sense that everything he said, and all that he wrote, was fashioned out of the years upon years of fieldwork—in prisons, on reservations, in the courts, where he listened to forgers, alcoholics, delinquent children, all others effectively called deviant.

He could thus listen, as few others could, because he understood the lives of these people from within the heart of his own experience. This, too, may have set him off from others in the tradition of social thinking he helped found. The first six chapters of this book are Lemert's own statement of his sociological principles, from the first essay in 1948, through the reassessment in the 1970s, to the two previously unpublished essays. This very compact survey of his thought in relation to the work of others reveals, still again, Edwin's way of tipping his head to the other side of things. Those who remember him will recall that, especially in the later years, Ed had a way of standing at a slight angle, his head perched to the side, his eyes set just above the immediate horizon. Though he did have back pain, which may have exaggerated this stance, he had no trouble with ears or eyes. That posture captured the two basic rules of his life and work. He was ever perched ready to look into whatever was about to occur before him, but he wanted always to see the event from some odd angle of his own making.

Thus, though Edwin Lemert was a founder of a school of criminology that today still ranks among the most influential, he tended to keep his distance from others in the field. As the essays of the first part of this book make clear, he allowed for the affinities between his thought and the more popular line called "labeling theory," but he was insistent about the differences. As time went on, he worried about the ways labeling theory could lapse into a meditation on all too local events without proper regard for the structures.

At the same time, in these same essays, it is easy to see how, though he appreciated the more structural vantage point of Robert Merton's ideas, Lemert went along only so far because of Merton's lack of attention to the dynamic individual. If there was a sociologist among his peers to whom he was closest, it was surely Erving Goffman, whose early writings are filled with references to Lemert. The two were friends, at least as much as two such different cowboys could have friends. They shared a complex sense of the social and personal moves at stake in the deviant career. And both, of course, believed that so-called deviance was a practice of the universal rules of social life, rules that ultimately refused to respect any categorical difference between the deviant and the normal. Yet, these broad affinities being given, Lemert would not go so far as Goffman did in limiting the practical contributions of the individual to his or her own sense of self.

Of all the essays here collected, the one that has always pleased me the most is

"Beyond Mead: The Societal Reaction to Deviance" (1974; chapter 3, "The Paradigm Reaches Its Limits," here). I like it for many reasons, not the least of which is its gemlike summaries of the ideas of those in relation to whom he situated himself—Merton, Goffman, Mead, Durkheim, the ethnomethodologists, the then-new British school of criminology, and (as always) his college teacher, W. F. Cottrell. At every turn, in the most compact language imaginable, Lemert treats these others with gentle respect in order to isolate the deficiency he wants to correct.

He felt then, and rightly so, that thinking in the sociology of deviance needed to go beyond Mead to a more robust structural attitude and do so without giving up the dynamic individual Mead and others had done so much to define. But Lemert pursued his idea, again, very much on the ground of evidence. Here, as elsewhere, the evidence is offered in the form of a story. In this case, it is the story of the California Youth Authority and the Department of Corrections. The issue at hand was the treatment of youthful offenders, in respect to which Lemert had definite ideas.

In his important report to the 1967 presidential commission, "Juvenile Court: Quests and Realities" (chapter 12, "Dilemmas of Intervention," here), Lemert took a strong stand against the administrative court. He referred to Roscoe Pound's classic essay "The Limits of Effective Legal Action" (1916) to support his own idea of "judicious nonintervention." Again, Lemert's deep respect of the individual was clear; and again, he had no dogmatic attitude. The expression meant not that there were no cases in which the courts must interfere with families but that they should do so cautiously. Judges must always be judicious, especially when a child is before them. Here, and again in "Why Children Should Be Kept Out of Court" (chapter 14), Lemert took his principled stand against overly aggressive administrative justice. These were an early warning that the carceral society refused to heed in its rush toward a "criminal justice system," shorn of real individuals, without even children.

Lemert's practical philosophy of the treatment of youthful offenders was clearly dear to his heart, for it was the example chosen to illustrate his warnings to colleagues in the field. Thus, the long ending sections of "Beyond Mead" tell the story of the figure he came to refer to, in later writings, as the "cow counties judge."

The setting for the story was a 1961 hearing before the California State Senate's Judiciary Committee, which was considering legislative changes recommended by a powerful commission of experts who sought, in effect, to overthrow the practice of judicious noninterference in the juvenile courts. The proposal was a step away from the family toward state administration. Members of the senate were wary of the proposal but unsure of the course to take. The commissioners seemed to have the upper hand. Then, at the crucial moment a single upstate judge came forth to testify.

A somewhat quaint, anachronistic figure in a black suit and a furled umbrella, he told in fine detail how he ran what was in effect an inquisitorial system of juvenile justice, ordering arrested youths into detention until by confessing their misdeeds they showed the remorse he considered necessary for their rehabilitation. The impact on a committee composed entirely of lawyers, former district attorneys, and a former judge was like that of a bomb in an echo chamber.

The law was changed but later modified. The story may seem to contradict Lemert's attitude of judicious noninterference, except for one thing. The cow counties judge was a real individual who brought home the truth and consequences of the administrative approach in vivid, human terms. Though stern, the cow counties judge was nonetheless a human presence in the lives of those children from whom he sought not blind punishment but remorse and a change of life.

But the story as told in Lemert's 1973 presidential address was meant, curiously, to make another point—one on the importance of structures. We who have read a lot of structuralism, as it is now called, might find this odd. But Lemert had the idea right. Structures are social forces and never abstractions. They always come down to real interactions. The consequences of an action affected by structural change—as the 1961 law was—are never clear to the naked eye. They explode before us only when we see them through the testimony of individuals—whether children or parents or the cow judges who determine the limits of their dynamic independence.

Structures are never simple. They always take on the concrete detail of "situations specified in time and space." That this is so is seen in the simple act of comparing the structures at work in the stories Lemert told—the effects of drinking on the potlatch status rituals of the Northwest Indians (chapter 7 here), the dilemmas of the check forger, the administrative cautions of the juvenile judge, among so many others. In each and every instance, Lemert goes beyond the local to the varieties of social control, in order to come back to the individual. He or she who would be judged deviant is a person like all others. What distinguishes such a person from the rest is a particular exposure to an effective disapproval. The cow judge is such a wonderful figure for Lemert's idea because he is so utterly unsentimental. He was quaint, anachronistic, inquisitorial. But he stood before the child, imposing disapproval with the full expectation of remorse and redemption.

In a day after the beginning of a new century, when crime is still with us but the criminal is lost in a bureaucratic system, Edwin Lemert offers a still useful vision. The cowboy sociologist who admired the cow counties judge teaches us still that the system we inhabit, whether normal or not, is directed in large measure by powerful enforcers; but it is also the habitat of real people, whether criminal or not.

Part I

Formation and Evolution of Societal Reaction Theory

Chapter 1

From Social Pathology to Deviance

This is neither the time nor the place to undertake a comprehensive survey of all the theories of sociopathic behavior in the light of their philosophical or logical integrity. Let it suffice to say that the most important requirements of any social theory are that it delimit the field of study and detail the process of effective causation. It occurred to the writer that the delimitation of the field by social pathologists might be studied in something like operational terms by ascertaining what subject matter is actually discussed as pathological phenomena in substantive chapters of textbooks and treatises on the subject. One simple way of doing this was to compute the total number of pathological persons in our society at some given year on the basis of estimates of various pathological populations supplied in general textbooks and special treatments on social pathology.

The procedure which was ultimately settled upon was to select ten of the most widely adopted textbooks in the field of social maladjustments, as determined by university and college class adoption figures, furnished by courtesy of the publishers of the books. From these a list of categories of social pathology was prepared in which the "problem" was measured by population estimates. For a few of the categories it was necessary to supplement the textbook estimates from other, usually monographic, sources. One or two estimates had to be made by the writer. Because the estimates were given for different years, the base was taken as of 1935, tedious interpolations which would be necessary to achieve a high degree of accuracy not being undertaken. The final total estimate was thus unavoidably crude. Altogether, there were thirty-three categories of social pathology which were sufficiently well defined to occur in two or more of the textbooks and which were conceived as discrete populations. Even from such a cursory canvass, it was apparent that the number of categories of pathology to be found is a function of

---

"Some Aspects of a General Theory of Sociopathic Behavior." *Proceedings of the Pacific Sociological Society*. Research Studies, State College of Washington, 16, 1 (1948): 23–9. Reprinted as originally published.

the diligence of the person doing the searching, and that, without much additional effort, the total categories could easily have been increased to forty or even fifty.

The grand total of all the estimates of populations in the sociopathic categories amounted to 104,020,324 out of a population of 127,250,232 in 1935. This means that approximately ten persons out of every twelve or thirteen were counted as sociopathic deviants during the period covered by the estimates. Though it might be said that some of the inclusions were not justified and that some estimates of the numbers of sociopathic persons in the population were exaggerated, exactly the opposite might be shown. For example, the estimates for several chronic diseases were omitted; there were no figures for ex-convicts, for persons on probation, for criminals in jails, and for dependent children in institutions and foster homes. If the lead of some writers had been followed and such groups as white-collar criminals, the obese and the ugly, pathological eaters, and those who engage in nonmarital sex relations had been included, it is plain that the number of pathological persons would not only have been equal to, but would have surpassed by many millions the actual numbers in our population in 1935.

There are, of course, certain explanations which immediately suggest that this fantastically large number of pathological persons in the population is more nominal than real. Obviously, there is overlapping in the figures, so that some persons were being counted twice, thrice, or many times. Yet, even if allowance is made for overlapping, by reducing the total to, say, sixty million or even forty million, a situation still exists wherein one person out of every three or four must be regarded as sociopathic. Instead of looking upon these statistical data as a dismal commentary upon the true state of the American population, however, one should regard them as the awkward and embarrassing consequences of the failure of social pathologists to delimit their field and to contrive meaningful and sociologically descriptive categories of pathology. They clearly point to the absence of any usable distinction between normal and abnormal human behavior, to the confusion of sociological with biological fields and other fields, and to an unconcern with the problem of priority and mutual exclusiveness in classifications where pathologies overlap in the same persons and groups.

In deviant behavior not complicated by biological disease or defect, it is questionable whether significant aspects of behavior have been employed as a basis for delimiting and classifying pathological social phenomena. This is especially true of such deviants as criminals, juvenile delinquents, prostitutes, gamblers, homosexuals, and migratory persons. Despite the theoretical pretense which some writers in this field have made of distinguishing social disorganization and personal disorganization, it is seldom clear whether they have in mind pathological behavior, pathological situations, or pathological persons in their discussions.

We may pertinently ask at this juncture whether the time has not come to break abruptly with the traditions of older social pathologists and abandon once and for all the archaic and medicinal idea that human beings can be divided into normal and pathological, or, at least, if such a division must be made, to divest the term "pathological" of its moralistic, unscientific overtones. As a step in this direction, the writer suggests that the concepts of social differentiation and individuation be rescued from the limbo of the older textbooks on sociology, dusted off and given scientific airing, perhaps being supplemented and given statistical meaning with the perfectly usable concept of deviation. There seems to be no cogent reason why the bulk of the data discussed in textbooks and courses on social pathology cannot be treated as a special phase of social and cultural differentiation and individuation and thus conveniently integrated with general sociological theory as taught in courses in introductory sociology.

Because some method must be found to distinguish that portion of differentiation which can be designated appropriately as falling within the field of social pathology, the second necessary postulate is that there is a space-time limited societal awareness and reaction to deviation, ranging from strong approval through indifference to strong disapproval. Thus, by further definition, sociopathic phenomena simply become differentiated behavior which, at a given time and in a given place, is socially disapproved, though the same behavior may be socially approved at other times and at other places, and for our society as a whole there may be no consensus as to whether the behavior is desirable or undesirable. One writer has already shown how specific definitions may be worked out in this way through the use of a "tolerance quotient."[1]

In order to exploit the concept of differentiation profitably, some way of conceiving it in sociocultural and personal contexts is necessary, inasmuch as the segments of deviant behavior in persons and groups cannot be treated alone. For example, it is clear even to the sociologically uninitiated that morphine addiction in a physically well person has a meaning quite apart from morphine addiction in a terminal cancer patient, both with respect to the societal reaction and the individual symbolic reaction. This suggests that many of the things taken as "value conflicts" in our culture in reality are space, time, and function qualifications of social norms, which are often necessary phases of societal integration. Furthermore, it guards us against being unduly exercised about culture conflicts or value conflicts which are not effectively expressed in social organization. As Linton[2] has shown, most value conflicts go in one synapse and out the other when they do not affect role and status of persons and groups.

Some socially disapproved differentiation of the behavioral sort is almost purely symptomatic and expressive of deep-lying, intra-psychic conflicts in individuals. The differentiae in these cases are polymorphous, capricious, and related to social and cultural factors in such complex symbolic ways as to defy cross-sectional analysis, at least at this stage of our development in sociology. In other instances sociopathic behavior as we have defined it seems to be largely a manifestation of social situations, by which we mean that pressures or stimuli external to the person are relatively more dynamic factors than internal ones, with the result that space and time become important factors. The great bulk of situational sociopathic behavior, if the concept is permissible, probably springs from situations involving culture conflict. Sociologists are far better equipped to analyze situational behavior, particularly as culture conflicts, than they are to make sense out of psychotic and neurotic behavior.

Situational analysis falls short in accounting for the recurrence of sociopathic behavior outside the situation of which it is a function and its integrated expression and persistence in the behavior of some persons. For this reason it is necessary to postulate a third general class of behavior, namely, systematic role- and status-oriented deviation, or professional pathological behavior. This leads directly into analysis of behavior systems in ways comparable to that which has been done for some occupations and rather adequately for some types of crime. It is here, in the analysis of systematic pathological behavior, that the conventional sociological concepts in their present form can be employed to their fullest advantage.

However, both situational analysis and behavior system analysis, as now conceived, leave unanswered the perplexing question of the genesis of the differential reactions made by people to the same social and cultural stimuli. Consequently, many theories, even though they take cognizance of the situation and the factors associated with behavior systems, shed little light upon the details of the process of effective causation in social pathology. They fail especially to account for the growth or elaboration of symptomatic or situational deviation into systematic deviation. This has not been due to any lack of preoccupation with the problem on the part of sociologists. Generally, the concept of organic process and interaction, as first set forth by Cooley in connection with social and personal disorganization, remains the foundation for thinking upon this subject. Unfortunately, analysis still rests pretty much at the level of reiteration and large generalization where Cooley put it down. There has been a poverty of subsidiary hypotheses derived from the "concept" and an almost complete absence of implementation of the idea in textbooks where it has been used as a frame of reference. Beyond the unsalutary effects of Cooley's philosophical predilections and stylistic idiosyncrasies, there has been a tendency of some of his followers to invoke the concept of interaction as a reified explanatory term, like instincts. For instance, Brown goes so far as to say, "Everything plays its role and gets its meaning in interaction, hence interaction becomes a chief concept in every explanation."[3] The position obviously is untenable in that it involves a contradiction of terms, quaintly enough, interactional determinism.

As a matter of fact, interaction is not a theory or explanation at all. It does little more than set down a condition of inquiry, telling us that dynamic analysis must supplement structural analysis, and is best understood as a necessary reaction to the reified metaphysical explanations of human behavior current among nineteenth-century writers. Further reason for rejecting interaction as a theory *per se* is that it results in a directionless inquiry ending in a morass of dog-in-the-mangerish variables, none of which have priority or provide a formula for prediction.

If the concept of process or interaction is to be at all usable, it must take form so that empirical referents for the concept can be found. It has to be translated into natural histories or life cycles or "limited possibilities" or, as in chemistry, "functions of complex variables." Such concepts will have to be transmuted into sociological as opposed to philosophical, biological, or other levels of conceptualization. In general terms this has already been done with more than casual success in Mead's systematic analysis of the symbolic process, undertaken empirically through the study of language as behavior. Furthermore, a number of writers and teachers of introductory sociology carefully devote space and time to discussions of the self as it develops out of reflective language behavior. Yet, with the possible exception of L. G. Brown, none of the social pathologists have systematically applied the concepts of self, role, status, and social participation to processual analysis of pathologically deviant behavior.

The solution to the problem of differential reactions of individuals in relation to their sociopathic conduct patently lies in the study of the symbolic process. The developmental sequence in the symbolic process can be separated into at least two sharply polarized or even categorical phases on the basis of differential symbolic reactions made to the same deviant behavior. These may be termed *primary deviation* and *secondary deviation.* Primary deviation can arise from a wide variety of "causes" and its value lies in the fact that it permits subsuming the wide and seemingly contradictory varieties of special theories of given sociopathic behavior under a more general class without the burdensome necessity of disproving or replacing these theories. Each theory may be a valid explanation for a certain family of cases when the primary deviation is the focus of interest. Thus, it can be freely admitted that persons come to drink alcoholic liquors excessively for many different reasons: death of loved ones, exposure to death in battle, the strain of business competition, family role ambivalence, inferiority feelings, nipple fixation, and many others. The symbolic concomitants which commonly distinguish deviation in its primary phase are the definitions of the behavior as adjuncts or accessories of socially acceptable roles. Such behavior may be troublesome to the individual and make heavy demands upon his capacities for self-acceptance and -enhancement, but the important point remains that the definitions do not produce symbolic reorganization at the level of general role conception. Pathological and normal behavior remain as strange, if somewhat tensional, bedfellows in the same person.

Secondary deviation may be said to exist when the person begins to employ his deviant behavior or a role based upon it *as a means of defense, attack, or adjustment to the overt and covert problems created by the societal reaction to it.* In effect, the original causes of the deviation recede in importance or give way to the central importance of the disapproval and isolating reactions of the community. A person who began to drink heavily because of anxieties over his professional competence now drinks heavily because of the failures due to his drinking and corresponding sense of guilt and introjected self-definitions.

There are a number of more or less substantiated special theories of pathology which collectively point to the operation of symbolic factors in producing the shift from primary to secondary deviation as they have been described here. Lindesmith's[4] theory, when pruned of its rationalistic preconceptions, says in essence for opiate addiction what has been said in general here. Blumel's[5] and Van Riper's[6] distinction between primary and secondary symptoms of stuttering, Bacon's[7] processual analysis of alcoholism, Clinard's[8] and Porterfield's[9] stress upon role conception as the dynamic factor in delinquency, Slavson's[10] theory of childhood maladjustment in relation to parental rejection, Bain's[11] concept of vicious circles and vicious cycles in compulsive neurotic behavior, to some extent Adamczyk's[12] distinction between individuated behavior as opposed to spontaneous group behavior, Kingsley Davis'[13] analysis of the sociology of prostitution, and Dai's[14] along with Boisen's[15] conception of a symbolic determinant in mental disease—all more or less conceptualize for specific pathologies the process postulated as generally operating in the transition from primary to secondary deviation.

In order to avoid the fallacy of reductionism, and in order to keep analysis at a sociological as well as a sociopsychological level, it will be necessary to relate the symbolic process to an objectively described societal reaction. This involves a study of social situations and society's control and welfare agencies from the standpoint of their average symbolic impact, their self-defining, invidious, and discriminating effects upon the deviant person. Obviously, this area of sociological research is almost completely untouched, although its importance is becoming increasingly appreciated.

NOTES

1. C. Van Vechten, "The Tolerance Quotient as a Device for Defining Certain Social Concepts," *American Journal of Sociology,* XLVI (1940), 35–39; E. Lemert, "Legal Commitment and Social Control, *Sociology and Social Research,* XXX (1946), 370–78.
2. R. Linton, *The Study of Man* (New York, 1936), p. 362.
3. L. Guy Brown, *Social Pathology* (New York, 1942), p. 9.
4. A. Lindesmith, *Opiate Addiction* (Bloomington, Ind., 1947).
5. C. S. Blumel, "Primary and Secondary Stuttering," *Proceedings of the American Speech Correction Association,* Vol. II (1932), pp. 91–102.
6. C. Van Riper, "The Growth of the Stuttering Spasm," *Quarterly Journal of Speech,* XXIII (1937), 70–73.
7. S. Bacon, "Alcoholism: Nature of the Problem," mimeographed abstract of address to Institute on Alcoholism, University of California at Los Angeles, 1947.
8. M. Clinard, "The Process of Urbanization and Criminal Behavior," *American Journal of Sociology,* XLVIII (1942), 203–13.
9. A. Porterfield, "Delinquency and Its Outcome in Court and College," *American Journal of Sociology,* XLIX (1943), 199–208.
10. S. Slavson, *An Introduction to Group Psychotherapy* (New York: The Commonwealth Fund, 1943), p. 7.

11. R. Bain, "Personality Development and Marriage," in C. Becker and R. Hill, *Marriage and the Family* (Boston, 1942), pp. 147 ff.

12. J. Adamczyk, *The Relation of Problem Solving Behavior to the Structuralization of Social Groups,* Ph.D. dissertation, Northwestern University, 1942.

13. K. Davis, "The Sociology of Prostitution," *American Sociological Review,* II (1937), 744–55.

14. B. Dai, "Personality Problems in Chinese Culture," *American Sociological Review,* VI (1941), 688–96.

15. A. Boisen, *The Exploration of the Inner World* (Chicago: Willett Clark and Company, 1936).

Chapter 2

Societal Reaction, Differentiation, and Individuation

A Sociological Approach to the Study of Sociopathic Behavior

The early tendency to regard sociology as a synthetic discipline which combines items of biological, psychological, psychiatric, geographic, and demographic knowledge in order to explain human behavior has pretty well disappeared. Sociologists now hold to the notion that theirs is a separate field of study requiring concepts and generalizations which are unique to this field. Sociologists now generalize at "their own level" rather than trying to reduce their generalizations to the level of other fields. The only remnants of the synthetic tradition, if it can be called that, lie in a certain amount of confusion over how to reckon theoretically with nonsociological factors which have a marginal or indirect bearing upon human behavior.

Our own position on this matter is that the direct or significant factors of sociopathic behavior are sociological or sociopsychological in nature, expressible by such concepts as social structure, group, role, status, and symbolic interaction. To the extent that factors falling outside of those which are strictly sociological must be taken into consideration in analyzing pathological human behavior, they must be related in a verifiable way to the sociological variables. Such factors as physical size and strength, biological anomalies, aggressiveness, hallucinations, monetary income, age, sex, and position in space can be applied in only a limited way to explain variation in social and cultural factors, which in turn are the chief interacting determiners of human behavior. Where variables

---

Excerpts from *Social Pathology: Systematic Approaches to the Study of Sociopathic Behavior*. New York: McGraw-Hill, 1951. Pp. 20–24, 51–52, 54–55, 58–61, 73–78. Reprinted as originally published by permission of the McGraw-Hill Companies.

such as the former must be taken into account, it must be shown how they affect social organization, role, status, social participation, self-definitions, and the other variables which we define as "sociological." The actual details of effective causation can be given at this last, a sociological or sociopsychological level. Starting with these assumptions as to the nature of the sociological approach and guided by the criteria of a systematic theory, we can now proceed to the series of propositions or postulates which are the elements of our theory of sociopathic behavior.

A General Statement of Our Theory

Stated in the most general way, our theory is one of social differentiation, deviation, and individuation. For a summary description we may turn to an excerpt from a paper by the present writer:[1]

> We may pertinently ask at this juncture whether the time has not come to break abruptly with the traditions of older social pathologists and abandon once and for all the archaic and medicinal idea that human beings can be divided into normal and pathological, or, at least, if such a division must be made, to divest the term "pathological" of its moralistic unscientific overtones. As a step in this direction, the writer suggests that the concepts of social differentiation and individuation be rescued from the limbo of older textbooks on sociology, dusted off, and given scientific airing, perhaps being supplemented and given statistical meaning with the perfectly usable concept of deviation. There seems to be no cogent reason why the bulk of the data discussed in textbooks and courses on social pathology cannot be treated as a special phase of social and cultural differentiation and thus conveniently integrated with general sociological theory as taught in courses in introductory sociology. . . .
>
> Because some method must be found to distinguish that portion of differentiation which can be designated as appropriately falling within the field of social pathology, the second necessary postulate is that there is a space-time limited societal awareness and reaction to deviation, ranging from strong approval through indifference to strong disapproval. Thus, by further definition, sociopathic phenomena simply become differentiated behavior which at a given time and place is socially disapproved even though the same behavior may be socially approved at other times and in other places.

To recapitulate, then, we start with the idea that persons and groups are differentiated in various ways, some of which result in social penalties, rejection, and segregation. These penalties and segregative reactions of society or the community are dynamic factors which increase, decrease, and condition the form which the initial differentiation or deviation takes. This process of deviation and societal reaction, together with its structural or substantive products, can be studied both from its collective and its distributive aspects. In the first instance, we are concerned with sociopathic differentiation; and, in the second, our concern is with sociopathic individuation.

The Postulates with Which We Start

In order to give further precision to the above statement, it can be resolved into a series of postulates. These postulates are simple statements of fact for which the writer feels no obligation to supply proof. They differ from axioms, upon which mathematical and symbolic systems are constructed, in that they contain empirical elements. They are the building blocks for the theory of this treatise and *ipso facto* they must be accepted as points of departure for the analysis which follows. The question as to whether these postulates are the relevant ones or whether they are too few must await answer until after the theory has been tested. The postulates are as follows:[2]

1. There are modalities in human behavior and clusters of deviations from these modalities which can be identified and described for situations specified in time and space.
2. Behavioral deviations are a function of culture conflict which is expressed through social organization.
3. There are societal reactions to deviations ranging from strong approval through indifference to strong disapproval.
4. Sociopathic behavior is deviation which is *effectively* disapproved.
5. The deviant person is one whose role, status, function, and self-definition are importantly shaped by how much deviation he engages in, by the degree of its social visibility, by the *particular* exposure he has to the societal reaction, and by the nature and strength of the societal reaction.
6. There are patterns of restriction and freedom in the social participation of deviants which are related directly to their status, role, and self-definitions. The biological strictures upon social participation of deviants are directly significant in comparatively few cases.
7. Deviants are individuated with respect to their vulnerability to the societal reaction because: (*a*) the person is a dynamic agent, (*b*) there is a structuring to each personality which acts as a set of limits within which the societal reaction operates.

The Place of This Theory in General Sociological Theory

In keeping with our high scientific resolve the various terms employed in stating our postulates are intended to be amoral and nonevaluational, having obvious statistical implications and derivations. There is no intimation that concepts like "restricted participation," "sociopathic behavior," or "deviation" connote either goodness or badness. The objective of this work is to study a limited part of deviation in human behavior and a certain range of societal reactions, together with their interactional products, and by the methods of science to arrive at generalizations about the uniformities in these events. The aim is to study sociopathic behavior in the same light as normal behavior and, by implication, with extensions or derivations of general sociological theory. By the same token, we hold that, with certain modifications in our frame of reference, variations from social norms in desirable and enviable directions should be explored as profitably as the more frequently studied sociopathic variations. The behavior of the genius, the motion-picture star, the exceptionally beautiful woman, and the renowned athlete[3] should lend itself to the same systematic analysis as that which is applied to the criminal, the pauper, or the sex delinquent.[4]

A question for parenthetical consideration is whether or not it is possible to apply our theory with logical extensions to the analysis of behavior systems and persons which are differentiated but which do not excite polarized reactions of social approbation or disapproval. In data like these the chief conditioning factors appear to be the special qualities of the societal reaction. Thus, for example, the primary influences in forming the occupational personality of a locomotive engineer are such things as time, mobility, and income. The small amount of dislike for the railroad man sometimes found in small towns has little to do with the formation of his role and self-conception.[5] Whatever may be the answer to our question, we can readily recognize the gains to be made by integrating the growing body of research on behavior systems of occupational and functional groups and the sort of trend in sociological analysis this book represents. Such an integration would broaden the possible scope of this kind of research and generalization to encompass such monographic studies as those of the railroader, the waitress, and the musician, as well as those of the professional thief, the hobo, or the beggar.[6]

The Relationship of Deviation and the Societal Reaction

The degree of deviation shown by an individual or a group can be taken as a partial gauge of the probable societal reaction. Other things being equal or ignored, a particularly heinous crime will arouse more public action than a mild one, or an increase in the number of traffic offenses will cause more vigorous policing of the community. In order to predict societal reactions, techniques for estimating deviation are necessary. However, few efforts have been made to measure deviational behavior. Hypothetically, the sum total of deviation in a given situation will consist of the variance of the actions from prescribed social norms multiplied by the number of persons who engage in such actions. Measured or informally estimated in this way, the deviation in disapproved categories should be reciprocated by a comparatively intense reaction from the aggregates and groups whose sanctions have been violated. However, there are at least two other factors which interact with the gross deviation to condition the extent and nature of the societal reaction. One of these is the social visibility of the deviation.

Social Visibility

In order for deviation to provoke a community reaction, it must have a minimum degree of visibility, that is, it must be apparent to others and be identified as deviation. A vast amount of sexual deviation in our society is clandestine and consequently escapes the public eye, which is to say that it has a low visibility, a fact probably related to the puritanical background of our culture. This is not to say that no social influence is present, since the deviant in such cases may still, through the action of covert symbolic processes, imagine the reaction of "others" to his behavior and acquire feelings of guilt or anxiety. However, he or she does avoid the traumatic impact of public identification as an immoral person and also evades the sequence of differential reactions and penalty which follow such an identification.

Criminal statistics are generally held to be unreliable for the very reason that such a vast amount of crime escapes the notice and records of the law enforcement agencies. Low-visibility crimes include hundreds of thousands of abortions, many sexual crimes, passing of counterfeit money, shortchanging of business patrons, confidence games, pocket picking, shoplifting, gambling, and many others.[7]

While many forms of criminal deviation remain concealed in our society, in other forms of deviation a high degree of visibility is present because of the intrinsic qualities of the behavior involved, because of the nature of the situation, or because of the physical and social characteristics of the persons involved. It is ordinarily believed that the misconduct of members of racial minorities receives more publicity than similar violations by majority-group persons. It has been the habit of many newspapers to call attention to the fact that a person committing a crime is a Negro or a Mexican, or an Indian, or an alien. This operates strongly to build up a stereotype of the group in question as being a criminally inclined "race" and thus heightens the societal reaction to their future violations. The low economic and unpropertied status of minority-group members means that they seldom appear as plaintiffs in civil and criminal proceedings and nearly always as defendants. This, too, heightens their visibility as deviants.

The member of an immigrant group living in an area not predominantly inhabited by persons of his own nationality is also likely to be more conspicuous when he transgresses the rules of society. The member of an upper social class is apt to have his behavior more carefully scrutinized for shortcomings when he is interacting with persons of low status than when he is with his compeers, although this probably varies a good deal.

A factor which has considerable effect in magnifying the visibility of any given deviation emerges from the adjustment which the deviants make to such a deviation. The adjustment consists of secondary, often habitual or unverbalized, responses which may be either compensatory in nature, or an integral part of a formalized deviant role. Reference intended here is to such things as the grimaces the stutterer makes in trying to speak; the bizarre posturings of crippled or blind persons, the mannerisms which the professional criminal elects to symbolize his difference from other members of society or from other criminals, or, finally, the flamboyant dress of the traditional prostitute.

. . .

THE SOCIETAL REACTION

The socially visible deviations within a group, community, or society stir its members to a wide variety of expressive reactions and attitudes, depending upon the nature of the deviations and the expectancies of the conforming majority. Admiration, awe, envy, sympathy, fear, repulsion, disgust, hate, and anger are felt and manifested by those confronted by departures from their sanctioned ways of behaving. These are the elemental stuff from which the societal reaction is compounded.

The Pristine Form of the Societal Reaction

In informally organized groups and communities there is a direct and spontaneous quality in the societal reaction which tends to be immediately relevant to the deviation. This continues to be the case, even in more formally organized groups and communities, so long as there is a close correspondence between the informal and formal organizations. Under these conditions the societal reaction tends to be a pure function of the interaction of deviation and the norms of the group which are transgressed. Other things being equal, the societal reaction will reciprocate in intensity the degree, amount, and visibility of the deviation. Beyond these, the compulsiveness of the norms violated or deviated from interacts to limit the severity of the societal reaction. Given constants and similarity of deviation, the public reaction in two different communities will vary with the respective importance attached to norms covering the deviations.

To illustrate what has been said in the preceding paragraph, we may take drunkenness for our example. Ordinarily, when a man is brought into court on a charge of "drunk and disorderly," he is warned or lectured and his case is dismissed. However, subsequent offenses are apt to result in fines and jail sentences. Ultimately, if his alcoholic disturbances persist over a long period of time, he may be placed in an institution.

This is a common pattern of reaction to drunken misdemeanants in many American communities. But from one community to another there may be variations in the policy for dealing with drunken persons. Drunkenness is handled with differing amounts of leniency because of the varying conceptions of the importance of sobriety. Some communities do not arrest drunks at all but hold them in protective custody until they are sober again. In communities with heavy contingents of foreign-born in the population, the public reactions to drunkenness may be mitigated by the receptive attitudes of these groups toward this behavior. On the other hand, in many Methodist communities in Kansas and Mormon communities in Utah, we see much greater public disapproval of drunkenness than in most other American communities.

In pursuing the more complex aspects of the societal reaction, some distinction must be observed between "innovating" and "recurrent" deviations. A sociopathic deviation which is entirely new and for which there is no historical antecedent often leaves a group or society at a loss for effective means of coping with it. This has often been the case where alcoholic liquors have been introduced by white men into primitive societies, leading to drunkenness which heretofore had been outside the experience of the group. Under conditions such as these the members of the group must rely or fall back upon informal expressions of their disapproval. These reactions may make the deviants uncomfortable and distressed but they do not necessarily impair their formal status. [See chapter 7 here.—eds.]

Recurrent deviations and the growth of a deviant population bring alterations in the culture and social organization of the community within which they occur. Mythologies, stigma, stereotypes, patterns of exploitation, accommodation, segregation, and methods of control spring up and crystallize in the interaction between the deviants and the rest of society. The informal societal reaction is extended and formalized in the routinized procedures of agents and agencies delegated with direct responsibility for penalizing and restraining or reforming the deviants. The status of the deviants is redefined, and special pariah roles may be assigned to them.

Despite the fact that when it first appears deviation can theoretically provoke approval, indifference, or disapproval, there is reason to believe that all innovations in behavior arouse some initial disapproval. The reason for this lies in the difficulty of immediately demonstrating the utility of the new behavior. Utility is a function of understanding the deviation and is not always at once apparent to the great majority of people.[8] Thus in the past many inventions, such as anesthesia and vaccination, were resisted by the public and even by members of the medical profession itself. Another reason why early departures from customary ways of behaving are unfavorably received by society or groups is that they upset a system of reciprocity between groups, extending to groups and persons who receive no direct value from the innovation. Moreover, the normative or value-systems of individuals may be so strongly reified that variations from expected behavior automatically awaken hostile reactions.

Once an innovation in behavior occurs and takes hold of a sizable number of persons, a dynamic interplay is observable between it and the social situation in which it takes place. Presumably there is a patterning in the sequence of events associated with the societal reaction. At least in such things as reform movements in urban politics there seems to be a similarity sufficiently recognizable to justify the terms "sequence" or "cycle." One attempt at analysis of the sequential aspects of communal reactions to disapproved behavior has been undertaken under the heading of "the natural history of a social problem." The deviation under consideration in this study was the appearance in Detroit, Michigan, of the pattern of family living in trailers and the growth of trailer camps in places where these families congregated and set up subcommunity organizations among themselves. The societal reaction to this new development was found to fall into three phases: (1) awareness, (2) policy determination, and (3) reform.

The time span between the first trailer-camp establishments and the peak of the community agitation and reaction to the "problem" was from ten to fifteen years. Visibility of the behavior was very low at first, then it tended to spread through geographic and social space until newspapers began to reflect the strong concern of many community groups at different social levels. As the hostility toward the inhabitants of these camps mounted, other groups were drawn into the situation, on the side of the trailer people as well as among their opponents. The chief advocates of the new behavior and defenders of the trailer dwellers were the companies manufacturing trailers and trailer equipment. Conflicts over policy gave rise to alignments of groups for and against various proposals to control the situation or to do away with the behavior. Finally, after a period of public controversy, the reaction to the "problem" tended to shift to an administrative level, with new ordinances and regulations put into effect by city and county officials. We are left to believe that the behavior which in its original form was disapproved of was finally integrated into the community culture.[9]

No One Sequence or Pattern in the Societal Reaction

While the analysis has much to commend it, there is some doubt as to whether it is a sufficient one. It is questionable whether the community reaction to variant behavior always follows the course and eventuates in the manner indicated by this research. The sequence described seems entirely too unilinear and mechanical. At least three possible end products of the community reaction are indicated: (1) ultimate acceptance of the variant behavior and its integration into the general, local, or special culture; (2) an unstable equilibrium or symbiotic relationship between the aberrant social organization and the normal; and (3) complete and unqualified rejection of the sociocultural novelty. The first alternative, which impressed the students of the Detroit situation, simply means that the deviation and societal reaction become a phase of social and cultural change. History records many similar instances of this sort. Trailer housing is not only well established in given localities but is pretty well accepted throughout our entire society. The use of lipstick, rouge, silk stockings, and smoking and drinking were all once confined to women with low social status or to prostitutes, yet today they are universally sanctioned as normal behavior for women of all classes. The Republican and Democratic parties in the United States have promoted and passed legislation in recent years which was once condemned as being socialistic and communistic. The proposals for graduated income taxes and the income tax generally were held to be radical and subversive in principle when first proposed; nevertheless, today these taxes are regarded as necessary parts of our whole financial structure.

Unstable Equilibrium in the Societal Reaction

The second large alternative, societal reaction, seems to be present in conjunction with many of our historically old "social problems," such as pauperism and many kinds of crime and prostitution, the forms of which have their roots in our European cultural antecedents. The societal reaction to these sociopathic behaviors in many areas is a compound of acceptance and rejection, frequently manifesting itself as the tacit tolerance of variant social patterns coupled with a nominal or formal disapproval and rejection. In this case the waxing deviation seems to have been halted at a certain point, giving rise to a tenuous integration between it and the older, accepted social organization. A situation obtains in which community tolerance is precariously stabilized just short of a critical point in the tolerance quotient at which collective action is taken.

The impasse which is reached in the societal reaction is partly explained by generalized culture conflict which affects such a large majority of the population that little consistent action is possible. This can be seen in ambivalent attitudes toward such things as begging and gambling. In the latter case most people realize that it is a costly and meaningless form of behavior, but the attitude is complicated by the fact that most people have gambled at some time or another. Even our churches have utilized gambling to raise money. In other words, gambling is both situational and systematic deviation. Consequently, fears are easily awakened that controls set up to eliminate the systematic gambling will be applied to gambling in other contexts. Drawing up legislation which will penalize the unwanted deviation without jeopardizing the status of the numerous casual participants is exceedingly difficult.

Other forms of sociopathic behavior are strictly systematic, and a sharp distinction can be made between the minority of persons who participate in it and the majority who do not. Here the explanation of the truncated societal reaction must be sought in the structuring of group relationships and the distribution of power within the community. The socially disapproved behavior in question may stir up a fairly strong and constant desire in the community for change and reform, but its importance in a reciprocal economy of group relations makes it impossible to root it out and destroy it.

. . .

SOCIOPATHIC INDIVIDUATION

The deviant person is a product of differentiating and isolating processes. Some persons are individually differentiated from others from the time of birth onward, as in the case of a child born with a congenital physical defect or repulsive appearance, and as in the case of a child born into a minority racial or cultural group. Other persons grow to maturity in a family or in a social class where pauperism, begging, or crime are more or less institutionalized ways of life for the entire group. In these latter instances the person's sociopsychological growth may be normal in every way, his status as a deviant being entirely caused by his maturation within the framework of social organization and culture designated as "pathological" by the larger society. This is true of many delinquent children in our society.[10]

> It is a matter of great significance that the delinquent child, growing up in the delinquency areas of the city, has very little access to the cultural heritages of the larger conventional society. His infrequent contacts with this larger society are for the most part formal and external. Quite naturally his conception of moral values is shaped and molded by the moral code prevailing in his play groups and the local community in which he lives . . . the young delinquent has very little appreciation of the meaning of the traditions and formal laws of society. . . . Hence the conflict between the delinquent and the agencies of society is, in its broader aspects, a conflict of divergent cultures.

The same sort of gradual, unconscious process which operates in the socialization of the deviant child may also be recognized in the acquisition of socially unacceptable behavior by persons after having reached adulthood. However, with more verbal and sophisticated adults, step-by-step violations of societal norms tend to be progressively rationalized in the light of what is socially acceptable. Changes of this nature can take place at the level of either overt or covert behavior, but with a greater likelihood that adults will preface overt behavior changes with projective symbolic departures from society's norm. When the latter occur, the subsequent overt changes may appear to be "sudden" personality modifications. However, whether these changes are completely radical ones is to some extent a moot point. One writer holds strongly to the opinion that sudden and dramatic shifts in behavior from normal to abnormal are seldom the case, that a sequence of small preparatory transformations must be the prelude to such apparently sudden behavior changes. This writer is impressed by the day-by-day growth of "reserve potentialities" within personalities of all individuals, and he contends that many normal persons carry potentialities for abnormal behavior, which, given proper conditions, can easily be called into play.[11]

Personality Changes Not Always Gradual

This argument is admittedly sound for most cases, but it must be taken into consideration that traumatic experiences often speed up changes in personality.[12] Nor can the "trauma" in these experiences universally be attributed to the unique way in which the person conceives of the experience subjectively. Cases exist to show that personality modifications can be telescoped or that there can be an acceleration of such changes caused largely by the intensity and variety of the social stimulation. Most soldiers undoubtedly have entirely different conceptions of their roles after intensive combat experience. Many admit to having "lived a lifetime" in a relatively short period of time after they have been under heavy fire in battle for the first time. Many generals have remarked that their men have to be a little "shooted" or "blooded" in order to become good soldiers. In the process of group formation, crises and interactional amplification are vital requisites to forging true, role-oriented group behavior out of individuated behavior.[13]

The importance of the person's conscious symbolic reactions to his or her own behavior cannot be overstressed in explaining the shift from normal to abnormal behavior or from one type of pathological behavior to another, particularly where behavior variations become systematized or structured into pathological roles. This is not to say that conscious choice is a determining factor in the differentiating process. Nor does it mean that the awareness of the self is a purely conscious perception. Much of the process of self-perception is doubtless marginal from the point of view of consciousness.[14] But however it may be perceived, the individual's self-definition is closely connected with such things as self-acceptance, the subordination of minor to major roles, and with the motivation involved in learning the skills, techniques, and values of a new role. *Self-definitions or self-realizations are likely to be the result of sudden perceptions and they are especially significant when they are followed immediately by overt demonstrations of the new role they symbolize.* The self-defining junctures are critical points of personality genesis and in the special case of the atypical person they mark a division between two different types of deviation.

Primary and Secondary Deviation

There has been an embarrassingly large number of theories, often without any relationship to a general theory, advanced to account for various specific pathologies in human behavior. For certain types of pathology, such as alcoholism, crime, or stuttering, there are almost as many theories as there are writers on these subjects. This has been occasioned in no small way by the preoccupation with the origins of pathological behavior and by the fallacy of confusing *original* causes with *effective* causes. All such theories have elements of truth, and the divergent viewpoints they contain can be reconciled with the general theory here if it is granted that original causes or antecedents of deviant behaviors are many and diversified. This holds especially for the psychological processes leading to similar pathological behavior, but it also holds for the situational concomitants of the initial aberrant conduct. A person may come to use excessive alcohol not only for a wide variety of subjective reasons but also because of diversified situational influences, such as the death of a loved one, business failure, or participating in some sort of organized group activity calling for heaving drinking of liquor. Whatever the original reasons for violating the norms of the community, they are important only for certain research purposes, such as assessing the extent of the "social problem" at a given time or determining the requirements for a rational program of social control. From a narrower sociological viewpoint the deviations are not significant until they are organized subjectively and transformed into active roles and become the social criteria for assigning status. The deviant individuals must react symbolically to their own behavior aberrations and fix them in their sociopsychological patterns. The deviations remain primary deviations or symptomatic and situational as long as they are rationalized or otherwise dealt with as functions of a socially acceptable role. Under such conditions normal and pathological behaviors remain strange and somewhat tensional bedfellows in the same person. Undeniably a vast amount of such segmental and partially integrated pathological behavior exists in our society and has impressed many writers in the field of social pathology.

Just how far and for how long a person may go in dissociating his sociopathic tendencies so that they are merely troublesome adjuncts of normally conceived roles is not known. Perhaps it depends upon the number of alternative definitions of the same overt behavior that he can develop; perhaps certain physiological factors (limits) are also involved. However, if the deviant acts are repetitive and have a high visibility, and if there is a severe societal reaction, which, through a process of identification is incorporated as part of the "me" of the individual, the probability is greatly increased that the integration of existing roles will be disrupted and that reorganization based upon a new role or roles will occur. (The "me" in this context is simply the subjective aspect of the societal reaction.) Reorganization may be the adoption of another normal role in which the tendencies previously defined as "pathological" are given a more acceptable social expression. The other general possibility is the assumption of a deviant role, if such exists; or, more rarely, the person may organize an aberrant sect or group in which he creates a special role of his own. *When a person begins to employ his deviant behavior or a role based upon it as a means of defense, attack, or adjustment to the overt and covert problems created by the consequent societal reaction to him, his deviation is secondary.* Objective evidences of this change will be found in the symbolic appurtenances of the new role, in clothes, speech, posture, and mannerisms, which in some cases heighten social visibility, and which in some cases serve as symbolic cues to professionalization.

Role Conceptions of the Individual Must Be Reinforced by Reactions of Others

It is seldom that one deviant act will provoke a sufficiently strong societal reaction to bring about secondary deviation, unless in the process of introjection the individual imputes or projects meanings into the social situation which are not present. In this case anticipatory fears are involved. For example, in a culture where a child is taught sharp distinctions between "good" women and "bad" women, a single act of questionable morality might conceivably have a profound meaning for the girl so indulging. However, in the absence of reactions by the person's family, neighbors, or the larger community, reinforcing the tentative "bad-girl" self-definition, it is questionable whether a transition to secondary deviation would take place. It is also doubtful whether a temporary exposure to a severe punitive reaction by the community will lead a person to identify himself with a pathological role, unless, as we have said, the experience is highly traumatic. Most frequently there is a progressive reciprocal relationship between the deviation of the individual and the societal reaction, with a compounding of the societal reaction out of the minute accretions in the deviant behavior, until a point is reached where ingrouping and outgrouping between society and the deviant is manifest.[15] At this point a stigmatizing of the deviant occurs in the form of name calling, labeling, or stereotyping.

The sequence of interaction leading to secondary deviation is roughly as follows: (1) primary deviation; (2) social penalties; (3) further primary deviation; (4) stronger penalties and rejections; (5) further deviation, perhaps with hostilities and resentment beginning to focus upon those doing the penalizing; (6) crisis reached in the tolerance quotient, expressed in formal action by the community stigmatizing of the deviant; (7) strengthening of the deviant conduct as a reaction to the stigmatizing and penalties; (8) ultimate acceptance of deviant social status and efforts at adjustment on the basis of the associated role.

As an illustration of this sequence the behavior of an errant schoolboy can be cited. For one reason or another, let us say excessive energy, the schoolboy engages in a classroom prank. He is penalized for it by the teacher. Later, due to clumsiness, he creates another disturbance and again he is reprimanded. Then, as sometimes happens, the boy is blamed for something he did not do. When the teacher uses the tag "bad boy" or "mischief maker" or other invidious terms, hostility and resentment are excited in the boy, and he may feel that he is blocked in playing the role expected of him. Thereafter, there may be a strong temptation to assume his role in the class as defined by the teacher, particularly when he discovers that there are rewards as well as penalties deriving from such a role. There is, of course, no implication here that such boys go on to become delinquents or criminals, for the mischief-maker role may later become integrated with or retrospectively rationalized as part of a role more acceptable to school authorities.[16] If such a boy continues this unacceptable role and becomes delinquent, the process must be accounted for in the light of the general theory of this volume. There must be a spreading corroboration of a sociopathic self-conception and societal reinforcement at each step in the process.

The most significant personality changes are manifest when societal definitions and their subjective counterpart become generalized. When this happens, the range of major role choices becomes narrowed to one general class.[17] This was very obvious in the case of a young girl who was the daughter of a paroled convict and who was attending a small Middle Western college. She continually argued with herself and with the author, in whom she had confided, that in reality she belonged on the "other side of the railroad tracks" and that her life could be enormously simplified by acquiescing in this verdict and living accordingly. While in her case there was a tendency to dramatize her conflicts, nevertheless there was enough societal reinforcement of her self-conception by the treatment she received in her relationship with her father and on dates with college boys to lend it a painful reality. Once these boys took her home to the shoddy dwelling in a slum area where she lived with her father, who was often in a drunken condition, they abruptly stopped seeing her again or else became sexually presumptive.

NOTES

1. Lemert, Edwin M., "Some Aspects of a General Theory of Sociopathic Behavior," *Proceedings of the Pacific Sociological Society,* 1948, Research Studies, State College of Washington, 16, No. 1, pp. 24*f.* [Reprinted here as chapter 2.—eds.]

2. While in general we found the social problems and the social disorganization viewpoints lacking in theoretical fulfillment, it is not our intention here to insist that all recent treatments of social pathology are without value and that "ours is the only theory." Several books on social pathology have presented fairly defensible theoretical positions. L. Guy Brown's *Social Pathology* is distinguished in the main for its internal consistency and interrelated framework of ideas, and for the integrity with which its central scheme is made the basis for each successive discussion of problem behavior. *Social Pathology,* by Stuart Queen and Jeannette Gruener, merits favorable comment for the simplicity and economy of its conceptual presentation, features which, as we have shown, are desirable in all theory. Whether their attempt to study social pathology exclusively in terms of social participation is an oversimplification remains to be seen. Certainly it is a necessary concept, as we shall try to show; but alone, at least as it has been used by others, it remains an incomplete formulation. Another position which deserves comment here because of its obvious bearing upon certain phases of our theory is the value-conflict conception of social problems. In this conception, chief emphasis is placed upon the clash of ideals, opinions, judgments, and meanings as the source of social problems. In our estimation this is a special variety of culture-conflict theory, and we freely recognize its importance in studying deviation. However, the value-conflict theory remains a highly generalized statement which fails to make a sharp delimitation of the field. For example, it does not tell us how much or what kind of conflict is necessary in order to have a social problem. No distinction is struck between effective value-conflicts and those which are purely spurious and have little or no effect upon the organization and interaction of groups and participating individuals. Furthermore, it makes no allowance for cultural inconsistencies or contradictory value systems within the same culture which are reciprocals or necessary derivatives of each other. For statements of the value-conflict view see Waller, W., "Social Problems and the Mores," *American Sociological Review,* 1, December 1936 pp. 922–933; Fuller, R., and R. Myers, "Some Aspects of a Theory of Social Problems," *ibid.,* 6, February 1941, pp. 24–32; Cuber, J., and R. Harper, *Problems of American Society,* 1948.

3. We lack a good concept to designate this kind of deviation. We think of such terms as "honorific behavior" or "emulative behavior" without being very satisfied with them.

4. We have raised the question in graduate seminars as to whether our theory is

applicable to the study of minority or ethnic groups. Generally this question has to be left unanswered. While ethnic groups are often comparable to the type of deviant groups in which we are interested, it is also true that in some cases their large size and occasional positions of considerable power in local areas mean that they differ significantly from the deviant groups we shall be studying.

5. See Cottrell, W. F., *The Railroader,* 1940.

6. It is only fitting to acknowledge the contribution which has been made by E. H. Sutherland in his criminological research by bringing before American sociologists the importance of behavior systems as research areas. See also Hollingshead, A. B., "Behavior Systems as a Field of Research," *American Sociological Review,* 4, December 1939, pp. 816–822.

7. Von Hentig, H., *Crime, Cause and Conditions,* 1947, p. 21.

8. Mowrer, E., *Disorganization, Personal and Social,* 1942, p. 28.

9. Fuller, R., and R. Myers, "The Natural History of a Social Problem," *American Sociological Review,* 6, June 1941, pp. 320–329.

10. Shaw, C., *The Natural History of a Delinquent Career,* Chicago, 1941, pp. 75–76. Quoted by permission of the University of Chicago Press, Chicago.

11. Brown, L. Guy, *Social Pathology,* 1942, pp. 44–45.

12. Allport, G., *Personality, A Psychological Interpretation,* 1947, p. 57.

13. Slavson, S. R., *An Introduction to Group Psychotherapy,* 1943, pp. 10, 229*ff.*

14. Murphy, G., *Personality,* 1947, p. 482.

15. Mead, G., "The Psychology of Punitive Justice," *American Journal of Sociology,* 23, March 1918, pp. 577–602.

16. Evidence for fixed or inevitable sequences from predelinquency to crime is absent. Sutherland, E. H., *Principles of Criminology,* 1939, 4th ed., p. 202.

17. Sutherland seems to say something of this sort in connection with the development of criminal behavior. *Ibid.,* p. 86.

Chapter 3

The Paradigm Reaches Its Limits

What I prefer to call the sociology of deviance now appears to be under attack from so many quarters, both for what it is and what it is not, that a sense of embattlement is inescapable. The diverse, perverse, and tangential nature of the criticisms makes it difficult to tell friend from foe. Sensitive to this state of affairs, Peter Manning (1973) in a review essay of surpassing excellence asserts that a grey fog has settled over the field. This I can discount as the natural fog of good men's minds; but his further allegations that the theoretical impetus of deviance sociology is spent and that a state of exhaustion and conceptual decay prevails, I found painful and much harder to reconcile with my proprietary interests.

I should say parenthetically that reading the essay left me spelled by the beauty of its words and niceties of expression, as well as overwhelmed by its sense of prophecy. It recalled me to an old auctorial ideal espoused by James Branch Cabell, namely that we should write beautifully of things as they are. But having had time to cast off Manning's spell, I conclude that sociologists sometimes write beautifully of things as they are not and that in striving for rhetorical symmetry their conclusions may go beyond what facts will support. In this case I must object that the allegations of its sadness and senility ignore the theoretical potential of deviance sociology, its continuing research output, its influence on the diversion movement in criminal justice, and its striking impact on younger, highly articulate sociologists in Britain. Granting the slow stain and constant erosion of all ideas, it seems to me that even with age deviance sociology still is "majestic in decay."

But without further pause on the decadence issue, I would like to deal with what may cause some of the faithful to cry sacrilege, namely the deficiencies of G. H. Mead's conception of symbolic interaction and their implications for the study of deviance. My purpose is not to add to the theoretical confusion but to clear some

---

"Beyond Mead: The Societal Reaction to Deviance." *Social Problems* 21, 4 (April 1974): 457–68. *Presidential Address, Society for the Study of Social Problems, Annual Meeting, August 1973.*

of it away, and hopefully free up sociological energies to exploit in the measure it deserves its least worked area, namely the societal reaction. In order to maximize the clarity of my discussion I will recap what the term has meant to me.

Some years ago in my early work on deviance I used the term societal reaction to comprehend a number of processes by which societies respond to deviants either informally or through their officially delegated agencies (Lemert, 1951). While communication of invidious definitions of persons or groups and the public expression of disapproval were included as part of the societal reaction, the important point was made that these had to be validated in order to be sociologically meaningful. Validation was conceived as effective social control taking form as isolation, segregation, penalties, supervision, or some kind of organized "treatment." In effect, this was a kind of middle range conceptual orientation to a body of data.

Societal reaction theory distinguished objective as well as subjective aspects of deviance, recognizing a relationship between the nature, degree, extent, and visibility of deviance and corresponding form and intensity of the societal reaction. It also allowed that attributes of deviants and the form of their deviance affected the way in which societal definitions were internalized, most easily seen in biological anomalies and physical handicaps. Among the objective influences on the societal reaction were noted technology, procedures, and limitation of agency personnel and resources. However, these did not get much elaboration or application, save in the discussion of changing tolerances for crime.

Then, as in my later work on deviance (Lemert, 1972), I emphasized the need to begin the analysis with the societal reaction, more particularly social control, rather than with etiology. Herein lay the distinctiveness of the societal reaction approach, which sought to show how deviance was shaped and stabilized by efforts to eliminate or ameliorate it. In retrospect, the break with structural conceptions of deviance and the traditional concern of sociology with causes was by no means complete. This I now believe to have been less a matter of theoretical asymmetry than an encounter with a perennial problem of sociological theory, namely how to establish a connection between symbolic systems, social systems, and physical systems, without denying the obvious fact that human beings make choices that affect as well as are affected by the system. According to John Scott's (1963) informed analysis, even the grand theorist of our age, Talcott Parsons, failed to reach an ultimate solution of this problem.

This question was pretty well obscured during the 1950s and 1960s, probably because of the tremendous growth in our national production and the belief that affluence was easily procurable for all, abetted by Keynesian economic theory aimed at little more than preventive maintenance of the marvelous machine making it all possible. But recently the avalanche of population growth, swift exhaustion of resources, environmental destruction, plus an "energy crisis" have made an awareness that human choices can either sustain or destroy the physical and technological basis on which they are made. Physical environments formerly taken as constants and merely limiting now can be seen changing in foreseeable time spans, and it becomes possible to speak of responses and feedback from the physical world. Even the vulgarization and deserved criticism of the ecology movement cannot quiet the deepening appreciation that man is inescapably part of a larger bio-physical system.

SYMBOLIC INTERACTION

Over the decades of the present century sociology moved steadily away from early social science, which had sought standing ground on biology, geography, and economics. Within sociology, social psychologists pushed farthest along this path, retaining only some nominal allegiance to organic and natural history analogies. And within social psychology, it has been those sociologists concerned with deviance who have laid the greatest and most exclusive emphasis on the sociopsychological process as the determining element in social life. It has been asserted that the one theme uniting the otherwise diverse views of labeling theorists, Neo-Chicagoans, or West Coast school, as they are variously called, is their fealty to the symbolic interactionism of G. H. Mead (Schur, 1969).

Nevertheless, it may be asked whether the prevailing definition of deviance as a group creation through labeling and the adoption of an "underdog" view of the symbolic process do not do a disservice to Mead. Labeling unfortunately conveys an impression of interaction that is both sociologistic and unilateral; in the process deviants who are "successfully labeled" lose their individuality; they appear, as Bordua (1967) says, like "empty organisms" or, as Gouldner (1968) puts it, "like men on their backs" (Walton 1973). The extreme subjectivism made explicit by the underdog perspective, reflecting sympathy for the victim and antipathy towards the establishment, also distorts by magnifying the exploitative and arbitrary features of the societal reaction. But more important, it leaves little or no place for human choice at either level of interaction.

Actually the difficulties may lie in the ambiguities and uncertainties of Mead's ideas themselves. While Mead reconciled the objective and the subjective in general terms by making self and other dual aspects of a common behavioral process, the specifics of the process with respect to choice making were far from clear. Other strictures inhere in Mead's conception of the societal other; his unformed ideas about society, primarily that of one generalized other, are a poor source for a modern theory of the societal reaction (Meltzer 1967; Kolb 1967). This is amply demonstrated in the dramatistic descriptions of the societal reaction which revolve around the idea of symbolic interaction.

THE DRAMATISTIC METAPHOR

Most of the currently held representations of the societal reaction are metaphors having in common a curious primitive quality. In his one article on the subject, Mead (1928) spoke of the "modern organization of taboo"; later Tannenbaum

(1937) called the process the dramatization of evil, equatable with ancient Hebraic scapegoating; Garfinkle (1956) depicted it as ceremonial degradation based on suprapersonal values of the tribe; others have termed the process stigmatization, victimization, exclusion, and conferral of an invidious property. Becker (1963) drew on a reconstructed incident of clan reaction to incest in the far off Melansian islands to epitomize the contingency of the labeling process. The anachronistic overtones in these figures are unmistakable.

While fabrication of a pristine state of affairs and the use of analogies and metaphors for purposes of analysis are inviting, it is also true that they may become the ties that bind; in this case the dramatistic metaphors, or life-as-a-theatre analysis, traceable from Mead's comparison of social interaction to dramatic play and games, carry reductionistic implications hard to evade. The inescapable concomitants of the play are a scenario, actors who play prescribed parts, striking conjunction of actions, outward expression of inner conceptions, and denouement to an unequivocal end. The significant implication is that the societal reaction rests upon a kind of programmed consensus, a point made explicit by the concepts employed in many studies of agencies of social control. When "others" are agents of groups their decisions and actions are seen as the expression of rules, "routine practices," "common typifications," "proverbial characterizations," or racial-class bias, all strongly reminiscent of Durkheimian collective representations. Reification of one locus of power, insistence on group sustaining functions of deviance and uncritical acceptance of custodial treatment institutions as "total" give a further cast of Durkheimian solidarity to groups against which deviants are said to stand as outsiders (for criticism of dramaturgic analysis, see Messinger, 1962, Zicklin, 1968, Garfinkel, 1967, 145ff.).

One consequence of the use of the above-mentioned analogies to describe the societal reaction is to restrict conflict to that between the group and the persons it seeks to label. No questions rise about possible effects of dissensus within the dominant group nor that generated by the intrusive claims of other groups. Becker's rules which create deviance appear as agreed upon, if not derived from an overarching establishment, at least from the subculture or occupational culture of the labelers; this despite knowledge that the salient problem for agents of social control such as police and court people is how to choose from among a plethora of rules at hand and how to find a basis for choice itself. There is little that I can find in labeling theory which deals with this kind of conflict and choice making in the context of a pluralism of groups so conspicuous in modern society.

ETHNOMETHODOLOGY—THE METHODOLOGY OF CULTURE

To say that revolutions in thought come to devour their own may overstate the case but there now comes a younger generation of ethnomethodologists, existentialists, or phenomenologists in sociology who attack labeling theory as insufficient explication of the societal reaction process. Sensitive to the fragmentation, divisiveness, and pluralism of the contemporary social world, these writers stress the fluidity and provisional nature of the dynamics by which good and evil, and conformity and deviance, emerge. While these thinkers are still allied with symbolic interactionism, they reject the Meadian concept of social role, and insist that "reality" lies under, beyond, or apart from institutional structures. Rules are replaced by concepts of "deeper rules," "relational rules," or preconceptions of social interaction (Douglas, 1970). In starkest form the ethnomethodologists assert that confrontations or collective action generating deviance are little more than negotiated understandings contrived in a world without meaning or which is "absurd" (Lyman and Scott, 1970).

The concomitant process has been called "work" or the "social construction of reality," situated in nature. Apart from this, however, clarification is meager, suggesting the difficulties which ethnomethodologists have in rising above a kind of raw "here and now" empiricism in the research application of their ideas. The low level of characterization of the stigmatization of clients at the hands of a welfare organization is described by one writer as a process of "muddling through." He concludes (Scott 1970):

> This, in turn, implies that one can only speak of constructed meanings of stigma in the sense that they are genuinely manmade.

As the term denotes, ethnomethodology contends that cultures or subcultures set fundamental rules for determining what is perceived as real. In arguing for this position its partisans deepen the entanglement of deviance study in reductionism and subjectivism. The denial of any objective reality is made explicit in a statement by Erich Goode (1969):

> The only reality available to individual consciousness is a subjective reality . . . meaning is read into every situation, event, object and phenomenon.

FURTHER DILEMMAS

Insofar as ethnomethodologists hold that constructions of deviance rest on perceptions or "grounds" which are determined by cultural or subcultural screens, their ideas turn into solipsisms, recapitulating the difficulty from which Mead tried to rescue Watsonian behaviorism. In a narrow sense it is true that culture sets up an apperceptive base from which those enculturated respond selectively to define good and evil independently of other aspects of the actions they perceive. Culture may provide people with meanings that keep them acting for long periods in ways that appear to be irrational, meaningless, or even fantastic. The pure culturologist or ethnomethodologist looking at such behavior concludes that culture or social construction of reality can make anything good or bad, denying that there is any standard common to mankind that affects his efforts.

This kind of generalization can be made true only by denying that man learns or responds on any other basis than what is symbolically transmitted. Actually it is only in cases where a cultural definition of what happens is reinforced by anticipated results that men are free to selectively define reality in this circular manner. In effect they may react as if only part of what happened actually happened, thus identifying a whole pattern of action as a cultural or perceptual phenomenon.

But as W. F. Cottrell (1972) convincingly demonstrates, while some of our responses depend on symbolically acquired meanings, others require for their validation direct feedback from our bodies or the physical world; and still other responses can be made or learned only through direct experience of the doing of them. From this point of view any pattern of human reaction to others, individual or collective, is a mixture or product of prior symbolically transmitted knowledge, past knowledge acquired from experience with the objective world and past knowledge acquired from experience with the objective world and newly invented meanings derived from immediate experience with the social and physical worlds.

CHANGE IN THE SOCIETAL REACTION

It is primarily by treating the societal reaction as a residue after all factors operating to produce it have occurred that the impression of its subjective symbolic character can be maintained. While granting that the residues of social action are symbolically transmitted, looking at the action from the perspective of change directs attention to its non-symbolic antecedents. This is made clear in Cottrell's (1972) words:

> If culture be treated as a residue . . . then of course what is found there includes all the norms, the results of all strivings, as well as all knowledge that will be symbolically transmitted. But how much of what was there yesterday is still there . . . How much of what is there now is new, now to be symbolically transmitted but not learned that way? . . . if . . . our model permits us to look elsewhere we may see that culture change was preceded by technological invention, or that certain kinds of deleterious social relationships were selected out of that culture when new knowledge made it possible to discover their influence . . . It is only in the comparative short run that culture can make anything good. . . .

A great many of the studies of agencies controlling deviance have been synchronous in nature, describing and analyzing portions and pieces of a social process. Many have been timeless and without provenience. Consequently when attention is turned to the rise and fall of moral ideas and the transformation of definitions of deviance, labeling theory and ethnomethodology do little to enlighten the process. This is especially true as it pertains to the interaction of groups. A sociopsychological model focused on symbolic interaction in the Mead tradition either leaves groups vague entities or psychologizes their action. This can be seen in the proposition that new moral and legal categories are the work of moral entrepreneurs or crusaders with a sense of mission to impose their morality on others (Becker 1963). One version of this idea has it that such crusaders seize on a single moral issue as a symbol for reform in an effort to preserve a common way of life threatened by social change. Motivation presumably is purely symbolic, monolithic, and divorced from distributive material or means considerations (Gusfield, 1966).

Looking beyond symbolic politics for pertinent theory on the societal reaction is scarcely more rewarding. Radical critics and those who write on the politicization of deviance properly have noted the superficiality of the moral crusader formulation, as well as faulting labeling theory generally for its neglect of conflict and power. But the alternative theory of so-called radical sociology I find very generalized, as well as doctrinaire. Neither the Marxian concept of class, the power elites of Mills, nor the new left "urban alliance" of blacks and students have much immediate or practical use for research into the dynamics of the societal reaction. At best they substitute ideologies for things like group rules and define power as outcome of action or an attribute rather than as a process, e.g., "power is the ability to enforce one's moral claims."

In sum, radical critics reify power only slightly less than those they criticize; and in order to dramatize their criticisms they sometimes get caught up in the subjective, phenomenological perspective they seek to reject. Indeed some recent radical critiques seem bent on restoring machismo to the deviants and distinguishing the stout hearted and red blooded deviants who defy the system from those who live in its chinks and crannies. But even those on the sinistral side who call for sociologists to stigmatize the oppressor instead of their victims compound contradictions of power by insisting that high ranking persons are deviant even though they admittedly hold the power indispensable to defining deviance (Liazos, 1972).

Empirical materials to aid in formulation of theory on the evolution of morals and law unfortunately are sparse, for history seldom has recorded the kinds of events relevant to the task. Yet that which is available: J. Hall's (1935) studies of the evolution of the law of theft, research on the growth of vagrancy laws (Chambliss, 1964), commission reports on the poor laws, recent English articles on the politics of deviance (Taylor and Taylor, 1973), my own work on change in the California Juvenile Court Law (1970), along with investigations into the origins and working of the Probation Subsidy Program in California, make it doubtful that the emergence of new morality and procedures for defining deviance can be laid to the creations of any one group, class, or elite. Rather they are the products of the interaction of groups. The working of legislatures reveal the multifaceted interaction they have with such groups as well as the complexities of their own internal interaction through committees, majorities, and minorities. Judges, court workers, administrators, and police further interact to qualify the effective reach of new substantive law by jurisdictional and procedural adaptations. To understand the interplay of many groups out of which materialize new categories of moral and legal control requires a model of interaction quite different than those fathered by the psychologically oriented thought of Mead or from those of the class conflict theorists.

GROUP INTERACTION

Group interaction is best understood as a process resting on evaluation in which individuals sort out their purposes or values in terms of their dependence on groups necessary for their satisfaction. In so doing they give up some values in order to satisfy others, at the least possible sacrifice. The pattern of group action which results will reflect the claims and power of all those involved in the interaction; and the priorities it follows often are at considerable variance from the value hierarchies of individual participants. When a chain of interaction occurs between groups, the disparity between values dominant in final action, and the values of any one group member may be enormous. Police may acquiesce in positions of legislation taken by their representative association which deeply offend their sense of morality and justice because other values which have been given precedence are at stake in concurrent legislation. Legislators, too, may be captured by their group commitments so that they must pass bills which are grossly contrary to values they personally espouse.

The order in which interests, claims, or values get satisfied reflects not only group allegiance but also the availability of means for their satisfaction and the costs of such means, measurable by time, energy, and other values expended. Laws and rules made by this kind of process often express the values and norms of no group or person but rather their dilemmas, compromises, expeditious adherence to procedures, and strictures of time and budgets. For this reason it becomes difficult or impossible to predict the emergence of new definitions and controls of deviance by introspecting or "taking the role of the other" to discover what is in the minds of those making the change. Nor can predictions be made successfully by imputing cultures, subcultures, or life styles to the agents of change.

What has been said is well illustrated by reference to the interaction of a variety of professional associations which took part in revising the Juvenile Court law in California in 1961, a change which narrowed the jurisdiction of the court and effectively modified definitions of delinquency (Lemert, 1970). Each association sorted out the proposed changes in terms of its own values, supporting or resisting according to whether the changes were seen as a means of achieving their existing values or called for sacrifices deemed intolerable. In the change, probation officers gave up their accustomed right to employ a number of informal procedures but got more power *vis-à-vis* the police in decisions to detain juveniles. Police lost this power but got badly needed clarification of arrest powers. Judges lost their considerable freedom to handle the court informally, but they along with interested attorneys gained by the introduction of guarantees of certain rights to minors. All three professional groups had splits for and against the changes, and their conflicting positions were arrived at for different reasons and in different ways. Ultimately resistance among probation officers disappeared because the resisters had to choose between continued opposition and preservation of their association, which it threatened to destroy. Opposition among judges centered around one of their members who remained against the changes throughout but ultimately chose not to risk loss of reputation among his other colleagues by protracted resistance. Police resistance, primarily among Juvenile Officers from the south state, got stymied by the structure of their lobbying committee, which was dominated by chiefs who were more concerned with evidentiary bills and a death penalty bill than they were with juvenile justice.

STRUCTURES AND THE SOCIETAL REACTION

It is clear from what has been said that social structures influenced the outcome of the legislation in question. This happened in several ways, such as limiting the access of some groups to the legislature, allocating power in a manner so that the decision of one committee was crucial, and the special autonomy to act given to the group which initiated the changes. However, here I wish to emphasize for theoretical reasons how structures become instrumentally important as vehicles or channels by which feedback from direct experience with the objective world modifies choice—in this instance how new structures affect dissemination of new knowledge which selects out old patterns or paradigms.

The movement to change the Juvenile Court law, although it had outside leadership, was something less than a moral crusade, nor could it be described realistically as a popular movement shaped by public opinion. Leaders were a few attorneys, some probation officers, correctional administrators, and college professors, from among whom was organized a commission within the California Youth Authority (CYA) and the Department of Corrections. Joint sponsorship by the two organizations and later loss of interest by the CYA top people in the movement made it much like an autonomous staff operation. Several of the attorneys were attracted to the movement in its early stages mainly from frustrating encounters with highhanded judges in juvenile courts, but the focus and articulation of the movement owed much to organizational features introduced with creation of the CYA.

In essence, the movement was a challenge to the traditional *parens patriae* conception of the juvenile court, although it was not so represented. Social action grew out of an accumulation of new facts and information that raised serious doubts about the efficacy of the basic philosophy of the court. The main source of such information was input at the Board created for a different purpose, to hear and dispose all cases referred to CYA. This, together with reports from its field consultant division, allowed staff and Board members for the first time, circa 1944, to develop a statewide impression of what the juvenile courts were like in fact and to begin to appreciate the discrepancies between their ideology and their performance. A number of Board members after repeatedly listening to stories of youth coming before them grew convinced that injustices were being done.

The problem of the Commission became one of convincing persons with power to change the law that this was true. Given this general stance, the Commission did in a sense try to reconstruct the symbolic reality of the juvenile court, chiefly by means of a statewide survey, hearings, and presentations before legislative committees. But their report was late in appearing and was not very good at that; and the Commission's presentations before the powerful Senate Judiciary Committee, a majority of whose members were opposed to any change, fell short.

The event which did more than any other to undercut and select out the existing *parens patriae* conception of the juvenile court came from the unsolicited testimony of a single upstate judge who had come to defend the old style court and fight the changes sought by the Commission. A somewhat quaint, anachronistic figure in a black suit and a furled umbrella, he told in fine detail how he ran what was in effect an inquisitorial system of juvenile justice, ordering arrested youths into detention until by confessing their misdeeds they showed the remorse he considered necessary for their rehabilitation. The impact on a committee composed entirely of lawyers, former district attorneys, and a former judge was like that of a bomb in an echo chamber.

This strongly indicates that when a radical change is contemplated on the basis of new ideas about reality, it most likely occurs when there is a validation of the ideas in direct sensory experience—in this case a living breathing judge of the type the commissioners ineptly tried to fix as an image. The situation was dramatic because it was so real and because it was not staged.

Legislators—at least those in California—are well accustomed to staged presentations and highly sophisticated efforts to create realities favorable to the causes of lobbyists. As a matter of fact, they have committee techniques of their own designed to cope with these, that which might be called counter staging, set up to give the impression of responding to the voices of the public. Underneath, legislators tend to be tough-minded; and the prevalence of lawyers among them sets rigorous standards for what will be accepted as facts or evidence. That they have problems of obtaining objective measures of the harmful effects of deviance and of consequences of proposed programs for its control none will deny. The problems face social scientists as well as legislators, but they do not seem sufficient reason to believe that legislators have no way of getting feedback from the objective world.

It remains to comment on the effects of direct experience with physical or ecological consequences of patterns of social control as influences on change. From these flow costs, by which is meant the time, energy, and money costs of means to implement various methods of control. In a context of change this refers to anticipated as well as experienced costs. An important principle is that changes in the definition and control of deviance may be due not to any alteration in value systems but to changes in their costs of satisfaction. An increase in costs, such as the time needed to deliver a youth to detention, may change the disposition of cases by police or probation officers even though their preferences are to follow an old pattern.

Anticipated changes in the costs of means to ends affected both the support for and opposition to the 1961 Juvenile Court law revision. Los Angeles county sheriff people favored the change because the new arrest procedures simplified and helped the efficiency of their delinquency control operations. Police, on the other hand, both north and south, were concerned that the 48-hour limit imposed in the new law for investigations prior to detention hearings would make their jobs impossible. And indeed this was the case so far as their old procedures were concerned, especially in counties like Los Angeles, which had set up a detention control unit within its probation department. As a result, it became harder to use the juvenile court as an adjunct for extra-legal police methods. "Weekenders," youth swept up by police and detained in order to break up or curb local disorders, tended to disappear as a category.

Judges, probation officers, supervisors, and county executives in many instances were painfully aware that the proposed law revision would cost a great deal more money in order to provide counsel for minors, engage court reporters, and prepare records for court hearings. How to raise such funds was a critical issue in a number of counties. The requirement of two and possibly three court hearings could only increase the workload of the court and probation department, which meant either more tax funds or greater expenditures of time and effort by court personnel from judges on down.

The strong opposition to the law change by police and probation officers in the southern part of the state came from recognition of the hard fact that it would end the use of jail for detention, which was an intrinsic feature of the delinquency control system there. This eventuality was felt keenly in Long Beach, where a new wing of the jail had been constructed for such a purpose.

Higher standards of proof mandated by the law change and the new power of probation officers to dismiss at intake meant that more time and care had to go into police investigations and reports. This was more fully appreciated after some experience with the new law, and it fostered a changed categorical attitude that "either you have a case, or you don't." An organizational reflection of this change was the decision of the Los Angeles Police to eliminate its juvenile bureau and turn its work over to the detective bureau.

Herein may lie one of the main outcomes of the 1961 law change, namely a growing tendency to redefine delinquency more exclusively as law violations, and to differentiate such cases from so-called delinquent tendencies cases, many of which began to be handled by other means. Comments now are heard from probation officers that "601's (the code term for such cases) are on their way out."

CONCLUSION

It has been my contention that existing theories of deviance are ill suited to account for the complexities of the societal reaction in modern society. In place of a sociopsychological model I have proposed a group interaction model and tried to show how it clarifies the shifting significance of ends and means and their costs in the emergence of new patterns of social control. The chief gain is a method for specifying the way in which human choices affect the societal reaction without generalizing the claims of others or reducing them to reified ideas of culture, class, or power. It also shows how costs of changes in social control feed back into decisions to make changes, without the necessity of relying on older deterministic conceptions of the effects of the physical world on the social.

The possibility exists that the special subject matter of procedural law change within a bureaucratic context of correctional agencies puts the group interaction model in a more favorable light than if it were applied to substantive legislation of a more obviously "moral" nature, such as marihuana laws, temperance laws, and anti-pornography statutes. Yet I note a recent study of the evolution of our marihuana laws which advisedly chooses an organizational perspective emphasizing bureaucratic utilitarian values in its explanation (Dickson, 1968). I am also reminded of A. M. Lee's (1944) older pluralistic analysis of the temperance movement, which still stands unreconciled with the symbolic crusade theory of the same phenomenon.

A study of social control in Cuba, touching on censorship and sex behavior, not only has challenged the validity of the notion of moral entrepreneurs but also accentuates the need to fit concepts of social control to the differentiation of interests and groups in particular societies (Looney, 1973). All of which tells me that deviance sociologists can do better with working tool concepts than with ambitious theory. They obviously "can't go home again" to old style structural, positivist sociology any more than conservative sociologists can stomach the extremes of labeling theory. But there may be a less pretentious midground on which to meet—if not they, then a less committed generation of sociologists yet to come.

REFERENCES

Becker, Howard
1963 Outsiders. Glencoe, Ill: Free Press.

Bordua, David
1967 "Recent trends: deviant behavior and social control." American Academy of Political and Social Science 57:149–163.

Chambliss, William
1964 "A sociological analysis of the law of vagrancy." Social Problems 12:67–77.

Cottrell, W. F.
1972 Technology, Man and Progress. Columbus: Charles Merrill Pubs.
Dickson, Donald
1968 "Bureaucracy and morality: an organizational perspective on a moral crusade." Social Problems 16:143–156.
Douglas, Jack, ed.
1970 Deviance and Respectability. New York, London: Basic Books.
Garfinkel, Harold
1956 "Conditions of successful degradation ceremonies." American Journal of Sociology 61:420–424.
Goode, Erich
1969 "Marihuana and the politics of reality." Journal of Health and Social Behavior 10:84.
Gouldner, Alvin
1968 "The sociologist as partisan: sociology and the welfare state." American Sociologist (May):103–116.
Gusfield, Joseph
1966 Symbolic Crusade. Urbana, Ill.: Univ. Illinois Press.
Hall, Jerome
1935 Theft, Law and Society. Indianapolis: Bobbs Merrill.
Kolb, William
1967 "A critical evaluation of Mead's 'I' and 'Me' concepts." In Symbolic Interaction (eds. Jerome Manis and Bernard Meltzer). Boston: Allyn and Baron.
Lee, A. M.
1944 Techniques of reform: an analysis of the new prohibition drive. American Sociological Review 9:60–69.
Lemert, Edwin
1951 Social Pathology. New York: McGraw-Hill.
1970 Social Action and Legal Change. Chicago: Aldine Pub. Co.
1972 Human Deviance, Social Problems and Social Control. 2nd ed. Englewood Cliffs, New Jersey: Prentice-Hall, Inc.
Liazos, Alexander
1972 "The poverty of the sociology of deviance: nuts, sluts and perverts." Social Problems 20:103–120.
Looney, Martin
1973 "Social control in Cuba." In Politics and Deviance (eds. Ian Taylor and Laurie Taylor). London: Penguin. 42–60.
Lyman, Standford, and Marvin Scott
1970 A Sociology of the Absurd. New York: Appleton-Century-Crofts.
Manning, Peter
1973 "Survey essay on deviance." Contemporary Sociology 2:123–128.
Mead, G. H.
1917–18 "The Psychology of Punitive Justice." American Journal of Sociology 23:577–602.
Meltzer, Bernard N.
1967 "Mead's social psychology." In Symbolic Interaction (eds. Jerome Manis and Bernard Meltzer). Boston: Allyn and Bacon.

Messinger, Sheldon
1962 "Life as Theater: Some Notes on the Dramaturgic Approach to Social Reality." Sociometry 25 (March):98–110.

Schur, Edwin
1969 "Reaction to deviance: a critical assessment." American Journal of Sociology 75:309–322.

Scott, John
1963 "Changing foundations of a Parsonian scheme of action." American Sociological Review. 28:716–734.

Scott, Robert A.
1970 "Construction of Conceptions of Stigma by Professional Experts." In Deviance and Respectability (ed. Jack Douglas). New York: Basic Books. 255–290.

Tannenbaum, Frank
1937 Crime and the Community. New York: Columbia University Press.

Taylor, Ian, and Laurie Taylor, eds.
1973 Politics and Deviance. London: Penguin.

Walton, Paul
1973 "The case of the weathermen: social reaction and radical commitment." In Politics and Deviance (eds. Ian Taylor and Laurie Taylor). London: Penguin.

Zicklin, Gilbert
1968 "A Conversation Concerning Face-to-Face Interaction." Psychiatry 31, 3 (August):263–249.

Chapter 4

Choice, Value, and Action: Problems in General Social Theory

I have observed to some of my colleagues that labeling theory seems to be largely an invention of its critics. By this I mean that with a few commendable exceptions critics tend to impute common ideas to a number of authors, including myself, whose writings in reality are quite diverse. Critics even derive hypotheses for us or enumerate our underlying assumptions, most recently reaching an impressive total of nine. Having done this, they proceed to demonstrate the logical, methodological, and empirical insufficiencies of the theory. When confronted, those who have been identified with the theory or "school," so called, must deny or refute that which they haven't said, or defend ideas they don't necessarily share or accept only with qualifications.

Recently the tone of criticism has grown more militant and aggressive. A kind of *delenda est*—Carthage must be destroyed—attitude prevails. Critics seem less interested in careful assessment than in attack and destruction (e.g., Gove, 1975). Alleged disregard for the "traditional" approach to deviance by labeling theorists presumably decrees that he who lives by the sword shall die by the sword. Up the counter-revolution!

Unhappily the revolutionary mood abets if not encourages carelessness and misrepresentation. Consider, for example, recent exchanges between Scheff and Gove concerning the pertinence of labeling theory for the study of mental disorders. When I first read Scheff's demurrer that Gove misrepresented his writings, I thought that he—Scheff—was being normally testy about his cherished ideas or showing some mild academic paranoia (Scheff, 1974). My impression changed when in a recent paper Gove stated that in my 1951 book I said: "Those labeled as mentally ill do not differ markedly from those who are not labeled and it is those

---

"Response to Critics: Feedback and Choice." From *The Uses of Controversy in Sociology,* ed. Lewis Coser and Otto Larsen. New York: Free Press, 1976. Pp. 244–49. Reprinted as originally published.

on the margin of society who are most readily labeled" (Lemert, 1951).[1] Curious after twenty-four years to see again what I had said, I reread the designated pages not once but four times. I found no such statements in them.

Lest I too was being only testy, I read carefully a 1969 article by Mendel and Rapport cited by Gove to show that the mentally ill in Los Angeles County are prescreened before commitment and not routinely hospitalized. This turned out to be true and it questions some of Scheff's conclusions, but what Gove doesn't tell us is that commitments varied consistently by day of the week and time of day, and by the professional background of the admitting officials. More importantly it showed that there was no relationship between professionally rated seriousness of mental symptoms and decisions to hospitalize.

Gove's net even brings up a statement by Goffman that labeling theorists fail to examine the "organizational havoc" done to families by mental symptoms, citing this to support the "psychiatric perspective" that persons in mental hospitals are truly sick in a medical sense. Again, what Gove leaves out is that psychiatrists don't examine the havoc either, and further, to quote Goffman, "claims and actions of the ill person are not necessarily bizarre in themselves, merely bizarre when coming from a particular person addressing himself to a particular family. . . . And bizarreness itself is not the issue" (Goffman, 1969).

Years ago the Institute for Propaganda Analysis had a name for Gove's citing practices: It was called card stacking.

Hirschi's recent indictment of labeling theory is less chargeable with misrepresentation; obviously he is a man who reads carefully what others say before he speaks, and he sticks to the text (Hirschi, 1975). I must, however, object to his choice of targets. Tannenbaum strikes me as a sitting duck for a man with as much methodological expertise as Hirschi. Alas, poor Tannenbaum, he wrote thirty-seven years ago, at a time when there was little beyond Shaw and McKay to draw on (Tannenbaum, 1938). Further, he was a historian, most at home with labor problems and foreign policy. Moreover he was not really trying to go beyond presentation of a point of view. And he *did* have a new idea, something attested to by the men who urged its publication: John Dewey, Walton Hamilton, and Thorstein Veblen.

I prefer to think that Hirschi is fighting on ground not of his own choosing against opponents who to him obstinately refuse to follow the rules of the scientific method. This surfaces in his recent assessment of the evidence for and against the application of labeling theory to juvenile delinquency. Hirschi takes labeling simply as a variable in the traditional positivist sense to see whether it causes delinquency. In passing he acknowledges that interaction exists, but to him it is nothing more than the interaction of variables: If X, then Y.

Like the early determinists, Hirschi ignores or denies the existence of choice in human action lest this make us slip back into murky supernatural thinking officially tabooed by science. Our task is to find invariate orders between factors; X causes Y and that's that!

But the process of choice is *not* invariate. Unfortunately the mechanical model of cause and effect has been in use for so long in our culture that it is very difficult to advocate models which take teleology into account. Perhaps, though, as W. F. Cottrell says, now that we can build missiles that hunt missiles we can accept the purposeful behavior that invented them. The idea that human beings respond selectively to symbolic feedback on their actions can give us a model that may contribute to better understanding of what takes place without compelling us to leave what we regard as scientific ground.

A beginning was made with George Herbert Mead's conception of symbolic interaction. This becomes more precise when we include evaluation and groups as well as individuals in the process. To me interaction means that acts and events do not have fixed meanings or consequences when feedback and choice intervene. This does not deny that such things as anxiety exist, or that boys break windows or take automobiles without permission, or that heroin users have withdrawal symptoms. It means rather that human beings exercise choice in responding to these—organizing events into "cases," making judgments as to their seriousness, applying administrative categories, and opting for one among different lines of action.

The issue is whether agents of social control make choices in doing these things and, if they do, what factors influence their choice. If I understand Hirschi correctly, he says that police make simple choices between arresting and not arresting juveniles based on legal criteria, namely seriousness and frequency of the offense. Presumably there is no need to study police to predict the volume and nature of delinquency; delinquency already exists; police passively acknowledge its existence and certify it.

A number of studies are cited to support this conclusion. However, in addition to seriousness of offense, arrest record, age, demeanor, probation status, department, and officer emerge in varying degrees as influences on dispositions. Black and Reiss (1970) discovered that when interaction occurred between police and complainants, arrests of juveniles were more likely, and interaction with black complainants was more apt to produce arrests than with white complainants.

In James Q. Wilson's study (1968) comparing police control of juveniles in eastern and western cities, either overlooked or ignored by Hirschi, large differences came to light in police discretion. Arrest and processing rates for juveniles ran 50 percent higher for western over eastern police, although crime rates did not differ markedly. The greater normalization of juvenile conduct in the East was influenced by different conceptions of the seriousness of offenses, what constituted a record, racial attitudes, local area recruitment of police, location of juvenile officers and their records, patrolling practices, interaction with other officers, and time costs involved in presentation of cases in court—English style by the police themselves.

Similar findings emerged in a study of cautioning juvenile offenders by police in England, mainly done in northern cities (Steer, 1970). Factors influencing choice were age, sex, and nature of the offense but not necessarily its seriousness. Prior offenses were not important unless they were similar to the one in question. Differences between rates of juveniles cautioned rather than arrested varied substantially from one police force to another.

Still another study in Toronto (Gandy, 1970) revealed that differences in the nature and outcome of police discretion in dispositions of juvenile cases varied with the administrative unit to which officers were assigned. Significant differences lay in the emphasis and weight given to similar criteria for choosing dispositions, in perception of the relative seriousness of certain types of behavior, and in the frequency with which certain courses of action were chosen.

When I examine juvenile arrest figures for the State of California I am puzzled, to say the least, by the insistence that police arrest mainly juveniles committing serious offenses. In the 1973 report of the Bureau of Criminal Statistics of 362,000 arrests, 32 percent were felony-level violations, 39 percent misdemeanor-level, and 29 percent delinquent tendencies, such as truancy, runaways, and beyond control. In Sacramento County in 1974 only 40 percent of minors placed in the juvenile hall were for law violations, as opposed to 60 percent for delinquent tendencies and "various other reasons." This, of course, doesn't reflect cases processed by probation and court without being placed in detention, more likely less serious.

These data are consistent with the 1963 Erikson-Empey study in southern California dealing with seriousness of self-reported, undetected delinquency in samples of those never in court, those there once, those on probation, and those in institutions. Court records were found not to reflect the seriousness and frequency of offenses, nor did the latter differentiate or account for those in institutions when measured by undetected offenses. This is supported by Sheridan's 1966 survey of fifteen correctional institutions showing that 30 percent of the child inmates had committed no law violations. Other studies have put this figure as high as 48 percent.

In general I have found that studies of police and juvenile court processing of minors do not contradict the societal reaction view of delinquency, that is, that choice-making by agents of social control, influenced by values, interactions with others, social organization, availability of means and their costs, affect the designation of minors as delinquent and the overall volume and rate of delinquency. The loose definition of delinquency—not even defined in eight states—plus the ambiguous image of the juvenile court have meant that a large number of diverse problems, some of them not even problems, get redefined or rationalized as delinquency and processed because there seems no other way to deal with them.

The number of studies which have been specifically designed to test propositions drawn from societal reaction theory is not large. Many of them are short-term, synchronous in nature, which may show interaction of variables but not how outcomes are produced by symbolic interaction and feedback. They may postdict but not predict, because findings at one point in a process are not those at another point.

Denther and Erikson (1959), for example, some years ago found that recruits in army camps tended to normalize, accommodate, and even protect ineffective, "schizoid" soldiers. But a similar, more extended study by David Schneider (1947) showed that while new recruits accommodated psychosomatic complainers in much the same way, over time, as soldiers assimilated masculinity values of the military, they rejected the complainers, forcing them either to shape up or seek official validation of their sick role through the medical department. The five-year study of schizophrenic women by Sampson, Towne, and Messinger (1962) reached a roughly similar conclusion, that is, that accommodations to deviance may change and break down through time, resulting in hospitalization.

A more impressive demonstration of the effects of feedback based on the discovery of new facts from research came out of the 1969 Mendel-Rapport study. When directors of the admitting center discovered that time of day and day of week were affecting staff recommendations for hospitalization of mental cases, they changed procedure so that weekend cases were held over for review by the Monday staff. Commitments dropped and came more in line with instituted purposes to discover resources and alternatives to avoid hospitalization.

It may be that there is reason to use traditional methodology to study the causes of actions I will cautiously call primary deviance. But I don't think that search for abstract or timeless and spaceless attributes like seriousness of the offense or of symptoms will ever prove fruitful. The best we can hope for is to discover the costs of certain kinds of actions—of the controllers as well as the controlled—and the conditions under which such knowledge will enter into evaluation and policy formation, and, of course, if and how they influence creation and change of definitions of deviance.

NOTE

1. The pages in question are 392–98 and are cited in the paper read by Gove at the Vanderbilt deviancy conference (1975).

REFERENCES

Black, Donald L. and Albert J. Reiss. "Police Control of Juveniles." *American Sociological Review* 35 (February 1970): 63–77.

Crime and Delinquency in California. Sacramento: Bureau of Criminal Statistics [State of California] 1973.

Dentler, Robert and Kai Erikson. "The Functions of Deviance in Groups." *Social Problems* 7 (Fall 1959): 98–107.

Erickson, Maynard L. and LaMar Empey. "Court Records, Undetected Delinquency, and Decision-Making." *Journal of Criminal Law, Criminology, and Police Science* 54 (December 1963): 456–69.

Gandy, John M. "The Exercise of Discretion by Police as a Decision-Making Process in the Disposition of Juvenile Offenders." *Osgoode Hall Law Journal* 8 (November 1970): 329–44.

Goffman, Erving. "The Insanity of Place." *Psychiatry* 32 (November 1969): 357–88.

Gove, Walter R. 1975. "Labelling and Mental Illness: A Critique." In *Labelling Deviant Behavior: The Evaluation of a Perspective,* ed. Walter Gove. New York: Sage-Halstead, 1975, 35–81.

Hirschi, Travis. "Labelling Theory and Juvenile Delinquency: An Assessment of the Evidence." In *Labelling Deviant Behavior: The Evaluation of a Perspective,* ed. Walter Gove. New York: Sage-Halstead, 1975, 181–203.

Lemert, Edwin M. *Social Pathology*. New York: McGraw-Hill, 1951.

Mendel, Werner and Samuel Rapport. "Determinants in the Decision for Psychiatric Hospitalization." *Archives of General Psychiatry* 20 (March 1969: 321–8).

Sampson, Harold, Sheldon Messinger, and Robert Towne. "Family Processes and Becoming a Mental Patient." *American Journal of Sociology* (July 1962): 88–96.

Scheff, Thomas. "The Labelling Theory of Mental Illness." *American Sociological Review* 39 (June 1974): 444–52.

Schneider, David. "The Social Dynamics of Physical Disability in Army Basic Training." *Psychiatry* 10 (August 1947): 323–33.

Sheridan, William H. "Juveniles Who Commit Non-Criminal Acts: Why Treat Them in a Correctional System?" *Federal Probation* XXXI (1967): 26–30.

Steer, David. *Police Cautions: A Study in the Exercise of Police Discretion.* Oxford: Blackwell, 1970.

Tannbenbaum, Frank. *Crime and the Community*. Boston: Ginn and Co., 1938.

Wilson, James Q. "The Police and the Delinquent in Two Cities." In *Controlling Delinquents,* ed. Stanton M. Wheeler and Helen M. Hughes. New York: Wiley, 1968, Chapter 7.

Chapter 5

Rules, Deviance, and Social Control Theory

What we call deviance sociology and its cognate the "new criminology" without question have turned the thinking of social scientists in new directions and have considerably influenced related fields, such as psychiatry. They may even be said to be legitimized perspectives or at least respectably competing paradigms for the study of a good deal of what in the past has been called social problems. However, at the same time it is clear to the informed and thoughtful observer that, despite its professional and lay claims, all is not well with deviance sociology; flaws and inconsistencies in its formulations have surfaced in a substantial body of critical literature not easily disregarded. Much of this has been aimed at labeling theory, largely using Howard Becker's (1963) ideas as its target of opportunity.

At the risk of seeming to destroy that which I am assumed to help create if not initiate, I must ask whether the revolutionary features of labeling theory are not more apparent than real and whether by failing to develop a theory of social control (and a more nuanced concept of societal reaction) it does not carry forward much of the older structural conception of deviance. This is most apparent in Becker's statement that groups create rules whose infraction constitutes deviance (1963: 1–18). Significantly, Merton (1971: 827) called this statement banal, and as such he found no difficulty in integrating labeling ideas into his older structural conception of social disorganization and deviance. Furthermore, when Becker succumbed to the temptations of the fourfold table (1963: 20) to elaborate his conception, he trapped himself in inconsistency by recognizing the existence of secret deviance while simultaneously asserting that deviance to be such must be labeled by others. This denies what is to me the central assumption of deviance sociology—namely, that the existence of deviance is always problematic and that it can't be separated from the defining action of others or from extant social definitions applied by individuals to their own behavior.

Previously unpublished.

In short, I argue here that Becker's oft-quoted formulation of deviance fails to capture the innovative thrust of deviance sociology and gives no more than a superficial impression of a qualitative jump away from structural conceptions of deviance. The time is ripe for a second revolt in deviance sociology that will clear away or shoot down some of the junk still orbiting in our thoughts about deviance. A beginning can be made with a brief survey of what can be safely said about rules, particularly as they relate to public policy and social control.

RULES IN PUBLIC POLICY AND SOCIAL CONTROL

That rules alone are not an adequate basis for predicting what people will do was recognized and provocatively documented by the legal realists many years ago, and while the shortcomings of their views are well known, it is also true that their main conclusions are taken for granted in present-day jurisprudence. This is particularly true when attention is directed to the practice of law or to law as a system of interacting groups that lay- and professional law people participate in, rather than concentrating on how judges reason and what court cases show.

Most recently, structural concepts such as role, institution, norms, and rules have come under attack by ethnomethodologists and phenomenologists, who, impressed by the pluralism of modern society, hold that social reality must be found under, beyond, or apart from rules. Unfortunately, the concepts they propose to replace rules—routine practices, proverbial characterizations, or relational rules—do not token a radical departure from structural analysis so much as they seek to adopt a deeper level of analysis. A moment's reflection will betray their similarity to such ideas as "latent culture patterns" or to Fuller's concept of implicit law (1968: 43–49, 50, 57*ff.*).

The insufficiency of a rules-oriented conception of deviance is further attested to by criticism that those designated as radical sociologists have leveled at labeling theory. They assert that the theory concentrates too much on the actions of middle management agents of social control and ignores their hidden commitments to larger power groups or dominant classes in our society. They urge that people ordinarily studied as deviants in reality should be considered as victims, and the study of deviance in general should be shifted to their exploiters. Whatever their oversights and undersights, the radical critics add to the conviction that deviance can't be fully understood through examining the application of rules alone—that something significant lies beyond the rules.

There is still more evidence of the inconstancy of rules, their dependence on other factors, and their dissociation from the process of social control. Consider, for example, the phenomenon of politicization, which has been elucidated by such writers as Gusfield (1967), Horowitz and Leibowitz (1968), and Spector and Kitsuse (1977). Given politicization of norms, deviants change into minority groups whose violation of laws are tactical moves against a hated establishment or symbolic affirmation of rights denied to them. Looking beyond the confines of American society to socialist societies old and new clearly conveys not only that rules may be politicized but that crime and deviance typically may get defined and controlled by processes in which rules are so attenuated as to be nonexistent. Nazi Germany, Soviet Russia, Cuba, and, above all, the People's Republic of China supply comparative data showing that such societies have in the past and do currently define and control crime and deviance by political, administrative, or informal means.

The comparative study of deviance is not well developed, and it is doubtful whether any of our current formulations of deviance would be up to the task, primarily because they make so little room for political or group interaction in the analysis of the social control of deviance. When cross-cultural comparisons are made, usually they are superficial and undertaken to show the superiority of our criminal justice system as we like to believe exists, or to show how easily politics compromises systems other than our own. Politics in the administration of the criminal law in our society is an embarrassment, or it is taken as signs of the pathology of the law or form of deviance itself. A case in point is Blumberg's (1967) likening of the practice of the criminal law to a con game, in that the defendant is beaten not by inequalities or race, class, and economics but by the reciprocities of the system. Recent statistics make us wonder whether it is not the defendant who is winning the battles of crime, but this does not alter the realities that due process of law is something quite different than represented to be and that rules and rights become values that are negotiated in complex interaction.

The illusion of the autonomy of law created by pure reason dies hard and still casts its pall over the social sciences. Dispelling the illusion by recognition that rules are a product of past political interaction and their current use or indeed nonuse is a consequence of group interaction is imperative for the development of working models for the study of deviance and crime. Deviance is much better defined operationally as a body of data that are the consequences of types of social controls and responses to them rather than as violations of rules or laws. Social control in this context of thought is a dynamic, creative process admitting of values and policy formation in all their permutations.

SOCIAL CONTROL AND VALUES

Some perceptive readers at this point may say that they like the sound of my music but are not so sure about the words, particularly in that the term *social control* is likely to be a slippery one and that abandoning the concepts of rules may make the waters of deviance study even muddier. But deviance can be made explicit by saying that human beings and their actions may become objects or subjects of disapproval, condemnation, penalties, ostracism, banishment, segregation, treatment, and unsolicited help or even friendly advice—that is, of social controls. When and where this occurs, there is a body of data for study. Space does not allow me to develop a whole statement of social control in this chapter, but the organizing factors can be enumerated as values, groups, and structures (note the plural use of the term). The central process is group interaction, whose subjective aspects are to be found in evaluation and choice (Cottrell 1972; Fuller 1964).

Some may object to the use of values in a theory of social control, insisting that this is simply to call rules by another name. Admittedly, there are those in the social sciences who believe that the term is spurious or tautological and adds nothing to the explanation of behavior. Surveys of values with questionnaires are quite likely to get little more than lip service to ideals of little predictive use. Furthermore, even when values are inferred from observation, the difficulty persists that they may become terms to describe uniformities in behavior and then be invoked to explain the behavior. How, then, can value be employed to avoid these difficulties?

Following W. F. Cottrell, I use the concept of value to mean that which within physical and biological limits influences choice (Cottrell 1972; Lemert 1973). Value is defined in terms of opportunity costs; that is, we know the value of a thing when we know what we will sacrifice to achieve it. To avoid a narrow economic meaning of the term, we must say that policymaking and social control or action by an agency are the result of all the choices made by all of those involved, in terms of all that must be sacrificed to reach a given end or a goal. This kind of orientation moves us beyond preoccupation with discretionary action by individual police officers, sentencing peculiarities of judges, or such things as the intent of the legislature.

With this kind of a model of social control, rules of law are no more than several among a variety of means to ensure the priority of certain values in political action. Such concepts as justice, due process, rights, duties, rule of law, reason, and presumption of innocence are no more than values whose priority, while high in our culture, remains problematic and whose negotiability emerges from the interaction of groups characteristically called agencies of law making, enforcement, and courts.

Willingness to consider rules of law as means to ends rather than as negotiable values is often imputed to police when they are criticized for employing illegal methods to get evidence and make their arrests. Yet, close inquiry reveals that illegality is far from rare in the actions of prosecutors, public defenders, and judges as well, to say nothing of criminal lawyers. This is shown in Sudnow's (1965) findings that criminal charges often get reduced to situationally included lesser offenses rather than to those that can be legally included. Judges may grant probation or jail sentences in violation of the penal code, as I learned years ago while studying check forgers in Los Angeles County. In response to my queries as to why this happens, I was told, "Who is going to object?" What this says is not that no one objected but that no groups with contravening values were organized to make their objections felt in the judicial process.

A social control theory of deviance bypasses questions of causation in favor of prediction or analysis of how it emerges in policy, sociolegal definitions, and sanctions or treatment and what happens thereafter. Some find this theory perturbing, for it seems to disregard the significance of the subjects' behavior or the actions of those who take on deviant status. But social control is always selective, and while it may be arbitrary, it is also based on objective determination of costs of actions and affronts to identifiable values of others. The study of the costs of extant or developing patterns of behavior, how they arise and enter as considerations in public policy or new legislation, is a valid social science task so long as these patterns are not arbitrarily called deviance or crime by the researchers, thus confusing what some think should be with what is.

REFERENCES

Becker, Howard S. *Outsiders: Studies in the Sociology of Deviance*. Glencoe, Ill.: Free Press, 1963.

Blumberg, Abraham. "The Practice of Law as a Confidence Game: The Organizational Cooptation of a Profession." *Law and Society Review* 1, no. 2 (June 1967): 15–40.

Cottrell, W. F. *Technology, Man, and Progress*. Upper Saddle River, N.J.: Merrill/Prentice Hall, 1972.

Fuller, Lon. *The Anatomy of the Law*. New York: Praeger, 1968.

———. *The Morality of Law*. New Haven, Conn.: Yale University Press, 1964.

Gusfield, Joseph. "Moral Passage: The Symbolic Process in Public Designations of Deviance." *Social Problems* 15, no. 2 (Fall 1967): 175–88.

Horowitz, Irving L., and Martin Leibowitz. "Social Deviance and Political Marginality." *Social Problems* 15 (Winter 1968): 280–96.

Lemert, Edwin M. "Cottrell and Social Problems." *Sociological Focus* 6, no. 4 (Fall 1973): 111–16.

Merton, Robert K. "Social Problems and Sociological Theory." In *Contemporary Social Problems,* ed. R. K. Merton and R. A. Nisbet. 3d ed. New York: Harcourt, Brace Jovanovich, 1971.

Spector, Malcolm, and John Kitsuse. *Constructing Social Problems*. Menlo Park, Calif.: Cummings, 1977.

Sudnow, David. "Normal Crimes: Sociological Features of the Penal Code in a Public Defender's Office." *Social Problems* 12, no. 3 (Winter 1965): 255–76.

Chapter 6

How We Got Where We Are: An Informal History of the Study of Deviance

THE EMERGENCE OF SOCIAL PATHOLOGY

The study of deviance by sociologists dates from the early 1950s, when it became differentiated from the more general study of social problems and began to replace older fields commonly known as social pathology and social disorganization. Social pathology had prevailed as a kind of textbook, academic perspective on social problems from the early part of the twentieth century until the 1930s. Borrowed from medicine, the conception drew an analogy between organisms and societies, allowing that the latter as well as the former could be either normal and "healthy" or, conversely, subject to diseases. Social pathologies included such conditions as blindness, deafness, and illness, as well as poverty, unemployment, alcoholism, prostitution, crime, and insanity. These deplored states presented themselves to society or its curative agencies primarily as individual cases of failure to adjust the normative demands and standards of ongoing society. The norms and values by which social pathologies were identified were largely taken for granted, without critical reflection, by early social scientists as well as by those working with maladjusted persons through welfare agencies.

The study of social pathology was substantially influenced by eighteenth-century Enlightenment ideas, nineteenth-century evolutionary theory, and a belief in progress or the perfectibility of human institutions. These ideas together with humanitarianism pervaded the climate of social reform, which was conspicuous in American life until about World War I. Social pathology had close ties with the then emerging field of social work, which went farthest in embracing a medical vocabulary and borrowed ideas such as "case study," social "diagnosis," and "treatment"

Previously unpublished.

for problems of individuals and families. But whatever success social workers may have had in using such medical ideas, social pathology as a field failed to generate significant hypotheses or produce any distinctive research. Rather, it served as a convenient rubric under which to bring together in textbook form a variety of discussions of discrete social problems organized pragmatically in terms of causes, effects, and proposed solutions.

Social pathology lost its hold on sociological thought for several reasons, though its impulse in social work is still alive. Generally, the sociopsychological assumption on which it rested—opposition of the incompetent or "antisocial" individual to society—gave way to the interactional psychology of James Mark Baldwin, Charles Horton Cooley, and George Herbert Mead, which made society and the individual both expressions of a common socializing process, now generally known as *symbolic interaction.* Beyond this, a growing commitment of sociologists to the scientific method, their sensitivity to the issue of cultural relativity, and confrontation with the disruptive changes resulting from the Great Depression of the 1930s made the social pathology view of social problems less and less tenable. A conviction that their work should be more rigorous and value-free led many sociologists away from the study of social problems and social pathology. Access to a mounting body of comparative materials in anthropology challenged the evolutionary idea of the superiority or progressive nature of Western societies. The rise of seemingly successful communist and fascist societies early in the twentieth century in Europe stimulated social criticism directed at American institutions and capitalist social systems generally. Finally, the effects of worldwide economic depression, beginning in 1929 and causing large-scale unemployment, made it increasingly difficult to sustain the idea that this and related problems followed from some failure of individuals to adapt to normal institutions.

SOCIAL DISORGANIZATION

The concept of social disorganization that competed with and then largely displaced social pathology was more suited for interpreting larger social influences at work as America passed through the Depression years, saw wars and revolutions abroad, and along with other Western nations drifted toward World War II. Its two main versions had been set down in the work of Charles Horton Cooley and the collaboration of W. I. Thomas and Florian Znaniecki. Cooley's ideas centered around the consequences that rapid means of communication and transportation had for local institutions and primary groups such as the family, neighborhood, and small community. Thomas and Znaniecki dealt more directly and empirically with the effects of war and migration on peasant groups and values, at the same time trying to account in theoretical terms for the difficulties Polish immigrants experienced in settling in American cities during the early twentieth century.

The theory of social disorganization stressed change, flux, dissensus, conflict, and uneven development of societies and cultures. Social disorganization and personal disorganization were viewed as organically interdependent, the latter being a symptom of the former. One of the more explicit formulations of social disorganization was that of cultural lag, proposed by William Fielding Ogburn to demonstrate how tension and strain emerged from rapid developments in science and technology without reciprocal changes or adaptations by the family, education, religious institutions, and law. A significant but little-known application of the cultural lag hypothesis appeared in the work of the legal realist school of American jurisprudence, whose representatives helped shape policy and legislation during the New Deal administrations of Franklin D. Roosevelt beginning in 1932. This zealous body of scholar administrators took the dominance of large-scale corporate enterprise in American society as a fait accompli and set themselves the task of discovering legal devices to facilitate the achievement of maximum efficiency by business and industry and to achieve a more equitable distribution of goods and services.

Another development that helped flesh out the theory of social disorganization took place at the University of Chicago, whose department of sociology led the field until the mid-1930s. Sociologists there carried out extensive empirical studies in urban ethnography and social ecology and evolved a zonal hypothesis to demarcate areas of the city where rates of social disorganization such as juvenile delinquency, crime, mental illness, and drug addiction were highest. Proponents of this early social disorganization theory believed that the problems they studied were outcomes of natural processes of competition, succession, and segregation whose net result was to weaken social controls in some areas and not others.

Studies in other cities did not bear out the findings on social disorganization in Chicago. Social ecology of that period failed to account sufficiently for the effects of culture and values in shaping neighborhoods and constituent communities, particularly in the case of the Italian American populations. In time, the then current statistical techniques used to differentiate and delineate disorganized social areas were shown to be defective. Finally, subsequent ethnographic research demonstrated that while crime and vice might be found largely in slum areas, closer analysis revealed considerable integration or social organization existed there as well—between illegal activities and those acceptable to the larger community, such as church participation, business, and civic leadership. This emerged clearly in connection with organized gambling, which, to use the term coined by Robert Merton (1949a), served a "latent function" of facilitating affluence or upward mobility by disadvantaged slum dwellers, thus fulfilling in devious ways the promise of American entrepreneurial "success" values.

The conception of social disorganization held its ground in the writing and teaching of sociologists well into the 1950s and still has its defenders. It had and has the virtue of keeping social thinkers alert to the salience and consequences of rapid social change in Western and other world cultures. However, by emphasizing continuous social transformation, advocates of this approach made it difficult to distinguish empirically the conditions of social organization, disorganization, and reorganization. Nor was the line between social and personal disorganization ever successfully drawn and demonstrated empirically. Generally, one must conclude that only in a society with a value consensus or an accepted set of goals and shared priorities is it even possible to specify the conditions, patterns of action, or individual behavior that are disorganized. Appreciation of this difficulty becomes clearer in considering an alternative way of thinking about social problems and deviance, well known to sociologists as *functionalism.*

FUNCTIONALISM: THE WISDOM OF THE EAST

While the conceptions of social pathology and social disorganization issued from the thought and writings of sociologists indigenous to middle America, reflecting its pragmatism and sensitivity to problems of the immediate environment, functionalism was a much more sophisticated creation of those identified with academic establishments of the eastern seaboard, especially Harvard and Columbia Universities. Functionalist theory subordinated questions of social problems, social disorganization, and deviance by ignoring social change as such and asserting the prior existence of a social system. This was derived from assumptions about the implicit necessities for the reciprocal working of the component institutions of society and for its survival as a whole. Insofar as the idea of social disorganization was retained or integrated with functionalism, it became synonymous with conflicts of values or interests, or simply role conflicts. Parameters of such conflicts, of course, fall within the social system. The term *social dysfunctions* sometimes replaced that of disorganization.

In contrast to those writing about social disorganization, the functionalists began with assumptions of integration, equilibrium (sometimes called *homeostasis*), and boundary maintenance as attributes of social systems. These ideas owed a good deal to Durkheim's assertions about the necessary conditions of the moral order (*conscience collective*) of society. According to these, an important function of deviance was the activation of mechanisms of social control that made those failing to conform to the demands of the moral order subject to exclusion and public reaction to their actions as illegitimate.

Whereas Talcott Parsons, the foremost exponent of social system analysis, believed that social controls brought the deviant back into line, Durkheim stated that reactions to deviance, such as punishment of crime, might have little direct effect on the deviant but rather were a means of keeping social cohesion intact and of preserving the collective conscience. Such reactions were symbolic in nature, reaffirming the legitimacy of salient social values. This strand of thought is important for functional interpretations that make deviance a natural product of social systems. It also helps account for the existence of historically venerable forms of deviance such as prostitution and gambling, which have persisted for centuries despite social disapproval and repressive measures. From this perspective, deviance has paradoxical dual functions: it disrupts a social system, but it also contributes to its survival by periodic reinforcement of its dominant values.

Kai Erikson (1962) has added a related function of deviance, which he calls "boundary maintenance," meaning that deviance and social control mark off the boundaries of a group or community, indicating where "good" lies and "bad" begins and who belongs to which group. All this is very much in the older Durkheimian mode. According to Erikson's analysis, the magnitude of social control bears little relation to the actual volume of deviance in a society. The proportionate number of deviants selected out for symbolic punishment or control remains constant over time. It was this idea plus his insistence that "audiences" confer the property of deviance on persons that makes Erikson's approach in effect a bridge between functionalism and labeling theory.

No discussion of functionalism and deviance would be complete without reference to Merton's (1949b) famous linkage of social structure and anomie, which held the center of the stage in American deviance research for over two decades. Merton, like Durkheim and Parsons, under whom he studied, subscribed to the idea that societies have common hierarchies of cultural values. Likewise, he insisted that deviance is a natural product of a type of social structure that attenuates commitment to institutional norms. But while Durkheim believed that anomie or a condition of normlessness derived from the complex division of labor within society, Merton attributed it to the discontinuity between cultural structure and social class structure, which blocks or frustrates efforts of members of the lower classes to achieve societally approved ends. Put simply, his theory holds that some persons, due to situational disadvantage, are unable to succeed in a very success-oriented culture, and so they deviate from its norms primarily to have a better chance at success.

Merton's method had the merit of starting with a body of data and formulating concepts relevant to the problem under study, for which reason his theory of deviance has been called "middle range." While empirical research did not bear it out, his underlying idea that socially engendered conflict or psychological "strain" may be an influence that under some conditions leads to differentiation and deviance retains, nevertheless, some plausibility. Merton was mainly concerned with alienation, the disruptive effects of anomie, and failures of social systems to fulfill their functional prerequisites in relation to the generation of deviance. The overlap of these ideas with those of social disorganization is easily seen.

The shortcomings of functional analysis are well known in sociology. Whether relationships claimed to exist between institutions or between institutions and individuals are necessary for the survival of society is difficult to prove. The only compete test of functional necessity is whether people can get along without some particular pattern of behavior, but opportunities to observe such a situation may not often occur, and for some aspects of culture they never do. Hence, saying what is dysfunctional or deviant in a functional sense may be little more than an informed opinion and, as with the assertions of some of the older social pathologists, suspect of concealing moral bias albeit in more sophisticated language.

Functional analysis also has to be faulted for its adherence to a mechanical model of cause and effect that has so long dominated the physical and biological sciences and still pervades the social sciences. Human beings portrayed as unique individuals seldom appear in functional analysis; rather, they are conceived as actors, roles, class members, whose actions largely flow from their position in a social structure. It is for this reason that critics have written of the functional approach to deviance as the method of "insiders-from-a-distance" (Matza 1969: 32; Davis 1972: 449).

All of this is not to say that functional analysis is without value or that social structures have no influence over what people do. However, it must be protested that social structures do not cause people to act or to act in any specific way. If functional necessities exist, living people have to recognize them and take action to satisfy them. This means that they give thought to them and choose from alternative courses of action, hopefully leading to "functional" adaptations. Sometimes their choices help reinforce and preserve a systematic way of action, and sometimes they don't.

So long as structures and situations remain constant or change only in some way that preserves overall equilibrium, certain facts such as divorce rates, suicide rates, or family expenditures stay fixed or change in predictable ways. But knowledge gained from such phenomena is of little use in anticipating or predicting the outcome of fresh, changing, or novel situations. Something else "functions" in such situations. Missing from functional analysis as far back as Durkheim is a conceptual place for what Cooley (1966 [1918]: 351–62) called "social intelligence." This appears as evaluation and choice by individuals; when put into a context of social organization, it can be seen best in the interaction of groups.

SOCIETAL REACTION THEORY: A VIEW FROM THE WEST

While the symbolic interactionism of Cooley and Mead had become the ascendant theme of American social psychology by 1930, its application to the study of deviance did not take place until the late 1940s. At this time, what later came to be known as societal reaction theory appeared (Lemert 1948, 1951), subsequently superseded by labeling theory. Some have converged the two theories by referring to a single "neo-Chicagoan school"; others have called it the Western school, and still others the Pacific Seminar. On balance, its origin seems most accurately located as a post–World War II development taking place among sociology faculty and graduate students initially at UCLA and somewhat later at the University of California, Berkeley.

At UCLA Leonard Broom, one of its first sociologists, had briefly used a text by L. Guy Brown (1942) entitled *Social Pathology: Personal and Social Disor-*

ganization to teach a course in social problems. When I joined the faculty, I took over the course and continued to use Brown's book. From this emerged some of the ideas on deviance that were incorporated into my own equally mistitled book, *Social Pathology: A Systematic Approach to the Theory of Sociopathic Behavior* (1951). My main purpose was to develop some articulated concepts that could be applied consistently to the analysis of different forms of what up to that time had been called social problems or social disorganization.

Brown's book advanced two seminal ideas, unfortunately submerged in a heavily redundant writing style. One was that the abnormal and the normal both should be studied as natural variations of human behavior. The other was the provocative idea that causes of problematic behavior should be ignored in favor of looking at the behavior in terms of the meaning its gets from social interaction—a remarkable idea for its time. From this he went on to state that abnormal behavior, through interaction, might become part of social organization and, conversely, that normal behavior might become an integral part of social or personal disorganization. In effect, this view was a sociological paraphrase of the paradox that evil can come from good and good from evil. It reflected Brown's close affinity with the older University of Chicago sociology that featured the study of crime, delinquency, and vice as natural phenomena.

Lest too much influence be credited to University of Chicago sociology and Mead's social behaviorism as fonts of deviance theory, note that Brown also drew substantially from the then current field theory of Kurt Lewin and J. F. Brown. L. Guy Brown also carried forward the value conflict theory of social problems developed by Richard C. Fuller, Richard R. Myers, and Willard Waller, which, descending from William Graham Sumner, held that cherished values and institutions had to be considered as causes of social problems (Brown 1942: 14, 56).

In my early writings (1948, 1951), I attempted to systematize in a rough way the study of deviance, primarily in terms of social differentiation and social control, and to discover the circumstances under which the latter gives meaning and shape and stability to socially evaluated differences of individuals and groups. In this connection, I proposed that primary deviance under specified conditions may differentiate into secondary deviance, in which role and self definitions change qualitatively in the process of adaptation to societal reaction and social control. Later John Kitsuse (1962), originally my student at UCLA, stated societal reaction theory in more explicitly interactionist terms. Then Kitsuse and another of my UCLA students, Aaron V. Cicourel, contributed the further idea that "rates of deviance" are socially produced by control agencies and should be studied as such (Kitsuse and Cicourel 1963).

From a somewhat different angle, Erving Goffman's (1961) study of the social world of mental patients and the characteristics of total institutions, published in book form while he was at the University of California, Berkeley, perhaps did more than any other single work to popularize the then new approach to deviance. By design and necessity, he adopted an unbalanced, highly partisan view of the plight of the mental patient, which he justified on the grounds that most of the literature at the time had been written by professional psychiatrists "on the other side." In so doing, he echoed a position taken many years earlier by Albion Small, who believed that there were times when the imbalance of interests in society required that social scientists align themselves with the position of the underprivileged.

Following Goffman came Howard S. Becker's (1963) lucid exposition of what has become imprinted in the minds of many sociologists as labeling theory. Becker, like Goffman, had been a student of Everett Hughes and Herbert Blumer at Chicago, and his westernization, if it occurred, took place while he was at the Stanford Institute for the Study of Social Problems, during which time he held the editorship of *Social Problems*. Becker's ideas, which he regarded more as a perspective than as a theory, were that social groups create deviance by making rules whose infraction becomes deviance and by applying the rules to particular people and labeling them as outsiders. Such rules originated from the activities of those he termed "moral entrepreneurs." He also made a distinction, later quite controversial, between rule breaking and deviance, the latter including labeling as such by society. Becker was more doctrinaire than Goffman in his insistence that sociologists must take the viewpoint of the deviant—or the "underdog," as he put it—although he also justified this stance on technical research grounds as well.

There is more continuity in the development of societal reaction and labeling theories than ordinarily believed. Many other sociologists than those mentioned here contributed to the rise of the new perspective on deviance, and in a sense it experienced a pervasive intellectual growth throughout the 1950s, at first unheralded, then unmistakably installed as a provocative theoretical alternative to the positivist and functionalist approaches to deviance. The most dramatic instance of this development happened in Britain, where American ideas on deviance became a stimulus for the organization of the National Deviancy Conferences and the rise of the so-called new criminology (Taylor, Walton, and Young 1974).

Whether and to what extent the new deviance sociology was an ideological outgrowth of post–World War II socioeconomic conditions can only be a subject for speculation. The accelerated growth of large-scale organizations and bureaucracies in industry, business, health, welfare, government, and law enforcement generally suggest that it might have been some form of dialectical response of social scientists to the declining power and freedom of individuals vis-à-vis organizations. Labeling theorists have been variously characterized as "humanist critical," "liberal pragmatic," "counterintellectual," "debunking," "antitechnical," and even "hip" by various commentators. But such designations are easier to apply in retrospect than they could have been at the time deviance sociology was in the making. Acquaintance with the diversity in the backgrounds and interests of those credited with its origin belies the notion that they shared a common ideology. To speak of them as a school strains the idea, as an English sociologist once reminded me a number of years ago, by making the startling and revealing observation that "in America the symbolic interactionists rarely speak to one another."

REFERENCES

Becker, Howard S. *Outsiders: Studies in the Sociology of Deviance*. Glencoe, Ill.: Free Press, 1963.

Brown, L. Guy. *Social Pathology: Personal and Social Disorganization*. New York: Crofts, 1942.

Cooley, Charles Horton. *The Social Process*. Carbondale: Southern Illinois University Press, 1966 [1918].

Davis, Nanette J. "Labeling Theory in Deviance Research: A Critique and a Reconsideration." *Sociological Quarterly* 13, no. 4 (Fall 1972): 447–74.

Erikson, Kai T. "Notes on the Sociology of Deviance." *Social Problems* 9, no. 4 (Spring 1962): 307–14.

Goffman, Erving. *Asylums: Essays on the Social Situation of Mental Patients and Other Inmates*. Garden City, N.Y.: Doubleday, 1961.

Kitsuse, John. "Societal Reaction to Deviant Behavior: Problems of Theory and Method." *Social Problems* 9, no. 3 (Winter 1962): 247–56.

Kitsuse, John, and Aaron V. Cicourel. "A Note on the Uses of Official Statistics." *Social Problems* 11, no. 2 (Fall 1963): 131–39.

Lemert, Edwin M. *Social Pathology: A Systematic Approach to the Theory of Sociopathic Behavior*. New York: McGraw-Hill, 1951.

———. "Some Aspects of a General Theory of Sociopathic Behavior." *Proceedings of the Pacific Sociological Society Research Studies, State College of Washington* 16 (1948): 23–29.

Matza, David. *Becoming Deviant*. Upper Saddle River, N.J.: Prentice Hall, 1969.

Merton, Robert K. "Manifest and Latent Functions." In Robert K. Merton, *Social Theory and Social Structure*. Glencoe, Ill.: Free Press, 1949a.

———. "Social Structure and Anomie." In Robert K. Merton, *Social Theory and Social Structure*. Glencoe, Ill.: Free Press, 1949b.

Taylor, Ian R., Paul Walton, and Jock Young. *The New Criminology: For a Social Theory of Deviance*. New York: Harper & Row, 1974.

Part II

Ethnographies of the Marginal

Chapter 7

Home Brew, Hoochinoo, and the Whiskey Feast: Indian Drinking

INTRODUCTION

The purpose of this monograph and the research it reports is to help fill the need for comparative study of the consumption of alcoholic beverages in different societies. This paper is therefore both descriptive and theoretically interpretative of the drinking behavior of the Indians living on the Northwest Coast of America. The observations are the product of field research conducted there during five months of 1951 and for shorter summer periods in 1952 and 1953. Contacts were made with bands and informants from the following tribal groups: Salish, Nootka, Kwakiutl, Tsimshian, and Haida. The most extensive observations and most intensive interviewing were carried on in three Salish tribes—the Homalthko, the Sliammon, and the Tlahoose—on the mainland of British Columbia between Bute Inlet and Powell River.

THE PATTERN OF DRINKING AND ITS FUNCTIONS

All available evidence seems to concur in placing the native peoples of the Northwest Coast of America among American Indians who in aboriginal times were without knowledge and techniques for brewing or distilling intoxicating beers or liquors. One exceptional note comes from reports on the Kwakiutl of Vancouver

---

Excerpts from *Alcohol and the Northwest Coast Indians*. University of California Publications in Culture and Society, volume 2, number 6. Berkeley: University of California Press, 1954. Pp. 305–10, 323–32. Reprinted by permission of University of California Press.

Island, who made a beverage of elderberry juice, black chitons, and tobacco, which they claimed "made them dizzy." However, white men who tried this concoction did not experience any feelings of intoxication.[1] Even allowing for the possibility that the drink was an intoxicant, it remains clear that at the time of initial contact of the Indians with white culture it was neither in widespread use in the coastal area nor indeed of any noticeable significance as a culture trait of the Kwakiutl.

The absence of primitive intoxicants in the Indian cultures of the area under consideration means that the study of drinking behavior becomes a study of white-Indian contact and acculturation. The historical data make this preeminently clear. Liquor was introduced into the Aleutian Islands and the northern coastal cultures sometime after 1741 by the Russian explorers and colonizers, and later in the south by the Spanish, English, and Americans.[2] There is evidence that the first reactions of the aborigines to liquor were those of distaste and suspicion of the motives of the persons who provided the liquor. These definitely were the reactions of the more northerly, warlike tribes, the Tlingit, Tsimshian, and Ilaida. In all likelihood they sprang from the easy perception of drunkenness as causing special vulnerability to attacks and raids by enemies. The common expectations of encountering surreptition, surprise, and trickery in dealings with persons outside their own tribe led the natives to refuse liquor offered to them lest it "put them in the power of the Russians."[3]

Be this as it may, the initial resistance of the coastal Indians to the use of liquor soon decayed, and by 1790 they had everywhere acquired a taste for it as well as the expectation of receiving it from white men with whom they had dealings. At first liquor was given to Indians by explorers in a spirit of hospitality and curiosity; but later the dispensing of liquor to Indians seems to have become a concomitant of trade or a means of ingratiating traders with the native population. After 1800 the intense competition of maritime traders for furs converted liquor into a basic item of barter; soon no trading ship was considered completely stocked without many casks of liquor aboard. Moreover, the Indians frequently entered into trade solely for the purpose of securing rum or whisky, particularly after their rudimentary needs for guns, ammunition, and metal artifacts had been satisfied.

The Hudson's Bay Company and the Northwest Company of Canada both apparently had some conception of preventing liquor from becoming a chief means of trade, mainly in the interests of building up some kind of inland empire based upon a continuing fur harvest made possible by a tenuous discipline of native trappers and hunters. The maritime fur traders had no such policy, and the situation on the coast was additionally complicated by intense competition between traders of several nationalities. New England traders, the "Boston men," not only were inclined to outbid most of their British and Russian competitors but also were quicker to raise the number of gallons of rum per skin necessary to woo the Indians into trading.

In 1812 the Northwest Company and the Pacific Fur Company agreed to refrain from the use of liquor in dealings with the Indians, but it was not until 1842 that any real control was instituted. At that time the Russian American Company and the Hudson's Bay Company entered into a compact whereby neither would use intoxicants as a trade item unless "compelled to" by outside competition—in other words, by the Americans. There is reason to believe that in the next ten or fifteen years liquor was indeed used much less extensively in trading with the Indians, particularly north of Victoria.[4] In the 1850s there came some rather remarkable and as yet incompletely explained migrations of whole bands of northern Indians to live in the vicinity of Victoria; and at least one historian has suggested that the collective desire of these Indians for liquor, which could be obtained more easily through illicit traffic in the inlets and bays around this settlement, may have been an important reason for the migrations and encampments.[5]

In 1858 the situation in regard to the liquor traffic with the Indians was again disturbed, by the heavy influx of Americans en route to the newly discovered gold fields of British Columbia. Being a rough lot and accustomed to riotous dissipation, these miners were quick to use liquor as a means of debauching native women. It became a practice at this time and for some time thereafter for Indian women to journey to Victoria almost solely for purposes of prostitution, by means of which they earned money to buy liquor to take back to their villages. Although legislation forbidding the giving or selling of spiritous liquors to the Indians of British Columbia was enacted in 1858, illegal trade in liquor with the Indians continued by one means or another. A rough measure of the dimensions of this trade comes from records which show that from 1858 to 1864 in Victoria alone there were 336 court cases of men arrested for selling liquor to Indians.[6]

One of the important consequences of the illegal dealing in liquor with the coastal Indians was the introduction of a wide variety of diluted and adulterated intoxicants and also noxious chemical substitutes for whisky and rum. As a matter of fact this began with the early fur trade when it became a practice to dilute rum with anywhere from three to ten parts water. After prohibitory legislation came into effect, solutions of camphor and tobacco with a little whisky flavoring quite often were sold as liquor. Mixtures containing bluestone vitriol, a copper compound, and nitric acid were sold to the natives in the Queen Charlotte Islands. Vanilla extract and Jamaica ginger, as well as Florida water and cologne, proved highly popular drinks with natives in some areas.[7]

The willingness of the natives to drink beverages of this kind reveals a great deal about the intensity of their desires for intoxicants and about the kinds of pleasures or satisfactions they sought in drinking. The pattern of rapid drinking apparent among the coastal natives may well have got its start from the dilution of the intoxicants they drank. In other words, in order to get the desired "kick" from the trade rum, it was necessary to drink a large quantity. The frequency of death and the great disorganization of behavior caused by drinking also is understandable in the light of the highly toxic and poisonous qualities of the beverages the Indians drank with gusto.

Public efforts at prohibiting liquor to the Indian population of the coast were further complicated by the purchase of Alaska by the United States in 1867. The

American troops sent to occupy the area, as well as others attracted to it, proved to be poorly disciplined and given to drunkenness, wild depredations, and gross immorality. Smuggling of liquor to the new territory became a common practice, along with bootlegging to the Indian population. However, perhaps an even more significant event was the introduction to the Indians of a technique for home-brewing liquor, reputedly by an intemperate soldier who had deserted or had been discharged from the military post at Fort Wrangell. This brew, known as hoochinoo,[8] was concocted from a variety of ingredients, such as molasses, flour, dried apples, rice, potatoes, salmonberries, blackberries, yeast powder, and sometimes hops. Sufficient water was added to the selected ingredients to make a thin batter. After fermentation took place, a sour, muddy, highly alcoholic liquor was produced. Distillation was accomplished through using coal-oil cans for retorts and kelp for condensation tubes. The Alaska Indians distilled hoochinoo for the white trade as well as for themselves; the technique soon diffused southward throughout the coastal area and inland and became the source of liquor for many bands.[9]

Source of Supply

Today the sources of intoxicants differ for Indian bands of the coast, depending upon their location, their economic status, and their relationships with other groups in nearby communities. In Alert Bay, for example, there seems to be little if any home-brewing. The ease with which bottled beer can be obtained and taken onto the reservation is betokened by the sight of small Indian boys pushing great wheelbarrow loads of beer bottles through the streets to sell at the secondhand store. Beer and whisky both are obtained by the Indians from white loggers and fishermen—especially the Norwegians—on a friendship basis. It is rare that the white intermediaries in such transactions make a charge for their services.

In other localities a class of semiprofessional or part-time bootleggers has risen to meet and exploit the demand for liquor among the Indian population. In Port Alberni on Vancouver Island, for example, there are white frequenters of bars, who, when they discover that an Indian has money, will give him a few drinks to whet his thirst and then charge him all the traffic will bear for the liquor he needs to keep him intoxicated. Bootlegging of this general sort is likely to flourish in or near large towns and cities. In the town of Hope, in the Fraser River Valley, with a population of 1,500, it is estimated that there are at least forty bootleggers, most of whom have an Indian clientele. In this town the staple item of liquor commerce is a gallon of cheap wine or, less frequently, a thirteen-ounce bottle of whisky, called a "mickey," both of which are usually sold at twice the market price.[10] Taxi drivers in Vancouver and in other cities occasionally secure liquor for their Indian fares, particularly if the Indian is willing to pay enough for the illegal drink—as much as twenty-five dollars is known to have been paid for a fifth of whisky. In some of the smaller towns the taxi driver's role and situation is especially conducive to bootlegging. The Indians are often lucrative fares, because of the distance of their reserves from town and because of their strong preference for using taxis when they have the money. Because taxi drivers compete keenly for their trade, the Indians can demand and receive credit. From this it is an easy extension of the relationship for them to insist that the drivers obtain liquor for them, and large numbers of them do so.

Enfranchised Indians, half-breeds, foreign-born males, and Chinese also enact the role of the bootlegger for the Indian. The racial and cultural marginality of such persons undoubtedly is a significant factor behind their willingness to violate the law in order to supply the Indian with liquor. The sexual deprivation of the Chinese men in the province, due to a shortage of Chinese women, acts as additional inducement for them to procure liquor for Indians. It is usually through such means and the promise of a bottle to carry back to the reserve with her that the Indian woman becomes a sexual partner of the Chinese.

Home-brewing in the coast area proper seems to be relied upon as a source of intoxicants in the more isolated reserves and where the economic level of the Indian population is low. My most abundant information on the practice bears on the three mainland bands mentioned earlier: the Homalthko, Tlahoose, and Sliammon. The techniques employed by these coastal Salish bands resemble in most important respects those described in detail by Honigmann and Honigmann for a community of inland Athapascan-speaking peoples: Brush, Salmon, Mountain, and River Indians living in the town of Delio (pseudonym) on the Alaskan highway.[11] The drink habitually brewed by the Churchouse Homalthko is a variety of malt beer, the chief ingredient, malt, being purchased in stores at Campbell River and Powell River, and at smaller stores in nearby settlements. In addition to malt, sugar, water, and yeast, part of the base is oranges and raisins. The brew is usually set in a small wooden keg—twenty-five years ago a tub was used—and concealed in the bush, in order, if possible, to avoid discovery by the police and to minimize the more immediate risk of its theft by other Indians. Brewing is usually done by women of the band who are hired by the men with a promise of sharing the brew when it is ready. In contrast to the Delio Indians, who leave the brew in its original keg, the Homalthko sometimes drain the brew into Scotch or other whisky bottles, on which the label is left intact. This variation of the Homalthko is related to their custom of drinking aboard their fishing boats, where drinking from an open keg of course is not feasible. Like the Delio Indians, the Homalthko are eager to drink their brew and often consume it when it is only seventeen hours old. The brew itself is a cloudy yellow and exudes a heavy, sour odor. I smelled a bottle of it but was unable to rise to the heights of scientific sacrifice necessary to sample it. The alcoholic content of this brew is unknown, but there can be no doubt that the Homalthko and their neighbors manage to get wonderfully intoxicated on it.

In preceding pages I have dwelt variously upon alcoholic drinking functions which center upon the possible conflicts and maladjustments that individual Indians experience in fulfilling their differing social roles. Such functions are negative in that they permit the person to escape, narcotize, or otherwise deal with his painful or unpleasant feelings and impulses. Yet beyond such functions as these there is a more positive set of functions which strike the observer of native drinking behavior. In some instances these merge with or tend to overlie the negative functions of the drinking and drunkenness; in others, they are paramount.

The more positive aspect of drinking materializes in relation to rank and status. Thus, for many Indians, drinking patently is a way of maximizing or maintaining their status in the eyes of others. From their mien and manner in pouring and downing large glasses of wine, beer, or whisky, many natives seem to be saying in effect: "Look, this is the way I drink." Histrionic drinking by some of the younger Indians apparently is an expression of their conception of their establishment as adult males; in others it is an assertion of equality with white persons. The impression is strong that drinking even today bears closely upon the older patterns of competition and rivalry that characterized Northwest Coast culture of the past. These patterns dispose the individual to be continuously alert to ways and means of validating his status. One way he attempts to do this is by conspicuous drinking; another is by a display of hospitality in which liquor figures as an item of wealth and prestige. At this point, individual functions of drinking coalesce with those pertaining to the group, community, or society; our discussion of necessity must shift to that level.

Sociocultural Functions of Drinking

The analysis of the drinking behavior of coastal Indians from the standpoint of the relationship of this behavior to situational conflicts and anxieties perplexing the individual at best permits only a partial grasp of the problem. The relation of these psychic phenomena to drinking behavior is far from being a direct one. In the aggregate they supply the cumulative animus to drink, and distributively they are a means for assessing differential tendencies to heavy drinking. However, they shed little light upon the pattern and collective dynamics of drinking. Perhaps, for our purpose, the impact of the different roles and statuses that have been discussed can be appraised more precisely in terms of cultural and occupational impacts that lead to social isolation. In other words, the significant conflicts associated with these roles are those which detach or threaten to detach the person from the family and the band. The central anxiety then becomes one of actual or imminent social isolation.

The sociocultural functions of drinking in native societies of the Northwest Coast are most profitably studied within the broader context of acculturation. This can be thought of as having begun in the last decade of the eighteenth century with the initiation of coastal fur trade and the colonization of the Aleutian Islands and Alaska by Russia. The period that followed proved to be a time of continuing crisis for native peoples of the area—a crisis which had multiple aspects. In the first of these the natives are seen coming into contact and necessary interaction with people whose culture displayed a marked technological superiority to their own. In the second are seen the consequences of the fur trade through which native societies literally came to be confronted with an embarrassment of riches—increments of wealth without precedent in their precontact cultural experience.

The first aspect of the crisis made itself felt in status problems which hitherto independent, ethnocentrically integrated tribal groups experienced interacting directly or indirectly with white traders and settlers whom they were forced to accept as their superiors. This problem, while minimal at first, was aggravated by the multiplication of the white population on the coast and by a series of clashes between Indians and whites in which the inexorable military power of the whites was conclusively demonstrated. Subsequent to this the tribal groups had to deal internally with the problem of the accumulation of wealth by bands and persons who previously had been poor by native criteria. The increase of these native equivalents of *nouveaux riches* individuals and bands placed a great strain upon the system of status differentiation which had served the coastal tribes before the white man came. It is not known just what this system was, but it can be inferred that it was a less complex, less formal prototype of the potlatch, in which public distribution of wealth on a reciprocal basis served a dual function of differentiating status and cementing social ties between individuals and tribal groups.[12]

A somewhat different kind of crisis, yet equal in importance to that already discussed, was the high native death rate due to smallpox and other epidemics which periodically swept the coast from 1785 on. The critical impact of these plagues, again, had both external and internal aspects. They were perceived by the Indians as calamities visited upon them by the white man, whose power was such that he suffered but little from them himself while hundreds and even thousands of Indians perished miserably. Within tribal groups the death of adult males in large numbers created serious problems in the filling of the social roles by which hereditary ranks and privileges[13] were preserved.

A hypothesis which I boldly suggest is that the several aspects of this large culture crisis effected an extreme formalization of the sociocultural systems of the natives of the Northwest Coast, expressed in a phenomenal expansion of the rank-potlatch system, together with an efflorescence of crest heraldry and woodcarving art directly functional in the differentiation of rank between individuals, families, clans, and tribes. In other words, with the decline or change in the status of Indian society relative to white society, and with the difficulty of transcultural estimation of status, there emerged a compulsive concern on the part of the Indians with the minutiae of internal rank position.[14] The rapid evolution of formal patterns expressing this concern was made possible in the early acculturation era by the absence of any direct attacks upon the social organization of the coastal tribes by white agencies and was facilitated by the aforementioned accretion of wealth. The coastal natives enjoyed a relative freedom—at least until the middle of the nineteenth century—to select from a variety of white culture traits and integrate them into an expanding potlatch-rank system.[15]

The Whisky Feast

In the development of the potlatch there are definite indications that the natives tended to select for use those white culture traits which in their estimation conferred upon their users something of the high status of the whites. Numerous material items of white manufacture became basic prestige gifts: Hudson's Bay blankets, bolts of cloth, guns, traps, sets of chinaware, pots, pans, sewing machines, barrels of molasses, sacks of flour, and bushels of fruit, for example. Whisky was precisely the kind of thing one would have expected to be included in native ceremonies for validating status claims, for it obviously had scarcity value and also importance as a culture trait of the dominant whites, whether they were Russian, English, or American. The native conception of liquor as a prestige item may have been considerably influenced by the husbandry of alcohol practiced by the Russians, in which the leaders were free to brew and drink liquor, and the followers had theirs carefully dispensed to them. In the Russians' poorly supplied Alaskan colonies, alcohol was very definitely a luxury. More than that, it was the chief means of social control by which employees of the Russian American Company were kept in perpetual debt and peonage.[16] Furthermore, the use of rum and whisky by Englishmen and Americans in trade with the natives was a direct education in its value.

Yet, despite the prestige value of liquor, there were difficulties in the way of using it in potlatches. Obtaining and accumulating a sufficient reserve was difficult because the sources of supply were uncertain. But more important than this was the easily perceived incompatibility of drunkenness, which resulted from gifts of whisky, with the deadly serious or sacred nature of the potlatch. Whisky gifts were much more easily integrated into the aboriginal pattern of the feast.

Among the more northern tribes of the coast, feasts operated importantly in the expression of interclan rivalry, and often they were given for no other purpose than to provide the host with an opportunity to display his wealth and insult his guests through speeches and songs. At such feasts, visitors were forced to gorge themselves with food or run the risk of taunts and insults if they could not eat all that was placed before them. Ladles of grease and snow were served to those whom the host especially wanted to humiliate. Later, when liquor was brought in by traders, barrels or hogsheads of whisky and rum were substituted for food at such "challenge feasts."[17]

We are fortunate in having at hand Viola Garfield's detailed description of a whisky feast given by a clan of the Tsimshian:[18]

> Such a liquor feast was given by 'A-ya'i-ax of the Gilutsa'u tribe. He was away trapping in the Portland Canal when his uncle gave a potlatch at Port Simpson. When he heard about it he was embarrassed because he had not had a part in it, and decided to give a feast on his own account.
>
> On his way home he met a schooner carrying liquor and traded all his pelts for rum. He then caught a great many seals and returned to the village, waiting until dark to

land so that no one would see him take the liquor ashore. The seals he threw on the beach. The people, seeing them, remarked, "Now you will have to give a seal feast," and he answered, "Yes, I will do that."

That night the people heard singing in 'A-ya'i-ax's house, but thought that he and his relatives were practicing for the seal feast. Early the next morning 'A-ya'i-ax sent messengers to all the houses of the Gilutsa'u tribe inviting everyone to the feast. He borrowed large iron kettles from the chief's house, filled them with water and set them on the fire. When the guests arrived they saw the kettles and thought that the seals were cooking. When they were all in, 'A-ya'i-ax said, "Take the kettles and throw them out." They were taken out and returned to the chief's house. Then the hogsheads of liquor were rolled out and the guests were astonished because they came expecting to eat seal. The members of the house of 'A-ya'i-ax began to sing their drinking songs and the liquor was served. The first drink was a small one called "a taste." As it was served the hosts sang, "Bring your own little liquor and try to pacify yourself with its small quantity. That will make me happy." This was sung in Nisqa since the pelts used to purchase the liquor had come from the Nisqa territory.

After the "taste," liquor was served in larger quantities to each guest. A small iron pot and a tall glass vessel (a quart beer stein?) were also used as drinking cups. The iron pot was called, "Raven's Nest" and the other cup, "Raven's intestines." The portions for the two chiefs, Nias-lgu-mi-k and Nias-nawa were served to them simultaneously to prevent any criticism about precedence. The name of each recipient was called out and each was expected to empty the measure immediately or be subject to ridicule. The guest receiving the liquor could call on a nephew or niece to help drink it, but then the vessel was given back to the host. If he succeeded in emptying it without help he could do anything he liked with the cup. He could throw it into the fire, break it or keep it.

Since no one had had breakfast, all the guests were soon drunk and sank where they were to sleep it off. When they went home 'A-ya'i-ax gave each family a portion of seal meat.

The singing of satirical and insulting songs was a more or less intrinsic feature of the whisky feast, for by such means it derived its social meaning. This is emphasized by an additional excerpt from the description of a rum feast of the Tsimshian:[19]

Nias-gane's brought in a Nass River song composer who stayed all winter making and teaching the people new songs for the feasts, particularly the taunting songs for the liquor feast. At this, the first of the series, the Ravens wore their hair done up as warriors. The crests and dances of the house were exhibited and the inability of other clans to equal the Ravens in wealth and generosity freely pointed out in song and speech. The father of Nias-gane's and his lineage furnished ten barrels of liquor for this feast. It was served to the guests in large ceremonial ladles, in which snow and grease were formerly mixed and presented as a challenge and an invitation to join a war party. During this feast taunting songs to the other clans were sung. To the Wolf clan they sang, "The Great Grizzly is groaning drunk inside the stomach of the Bullhead (Raven)." Nias-xsan, a Blackfish, had announced a potlatch which he had not been able to give so this was called to mind by the song remark, "The Blackfish had risen and spouted and that's all we saw of him. He has gone away ashamed after trying to upset our canoe." The Laxse'la Ravens gave liquor to the Laxse'la Eagles singing, "It is your own Ravens who are doing this to you," that is, people from your own ancient village or tribe. Nias-gugwina't had started a dwelling which he had been unable to finish, so they sang of his house, "Though he is a Frog (also Raven clan member) he is not able to build a house as we are. Don't you know that it is the little Raven who is doing this to you, you who try to imitate me, but cannot complete your house, Big Frog?"

A drinking song which may have a special historical significance is the Fireweed song that reportedly originated near the headwaters of the Skeena River. Its content again stresses the emulative value which the possession of liquor and knowledge of its manufacture held for the coastal peoples of the North:

The Fireweed people will drink fermented juice with the
  Wolf and the Raven tribes.
Why think you that we know not how to brew it?
We walk proudly because we have made it for a long time.

This song is said to resemble strongly a Chinese street tune and to have a strange and alien sound when heard among other Indian songs. At the same time, like other songs sung in foreign languages by the northern coastal Indians, it is reminiscent of certain exotic Russian songs. Undoubtedly there were Russian influences at work in the origin and growth of drinking songs of the Northwest Coast natives, although the extent of these influences must remain problematical.[20] It is certain, however, that there was a diffusion of Russian drinking songs into the Aleutian Islands, where to this day at native drinking parties songs are sung in Russian. These for the most part are obscene and are sung by the men. When the Aleut women join in singing at drinking parties they sing Russian church hymns.[21]

Whisky feasts were given by the Haida and also by the Tsimshian, presumably activating similar interclan rivalry. In all probability the drinking bouts of the Tlingit and those of the Bella Bella also took this form.[22] In fact, it can be said with fair probability that the whisky feast spread throughout all the native cultures north of Cape Mudge as far as the Aleutian area. Several Kwakiutl informants noted the historical occurrence of whisky feasts for their tribe, and one informant described a drinking ritual and ethic similar to that of the Tsimshian which was followed by tribes at Kingcome Inlet.

It seems clear that the Kwakiutl did not compose special drinking songs to be sung at the whisky feast as did the Tsimshian. However, they do boast of drinking songs, which, as they are sung today, are primarily love songs rather than musical epitomes of clan rivalry. I managed to secure rough translations of two of these which originally were composed by an older Kwakiutl woman from Kingcome Inlet:

Si-hi-das Wine [Song for Home-Brew]
Squeeze the wine [home-brew] out,
Squeeze it again.
Squeeze it again and give me some to drink,
And then give me one cup more
And then I will be drunk (pass out).

Kwasika'antlakwala (I Am Crying for My Loved One)
I was drinking last night
With whisky in my system over night,
Just for my loved one.
I was crying last night
With tears on my cheek,
Just for my loved one.

These songs are sad rather than rollicking, running definitely to a minor key. They can be a lament for a close relative, a brother or a sister, as well as for a sweetheart. The impression given was that such songs might either be sung by groups or by pairs making love. A nominal similarity to these songs exists in Nootka drinking songs in that the latter are known by the same term as love songs—*tapyik*. However, the Nootka drinking songs in reality seem to be adaptations of *tama* songs, humorous and satirical music which traditionally was sung at a girl's first menstruation.[23]

Some of the Salish Indians whom I interviewed at the provincial prison told me that drinking songs were sung among the Salish in the Fraser River area. I was unable to get translations of these, but in the summer of 1953 I was fortunate enough to be able to tape record two Salish drinking songs; one was a Comox song, the other was a song known to both the Homalthko and the Sliammon. No literal translation could be had of the Comox song, but it was established that it was a song sung by a whole group at a drinking party as they pass the whisky bottle round the circle of drinkers and each takes his turn. The phrases are comments on the receding amounts of whisky left in the bottle after each successive drink. The drinkers measure the levels carefully and finally intone the emptying of the bottle with the final drink. This obviously is a song of fellowship.

The second song was sung for me by a man about fifty-five years of age, who learned it from his grandfather, a former chief of the Sliammon tribe. It follows:

Chief Johnson's Drinking Song
Give me a drink, I am afraid to go.
We keep on going. Come closer to me and drink.
I'm drunk now, I'm drunk now, and we have a pretty good time.
I am afraid to drink, but still I like to drink.
I don't like to drink, but I have to drink the whisky.
Here I am singing a love song, drinking, drinking, drinking.
I didn't know that whisky was no good, and still I was drinking it.

I found out that whisky is no good.
Come, come closer to me, my slaves,
And I'll give you a drink of whisky.
Here we are drinking now.
Have some more, some more of my whisky,
Have a good time with it.
Come closer to me, come closer to me, my slave.
We are drinking now, we feel pretty good.
Now you feel just like me.

From the references in this song it can be inferred that it is quite old, dating from the time when slaves were still held by the coastal natives. Although the singer speaks of it as a love song, the song seems to be more of a soliloquy of loneliness. Of course, it could be a love song if the slaves mentioned were female slaves, but none of the Indians present when it was sung for me could answer this question. In any event, the function of whisky drinking in diminishing social distance between the singer and his slaves and in dissipating his sense of loneliness seems clear enough in the words.

The drinking songs of the Kwakiutl, some of those of the Tlingit, and perhaps those of the Salish suggest another possible function of the whisky feast or drinking party aside from that of acting as a vehicle for the expression of stylized hostility between clan groups. This, in short, refers to a function related to the sociopsychological impacts of the expanding rank-potlatch system of the coastal cultures. There is good reason to believe that this expansion of formal social organization, implemented by emulative display and distribution of material wealth, proved to be exceedingly onerous for clans, families, and individuals who had to support it.[24] This was truer in some areas than others. For example, among the southern Kwakiutl the potlatch-rank system entangled individuals in a complicated debt structure at high interest rates, and highly individualized rivalries between clan and tribal chiefs were not uncommon. Jealousies, feuds, and even murders were some of the more overt signs of internal cleavages and personal strain accompanying the enlargement and extreme formalization of the potlatch-rank institution.[25] At the same time, other sources of cleavage, divisiveness, and personal anxiety arose out of the epidemic diseases and the intensification of warfare that followed the acquisition of weapons from whites.

The facts at hand and certain inferences led me to ask whether initial impacts of white culture on the native social systems of the Northwest Coast did not give rise to anomal and divisive tendencies or exaggerate those already present in such a way as to complicate the native individual's task of dealing with demands of his culture. This might be described as a problem of finding opportunity for a more organic expression of personality, or it might be described as a frustration of the striving of the individual for personal *esteem,* which is a more subjective desideratum of informal social interaction. Such esteem stands in contrast to *prestige,* which is derived from or synonymous with the standardized rewards of a formal role.[26]

From this point of view the whisky feast and the drinking party may be seen as offering an informal situation in which some kind of spurious "intimatization" could occur within or tangential to the framework of the more formal roles and organization of native society. By virtue of their primary or pseudoprimary group properties, the whisky feast and the drinking party allowed persons more freely and without subsequent penalty (a point to be developed later) to give vent to idiosyncratic feelings, impulses, and strivings. The fact that personal aggression and conflict figured in these does not necessarily invalidate the concept that the drinking group was in effect a species of primary group.

Such an interpretation must get its validity from the character of the feast as it was used by coastal Indians, a subject on which the available ethnographic data are none too clear. However, it does seem certain that the feast was informal rather than formal; furthermore it was a place where "people had fun." Also, the feast was a claim which lower-ranking persons had upon the higher-ranking members of the tribe or band. In horseplay and other antics carried on during feasts, status differentials were sometimes disregarded or even reversed. Persons who had no chance to employ formal procedures for expressing hostility could during the feast vent their displeasure through gossip, anecdotes, mock-serious speeches, and innuendo; by such means they could criticize and expose the foibles and weaknesses of those with prestige and high status. Although more data are needed to clarify the point, this may tell us a good deal about differential drinking between low- and high-ranking persons in the coastal societies. A very important point is that a person could not refuse to invite another to a feast simply because he did not like him. To do so was the equivalent of socially ostracizing the person, and social ostracism was imposed only on those who became completely *persona non grata* in the estimation of the whole community. In keeping with the emphasis of the culture, the release from personal strain and the expression of unintegrated impulses by the person took place within a structured situation and a group context.[27]

This social context among the Tlingit, and also among the Tsimshian, featured certain cross-moiety relationships resting upon the father-child and paternal-affinal bonds. Thus, children of men of the same sib, although because of matrilineal descent belonging to different moieties, nonetheless were supposed to form a particularly close and happy group and to be "like brothers." At more convivial feasts they often sat together and enlivened proceedings with buffoonery and all sorts of jokes, teasing, and horseplay. The designation used in such interaction, "Kagwantan's children" (children of the father's sib) unquestionably carried a strong sentimental appeal. Significantly, drinking songs were addressed to the child of a sib, usually one's own.[28]

NOTES

1. Edward Curtis, *Salishan Tribes of the Coast*. Vol. 9 of *The North American Indian*, 20 vols. (Cambridge, Mass.: Harvard University Press, 1913), 40.

2. F. W. Howay, "The Introduction of Intoxicating Liquors amongst the Indians of the Northwest Coast," *British Columbia Historical Review,* 6 (1942), 157–169.

3. F. H. von Langsdorff, *Voyages and Travels in Various Parts of the World . . .* (Carlisle, Penn., 1817) p. 396; Ross Cox, *The Columbia River* (2 vols., London, 1832), pp. 291*ff*. The Tlingit may have refused liquor in very early contacts with the Russians because of an awareness of the way in which it was used to keep the fur hunters under peonage in the Aleutian colonies.

4. G. E. Shankel, "The Development of Indian Policy in British Columbia" (Ph.D. diss., University of Washington, 1945) p. 89.

5. *Ibid.*, p. 93.

6. Frederick Whymper, *Travels and Adventures in the Territory of Alaska* (London, 1968), p. 36.

7. Frances Poole, *The Queen Charlotte Islands* (ed. John W. Lydon; London, 1872), p. 233; Thomas Crosby, *Among the An-ko-me-nums* (Toronto: Briggs, 1907), p. 129; C. E. Barrett-Lennard, *Travels in British Columbia, with the Narrative of a Voyage around Vancouver Island* (London, 1862), p. 49; Minor Bruce, *Alaska* (Seattle, Wash., 1895), p. 97.

8. The term *hoochinoo* apparently was derived from the name of a Tlingit Indian tribe that lived in the southwestern part of Admiralty Island off the Alaskan coast, a tribe notorious for its truculence and manufacture of fiery home-brew. Sheldon Jackson, *Alaska and the Missions of the North Pacific Coast* (New York, 1880), pp. 241–242. Another translation of the term is "bear's nest," referring to the kind of place in which the drink was made. Jeanette Nichols, *History of Alaska* (Cleveland: Clark, 1924), p. 106.

9. H. H. Bancroft, *History of Alaska* (San Francisco, 1886), pp. 621–622. One writer states that the Russians taught the Alaskan Indians how to make quass, but this is not corroborated by other sources. Quass is a thin, sour beer made by pouring warm water over rye or barley. The Russian spelling is *kvass*. See Bruce, *op. cit.*

10. Personal communication from William Duff, Provincial Museum of British Columbia, Vancouver, B.C.

11. J. J. Honigmann and Irma Honigmann, "Drinking in an Indian-White Community," *Quarterly Journal of Studies on Alcohol,* 5 (1945), 575–619.

12. The potlatch was a focal, integrating ritual pattern throughout Northwest Coast cultures. As observed and recorded in the latter part of the nineteenth century it involved ceremonial giving of gifts by high-ranking persons or chiefs to validate a claim to a certain name or to a position or to a seat in a potlatch house for himself or one of his relatives. The value of the gifts was carefully adjusted to the rank of the person receiving the gift. High-ranking persons of other tribes who received presents were under moral obligation to return gifts of equal or greater value at a later potlatch.

There is an increasing weight of opinion and evidence that before the coming of the white man the potlatch was not the same as it was later. Present-day Nootka have stated that in "very early times" potlatches were given infrequently and that the gifts handed out were of small value. The Bella Coola in the early part of the present century complained that "today everyone is a chief," meaning that in early times only a few persons were able to give potlatches and now everyone can do so. Philip Drucker, "Rank, Wealth and Kinship in Northwest Coast Society," *American Anthropologist*, 41 (1939), 56–64; *idem, The Northern and Central Nootkan Tribes*, Bulletin 144 (Washington, D.C.: Bureau of American Ethnology, 1951), pp. 13, 376; T. F. McIlwraith, *The Bella Coola Indians,* I, 3 vols. (Toronto: University of Toronto Press, 1948), p. 205; Wendell Endicott, *Adventures in Alaska and Along the Trail* (New York: Stokes, 1928), p. 84.

13. Drucker, *The Northern and Central Nootkan Tribes,* p. 12; among the Kwakiutl, many potlatch seats became vacant or had to be filled by women.

14. This hypothesis was suggested by Cottrell's study of the railroader, in which he found that the prestige, power, and income of persons engaged in railroading in recent decades have declined in comparison with those in other occupations, and that this has led to an increasing proliferation of technologically irrelevant job classifications within the railroad industry, in some of which the pay differences are as small as one-half cent per hour. W. F. Cottrell, *The Railroader* (Stanford University Press, 1940), pp. 88–90.

15. The more recent data on primitive cultures of the Northwest Coast indicate that the elaborate development of the wood-carving art, crest heraldry, totem poles, even clans and secret societies, may be of comparatively late origin. Marius Barbeau, *Totem Poles,* National Museum of Canada, Anthropological Series 30, Vol. II Bulletin 119, n.d., pp. 762–766, 825–828; *idem,* "Totem Poles a Recent Art of the Northwest Coast of America," *Geographical Review,* 20 (1930), 258–272; M. J. Herskovitz, *Man and His Works* (New York: A. Knopf, 1949), pp. 480–481. Although there is evidence, already cited, that the complex evolution of the potlatch is also recent, the only explicit treatment of the potlatch as an accultural reaction is that by F. E. La Violette, "Missionaries and the Potlatch," *Queen's Quarterly,* 58 (1951), pp. 237–251. For an informal record of the manner in which late-nineteenth-century potlatching became a symbol of the "old way of life" for the Kwakiutl, see William Halliday, *Potlatch and Totem* (Toronto: Dent, 1935). My preferred interpretation differs from that of La Violette in that I place the period of intense culture crisis before the period of intensive missionary work, which was well after the middle of the nineteenth century. La Violette himself (*op. cit.,* p. 241) suggests this when he states that the desire for white missionaries was present among Oregon and Fraser River Indians by 1830; Bishop Veniaminoff makes a smallpox epidemic in 1835 the "boundary line where the reign of dark ignorance ended and the progress of civilization began for the Tlingit." See his "Letters about the Islands of the Unalaska District," Pt. 2 of *Russian America IV,* trans. Ivan Petrov (ms. Bancroft Library, University of California, Berkeley, n.d.), p. 11. As early as 1800 the Tlingit had a "passion for European clothes," and high-ranking chiefs always wore them when meeting Europeans (*ibid.*, p. 8). See also "Records of Baptisms of Early Days of the Russian Occupation of Sitka," in "Alaska Archives from Unalaska and St. Paul Island", pp. 2, 8, 11; this suggests that these Indians were concerned with or struggling with the problem of their status in relation to whites a long while before their Christianization.

16. Hector Chevigny, *Lord of Alaska* (New York: Viking, 1942), pp. 51, 52, 86; Henry Elliott, *A Report on the Condition of Affairs in the Territory of Alaska* (Washington, D.C.: 1875), pp. 230–231; S. B. Okun, *The Russian American Company* (Cambridge: Harvard University Press, 1951), pp. 177–179.

17. One writer gives 1864 as the date of the first whisky feast on the Northwest Coast. W. H. Collison, *In the Wake of the War Canoe* (New York: Dutton, 1916), p. 33. However, whisky feasts are known to have been given at least twenty-five years before this and probably were held even earlier. One source reports that in 1840 at the Hudson's Bay Company

post on the "Stakin" River the local Indians (Tsimshian) gave a whisky feast in which a hogshead of whisky four feet high was emptied in one day. Eloise Harvey, *Life of John McLaughlin* (ms. Bancroft Library, University of California, Berkeley, n.d.).

18. Viola Garfield, *Tsimshian Clan and Society,* University of Washington Publications in Anthropology, Vol. 7, No. 3 (February, 1939), 208–209.

19. *Ibid.,* 200–201.

20. Marius Barbeau, *Alaska Beckons* (Caldwell Canyon, Id.: Caxton, 1947), p. 193. Some features of the Tsimshian whisky feast carry more than a hint of Russian drinking ritual and suggest something of the extent of Russian cultural influences in its development. Baranoff, the famous leader of the Russian colonies in Alaska, is reported to have on some occasions filled large iron kettles with liquor and called all of his "children," the *promyshleniki* (fur hunters), to come and drink from the common source. The Tlingit around Sitka in the 1870s customarily used the Russian term *prasnik* for their drinking carousals. See Bancroft, *op. cit.,* pp. 570, 622; Hector Chevigny, *op. cit.,* pp. 80–81; Washington Irving, *Astoria* (Portland, Ore.: Binfords and Mort, 1951), pp. 421–422.

21. Information supplied by Gordon Marsh, University of British Columbia.

22. For the Haida see Collison, *op. cit.,* p. 216; also Poole, *op. cit.,* p. 313; Tlingit drinking songs for dancing at a feast are recorded in J. R. Swanton, *Tlingit Myths and Texts,* Smithsonian Institution, Washington, D.C.: Bureau of American Ethnology, Bulletin 39 (1909), pp. 397, 398, 401–405, 414; Bella Bella drinking bouts are mentioned in Poole, *op. cit.,* p. 184. Specific references to a whisky feast held by the Tlingit is found in E. R. Skidmore, *Alaska, the Sitkan Archipelago* (1885), p.179.

23. Drucker, *The Northern and Central Nootkan Tribes* (New York: Appleton, 1940), pp. 141–142; Ford, *op. cit.,* p. 147.

24. Irving Goldman, "The Alkatcho Carrier of British Columbia," in Ralph Linton (ed.), *Acculturation in Seven American Indian Tribes* (New York: Appleton, 1940), p. 345.

25. McIlwraith, *op. cit.* Drucker has pointed out that competitive and "vengeance" potlatching are absent from Nootka culture; furthermore, he believes that the picture of the highly aggressive, paranoid Kwakiutl is overdrawn. The personality ideal of the Nootka is that of a nonaggressive, nonviolent person, and evidences of the same ideal are found throughout the culture area. Drucker, *op. cit.,* pp. 371, 453–457. For a description of coastal culture in which rivalry and competitive threat appear to be ubiquitous, see M. W. Smith, "The Puyallup of Washington," in Ralph Linton (ed.), *op. cit.,* chap. 1. In further contrast to Drucker's statement on the subject, Ford writes that the Kwakiutl encouraged strong aggressiveness in their children but that it was aggressiveness and rivalry within limits—limits which were very sharply drawn. Ford, *op. cit.,* p. 77. My own point of view, that the ritual cultures of the Northwest Coast as a whole were rigorous, demanding, and stressful for the individual, I have stated elsewhere. E. M. Lemert, "Stuttering among North Pacific Coastal Indians," *Southwestern Journal of Anthropology*, 8 (Winter, 1952), 429–441.

26. Kingsley Davis, *Human Society* (New York: Macmillan, 1949), pp. 93–94.

27. Ford, *op. cit.,* pp. 192–195; Pettitt, *op. cit.,* 86–87. See also the songs associated with drinking among the Tlingit in Swanton, *op. cit.*

28. Fredericka de Laguna, "Some Dynamic Forces in Tlingit Society," *Southwestern Journal of Anthropology*, 8 (Spring, 1952), 9–12.

Chapter 8

Fast Living, Big Spending, and Life on the Edge: The Check Forger

The concept of behavior systems in crime was first approximated in this country in Hall's analysis of several types of larceny in terms of their historical, legal, and social contexts (Hall 1952). Later the concept was made explicit and formulated into a typology by Sutherland (1937b) and by Sutherland and Cressy (1955; also Bonger 1916, pp. 579–589; Lindesmith and Dunham 1941; Puibarand 1893). Although this has hitherto inspired only a few monographic studies, there seems to be a growing consensus that focusing attention on specific orders of crime or making behavior systems that unit of study holds considerable promise for criminological research (Reckless 1955, p. 134)

Because this paper proposes to assess the usefulness of Sutherland's formulation of the behavior system in analyzing or understanding the behavior of the systematic check forger, the typology outlined in his study of the professional thief will be employed. The five elements of the behavior system of the thief are as follows: (1) stealing is made a regular business; (2) every act is carefully planned, including the use of the "fix"; (3) technical skills are used, chiefly those of manipulating people; this differentiates the thief from other professional criminals; (4) the thief is migratory but uses a specific city as a headquarters; (5) the thief has criminal associations involving acquaintances, congeniality, sympathy, understandings, rules, codes of behavior, and a special language (Cavan 1948, ch. 5; Clinard 1957, pp. 256–262; Elliott 1942, ch. 4; Maurer 1955; Reckless 1955; Sutherland 1937a, 1937b; Von Hentig 1943).

Altogether seventy-two persons currently serving sentences for check forgery and writing checks with insufficient funds were studied. Three additional check offenders were contacted and interviewed outside of prison. The sample included

---

"The Behavior of the Systematic Check Forger." *Social Problems* 6,2 (Fall 1958): 141–49.

eight women and sixty-seven men, all of whom served time in California correctional institutions.

Thirty of the seventy-five check criminals could be classified as systematic in the sense that they (1) thought of themselves as check men; (2) had worked out or regularly employed a special technique of passing checks; (3) had more or less organized their lives around the exigencies or imperatives of living by means of fraudulent checks. The remaining forty-five cases represented a wide variety of contexts in which bogus check passing was interspersed with periods of stable employment and family life, or was simply an aspect of alcoholism, gambling, or one of a series of criminal offenses having little or no consistency.

FINDINGS

Projected against the typology of professional theft, the behavior of the persons falling into the systematic check forgery category qualified only in a very general way as professional crime. In other words, although it is possible to describe these forgeries as *systematic,* it is questionable whether more than a small portion of them can be subsumed as *professional* under the more general classification of professional theft. A point-by-point comparison will serve to bring out the numerous significant differences between systematic forgery and professional theft.

1. *Forgery as a "regular business."* It is questionable whether check men look upon their crimes as a "regular business" in the same way as do members of "other occupational groups" who "wish to make money in safety." (Sutherland and Cressey 1955, p. 240) In virtually all cases the motivation proved to be exceedingly complex. This fact was self-consciously recognized and expressed in different ways but all informants revealed an essential perplexity or conflict about their criminal behavior. The following statement may be taken as illustrative:

> Nine out of ten check men are lone wolves. Those men who work in gangs are not real check men. They do it for money; we do it for something else. It gives us something we need. Maybe we're crazy. . . .

The conflicts expressed involved not merely the rightness or wrongness of behavior; they also disclosed a confusion and uncertainty as to the possibility of living successfully or safely by issuing false checks. All of the cases, even the few who had a history of professional thieving, admitted that arrest and imprisonment are inevitable. None knew of exceptions to this, although one case speculated that "It might be done by an otherwise respected business man who made one big spread and then quit and retired."

The case records of the systematic check forgers gave clear testimony of this. Generally they had but short-lived periods of freedom, ranging from a few months to a year or two at the most, followed by imprisonment. Many of the cases since beginning their forgery careers had spent less total time outside prisons than within, a fact corroborated by the various law-enforcement officers queried on the point.

Many of the check men depicted their periods of check writing as continuous sprees during which they lived "fast" and luxuriously. Many spoke of experiencing considerable tension during these periods, and two cases developed stomach ulcers which caused them to "lay off at resorts." A number gambled and drank heavily, assertedly to escape their internal stress and sense of inevitable arrest. A number spoke of gradual build-up of strain and a critical point just before their arrest at which they became demoralized and after which they "just didn't care any more" or "got tired of running." The arrests of several men having a very long experience with checks resulted from blunders in technique of which they were aware at the time they made them. Some of the men gave themselves up to detectives or F.B.I. agents at this point.

In general the picture of the cool, calculating professional with prosaic, matter-of-fact attitudes towards his crimes as a trade or occupation supported by rationalizations of a subculture was not valid for the cases in question.

2. *Planning as an aspect of forgery.* In regard to the second element of professional theft—planning—the behavior of check forgers is again divergent. Actually the present techniques of check passing either preclude precise planning or make it unnecessary. Although systematic check passers undeniably pay careful attention to such things as banking hours, the places at which checks are presented, and the kinds of "fronts" they employ, these considerations serve only as generalized guides for their crimes. Most informants held that situations have to be *exploited as they arise,* with variation and flexibility being the key to success. What stands out in the behavior of systematic check forgers is the rapid tempo—almost impulsiveness—with which they work.

The cases seemed to agree that check forgers seldom attempt to use the "fix" in order to escape the consequences of their crimes. The reason for this is that although one or a small number of checks might be made good, the systematic forger has too many bad checks outstanding and too many victims to mollify by offering restitution. Although the forger may be prosecuted on the basis of only one or two checks, ordinarily the prosecuting attorney will have a choice of a large number of complaints upon which to act. About the best the check forger can hope for through fixing activities is a short sentence or a sentence to jail rather than to prison.

3. *Technical skills.* Although the systematic check man relies upon technical skills—those of manipulating others—these are usually not of a high order, nor do they require a long learning period to master. From the standpoint of the appearance of the check or the behavior involved at the time of its passing, there need, of course, be no great difference between passing a bad check and passing a good check. This is particularly true of personal checks, which are at least as favored as payroll checks by check men.

When check men impersonate others or when they assume fictitious roles, acting ability is required. To the extent that elaborate impersonations are relied upon by the forger, his check passing takes on qualities of a confidence game. Most of the check men showed strong preference, however, for simple, fast-moving techniques. A number expressed definite dislike for staged arrangements, such as that of the "out of town real estate buyer" or for setting up a fictitious business in a community, then waiting several weeks or a month before making a "spread" of checks. As they put it, they "dislike the slow build-up involved."

4. *Mobility*. Like the thief, the systematic forger is migratory. Only one check man interviewed spoke of identifying himself with one community, and even he was reluctant to call it a headquarters. Generally check men are migratory within regions.

5. *Associations*. The sharpest and most categorical difference between professional theft and systematic forgery lies in the realm of associations. In contrast to pickpockets, shoplifters, and con men, whose criminal techniques are implicitly cooperative, most check men with highly developed systems work alone, carefully avoiding contacts and interaction with other criminals. Moreover, their preference for solitude and their secretiveness gives every appearance of a highly generalized reaction; they avoid not only cooperative crime but also any other kinds of association with criminals. They are equally selective and cautious in their contacts and associations with the noncriminal population, preferring not to become involved in any enduring personal relationships.

A descriptive breakdown of the thirty check forgers classified as systematic bears out this point. Only four of the thirty had worked in check passing gangs. Two of these had acted as "fences" who organized the operations. Both were close to seventy years old and had long prison records, one having been a receiver of stolen property, the other having worked as a forger. Both had turned to using gangs of passers because they were too well known to detectives either to pass checks themselves or to permit their handwriting to appear on the checks. The other two forgers who had worked in gangs were female drug addicts who had teamed up with other female addicts.[1]

Three other systematic check forgers did not work directly with other criminals but had criminal associations of a *contractual* nature. One old-time forger familiar with the now little-used methods for forging signatures and raising checks usually sold checks to passers but never had uttered (passed) any of his own forgeries. Two men were passers who purchased either payroll checks from a "hot printer" or stolen checks from burglars. Apart from the minimal contacts necessary to sell or obtain a supply of checks, all three men were lone operators and very seclusive in their behavior.

Six of the thirty systematic forgers worked exclusively with one other person, usually a girl or "broad."[2] The check men seemed to agree that working with a girl was equivalent to working alone. These pairs ordinarily consisted of the check man and some girl not ordinarily of criminal background with whom he had struck up a living arrangement and for whom he felt genuine affection. The girl was used either to make out the checks or to pass them. In some cases she was simply used as a front to distract attention. Some men picked up girls in bars or hotels and employed them as fronts without any knowledge.

The remaining seventeen of the thirty systematic check forgers operated on a solitary basis. The majority of these argued that contact with others is unnecessary to obtain and pass a supply of checks. Most of them uttered personal checks. However, even where they made use of payroll or corporation checks they contrived to manufacture or obtain them without resorting to interaction with criminal associates or intermediaries. For example, one Nisei check man arranged with a printer to make up checks for a fraternal organization of which he represented himself as secretary-treasurer. Another man frequented business offices at noon time, and when the clerk left the office, helped himself to a supply of company checks, in one instance stealing a check writing machine for his purposes.

It was difficult to find evidence of anything more than rudimentary congeniality, sympathy, understandings, and shared rules of behavior among the check forgers, including those who had worked in gangs. Rather the opposite seemed true, suspicion and distrust marking their relationships with one another. One organizer of a gang, for example, kept careful account of all the checks he issued to his passers and made them return torn off corners of checks in case they were in danger of arrest and had to get rid of them. Only two of the thirty forgers indicated that they had at times engaged in recreational activities with other criminals. Both of these men were lone wolves in their work. One other lone wolf stated that he had on occasion had dinner with another check man he happened to know well and that he had once or twice entered into a rivalry with him to see who could pass a check in the most difficult place.

The two men who had organized gangs of check passers worked with a set of rules, but they were largely improvised and laid down by the fence rather than voluntarily recognized and obeyed by the passers. The other check men with varying degrees of explicitness recognized rules for passing checks—rules learned almost entirely on an individual trial-and-error basis. The informants insisted that "you learn as you go" and that one of the rules was "never use another man's stunt."

Such special morality as was recognized proved to be largely functional in derivation. Thus attitudes toward drinking and toward picking up women for sexual purposes were pretty much the result of individual perceptions of what was likely to facilitate or hamper the passing of checks or lead to arrest. Many of the men stated that since they were dealing primarily with business, professional, and clerical persons, their appearance and behavior had to be acceptable to these people. "Middle class" is probably the best term to describe their morality in most areas.

Careful inquiries were made to discover the extent to which the check men were familiar with and spoke an argot. Findings proved meager. Many of the men had a superficial acquaintance with general prison slang, but only four men could measurably identify and reproduce the argot of check forgery or that of thieves. Three more could be presumed to have some familiarity with it. Only one of these spoke the argot in the prison setting. Another said that he never used the argot either in prison or on the outside, except years previously when once in a great while he had "let down at a thieves' party." There were only two men who spoke of themselves as being "on the scratch."[3]

INTERPRETATION

How can these findings be reconciled with the specific statement of Sutherland's informant (Sutherland 1937a, p. 77)[4] that "laying paper" is a form of professional theft most often worked in mobs? The answer to this apparent contradiction requires that a distinction be made between forgery of *the nineteenth and early twentieth centuries and that of the present day.* In the past forgery was a much more complex procedure in which a variety of false instruments such as bank notes, drafts, bills of exchange, letters of credit, registered bonds, and post office money orders as well as checks were manufactured or altered and foisted off. A knowledge of chemicals, papers, inks, engraving, etching, lithography, and penmanship as well as detailed knowledge of bank operations were prime requisites for success. The amounts of money sought were comparatively large, and often they had to be obtained through complex monetary transactions (Dilnot 1929). The technological characteristics of this kind of forgery made planning, timing, specialization, differentiation of roles, morale, and organization imperative. Capital was necessary for living expenses during the period when preparations for the forgeries were being made (Pinkerton 1905, 1884, pp. 338–441; Dilnot 1929). Intermediates between the skilled forger and the passers were necessary so that the latter could swear that the handwriting on the false negotiable instruments was not theirs and so that the forger himself was not exposed to arrest. A "shadow" was often used for protection against the passer's temptation to abscond with the money and in order to alert the others of trouble at the bank.[5] "Fall" money was accumulated and supplied to assist the passer when arrested. Inasmuch as forgery gangs worked together for a considerable length of time, understandings, congeniality, and rules of behavior, especially with regard to the division of money, could and did develop. In short, professional forgery was based upon the technology of the period.

Although precise dating is difficult, the heyday of professional forgery in this country probably began after the Civil War and lasted through the 1920's (Speare 1927). It seems to have corresponded with the early phases of industrialization and commercial development before business and law-enforcement agencies developed methods and organization for preventing forgery and apprehending the offenders. Gradually technological developments in inks, papers, protectographs, and check-writing machines made the forging of signatures and the manufacture of false negotiable instruments more difficult. According to one source, for example, raised drafts have been virtually nonexistent since 1905 (Speare 1927). Similarly, at the present time raising of checks is quite rare. The establishment of a protective committee by the American Bankers Association in 1894, related merchants' protective agencies, and improvements in police methods have made the risks of organized professional forgery exceedingly great (Maurer 1941; Pinkerton 1905).

Check gangs have always been vulnerable to arrest but this vulnerability has been multiplied many times by the large amounts of evidence left behind them in the form of countless payroll checks. Vulnerability is also heightened by the swiftness of communication today. If one person of a check-passing gang is arrested and identifies his associates, it becomes a relatively simple matter for police to secure their arrest. A sexually exploited and angered female companion may easily do the same to the check man. This goes far to explain the extreme seclusiveness of systematic check forgers and their almost abnormal fear of stool pigeons or of being "fingered." The type of persons who can be engaged as passers—unattached women, bar waitresses, drug addicts, alcoholics, petty thieves, and transient unemployed persons—also magnifies the probabilities that mistakes will be made and precludes the growth of a morale which might prevent informing to the police. These conditions also explain the fact that when the forger does work with someone it is likely to be one other person upon whom he feels he can rely with implicit confidence. Hence the man-woman teams in which the woman is in love with the man, or the case of the two homosexual girls, or of the two brothers mentioned previously.

Further evidence that organized forgery is a hazardous type of crime, difficult to professionalize under modern conditions, is indicated by the fact that the organizer or fence is apt to be an older criminal with a long record, whose handwriting methods are so well known that he has no choice other than to work through passers. Even then he does it with recognition that arrest is inevitable.

A factor of equal importance in explaining the decline of professional organized forgery has been the increasingly widespread use of business and payroll checks as well as personal checks. Whereas in the past the use of checks was confined to certain kinds of business transactions, mostly involving banks, today it is ubiquitous. Attitudes of business people and their clerical employees have undergone great change, and only the most perfunctory identification is necessary to cash many kinds of checks. Check men recognize this in frequent unsolicited comments that passing checks is "easy." Some argue that the form of the check is now relatively unimportant to passing it, that "you can pass a candy bar wrapper now days with the right front and story."[6] It is for this reason that the systematic check man does not have to resort to criminal associates or employ the more complex professional procedures used in decades past.

These facts may also account for the presence among lone-wolf check forgers of occasional persons with the identification, orientation, skills, codes, and argot of the thief. Case histories as well as the observations of informants show that older professional criminals in recent decades have turned to check passing because they face long sentences for additional crimes or sentencing under habitual criminal legislation. They regard checks as an "easy racket" because in many states conviction makes them subject to jail sentences rather than imprisonment. Check passing may be a last resort for the older criminal.

The presence of the occasional older professional thief in the ranks of check forgers may actually token a general decline and slow disappearance of professional thieving. One professional thief turned check passer had this to say:

> I'm a thief—a burglar—but I turned to checks because it's getting too hard to operate. Police are a lot smarter now, and they have better methods. People are different nowadays too; they report things more. It's hard to trust anyone now. Once you could trust cab drivers; now you can't. We live in a different world today.[7]

THE CHECK FORGER AS AN ISOLATE

The preference of many systematic check forgers for solitary lives and their avoidance of primary-group associations among criminals may also be explicable in terms of their educational characteristics and class origins. The history of forgery reveals that in medieval times it was considered to be the special crime of the clerical class, as indeed it had to be inasmuch as the members of this class monopolized writing skills (Tout 1919, pp. 5–31). It also seems to be true from the later history of the crime that it has held a special attraction for more highly educated persons, for those of higher socioeconomic status and those of "refined" or artistic tastes.[8] The basic method of organized forgery is stated to have been invented and perfected in England, not by criminals but by a practicing barrister of established reputation in 1840 (Dilnot 1930; Rhodes 1934). An early gang of forgers organized by a practicing physician is also described by Felstead (1926). A number of studies directed to the differentiating characteristics of check criminals point to an "above average" intelligence and formal education. This refers to the general population as well as to the criminal populations with which they have been compared (Berg 1944; Fox 1946; Hooton 1939, p. 87; Lawes 1938, p. 40).

All of this is not to say that less educated persons do not frequently pass bad checks but rather that the persons who persist in the behavior and develop behavior systems of forgery seem much more likely than other criminals to be drawn from a segment of the population distinguished by a higher socioeconomic status. Generally this was true of the systematic forgers in this study. Eight of the thirty had completed two or more years of college. Fourteen of the thirty had fathers who were or had been in the professions and business, including a juvenile court judge, a minister, a postmaster of a large city, and three very wealthy ranch owners. One woman came from a nationally famous family of farm implement manufacturers. Four others had siblings well established in business and the professions, one of whom was an attorney general in another state. Two of the men had been successful businessmen themselves before becoming check men.

The most important implication of these data is that systematic check forgers do not seem to have had criminal associations (Lemert 1953, 1956). For this reason, as well as for technical reasons, they are not likely to seek out or to be comfortable in informal associations with other criminals who have been products of early and lengthy socialization and learning in a criminal subculture. It also follows that their morality and values remain essentially "middle" or "upper" class and that they seldom integrate these with the morality of the professional criminal. This is reflected in self-attitudes in which many refer to themselves as "black sheep" or as a kind of Dr. Jekyll-Mr. Hyde person. Further support for this interpretation comes from their status in prison where, according to observations of themselves and others, they are marginal so far as participation in the primary groups of the prison is concerned.

CONCLUSION

The cases and data presented suggest that present-day check forgery exists in systematic form but does not appear to be a professional behavior system acquired or maintained through associations with other criminals. The technical demands of contemporary check forgery preclude efficient operation on an organized, cooperative basis. In addition to these factors the class characteristics and backgrounds of systematic forgers incline them to avoid intimate association with other criminals.

NOTES

1. One may question whether they were systematic check forgers in a true sense; other informants state that "such people are not real check men; they are just supporting a habit." Their self-definitions and the organization of their lives centers around drug addiction rather than forgery.

2. One of the "pair" workers consisted of two homosexual females. The other non–man-woman pair was made up of two brothers, both of whom had substantial prison records. They worked up and down the West Coast, alternating in making out checks and playing the part of passer.

3. The attitude of the lone wolf check man toward the argot is illustrated by the following quotation:

> It's just the older men in her [San Quentin] who use argot, or some of the young guys who think they are tough. I know the argot but when I hear it I tell them to talk English. Most people on the outside know it anyway. Why call a gun a heater? What is gained by it . . . ?

These findings coincide with Maurer's (1941). He states that the argot of check forgery is relatively unspecialized and that forgers seldom have an opportunity to use it.

4. Maurer (1941) refers to check forgery as a branch of the "grift," and also speaks of professional forgers without, however, defining the term. Yet he recognizes that check forgers are usually lone wolves.

5. Pinkerton (1905) enumerates the following roles of the forgery gang: (1) backer, (2) forger, (3) middleman, (4) presenter, (5) shadow; Maurer (1941) without specifying the

historical period to which his description applies, distinguishes the following as check forger roles: (1) connection, (2) fence, (3) passer.

6. Detectives in Santa Monica, California showed the writer a collection of checks successfully passed with such signatures as: "I. M. A. Fool," "U. R. Stuck," and others not printable. For a discussion of the crudeness of bogus checks accepted by business people see Clinard 1957.

7. There is evidence that there has been a sharp absolute decline in the number of pickpockets in recent years and that most of the so-called "class cannons" (highly skilled) operating now are fifty years of age or over (Maurer 1955).

8. This is the thesis of Rhodes (1934); two of the four participants in the famous Bank of England forgery in 1873 were college educated, one being a Harvard graduate. See Dilnot (1929); forgers coming from "good" families are described by Adam (1908a); fourteen of the nineteen persons tried for forgery at Newgate Prison in England during the later eighteenth and early nineteenth centuries were what can be termed "middle" and "upper" class, including three army or navy officers (one who commanded the royal yacht of Queen Caroline, consort of George IV), one banker, one physician Cambridge graduate, one prosecuting attorney, two engravers (one by appointment to George III), three "gentlemen" of good connections; and three bank clerks. Two of the three men who had "poor parents" had married women of "good means." Tegg (1841) and Bonger (1916, pp. 429, 430, 437) give data from France and Italy which support this idea. A number of writers have commented on the fact that forgery has been quite common among the educated classes of India, particularly the "wily Brahmins" (Adam 1908, Edwards 1924, pp. 3–6, 16).

REFERENCES

Adam, H. L. 1908a. *Oriental Crime* (London: T. Werner Laurie).

———. 1908b. *The Story of Crime* (London: T. Werner Laurie).

Berg, I. 1944. "A Comparative Study of Forgery," *Journal of Applied Psychology,* 28, 232–238.

Bonger, W. A. 1916. *Criminality and Economic Conditions* (Boston: Little, Brown).

Cavan, R. S. 1948. *Criminology* (New York: Crowell).

Clinard, M. B. 1957. *Sociology of Deviant Behavior* (New York: Rinehart).

Dilnot, G. 1929. *The Bank of England Forgery* (New York: Scribners).

———. 1930. *The Trial of Jim the Penman* (London: Geoffrey Bles).

Edwards, S. M. 1924. *Crime in India* (London: Oxford University Press).

Elliott, M. 1942. *Crime in Modern Society* (New York: Harper and Bros.).

Felstead, T. S. 1926. In *Famous Criminals and Their Trials* (New York: Doran).

Fox, V. 1946. "Intelligence, Race and Age as Selective Factors in Crime," *Journal of Criminal Law and Criminology,* 37 (July–August, 1946), 141–152.

Fregier, H. A. 1840. *Les Classes Dangereuses de la population dans les grandes villes* (Paris: Chex J. B. Balliére).

Hall, Jerome. 1952. *Theft, Law and Society,* 2nd Ed. (Indianapolis: Bobbs-Merrill).

Hardless and Hardless. 1920. *Forgery in India* (Chunar: Sanctuary).

Hooton, E. A. 1939. *The American Criminal,* Vol. I (Cambridge: Harvard University).

Lawes, L. 1938. *Life and Death in Sing Sing* (New York: Sun Dial Press).

Lemert, E. 1953. "An Isolation and Closure Theory of Naive Check Forgery," *Journal of Criminal Law and Criminology,* 44 (September–October), 296–307.

———. 1956. "Generality and Specificity in Criminal Behavior: Check Forgery Considered," paper read before American Sociological Society, September.

Lindesmith, A. R., and H. W. Dunham. 1941. "Some Principles of Criminal Typology," *Social Forces,* 19 (March), 307–314.

Maurer, D. W. 1941. "The Argot of Check Forgery," *American Speech,* 16 (December), 243–250.

———. 1955. *Whiz Mob* (Gainesville, Florida: American Dialect Society, No. 24).

Pinkerton, W. A. 1905. "Forgery," paper read before Annual Convention of the International Association of Chiefs of Police, Washington, D.C.

———. 1884. *Thirty Years a Detective* (New York: G. W. Carleton).

Puibaraud, L. 1893. *Les Malfaiteurs de profession* (Paris: E. Flammarion).

Reckless, W. C. 1955. *The Crime Problem,* 2nd Ed. (New York: Appleton Century).

Rhodes, H. T. F. 1934. In *The Craft of Forgery* (London: J. Murray).

Speare, J. W. 1927. *Protecting the Nation's Money* (Rochester: Todd Protectograph Co.).

Sternitsky, J. L. 1955. *Forgery and Fictitious Checks* (Springfield: Charles C. Thomas).

Sutherland, E. H. 1937a. *The Professional Thief* (Chicago: University of Chicago).

———. 1937b. "The Professional Thief," *Journal of Criminal Law and Criminology,* 28 (July–August), 161–163.

. 1947. *Principles of Criminology,* Rev. (New York: Lippincott).

Sutherland, E. H., and D. Cressey. 1955. *Principles of Criminology,* 5th Ed. (New York: Lippincott).

Tegg, T. 1841. *The Chronicles of Crime,* Vols. I, II (London: Camden Pelham).

Tout, T. F. 1919. *Medieval Forgers and Forgeries,* Bulletin of the John Rylands Library, 5, 3, 4.

Von Hentig, H. 1943. "The Pickpocket: Psychology, Tactics and Technique," *Journal of Criminal Law and Criminology,* 34 (May–June), pp. 11–16.

Chapter 9

You Are Not One of Us: Paranoia and Exclusion

One of the few generalizations about psychotic behavior which sociologists have been able to make with a modicum of agreement and assurance is that such behavior is a result or manifestation of a disorder in communication between the individual and society. The generalization, of course, is a large one, and, while it can be illustrated easily with case history materials, the need for its conceptual refinement and detailing of the process by which disruption of communication occurs in the dynamics of mental disorder has for some time been apparent. Among the more carefully reasoned attacks upon this problem is Cameron's formulation of the paranoid pseudocommunity (1943).

In essence, the conception of the paranoid pseudocommunity can be stated as follows:[1]

Paranoid persons are those whose inadequate social learning leads them in situations of unusual stress to incompetent social reactions. Out of the fragments of the social behavior of others the paranoid person symbolically organizes a pseudocommunity whose functions he perceives as focused on him. His reactions to this *supposed community* of response which he sees loaded with threat to himself bring him into open conflict with the actual community and lead to his temporary or permanent isolation from its affairs. The "real" community, which is unable to share in his attitudes and reactions, takes action through forcible restraint or retaliation *after* the paranoid person "bursts into defensive or vengeful activity" (Cameron 1943).

That community to which the paranoid reacts is "pseudo" or without existential reality is made unequivocal by Cameron when he says:

> As he (the paranoid person) begins attributing to others the attitudes which he has towards himself, he unintentionally organizes these others into a functional community,

---

"Paranoia and the Dynamics of Exclusion." *Sociometry* 25,1 (March 1962): 2–20. Reprinted as originally published.

> a group unified in their supposed reactions, attitudes and plans with respect to him. He in this way organizes individuals, some of whom are actual persons and some only inferred or imagined, into a whole which satisfies for the time being his immediate need for explanation but which brings no assurance with it, and usually serves to increase his tensions. The community he forms not only fails to correspond to any organization shared by others but actually contradicts this consensus. More than this, the actions ascribed by him to its personnel are not actually performed or maintained by them; *they are united in no common undertaking against him.* (1943; Italics ours.)

The general insightfulness of Cameron's analysis cannot be gainsaid and the usefulness of some of his concepts is easily granted. Yet a serious question must be raised, based upon empirical inquiry, as to whether in actuality the insidious qualities of the community to which the paranoid reacts are pseudo or a symbolic fabrication. There is an alternative point of view, which is the burden of this paper, namely that, while the paranoid person reacts differentially to his social environment, it is also true that "others" react differentially to him and his reaction commonly if not typically involves covertly organized action and conspiratorial behavior in a very real sense. A further extension of our thesis is that these differential reactions are reciprocals of one another, being interwoven and concatenated at each and all phases of a process of exclusion which arises in a special kind of relationship. Delusions and associated behavior must be understood in a context of exclusion which attenuates this relationship and disrupts communication.

By thus shifting the clinical spotlight away from the individual to a relationship and a process, we make an explicit break with the conception of paranoia as a disease, a state, a condition, or a syndrome of symptoms. Furthermore, we find it unnecessary to postulate trauma of early childhood or arrested psychosexual development to account for the main features of paranoia—although we grant that these and other factors may condition its expression.

This conception of paranoia is neither simple *a priori* theory nor is it a proprietary product of sociology. There is a substantial body of writings and empirical researches in psychiatry and psychology which question the sufficiency of the individual as primary datum for the study of paranoia. Tyhurst (1957), for example, concludes from his survey of this literature that reliance upon intrapsychic mechanisms and the "isolated organism" have been among the chief obstacles to fruitful discoveries about this disorder. Significantly, as Milner (1949) points out, the more complete the investigation of the cases the more frequently do unendurable external circumstances make their appearance. More precisely, a number of studies have ended with the conclusions that external circumstances—changes in norms and values, displacement, strange environments, isolation, and linguistic separation—may create a paranoid disposition in the absence of any special character structure (Pederson 1946). The recognition of paranoid reactions in elderly persons, alcoholics, and the deaf adds to the data generally consistent with our thesis. The finding that displaced persons who withstood a high degree of stress during war and captivity subsequently developed paranoid reactions when they were isolated in a foreign environment commands special attention among data requiring explanation in other than organic or psychodynamic terms (Kine 1951; Listivan 1956).

From what has been said thus far, it should be clear that our formulation and analysis will deal primarily with what Tyhurst (1957) calls paranoid patterns of behavior rather than with a clinical entity in the classical Kraepelinian sense. Paranoid reactions, paranoid states, paranoid personality disturbances, as well as the seldom-diagnosed "true paranoia," which are found superimposed or associated with a wide variety of individual behavior or "symptoms," all provide a body of data for study so long as they assume priority over other behavior in meaningful social interaction. The elements of behavior upon which paranoid diagnoses are based—delusions, hostility, aggressiveness, suspicion, envy, stubbornness, jealousy, and ideas of reference—are readily comprehended and to some extent empathized by others as social reactions, in contrast to the bizarre, manneristic behavior of schizophrenia or the tempo and affect changes stressed in manic-depressive diagnoses. It is for this reason that paranoia suggests, more than any other forms of mental disorder, the possibility of fruitful sociological analysis.

DATA AND PROCEDURE

The first tentative conclusions which are presented here were drawn from a study of factors influencing decisions to commit mentally disordered persons to hospitals, undertaken with the cooperation of the Los Angeles County Department of Health in 1952. This included interviews by means of schedules with members of 44 families in Los Angeles County who were active petitioners in commitment proceedings and the study of 35 case records of public health officer commitments. In 16 of the former cases and in seven of the latter, paranoid symptoms were conspicuously present. In these cases family members and others had plainly accepted or "normalized" paranoid behavior, in some instances longstanding, until other kinds of behavior or exigencies led to critical judgments that "there was something wrong" with the person in question, and, later, that hospitalization was necessary. Furthermore, these critical judgments seemed to signal changes in the family attitudes and behavior towards the affected persons which could be interpreted as contributing in different ways to the form and intensity of the paranoid symptoms.

In 1958 a more refined and hypothesis-directed study was made of eight cases of persons with prominent paranoid characteristics. Four of these had been admitted to the state hospital at Napa, California, where they were diagnosed as paranoid schizophrenic. Two other cases were located and investigated with the assistance of the district attorney in Martinez, California. One of the persons had previously been committed to a California state hospital, and the other had been held on an insanity petition but was freed after a jury trial. Added to these was one so-called "White House case," which had involved threats to a President of the United States, resulting in the person's commitment to St. Elizabeth's Hospital in

Washington, D.C. A final case was that of a professional person with a history of chronic job difficulties, who was designated and regarded by his associates as "brash," "queer," "irritating," "hypercritical," and "thoroughly unlikeable."

In a very rough way the cases made up a continuum ranging from one with very elaborate delusions, through those in which fact and misinterpretation were difficult to separate, down to the last case, which comes closer to what some would call paranoid personality disturbance. A requirement for the selection of the cases was that there be no history or evidence of hallucinations and also that the persons be intellectually unimpaired. Seven of the cases were of males, five of whom were over 40 years of age. Three of the persons had been involved in repeated litigations. One man published a small, independent paper devoted to exposures of psychiatry and mental hospitals. Five of the men had been or were associated with organizations, as follows: a small-town high school, a government research bureau, an association of agricultural producers, a university, and a contracting business.

The investigations of the cases were as exhaustive as it was possible to make them, reaching relatives, work associates, employers, attorneys, police, physicians, public officials and any others who played significant roles in the lives of the persons involved. As many as 200 hours each were given to collecting data on some of the cases. Written materials, legal documents, publications and psychiatric histories were studied in addition to the interview data. Our procedure in the large was to adopt an interactional perspective which sensitized us to sociologically relevant behavior underlying or associated with the more apparent and formal contexts of mental disorder. In particular we were concerned to establish the order in which delusions and social exclusion occur and to determine whether exclusion takes conspiratorial form.

THE RELEVANT BEHAVIOR

In another paper (Lemert 1946) we have shown that psychotic symptoms as described in formal psychiatry are not relevant bases for predictions about changes in social status and social participation of persons in whom they appear. Apathy, hallucinations, hyperactivity, mood swings, tics, tremors, functional paralysis or tachycardias have no intrinsic social meanings. By the same token, neither do such imputed attributes as "lack of insight," "social incompetence," or "defective role-taking ability" favored by some sociologists as generic starting points for the analysis of mental disorders. Rather, it is behavior which puts strain on social relationships that leads to status changes: informal or formal exclusion from groups, definition as a "crank," or adjudication as insane and commitment to a mental hospital. This is true even where the grandiose and highly bizarre delusions of paranoia are present. Definition of the socially stressful aspects of this disorder is a minimum essential, if we are to account for its frequent occurrence in partially compensated or benign form in society, as well as account for its more familiar presence as an official psychiatric problem in a hospital setting.

It is necessary, however, to go beyond these elementary observations to make it pre-eminently clear that strain is an emergent product of a relationship in which the behaviors of two or more persons are relevant factors, and in which the strain is felt both by ego and *alter* or *alters*. The paranoid relationship includes reciprocating behaviors with attached emotions and meanings which, to be fully understood, must be described cubistically from at least two of its perspectives. On one hand the behavior of the individual must be seen from the perspective of others or that of a group, and conversely the behavior of others must be seen from the perspective of the involved individual.

From the vantage of others the individual in the paranoid relationship shows:

1. A disregard for the values and norms of the primary group, revealed by giving priority to verbally definable values over those which are implicit, a lack of loyalty in return for confidences, and victimizing and intimidating persons in positions of weakness.
2. A disregard for the implicit structure of groups, revealed by presuming to privileges not accorded him, and the threat or actual resort to formal means for achieving his goals.

The second items have a higher degree of relevancy than the first in an analysis of exclusion. Stated more simply, they mean that, to the group, the individual is an ambiguous figure whose behavior is uncertain, whose loyalty can't be counted on. In short, he is a person who can't be trusted because he threatens to expose informal power structures. This, we believe, is the essential reason for the frequently encountered idea that the paranoid person is "dangerous" (Dentler and Erikson 1959).

If we adopt the perceptual set of ego and see others or groups through his eyes, the following aspects of their behavior become relevant:

1. the spurious quality of the interaction between others and himself or between others interacting in his presence;
2. the overt avoidance of himself by others;
3. the structured exclusion of himself from interaction.

The items we have described thus far—playing fast and loose with the primary group values by the individual, and his exclusion from interaction—do not alone generate and maintain paranoia. It is additionally necessary that they emerge in an interdependent relationship which requires trust for its fulfillment. The relationship is a type in which the goals of the individual can be reached only through cooperation from particular others, and in which the ends held by others are realizable if cooperation is forthcoming from ego. This is deduced from the general proposition that cooperation rests upon perceived trust, which in turn is a function of communication (Loomis 1959). When communication is disrupted by exclusion, there is a lack of mutually perceived trust and the relationship becomes dilapidated or paranoid. We will now consider the process of exclusion by which this kind of relationship develops.

THE GENERIC PROCESS OF EXCLUSION

The paranoid process begins with persistent interpersonal difficulties between the individual and his family, or his work associates and superiors, or neighbors, or other persons in the community. These frequently or even typically arise out of bona fide or recognizable issues centering upon some actual or threatened loss of status for the individual. This is related to such things as the death of relatives, loss of a position, loss of professional certification, failure to be promoted, age and physiological life cycle changes, mutilations, and changes in family and marital relationships. The status changes are distinguished by the fact that they leave no alternative acceptable to the individual, from whence comes their "intolerable" or "unendurable" quality. For example: the man trained to be a teacher who loses his certificate, which means he can never teach; or the man of 50 years of age who is faced with loss of a promotion which is a regular order of upward mobility in an organization, who knows that he can't "start over"; or the wife undergoing hysterectomy, which mutilates her image as a woman.

In cases where no dramatic status loss can be discovered, a series of failures often is present, failures which may have been accepted or adjusted to, but with progressive tension as each new status situation is entered. The unendurability of the current status loss, which may appear unimportant to others, is a function of an intensified commitment, in some cases born of an awareness that there is a quota placed on failures in our society. Under some such circumstances, failures have followed the person, and his reputation as a "difficult person" has preceded him. This means that he often has the status of a stranger on trial in each new group he enters, and that the groups or organizations willing to take a chance on him are marginal from the standpoint of their probable tolerance for his actions.

The behavior of the individual—arrogance, insults, presumption of privilege and exploitation of weaknesses in others—initially has a segmental or checkered pattern in that it is confined to status-committing interactions. Outside of these, the person's behavior may be quite acceptable—courteous, considerate, kind, even indulgent. Likewise, other persons and members of groups vary considerably in their tolerance for the relevant behavior, depending on the extent to which it threatens individual and organizational values, impedes functions, or sets in motion embarrassing sequences of social actions. In the early generic period, tolerance by others for the individual's aggressive behavior generally speaking is broad, and it is very likely to be interpreted as a variation of normal behavior, particularly in the absence of biographical knowledge of the person. At most, people observe that "there is something odd about him," or "he must be upset," "or he is just ornery," or "I don't quite understand him" (Cumming and Cumming 1957).

At some point in the chain of interactions, a new configuration takes place in perceptions others have of the individual, with shifts in figure-ground relations. The individual, as we have already indicated, is an ambiguous figure, comparable to textbook figures of stairs or outlined cubes which reverse themselves when studied intently. From a normal variant the person becomes "unreliable," "untrustworthy," "dangerous," or someone with whom others "do not wish to be involved." An illustration nicely apropos of this came out in the reaction of the head of a music department in a university when he granted an interview to a man who had worked for years on a theory to compose music mathematically:

> When he asked to be placed on the staff so that he could use the electronic computers of the University *I shifted my ground* . . . when I offered an objection to his theory, he became disturbed, so I changed my reaction to "yes and no."

As is clear from this, once the perceptual reorientation takes place, either as the outcome of continuous interaction or through the receipt of biographical information, interaction changes qualitatively. In our words it becomes *spurious,* distinguished by patronizing, evasion, "humoring," guiding conversation onto selected topics, underreaction, and silence, all calculated either to prevent intense interaction or to protect individual and group values by restricting access to them. When the interaction is between two or more persons in the individual's presence it is cued by a whole repertoire of subtle expressive signs which are meaningful only to them.

The net effects of spurious interaction are to:

1. stop the flow of information to ego;
2. create a discrepancy between expressed ideas and affect among those with whom he interacts;
3. make the situation or the group image an ambiguous one for ego, much as he is for others.

Needless to say this kind of spurious interaction is one of the most difficult for an adult in our society to cope with, because it complicates or makes decisions impossible for him and also because it is morally invidious.[2]

The process from inclusion to exclusion is by no means an even one. Both individuals and members of groups change their perceptions and reactions, and vacillation is common, depending upon the interplay of values, anxieties and guilt on both sides. Members of an excluding group may decide they have been unfair and seek to bring the individual back into their confidence. This overture may be rejected or used by ego as a means of further attack. We have also found that ego may capitulate, sometimes abjectly, to others and seek group re-entry, only to be rejected. In some cases compromises are struck and a partial reintegration of ego into informal social relations is achieved. The direction which informal exclusion takes depends on ego's reactions, the degree of communication between his interactors, the composition and structure of the informal groups, and the perceptions of "key others" at points of interaction which directly affect ego's status.

ORGANIZATIONAL CRISIS AND FORMAL EXCLUSION

Thus far we have discussed exclusion as an informal process. Informal exclusion may take place but leave ego's formal status in an organization intact. So long as this status is preserved and rewards are sufficient to validate it on his terms, an uneasy peace between him and others may prevail. Yet ego's social isolation and his strong commitments make him an unpredictable factor; furthermore the rate of change and internal power struggles, especially in large and complex organizations, means that preconditions of stability may be short lived.

Organizational crises involving a paranoid relationship arise in several ways. The individual may act in ways which arouse intolerable anxieties in others, who demand that "something be done." Again, by going to higher authority or making appeals outside the organization, he may set in motion procedures which leave those in power no other choice than to take action. In some situations ego remains relatively quiescent and does not openly attack the organization. Action against him is set off by growing anxieties or calculated motives of associates—in some cases his immediate superiors. Finally, regular organizational procedures incidental to promotion, retirement or reassignment may precipitate the crisis.

Assuming a critical situation in which the conflict between the individual and members of the organization leads to action to formally exclude him, several possibilities exist. One is the transfer of ego from one department, branch or division of the organization to another, a device frequently resorted to in the armed services or in large corporations. This requires that the individual be persuaded to make the change and that some department will accept him. While this may be accomplished in different ways, not infrequently artifice, withholding information, bribery, or thinly disguised threats figure conspicuously among the means by which the transfer is brought about. Needless to say, there is a limit to which transfers can be employed as a solution to the problem, contingent upon the size of the organization and the previous diffusion of knowledge about the transferee.

Solution number two we call encapsulation, which, in brief, is a reorganization and redefinition of ego's status. This has the effect of isolating him from the organization and making him directly responsible to one or two superiors who act as his intermediators. The change is often made palatable to ego by enhancing some of the material rewards of his status. He may be nominally promoted or "kicked upstairs," given a larger office, or a separate secretary, or relieved of onerous duties. Sometimes a special status is created for him.

This type of solution often works because it is a kind of formal recognition by the organization of ego's intense commitment to his status and in part a victory for him over his enemies. It bypasses them and puts him into direct communication with higher authority who may communicate with him in a more direct manner. It also relieves his associates of further need to connive against him. This solution is sometimes used to dispose of troublesome corporation executives, high-ranking military officers, and academic *personae non gratae* in universities.

A third variety of solutions to the problem of paranoia in an organization is outright discharge, forced resignation or non-renewal of appointment. Finally, there may be an organized move to have the individual in the paranoid relationship placed on sick leave, or to compel him to take psychiatric treatment. The extreme expression of this is pressure (as on the family) or direct action to have the person committed to a mental hospital.

The order of the enumerated solutions to the paranoid problem in a rough way reflects the amount of risk associated with the alternatives, both as to the probabilities of failure and of damaging repercussions to the organization. Generally, organizations seem to show a good deal of resistance to making or carrying out decisions which require expulsion of the individual or forcing hospitalization, regardless of his mental condition. One reason for this is that the person may have power within the organization, based upon his position, or monopolized skills and information,[3] and unless there is a strong coalition against him the general conservatism of administrative judgments will run in his favor. Herman Wouk's novel of *The Caine Mutiny* dramatizes some of the difficulties of cashiering a person from a position of power in an essentially conservative military organization. An extreme of this conservatism is illustrated by one case in which we found a department head retained in his position in an organization even though he was actively hallucinating as well as expressing paranoid delusions.[4] Another factor working on the individual's side is that discharge of a person in a position of power reflects unfavorably upon those who placed him there. Ingroup solidarity of administrators may be involved, and the methods of the opposition may create sympathy for ego at higher levels.

Even when the person is almost totally excluded and informally isolated within an organization, he may have power outside. This weighs heavily when the external power can be invoked in some way, or when it automatically leads to raising questions as to the internal workings of the organization. This touches upon the more salient reason for reluctance to eject an uncooperative and retaliatory person, even when he is relatively unimportant to the organization. We refer to a kind of negative power derived from the vulnerability of organizations to unfavorable publicity and exposure of their private lines that are likely if the crisis proceeds to formal hearings, case review or litigation. This is an imminent possibility where paranoia exists. If hospital commitment is attempted, there is a possibility that a jury trial will be demanded, which will force leaders of the organization to defend their actions. If the crisis turns into a legal contest of this sort, it is not easy to prove insanity, and there may be damage suits. Even if the facts heavily support the petitioners, such contests can only throw unfavorable light upon the organization.

THE CONSPIRATORIAL NATURE OF EXCLUSION

A conclusion from the foregoing is that organizational vulnerability as well as anticipations of retaliations from the paranoid person lay a functional basis for conspiracy among those seeking to contain or oust him. Probabilities are strong that a coalition will appear within the organization, integrated by a common commitment to oppose the paranoid person. This, the exclusionist group, demands loyalty, solidarity and secrecy from its members; it acts in accord with a common scheme and in varying degrees utilizes techniques of manipulation and misrepresentation.

Conspiracy in rudimentary form can be detected in informal exclusion apart from an organizational crisis. This was illustrated in an office research team in which staff members huddled around a water cooler to discuss the unwanted associate. They also used office telephones to arrange coffee breaks without him and employed symbolic cues in his presence, such as humming the Dragnet theme song when he approached the group. An office rule against extraneous conversation was introduced with the collusion of supervisors, ostensibly for everyone, actually to restrict the behavior of the isolated worker. In another case an interview schedule designed by a researcher was changed at a conference arranged without him. When he sought an explanation at a subsequent conference, his associates pretended to have no knowledge of the changes.

Conspiratorial behavior comes into sharpest focus during organizational crises in which the exclusionists who initiate action become an embattled group. There is a concerted effort to gain consensus for this view, to solidify the group and to halt close interaction with those unwilling to completely join the coalition. Efforts are also made to neutralize those who remain uncommitted but who can't be kept ignorant of the plans afoot. Thus an external appearance of unanimity is given even if it doesn't exist.

Much of the behavior of the group at this time is strategic in nature, with determined calculations as to "what we will do if he does this or that." In one of our cases, a member on a board of trustees spoke of the "game being played" with the person in controversy with them. Planned action may be carried to the length of agreeing upon the exact words to be used when confronted or challenged by the paranoid individual. Above all there is continuous, precise communication among exclusionists, exemplified in one case by mutual exchanging of copies of all letters sent and received from ego.

Concern about secrecy in such groups is revealed by such things as carefully closing doors and lowering of voices when ego is brought under discussion. Meeting places and times may be varied from normal procedures; documents may be filed in unusual places and certain telephones may not be used during a paranoid crisis.

The visibility of the individual's behavior is greatly magnified during this period; often he is the main topic of conversation among the exclusionists, while rumors of the difficulties spread to other groups, which in some cases may be drawn into the controversy. At a certain juncture steps are taken to keep the members of the ingroup continually informed of the individual's movements and, if possible, of his plans. In effect, if not in form, this amounts to spying. Members of one embattled group, for example, hired an outside person unknown to their accuser to take notes on a speech he delivered to enlist a community organization on his side. In another case, a person having an office opening onto that of a department head was persuaded to act as an informant for the nucleus of persons working to depose the head from his position of authority. This group also seriously debated placing an all-night watch in front of their perceived malefactor's house.

Concomitant with the magnified visibility of the paranoid individual come distortions of his image, most pronounced in the inner coterie of exclusionists. His size, physical strength, cunning, and anecdotes of his outrages are exaggerated, with a central thematic emphasis on the fact that he is dangerous. Some individuals give cause for such beliefs in that previously they have engaged in violence or threats; others do not. One encounters characteristic contradictions in interviews on this point, such as: "No, he has never struck anyone around here—just fought with the policemen at the State Capitol," or "No, I am not afraid of him, but one of these days he will explode."

It can be said parenthetically that the alleged dangerousness of paranoid persons storied in fiction and drama has never been systematically demonstrated. As a matter of fact, the only substantial data on this, from a study of delayed admissions, largely paranoid, to a mental hospital in Norway, disclosed that "neither the paranoiacs nor paranoids have been dangerous, and most not particularly troublesome" (Ödegard 1958). Our interpretation of this, as suggested earlier, is that the imputed dangerousness of the paranoid individual does not come from physical fear but from the organizational threat he presents and the need to justify collective action against him.[5]

However, this is not entirely tactical behavior—as is demonstrated by anxieties and tensions which mount among those in the coalition during the more critical phases of their interaction. Participants may develop fears quite analogous to those of classic conspirators. One leader in such a group spoke of the period of the paranoid crisis as a "week of terror," during which he was wracked with insomnia and "had to take his stomach pills." Projection was revealed by a trustee who, during a school crisis occasioned by discharge of an aggressive teacher, stated that he "watched his shadows," and "wondered if all would be well when he returned home at night." Such tensional states, working along with a kind of closure of communication within the group, are both a cause and an effect of amplified group interaction which distorts or symbolically rearranges the image of the person against whom they act.

Once the battle is won by the exclusionists, their version of the individual as dangerous becomes a crystallized rationale for official action. At this point misrepresentation becomes part of a more deliberate manipulation of ego. Gross misstatements, most frequently called "pretexts," become justifiable ways of getting his cooperation, for example, to get him to submit to psychiatric examination or detention preliminary to hospital commitment. This aspect of the process has been effectively detailed by Goffman (1959), with his concept of a "betrayal funnel" through which a patient enters a hospital. We need not elaborate on this, other than to confirm its occurrence in the exclusion process, complicated in our cases by legal strictures and the ubiquitous risk of litigation.

THE GROWTH OF DELUSION

The general idea that the paranoid person symbolically fabricates the conspiracy against him is in our estimation incorrect or incomplete. Nor can we agree that he lacks insight, as is so frequently claimed. To the contrary, many paranoid persons properly realize that they are being isolated and excluded by concerted interaction, or that they are being manipulated. However, they are at a loss to estimate accurately or realistically the dimensions and form of the coalition arrayed against them.

As channels of communication are closed to the paranoid person, he has no means of getting feedback on consequences of his behavior, which is essential for correcting his interpretations of the social relationships and organization which he must rely on to define his status and give him identity. He can only read overt behavior without the informal context. Although he may properly infer that people are organized against him, he can only use confrontation or formal inquisitorial procedures to try to prove this. The paranoid person must provoke strong feelings in order to receive any kind of meaningful communication from others—hence his accusations, his bluntness, his insults. Ordinarily this is non-deliberate; nevertheless, in one complex case we found the person consciously provoking discussions to get readings from others on his behavior. This man said of himself: "Some people would describe me as very perceptive, others would describe me as very imperceptive."

The need for communication and the identity which goes with it does a good deal to explain the preference of paranoid persons for formal, legalistic, written communications, and the care with which many of them preserve records of their contacts with others. In some ways the resort to litigation is best interpreted as the effort of the individual to compel selected others to interact directly with him as equals, to engineer a situation in which evasion is impossible. The fact that the person is seldom satisfied with the outcome of his letters, his petitions, complaints and writs testifies to their function as devices for establishing contact and interaction with others, as well as "setting the record straight." The wide professional tolerance of lawyers for aggressive behavior in court and the nature of Anglo-Saxon legal institutions, which grew out of a revolt against conspiratorial or star-chamber justice, mean that the individual will be heard. Furthermore his charges must be answered; otherwise he wins by default. Sometimes he wins small victories, even if he loses the big ones. He may earn grudging respect as an adversary, and sometimes shares a kind of legal camaraderie with others in the courts. He gains an identity through notoriety.

REINFORCEMENT OF DELUSION

The accepted psychiatric view is that prognosis for paranoia is poor, that recoveries from "true" paranoia are rare, with the implication that the individual's delusions more or less express an unalterable pathological condition. Granting that the individual's needs and dispositions and his self-imposed isolation are significant factors in perpetuating his delusional reactions, nevertheless there is an important social context of delusions through which they are reinforced or strengthened. This context is readily identifiable in the fixed ideas and institutionalized procedures of protective, custodial, and treatment organizations in our society. They stand out in sharpest relief where paranoid persons have come into contact with law enforcement agencies or have been hospitalized. The cumulative and interlocking impacts of such agencies work strongly to nurture and sustain the massive sense of injustice and need for identity which underlie the delusions and aggressive behavior of the paranoid individual.

Police in most communities have a well-defined concept of cranks, as they call them, although the exact criteria by which persons are so judged are not clear. Their patience is short with such persons: in some cases they investigate their original complaints and if they conclude that the person in question is a crank they tend to ignore him thereafter. His letters may be thrown away unanswered, or phone calls answered with patronizing reassurance or vague promises to take steps which never materialize.

Like the police, offices of district attorneys are frequently forced to deal with persons they refer to as cranks or soreheads. Some offices delegate a special deputy to handle these cases, quaintly referred to in one office as the "insane deputy." Some deputies say they can spot letters of cranks immediately, which means that they are unanswered or discarded. However, family or neighborhood quarrels offer almost insoluble difficulties in this respect, because often it is impossible to determine which of two parties is delusional. In one office some complainants are called "fifty-fifty," which is jargon meaning that it is impossible to say whether they are mentally stable. If one person seems to be persistently causing trouble, deputies may threaten to have him investigated, which, however, is seldom if ever done.

Both police and district attorney staffs operate continuously in situations in which their actions can have damaging legal or political repercussions. They tend to be tightly ingrouped and their initial reaction to outsiders or strangers is one of suspicion or distrust until they are proved harmless or friendly. Many of their office procedures and general manner reflect this—such as carefully recording in a log book names, time, and reason for calling of those who seek official interviews. In some instances a complainant is actually investigated before any business will be transacted with him.

When the paranoid person goes beyond local police and courts to seek redress through appeals to state or national authorities, he may meet with polite evasion, perfunctory treatment of his case or formalized distrust. Letters to administrative people may beget replies up to a certain point, but thereafter they are ignored. If letters to a highly placed authority carry threats, they may lead to an investigation by security agencies, motivated by the knowledge that assassinations are not unknown in American life. Sometimes redress is sought in legislatures, where private bills may be introduced, bills which by their nature can only be empty gestures.

In general, the contacts which the delusional person makes with formal organizations frequently disclose the same elements of shallow response, evasion or distrust which played a part in the generic process of exclusion. They become part of a selective or selected pattern of interaction which creates a social environment of uncertainty and ambiguity for the individual. They do little to correct and much to confirm his suspicion, distrust and delusional interpretations. Moreover, even the environment of treatment agencies may contribute to the furtherance of paranoid delusion, as Stanton and Schwartz (1954) have shown in their comments on communication within the mental hospital. They speak pointedly of the "pathology of communication" brought about by staff practices of ignoring explicit meanings in statements or actions of patients and reacting to inferred or imputed meanings, thereby creating a type of environment in which "the paranoid feels quite at home."

Some paranoid or paranoid-like persons become well known locally or even throughout larger areas to some organizations. Persons and groups in the community are found to assume a characteristic stance towards such people—a stance of expectancy and preparedness. In one such case, police continually checked the whereabouts of the man and, when the governor came to speak on the courthouse steps, two officers were assigned the special task of watching the man as he stood in the crowd. Later, whenever he went to the state capitol, a number of state police were delegated to accompany him when he attended committee hearings or sought interviews with state officials.[6] The notoriety this man acquired because of his reputed great strength in tossing officers around like tenpins was an obvious source of pleasure to him, despite the implications of distrust conveyed by their presence.

It is arguable that occupying the role of the mistrusted person becomes a way of life for these paranoids, providing them with an identity not otherwise possible.

Their volatile contentions with public officials, their issuance of writings, publications, litigations in *persona propria,* their overriding tendency to contest issues which other people dismiss as unimportant or as "too much bother" become a central theme for their lives, without which they would probably deteriorate.

If paranoia becomes a way of life for some people, it is also true that the difficult person with grandiose and persecutory ideas may fulfill certain marginal functions in organizations and communities. One is his scapegoat function, being made the subject of humorous by-play or conjectural gossip as people "wonder what he will be up to next." In his scapegoat role, the person may help integrate primary groups within larger organizations by directing aggressions and blame towards him and thus strengthening feelings of homogeneity and consensus of group members.

There are also instances in which the broad, grapeshot charges and accusations of the paranoid person function to articulate dissatisfactions of those who fear openly to criticize the leadership of the community, organization, or state, or of the informal power structures within these. Sometimes the paranoid person is the only one who openly espouses values of inarticulate and politically unrepresented segments of the population (Marmor 1958). The "plots" which attract the paranoid person's attention—dope rings, international communism, monopolistic "interests," popery, Jewry, or "psychopoliticians"—often reflect the vague and ill-formed fears and concerns of peripheral groups, which tend to validate his self-chosen role as a "protector." At times in organizational power plays and community conflicts his role may even be put to canny use by more representative groups as a means of embarrassing their opposition.

THE LARGER SOCIO-CULTURAL CONTEXT

Our comments draw to a close on the same polemic note with which they were begun, namely, that members of communities and organizations do unite in common effort against the paranoid person prior to or apart from any vindictive behavior on his part. The paranoid community is real rather than pseudo in that it is composed of reciprocal relationships and processes whose net results are informal and formal exclusion and attenuated communication.

The dynamics of exclusion of the paranoid person are made understandable in larger perspective by recognizing that decision making in American social organization is carried out in small, informal groups through casual and often subtle male interaction. Entree into such groups is ordinarily treated as a privilege rather than a right, and this privilege tends to be jealously guarded. Crucial decisions, including those to eject persons or to reorganize their status in larger formal organizations, are made secretly. The legal concept of "privileged communication" in part is a formal recognition of the necessity for making secret decisions within organizations.

Added to this is the emphasis placed upon conformity in our organization-oriented society and the growing tendency of organization elites to rely upon direct power for their purposes. This is commonly exercised to isolate and neutralize groups and individuals who oppose their policies both inside and outside of the organization. Formal structures may be manipulated or deliberately reorganized so that resistant groups and individuals are denied or removed from access to power or the available means to promote their deviant goals and values. One of the most readily effective ways of doing this is to interrupt, delay or stop the flow of information.

It is the necessity to rationalize and justify such procedures on a democratic basis which leads to concealment of certain actions, misrepresentation of their underlying meaning and even the resort to unethical or illegal means. The difficulty of securing sociological knowledge about these techniques, which we might call the "control behind the controls," and the denials by those who use them that they exist are logical consequences of the perceived threat such knowledge and admissions become to informal power structures. The epiphenomena of power thus become a kind of shadowy world of our culture, inviting conjecture and condemnation.

CONCLUDING COMMENT

We have been concerned with a process of social exclusion and with the ways in which it contributes to the development of paranoid patterns of behavior. While the data emphasize the organizational forms of exclusion, we nevertheless believe that these are expressions of a generic process whose correlates will emerge from the study of paranoia in the family and other groups. The differential responses of the individual to the exigencies of organized exclusion are significant in the development of paranoid reactions only insofar as they partially determine the "intolerable" or "unendurable" quality of the status changes confronting him. Idiosyncratic life history factors of the sort stressed in more conventional psychiatric analyses may be involved, but equally important in our estimation are those which inhere in the status changes themselves, age being one of the more salient of these. In either case, once situational intolerability appears, the stage is set for the interactional process we have described.

Our cases, it will be noted, were all people who remained undeteriorated, in contact with others and carrying on militant activities oriented towards recognizable social values and institutions. Generalized suspiciousness in public places and unprovoked aggression against strangers were absent from their experiences. These facts, plus the relative absence of "true paranoia" among mental-hospital populations, leads us to conclude that the "pseudocommunity" associated with random aggression (in Cameron's sense) is a sequel rather than an integral part of paranoid patterns. They are likely products of deterioration and fragmentation of personality appearing, when and if they do, in the paranoid person after long or intense periods of stress and complete social isolation.

NOTES

The research for this paper was in part supported by a grant from the California State Department of Mental Hygiene, arranged with the assistance of Dr. W. A. Oliver, Associate Superintendent of Napa State Hospital, who also helped as a critical consultant and made the facilities of the hospital available.

1. In a subsequent article Cameron (1959) modified his original conception, but not of the social aspects of paranoia, which mainly concern us.
2. The interaction in some ways is similar to that used with children, particularly in "*enfant terrible*." The function of language in such interaction was studied by Sapir (1915) years ago.
3. For a systematic analysis of the organizational difficulties in removing an "unpromotable" person from a position see (Levenson 1961).
4. One of the cases in the first study.
5. *Supra*, p. 3.
6. This technique in even more systematic form is sometimes used in protecting the President of the United States in "White House cases."

REFERENCES

Cameron, N. 1943. "The Paranoid Pseudocommunity," *American Journal of Sociology,* 46, 33–38.

———. 1959. "The Paranoid Pseudocommunity Revisited," *American Journal of Sociology,* 65, 52–58.

Cumming, E., and J. Cumming. 1957. *Closed Ranks*, Cambridge, Mass.: Harvard Press, Ch. VI.

Dentler, R. A., and K. T. Erikson. 1959. "The Functions of Deviance in Groups," *Social Problems,* 7, 102.

Goffman, E. 1959. "The Moral Career of the Mental Patient," *Psychiatry* 22, 127 ff.

Jaco, E. G. 1957. "Attitudes Toward, and Incidence of Mental Disorder: A Research Note," *Southwestern Social Science Quarterly,* June, p. 34.

Kine, F. F. 1951. "Aliens' Paranoid Reaction," *Journal of Mental Science,* 98, 589–594.

Lemert, E. 1946. "Legal Commitment and Social Control," *Sociology and Social Research,* 30, 33–338.

Levenson, B. 1961. "Bureaucratic Succession," in *Complex Organizations,* A. Etzioni, (ed.), New York: Holt, Rinehart and Winston, 362–395.

Listivan, I. 1956. "Paranoid States: Social and Cultural Aspects," *Medical Journal of Australia,* 776–778.

Loomis, J. L. 1959. "Communications, The Development of Trust, and Cooperative Behavior," *Human Relations,* 12, 305–315.

Marmor, J. 1958. "Science, Health and Group Opposition" (mimeographed paper).

Milner, K. O. 1949. "The Environment as a Factor in the Etiology of Criminal Paranoia," *Journal of Mental Science,* 95, 124–132.

Ödegard, Ö. 1958. "A Clinical Study of Delayed Admissions to a Mental Hospital," *Mental Hygiene,* 42, 66–77.

Pederson, S. 1946. "Psychological Reactions to Extreme Social Displacement (Refugee Neuroses)," *Psychoanalytic Review,* 36, 344–354.

Sapir, E. 1915. "Abnormal Types of Speech in Nootka," *Canada Department of Mines, Memoir* 62, No. 5.

Stanton, A. H., and M. S. Schwartz. 1954. *The Mental Hospital,* New York: Basic Books, 200–210.

Tyhurst, S. J. 1957. "Paranoid Patterns," in A. H. Leighton, J. A. Clausen, and R. Wilson (eds.), *Exploration in Social Psychiatry,* New York: Basic Books, Ch. II.

Chapter 10

Sociologists on the Trail of Evil

My purpose in the writings that follow is to discuss whether evil can be subjected to sociological analysis and, more precisely, whether it can be studied with the existing methods of social science as an extension of the study of deviance and social control. Put as a query, I ask whether our understanding of deviance can be deepened or broadened by the inclusion of evil as part of its subject matter. In short, does the study of evil help complete the sociological account of what happens when there is deviance?

For some sociologists, perhaps most, such questions will appear to be regressive, or a circling back to an earlier era of thinking when a number of writers more or less took the existence of evil for granted. I refer here to turn-of-the-century books of social reformers in which they wrote of the "social evils," such as prostitution, gambling, and drunkenness, sometimes explicitly attributing the latter to the "demon rum."

In contrast to these writings, those of persons identified with the social science movement of the post–Civil War period reflected growing commitment to the philosophy of the early physical and biological sciences that rejected explanations of human behavior based on other than natural phenomena. The ascendancy of rationalism as the underlying premise of Western thought became so complete that references to supernatural explanations of events by social scientists were likely to put them at risk professionally.

There are particular reasons why present-day sociologists have avoided the topic of evil, apart from their allegiance to the rigors of the scientific method and its associated philosophy of positivism. One is the prevalence of cultural relativism as a predominant perspective. An extension of this is the reluctance of sociologists openly to apply terms like "bad," "immoral," or "evil" except in descriptive or analytical contexts. Sociologists often have been at their best playing the

---

Excerpts from *The Trouble with Evil: Social Control at the Edge of Morality*. Albany, NY: State University of New York Press, 1997. Pp. 1–15, 159–164.

role of the demystifier or the unmasker, who exposes the dilapidation and gaps between moral principles and human action. In so doing at times they have dealt heavily in irony and paradox, especially in discussions of deviance. Finally, sociologists have excluded possible concern with evil by conceiving social control and deviance in terms of rules, rule compliance, and conformity, which while relevant to the study of bureaucratized society, scarcely allow comprehension of morality and evil in a broader universalistic sense.

Despite the formidable hindrances to the enterprise, a small number of sociologists have boldly confronted the subject of evil both as a substantive issue as well as analytical. Among the very first, if not the first, sociologists to write on evil as a distinctive topic was E. A. Ross, whose work *Sin and Society* appeared in 1907. For Ross (p. 98), evil was essentially the equivalent of sin, something he defined as "conduct which harms another." Sin, he said, is not self-limiting, as is the case with vice; hence, "Satan's main onset today is on the side of sin rather than vice."

However outdated the post-Victorian Ross's words sound today, nevertheless, his empirical referents for sin were surprisingly modern, being directed at the lack of accountability and control of corporations—a condition that, he said, "transmits the greed of investors but not their conscience" (p. 102). Seeking to fashion a corporate morality, he spoke of monopoly as a "fiduciary sin," along with such practices as rebates, dummy directors, flaunting of factory laws, insurance thievery, inoperative mine inspection laws, and laws for tenement reform.

Ross was essentially a social critic/reformer perturbed by the depredations of the so-called robber barons of the time and their large-scale business and industrial combinations. In a sense his tactics were like those of General Custer's, who "rode to the sound of the guns." His theoretical premises came from French social psychology, which opposed the individual to society as "anti-social" and needing socialization into its fabric. Like some of the other sociologists of his time, he was little deterred from designating evil and evildoers as he saw them and urging their social control.

More than half a century passed before any sociologist appeared in print to argue for the creation of a sociology of evil. The first such publications in what might be called the modern era were written by Kurt Wolff for Italian and French journals (1964, 1967); his English statement came in 1969, "For a Sociology of Evil," published in a psychological rather than a sociological journal. Among other concerns Wolff stressed the need to study alienation and the misdirection Weber's (1958) idea of a value-free society had given to sociology.

In 1978 came the first lengthy discourse on evil *per se* by Stanford Lyman: *The Seven Deadly Sins: Society and Evil.* While the background rationale in this, and to a lesser extent in Wolff's papers, did not exclude concern with the corporate misdoings condemned as evil by Ross, it nevertheless changed to reflect existentialist misgivings about the mission of sociology itself and to feature the alienated nature of the human condition engendered by a corporate-based world. Thus Lyman charged sociology with lacking an awareness and a language for confronting the ubiquitous erosion of meaning resulting from the rationalizing, "scientizing," and bureaucratizing of human activity.

Lyman (1978, viii) does not match Ross's crisp definition of sin. Rather he stated that "Evil is let loose whenever the capacity to criticize is subverted." He then calls evil a "structure of alienating sins." The reader must then find definitions or delineations for each of the seven deadly sins in succeeding chapters of the book, some of which are clear, some necessarily ambiguous.

Overall a reader of *The Seven Deadly Sins,* although likely to be enchanted by the author's lyrical style and erudition, is left uncertain as to his intent. One cannot tell whether the writer is claiming the existence of an objective standard of good by which evil can be judged or merely describing social dramas of good and evil with the implied need to look behind the dramas to decipher true evil. This may follow from a reluctance by Lyman to abandon his "sociology of the absurd" perspective (1989), or it may simply be the inability to rise above one of the salient features Lyman attributes to the "mood" of modern dramas of evil, namely its ambiguity.

A heady conclusion from reading *The Seven Deadly Sins* is that the closer one gets to the subject of evil, the finer its analysis, the more ambiguous it becomes. As I will try to show, this inheres in the process of its ascription and the sociocultural context out of which any formulation or imputation of evil comes.

Other attributes of emergent evil in modern society that have been recognized by sociologists are those of scale and impersonality. They acquire their meaning from the large numbers of Jews and ethnic minorities put to death by German Nazis in World War II and cases of wholesale massacres of civilians during the Viet Nam War. Everett Hughes (1971, 1962) contended with the question, somewhat obliquely put, why otherwise "good" people in Germany tolerated the operation of the death camps. In answer to his own question he concluded that the problem revolved around "dirty work" and implied that in various forms and degrees it exists in all societies. It exists because ordinary people avoid thinking and talking about such things lest group solidarity be threatened. Moreover the greater the social distance between ordinary people and those the object of dirty work, the more likely an implicit mandate will be given to those who carry it out, in this case persons who are isolated from groups other than their own. Hughes also stated that dirty work people tend to be social failures.

Whether Nazi organizations and administration of the Holocaust were staffed primarily by social failures or evil people is a debatable point, considering the wide variety of workers. Non-Germans and victims themselves, including Jews, worked in collecting, transporting, and killing victims of the holocaust. Beyond this is the nagging question of whether persons playing roles and obeying directives in large-scale organizations can be shown to work by evil intent or to commit manifestly evil acts. This is the painful theme encountered in Hannah Arendt's (1965, p. 287) study of the Eichman trial in Israel, which she subtitled *A Report of the Banality of Evil:*

> when I speak of the banality of evil, I do so only on a strictly factual level, pointing to a phenomenon which stared one in the face at the Eichman trial. Eichman was not Iago and not Macbeth, and nothing would have been farther from his mind to determine with Richard III, "to prove a villain."

Lewis Coser (1969), who was equally concerned with Nazi genocidal projects, proposed a somewhat different solution to Hughes's query about the tolerance of evil by presumably good people. This was "structured visibility," which hides or protects people from sensual overload. He posited the existence of limits to the "span of sympathy" ordinary people have for remote victims of evil. Finally, Coser offered the idea that apocalyptic evil of such massive scope implies that victims "must have done something" to deserve such treatment. However, he does not tell us whether such reactions are themselves evil, merely how they make evil possible.

SANCTIONS FOR EVIL

What Hughes, Coser, and some other sociologists were saying is that, given certain circumstances and beliefs, almost any human being is capable of ignoring, minimizing, or tolerating the evil practices of others. In a somewhat different way, Arendt specified how evil can result from the dispassionate, workaday motivations and ambitions of bureaucrats. A line of thought less passive than that of the sensory-removed audience and the mindless bureaucrat runs through another publication of a group of social scientists that includes sociologists, namely *Sanctions for Evil* (Sanford and Comstock 1971). This develops a common theme that doers of evil actually are sanctioned by other members of society who negatively evaluate and dehumanize other groups of people.

Among the sociologists contributing to the volume, Smelser (1971) somewhat legalistically defined evil as the use of coercion, force, and violence that exceeds institutional or legal "limits," or their use by persons without authority to do so. The result is destructiveness. A condition necessary for such an eventuality is a belief that some enemy is evil, intelligent, and omnipotent. At the same time the perpetrator of evil holds to a belief in his own omnipotence and moral superiority. Illustrations are Christian militancy, Nazism, and vigilantism. Precipitation of evil follows from its legitimation, authorization, and rationalization.

Granting its conceptual symmetry, the most that can be concluded from all of this is that evil (read destructiveness) is the outcome of the process of collective behavior and group conflict. It remains unclear as to what is gained by introducing the term evil into such analysis, especially since the author gives no standard for determining what the limits of force are. Similarly no standard is given for judging the meaning of "unauthorized" actions involving destruction, such as the Boston Tea Party by revolutionary Americans.

Troy Duster (1971), by assuming that the absence of guilt is necessary for evil action, outlines a hypothetical state that, in the manner of Garfinkel's (1956) "Conditions of Successful Degradation Ceremonies," proposes "Conditions of a Guilt Free Massacre." He sets down six such conditions, ranging from public faith in the organizational arm of violence, downgrading of individual grounds for action, fragmentation of distributive responsibility in organizations, secrecy, a vulnerable population, and developing a motivation for massacre.

Duster somewhat perversely raises but does not answer the questions about the corporate responsibility for destructive actions. He leaves the issue unclear as to whether groups can experience guilt or be held guilty. In sum he merely shows how a number of people can be shown to have massacred others without a pronouncement of guilt or a sense of guilt in the acting persons. While Duster's piece is a plausible enough formulation, whether it fits the actual history of massacres, he does not question nor even discuss. Off hand a significant exception comes to mind in the massacres of White settlers by Native Americans, who were highly individualistic in war-making and without much if any corporate organization in Duster's sense of the term.

A somewhat more Olympian sociological analysis of evil by Robert Bellah (1971) looks to the communal foundations of American society in a search for the sanctions of evil. These he finds in intrapsychic repression connected with the exclusion or rejection of some groups by others, originally on simple religious grounds, later in history on the high moral grounds of religious piety, and finally on the basis of economic success or failure. Bellah readily admits that all societies have a "dialectic of inclusion and exclusion" but argues that this can be overcome by creating a new open society and a "new man." Bellah is forgiving towards the principals in the killing of villagers in the Viet Nam War, allowing that "we too might have acted as they did." However, not so for those who "failed to create punitive sanctions" and take action against the evildoers.

A conclusion from the writings of sociologists so far cited is that they tend to take the nature of evil for granted or see it broadly as harm or destructiveness. As such, evil emerges as a product of universalistic intrapsychic processes associated with group identities and the projection of primitive aspects of the person onto scapegoat groups. The concomitant destructiveness is "sanctioned," abetted, or even forgiven by humanization, fragmented responsibility, sensual overload, low visibility, or by lack of sanctions against evil acts.

While these sociologists concerned with evil do not quite endow man the social animal with original sin, they make it clear that given certain sociopsychological circumstances he is prone to evil—a kind of "there but for the grace of God go I" perception or one of "it could happen to anyone." In a paradoxical way they are caught up in the positivism of conventional methods of analysis, and, by finding causes for given behavior, inescapably mitigate the evil they identify and decry. They humanize that which has to be dehumanized to be evil. In so doing, however, sophisticated their approaches, they do little to dispel the cloud of ambiguity that has hung over the subject for centuries.

THE ROOTS OF EVIL

I prolong my critical search of the sociological literature on evil to include the work of Ervin Laub (1989), *The Roots of Evil,* who, although writing from a psychological vantage point, incorporates a variety of societal, cultural, and group concepts in his comparative study of mass killings. This has the special merit of concentrating on data with a known provenance from which relevant concepts are derived. As the title of the book suggests, Laub writes with an eye to the moral history or evolution of human violence in its collective aspects. Laub says that individuals have potentialities for good and for evil, likewise groups. The direction they take is influenced by various factors: economic hardship, nationalism, ideology, motivations of perpetuators and bystanders, cultural self-concepts, and others.

Laub concedes that evil is not a scientific concept and that it has no agreed-on meaning, but that the idea of evil is part of the human heritage. A *non sequitur* nevertheless follows: "the essence of evil is the destruction of human beings." Added to this is the idea that the evil of group violence has a potential for growth much like a geometrical progression. In common with sociologists previously cited, Laub has some logical difficulties with the relationship of individual and group motivation but overrides these by saying that groups are like individuals so far as the optional development of good and evil is conceded.

Starkly considered, Laub's work does little more than append the term evil to its title and make some passing contextual references to it. It is, properly seen, a study of mass killings, defensible and praiseworthy as scholarship, but not as an understanding of evil. While an admitted feature of evil is incomprehensibility, Laub obviously believed that it can be made comprehensible. Thus he, along with sociologists, knowingly or unknowingly removed part of its core meaning.

EVIL AS TRANSCENDENCE

Two sociologists have moved perceptibly away from broad causational explanations of evil to focus on its special sociopsychological concomitants as they relate to deviance and crime. In so doing they reflect ideas traceable to philosophy and literature, particularly French literature, that revolve around problems of validating human existence and repairing attenuated identity.

Shoham (1979) in his work *Salvation Through the Gutters,* draws heavily on psychodynamic psychology and myths along with ideas from Nietzsche to account for the evil dimensions of human acts. Such deviance is transcendental or heroic in nature and follows from "ontological prodding of the self" in persons whose lives are devoid of meaning and reality. Negative acts, such as murder or arson, because of their basic ontological significance, give structure, meaning, or social substance to eroded identity. "Playing evil roles" in this way becomes an act of self-definition.

The theme of Shoham's work, figuratively put in the title of his book, was among other things influenced by the literature now grown to legendary proportions surrounding the life of Jean Genet. Genet and his varied literary chroniclers more or less colluded to fashion a grand moral paradox or ethical inversion in which "betrayal, theft, and homosexuality" are converted into saintliness, allegedly due to the intensity and purity of motivation to pursue such actions. Genet thus sought to glorify depravity as a means to achieve a sense of sovereignty, to transcend his low status and spoiled identity as defined by ordinary moral standards.

Genet's depiction (Dort, 1979) of his emergent superdeviant motivations stands as a delight to remaining partisans of labeling theory:

> In order to weather my desolation, I withdrew more deeply into myself. I worked out inadvertently a rigorous discipline I have used ever since. So to every charge brought against me, unjust though it were, from the bottom of my heart I would answer "guilty." No sooner had I pronounced the word or phrase signifying it, when I myself felt the need to become what I had been accused of being.

Shoham incorporates such material on Genet into a kind of existentialist explanation of deviance resulting from separation of the ego from others and the resultant striving for congruence between them. This takes the author on a wide-ranging discussion of the works of Jung and neo-Freudians, as well as of religion, philosophy, and criminology. There is little systematic use of empirical data in the discussions.

CRIME AS DOING EVIL

The most striking and in many ways captivating challenge to conventional studies of crime appeared with Katz's (1988) volume on *Seductions of Crime* subtitled *The Moral and Sensual Attractions of Evil.* If the author does not fly in the face of positivist criminology, he certainly grievously faults it for its sins of omission. In essence he claims that prevailing studies of crime are insufficient or poorly grounded. They lack empirical substance, primarily because they ignore "Evil . . . as lived in everyday realities of society" (p. 10).

However, evil *per se* is less featured in Katz's discussions than the subjective states or "foregound factors" which accompany, precede, or induce various crimes by reason of their seductive qualities. These vary depending on the nature of the crime subjected to analysis, consisting of "sneaky thrills," "magic of violence," "transcendence on the field," "sovereignty," "spirit of street elites," "transcendent fascinations," "moral dominance" or "moral advantage," "moral meanness," "dizzying moral emotions," and "cosmological control."

Katz stretches his term for evil considerably when he speaks of inspiring dread as "moral advantage" (pp. 88 ff) gained by threat and violence. In his descriptions these sound much more like simple intimidation, menace, open defiance, or provocation. However, such characteristics are scarcely applicable to the "thrills" experienced by teenage shoplifters, since there is little or no interaction between them and their proprietary victims. Intimidation practiced by "street elites" on the other hand obviously requires victims or an audience. Likewise, "doing stickup" robbery by its nature requires victims as well as specific kinds of situations. But here there may be a technical or instrumental need for dominance in the sense of using skilled threats to obtain money or other valuables. Katz, however, argues in some detail against the stumbling block idea that robbers evolve their techniques rationally to any significant degree.

Katz properly calls attention to the importance of feelings, emotions, and nuances of meaning important to the commission of some but not all forms of crime, especially as they bear on the subjective needs of offenders which are satisfied by their violent actions. Many of these concomitants are implicit rather than explicit and have to be inferred from analysis of cases. Katz alleges (p. 11) to have used the method of analytic induction for this purpose but unfortunately gives only his results rather than demonstrating stepwise his use of data in a critical fashion.

It is possible to apply alternative explanations to Katz's material on stickups by Blacks. One of these directs attention to the situational particulars of such crimes. A goodly proportion of the victims of robberies and robbery-homicides are known to the offender and occur in residences; likewise the two in many cases live in close proximity to one another. Such facts are consistent with Donald Black's (1983) theory of crime as social control in which offenders seek to redress specific wrongs done them by particular others.

It is true that Katz employs the concept of social control but primarily as a dramatic act by an offender to assert control over the chaos in his personal life, who like Shakespeare's protagonist "takes arms against a sea of troubles and by opposing seeks to end them." What Katz fails to explore is that the stickup offender in his reaction to chaos may be opting for the specific negative identity of jail or prison inmate by the seeming irrational manner in which he performs the crime. He may be responding to high stress levels that ultimately go with his "hardman" image or identity.

In such a case, maintaining the hardman identity grows unbearable not only because of stress but because the rewards of stickup over time lose their validating effects for the self. Katz inadvertently recognized this when he noted the instance of a harassed robber who expressed relief on his arrest and by citing Laurie Taylor's (1984, p. 180) observation from English research that some such "villains" at critical points harbor a death wish so that they deliberately increase their visibility and thereby the likelihood of detection. These interpretations clearly are not consistent with the idea that the stickup man is imposing "disciplined control" by force of his personality over his chaotic life situation. Rather he is openly engineering a change of identity as an escape from his present life situation.

All of this reflects an underlying problem with Katz's type of analysis in that he sees transcendence as a state or a condition that explains criminal acts. His analysis is synchronic rather than diachronic and overlooks the possibility now entertained by some writers (Olson & Rouner, 1981; Griffin, 1991) that transcendence must be seen as a process, or possibly as part of a process. Thus the same actions may have different meanings at different stages of a process or of a criminal career. Unless this is known, a kind of time or "phase" bias may affect case history data.

In my older study (Lemert, 1972) of systematic check forgers I found that they moved through a cycle of rising stress coupled with declining satisfaction with their "fast" life style composed of indulgence in fine clothes, first-class air travel, staying at fine hotels, gambling, and intercourse with women available on short acquaintance. Mounting stress came from the ubiquitous threat of arrest, while declining life satisfaction resulted from compounding social isolation imposed by the forger's high mobility, use of false identities, and closely guarded interpersonal interaction precluding the intimate validation of self. Finally, identity itself eroded to a point of crisis, at which time arrest usually occurred. This allowed reidentification in socially realistic, albeit negative, terms.

At the time I did this research and writing I realized that the robber's ultimate problem was analogous to that of the committed check forger in that both become isolated, although for different reasons. Further study may very well reveal that the robber's reputation as a hardman or as "somewhat crazy" (Katz's term) gets fed by his intimidation of personal associates as well as by his crime victims; this, complicated by his violent treatment of women, magnifies his social isolation and alienation in his own world. Thus while it emerges in a different context, critical social isolation of the stickup criminal may have the effect of precipitating an identity crisis much as it does for the systematic check forger.

The brief comparisons I have drawn here between stickup criminals and systematic check forgers necessarily raise questions about the sufficiency of the concept of transcendence as an explanation of evil. There are certainly "sensual dynamics" associated with bad check passing in the form of thrills, excitement, and gamelike exhilaration that qualify as transcendence. However, ordinarily there is no visible "moral advantage" over victims as with stickups because the bogus nature of the bad checks is discovered only later. Nor does the crime produce violence; check forgers seldom if ever possess weapons and, in interviews, protest that they "could never hurt anyone." With passing time the check forger's active criminal life does not become chaotic so much as empty and meaningless.

Although transcendence is a recognizable aspect of the check forger's criminal experience, he does not typically have an antecedent illicit life style attributed by Katz to street elites, "bad ass niggers," and stickup criminals. According to my early findings, habitual check criminals often came from middle-class backgrounds and in some cases were highly educated. A final dissenting note is that while such criminals may have been attracted "sensually" to bogus check passing, they did not find it morally seductive; to the contrary they were typically perplexed and deeply perturbed by the moral contradictions between their crimes and their conventional upbringing.

From what I have said and what research likely would show, transcendence can be the concomitant of a number of different crimes that vary greatly in the extent to which they can be characterized as evil. Moreover the need for transcendence may be a secondary effect of a crime as well as a cause, a confusion best eliminated by following some form of process or extended, trouble case analysis.

Common knowledge grants that transcendence is not exclusively a feature of evil crimes; it occurs in the lives of conventionally moral persons. Mystical experiences happen to people making up the normal population in many cultures and, as William James (1977) wrote, are institutionalized as religious expression. Artists and musicians attest to "moments of truth" in their creative moods; linebackers on professional football teams are known to "go a little crazy" prior to game time, yet revert to peaceful family life afterwards. Indeed even professors may transcend their sedate milieus, as in the case of Erving Goffman, whom Bennett Berger (1971, p. 136) referred to as pursuing his observations and writings with "demonic detachment."

While Katz fathered a host of fresh ideas for the study of crime, he made no effort and did little to clarify the idea of evil; if anything, like others writing on the topic, he has added ambiguity to the term. A pertinent query is why he chose to use the word in the title of his book and intermittently in his discussions, for in likelihood they could have been put just as well without invoking the notion of evil. Questions of this sort turn attention to the author's purpose in writing his book, his mission, if you will, and to the audience he addresses, as well as to the larger purpose he conveyed by his writing style. It shifts attention way from evil *per se* to its rhetoric.

THE RHETORIC OF EVIL

Lyman's writings on sin and evil stirred little lasting interest among sociologists or among those in its most relevant area, deviance and criminology; but in one respect they were ahead of their time. I refer to his urgent call for a rhetoric evil. As he put the matter (1978, viii):

> we lack a rhetoric of criticism for social evils . . . a rhetoric that grasps the structures of consciousness, the phenomenology of history and the dramaturgy of contemporary scenes. . . . Such a new rhetoric . . . would take evil as a topic in its own right, seeking to uncover its historical backgrounds, describe its social forms and architectonics, and examine its supports and strengths.

It is only recently that sociologists and researchers in the field of communications have given a "new turn" to rhetoric or returned to its study with new perspectives. In the past, rhetoric suffered ill repute among scientists, who often treat it with derision or as an antithesis to logic, reason, and objective communication. Current rhetorical studies, while focusing on how best to persuade an interested, informed, and judicious audience, now analyze written and oral materials to decipher how they are qualified and given epiphenomenal meaning by their format and style (Simon, 1989; Hunter, 1990).

Gusfield (1967, 1988, 1981), for example, portrayed how a kind of special rhetoric develops as part of the culture of social problems, such as drunk driving, but was content merely to point to its deficiencies. Lyman (1978) seemingly is the only sociologist self-consciously to undertake the task of creating a rhetoric of evil. Whether he succeeded is dubious, and if he did, it was a fractured rhetoric.

A careful reading of Lyman's discussion of the various sins of mankind shows that he employed two vocabularies, one historical and morally descriptive, another conceptualizing such things as overeating, addiction to drugs, and alcoholism with terms taken from texts on deviance and abnormal psychology. The "rhetoric" appears in captions that combine the two vocabularies, such as Gluttony and Social Structure, The Social Construction of Gluttony, and Absolution from the Sin of Gluttony: Strategies of Excuse and Justification. The text itself is threaded with sermonizing frequently in the manner of Old Testament prophets, fittingly conveyed by the last word in his book, "Amen."

* * *

Writing about evil while adhering to the method of science is no easy task, for the simple reason that evil is a mystical idea that loses an important part of its meaning when it is defined solely as an objective phenomenon. To do so omits a subjective element having to do with special feelings and emotions that defy generalization. These cannot be captured by defining evil as harm because harm is defined as evil, leaving a tautology, which is rejected by scientists, who insist on defining a phenomenon in terms of its operations.

Bridging the gap between the mystical and the real is helped by noting William James' concept of religious experience as ineffable, which can only be expressed by passive terms such as awe or reverence. In contrast, evil, while it is a variety of mystical experience, is active not passive; its dominant emotion is fear rising to panic and an urgent demand for action.

This occurs when the premonitory emotions of evil experienced by individuals are transformed into a collective expression through a process of social interaction. This process is one of contested meanings and of emergent consensus. It is influenced by fixed background factors as well as by problematic foreground factors. Among the former are nighttime fears derived from evolutionary memories, which can be observed in small children. Later their fear of the dark generalizes to the color black as a premonitor of evil, which, along with red, signals danger.

The folk recognition of the evil eye, conveyed by overgazing, along with negative charisma, illustrates the play of foreground factors in the perception of evil. Cultures "exploit" such factors; but more particularly, groups or individuals do so. Exploitation ranges from modern films made to horrify adolescent movie-goers to the conjurations of sorcerers, who wear black clothing, roam the night, and deliver evil incantations and potions to others.

As I explained in the preface of my book, its subject matter evolved from a number of sources and finally came to rest on the topics of witchcraft and sorcery, which flourished in Africa and in Melanesia. Unfortunately the resting place is a shaky one inasmuch as no agreement exists as to the meanings of sorcery and witchcraft, and some writers use them interchangeably.

One solution to the confusion of the terms is to subsume them under the concept of magic, or to follow Kluckhohn, who distinguished different kinds of witchcraft as forms of wizardry. Another solution for the inconsistent use of the concepts of witchcraft and sorcery is to speak, write, or think of the three terms as the several ways in which power over others is exercised, and becomes a means of social control. An issue growing out of this is whether such means of social control is sufficiently regularized to consider it to be legal control.

Another line that leads out of the confusion between witchcraft and sorcery lies in use of the sociological term status. By this token witches have only adventitious or putative status, socially created by suspicion, blame, and the potential for collective attack. These vary with community fears and are in turn influenced by changing socioeconomic conditions.

Viewed sociologically, sorcerers have an established status, albeit a marginal one; they are socially accepted specialists who live by exploiting the fears of others in the community. It is the sense of having exploited that generates distrust of the sorcerer and the possibility of retaliation, which, however, he minimizes by distancing himself from others.

THE WITCH HUNT AS SOCIAL CONTROL

Witch hunts were collective movements to control witches and witchcraft, and were largely confined to Africa. They had cult-like features but differed from cargo cults found in Melanesia. As forms of social control they aimed at inducing local peoples to give up their evil practices. This was done by harrassment and sometimes the execution of the supposed "witches." The forms that the witch hunt took were influenced by the authority of native monarchs and restricted by the policies of colonial administrators in Africa. In New Guinea and Papua, where colonialism came late and where sorcery was available to all, no witch hunts materialized; at most cargo cults there resembled witch hunts in regard to the extraction of money by leaders from their followers.

Conclusions about leadership in Melanesian societies are necessarily tentative and subject to exceptions. It was affected by the ubiquitous competition for status among followers as well as among leaders. At the same time this motivation to excel was counterbalanced by allegiance to the values of equivalence. These values emerged or were satisfied in translocal gift exchanges around which socioeconomic life was organized.

Competition of the sort attributed to Melanesians was charged with emotions of anger and distrust, whose expression did not typically precipitate conflict but rather became a stimulus to remedial gift giving. Here one sees a reflection of the stark differences between Southeast Asian cultures and those of the West. Thus for many Melanesian cultures emotions followed a categorically different pattern than in Western cultures. For people of these cultures anger, hatred, and distrust were an integral part of ordinary, recurrent social relationships as well as a means to initiate such relationships. Civility and amity stood low in the scale of Melanesian values, removed by many centuries from the culture of civility that emerged in eighteenth-century Europe. Savagery was far from being a mere state of unenlightenment for Melanesians; rather it had features of cultlike ecstasy.

The values pertaining to this distinctive savagery were those of the warrior class, whose intermittent satisfaction fluctuated with skirmishing, raiding, and warfare. The shifting periods of warfare and quiescence gave rise to alternating patterns of indulgence in violence, killing, and destruction of enemy houses, trees and gardens, followed by uneasy peace. The labile nature of the accompanying emotions may be regarded as an integral part of a warfare complex whose values were maintained by the hegemony of the warrior group. The endemic nature of Melanesian warfare followed from the lack of formal means or overriding authority necessary to bring it to an end. This contrasts sharply with the already noted formality of the Japanese people, who employ linguistic forms, bowing, verbal apologies, and carefully segregated social relationships to control conflict.

One must acknowledge that patterns of intermittent warfare did not hold for all Melanesian tribes. There were those in which warfare was persistent. Information is not available as to whether individual competition and rivalry were present in societies organized for continuous war making. However, there is evidence that the incidence of sorcery was much lower in societies with martial cultures than in those that periodically resumed social contacts with their erstwhile enemies. The greater reliance on sorcery for purposes of social control occurred more frequently in societies whose members interacted with former foes.

There were Melanesian societies that did not rely on violence and sorcery as means of social control. A broad view indicates that shaming was more often or more widely distributed as a means of social control than any other. Whether its effects were more successful than sorcery is hard to say. However, it is clear that the effects of sorcery, according to native belief, were more fateful, since they were likely to produce disease, death, or misfortune.

Shaming depended for its success on the vulnerability of those who were shamed. This in turn depended on socialization of the child. Orphans and others missing such influence often were untouched by shaming. Migratory workers could very well outgrow sensitivity to shaming, likewise "rubbish men" who were social dropouts and who did not live by the competitive ethic.

A remarkable feature of social control found throughout the area of New Guinea and Papua was the resort to self-destructive behavior on the part of individuals who felt aggrieved by others or by their failure to meet due obligations. Such persons' responses ranged from giving away money to a kind of vengeance suicide.

Peoples of the West have some general familiarity with the traditional suicide rituals of the Japanese, so-called *hara kiri;* but examined carefully, they differ from Melanesian shaming reactions. Melanesians inflict shame on others by turning their own anger into self-demeaning and self-destructive actions, not to erase their shame so much as to project it onto the offending others.

Suicide can have a number of different meanings even within the same culture. Melanesian self-directed destructiveness and immolation can be interpreted as a form of transcendence—a reaching for ultimate experience or a final resolution of life conflicts. The same holds for Japanese under certain circumstances, when they commit suicide, not necessarily to expunge shame but to achieve some pinnacle of ecstasy—as when teenage lovers leap into a volcano. It is shown even more graphically by a present day film, *Realm of the Senses,* in which a Japanese prostitute cuts off the genitals of her lover in the final act of a tempestuous love affair.

Japanese and Melanesian instances of transcendence underscore the many shapes that such experience takes in other cultures, from adolescent thrills felt with shoplifting to the fulminations of great leaders, who are "overcome by their belief in themselves" (Nietzsche's phrase). It is for this reason along with others that transcendence is recognized as a process rather than as a state of a condition. Furthermore, whether transcendence is evil depends on the meaning it acquires in social interaction.

In broad perspective it is unfortunate but true that many questions can be raised about aspects of Melanesian cultures for which answers cannot be found in published ethnographies of the area. This does not fault the field workers who gathered the available knowledge. Rather it is a commentary on the impossible task before them, faced as they have been with the diversity of cultures to record and the rapid rate at which they changed after World War II contacts.

Fairness and the pleasure from the opportunity to read their accounts leads me to applaud the richness and intriguing variety of the ethnographers' data that are available. On the down side I must say or admit that their reluctance or failure to make cross-cultural comparisons was a disappointment. Conversations with some of my anthropological friends suggest that this may have been naiveté on my part. On the other hand it may harken back to the time when I and a few others believed that combined training in the fields of sociology and anthropology was, as is now said, "the way to go."

REFERENCES

Arendt, Hannah. *Eichmann in Jerusalem: A Report on the Banality of Evil*. London: Penguin Books 1965.

Bellah, Robert N. "Evil and the American Ethos." In *Sanctions for Evil: Sources of Social Destructiveness,* ed Nevitt Sanford and Craig Comstock. Boston: Beacon Press, 1971.

Berger, Bennett. *Looking for America: Essays on Youth, Suburbia, and Other American Obsessions*. Englewood Cliffs, NJ: Prentice-Hall, 1971.

Black, Donald. "Crime as Social Control." In Donald Black, *Toward a General Theory of Social Control*. Volume 2: *Selected Problems*. Orlando: Academic Press, 1983, 1–27.

Coser, Lewis. "The Visibility of Evil." *Journal of Social Issues* 25 (1969): 101–9.

Dort, Bernard. "Genet: The Struggle with Theater." Tr. by Ruth Goldfarb. In *Genet: A Collection of Critical Essays,* ed Peter Brooks and Joseph Halpern. Englewood Cliffs, NJ: Prentice-Hall, 1979, 114–28.

Duster, Troy. "Conditions for a Guilt-Free Massacre." In *Sanctions for Evil: Sources of Social Destructiveness,* ed Nevitt Sanford and Craig Comstock. Boston: Beacon Press, 1971, 25–36.

Garfinkel, Harold. "Conditions of Successful Degradation Ceremonies." *American Journal of Sociology,* 61,5 (1956): 420–24.

Griffin, David Ray. *Evil Revisited: Responses and Reconsiderations*. Albany: State University of New York Press, 1991.

Gusfield, Joseph. "Constructing Ownership of Social Problems: Fun and Profit in the Welfare State." *Social Problems* 36,5 (December 1988): 431–41.

———. *The Culture of Public Problems*. Chicago: University of Chicago Press, 1981.

———. "Moral Passage: The Symbolic Process in the Public Designation of Deviance." *Social Problems* 15, 2 (Fall 1967): 175–88.

Hughes, Everett. "Good People and Dirty Work." *Social Problems* 10, 1 (Summer 1962): 3–11.

———. *The Sociological Eye: Selected Papers*. Chicago: Aldine, 1971.

Hunter, Albert. *The Rhetoric of Social Research*. New Brunswick, NJ: Rutgers University Press, 1990.

James, William. *The Varieties of Religious Experience: A Study of Human Nature*. New York: Penguin, 1982 [1977].

Katz, Jack. *The Seductions of Crime: The Moral and Sensual Attractions of Evil*. New York: Basic Books, 1988.

Laub, Ervin. *The Roots of Evil*. New York: Cambridge University Press, 1989.

Lemert, Edwin M. "The Behavior of the Systematic Check Forger." In Edwin M. Lemert, *Human Deviance, Social Problems, and Social Control*. 2nd ed. Englewood Cliffs, NJ: Prentice-Hall, 1972.

Lyman, Stanford. *The Seven Deadly Sins: Society and Evil*. New York: St. Martins Press, 1978.

Lyman, Stanford and Marvin Scott. *Sociology of the Absurd*. 2nd ed. Dix Hills, NJ: General Hall, 1989.

Olson, Alan M. and LeRoy Rouner, eds. *Transcendence and the Sacred*. Notre Dame, IN: University of Notre Dame Press, 1981.

Ross, E. A. *Sin and Society*. Boston and New York: Houghton-Mifflin, 1907.

Sanford, Nevitt and Craig Comstock, eds. *Sanctions for Evil: Sources of Social Destructiveness*. Boston: Beacon Press, 1971.

Shoham, S. Giora. *Salvation Through the Gutters: Deviance and Transcendence*. Washington, DC: Hemisphere Publishing Co., 1979.

Simon, Herbert, ed. *Rhetoric in the Human Sciences*. London: Sage, 1989.

Smelser, Neil J. "Some Determinants of Destructive Behavior." In *Sanctions for Evil: Sources of Social Destructiveness,* ed. Nevitt Sanford and Craig Comstock. Boston: Beacon Press, 1971, 15–24.

Taylor, Laurie. *In the Underworld*. London: Basic Blackwell, 1984.

Weber, Max. *The Protestant Ethic and the Spirit of Capitalism*. Translated by Talcott Parsons. With a foreword by R. H. Tawney. New York: Scribners, 1958.

Wolff, Kurt. "For a Sociology of Evil." *Journal of Social Issues* 25,1 (1969): 111–25.

———. "Note sul Profilarsi di una Nuova Scienza Sociale." *Centro Sociale* 55 (1964): 30–40.

———. "Pour une Sociologie du Mal." *L'Homme et la Societe* 4 (1967): 197–213.

Chapter 11

Alcohol Comes to the South Seas

Although not entirely strangers to the experience of intoxication, thanks to their native drink, *kava,* Polynesians must be counted among those peoples without knowledge of alcoholic beverages prior to their contacts with Europeans and Americans. The first among them to taste liquor were chiefs and royalty who had been invited as guests aboard ships of early voyagers to the Pacific area. In most instances, they found it unpalatable or even repellent. Comte Louis Antoine de Bougainville, one of the first Europeans to land in Tahiti, described the native reaction to French wine and brandy: "J'en dirois autant de leurs boissons; . . . ils n'en consoissent d'autre que l'eau: l'odeur feule du vin et de l'eau-de-vie leur donnoit de la repugnance."[1] Similar observations were recorded by Joseph Banks, who accompanied Wallis and Cook on his voyage to Tahiti: "Drink they have none, except water and coconut juice, nor do they have any method of intoxication among them. Some there were who drank pretty freely of our liquors and in a few instances became very drunk, but seemed far from pleased with their intoxication, the individuals afterwards shunning a repetition of it, instead of greedily desiring it, as most Indians are said to do."[2]

Approximately fifteen to twenty years after these observations were recorded in 1791, liquor was first introduced to the Hawaiians by a Captain "Maxhalawell" at Kailua on the large island of Hawaii. Kamakau, a native historian, wrote graphically of the incident:

> When Kamehameha was residing at Kailua, a vessel was seen off Keahole Point, when Kamehameha with his foreigners set out to meet it, these being Young and Davis. . . . [I]t was on this vessel that Kamehameha first tasted liquor with the aid of foreigners; the canoe men also drank liquor at this time for the first time. The canoe came back with Kamehameha. . . . When the people and chiefs saw that Kamehameha was not acting his usual way. The people thought he had gone insane, so the people

---

This unpublished essay was originally titled "Alcohol and Social Control in Polynesia, 1800–1960"

cried out "Woe! Woe! Woe! You have lost your reason. You are red in the face. Woe is you."

Those who came back from the vessel replied: "It was the exhilarating water from the foreigners. It was the sparkling water from the foreigners. It was the dancing waters from the foreigners."[3]

Whatever early dislike Polynesians may have had for liquor soon changed to avid liking. It quickly became an article of commerce, as well as ready means by which foreigners gained and kept the goodwill of chiefs and nobles. Kamakau refers to Kalanimoke as the first of the chiefs to purchase liquor from a vessel anchored at Kailua; he further states that the exchange of food for "something to get intoxicated with," such as bananas, potatoes, melons, pineapples, sugar cane, mountain apples, and *poha* berries, became well known over the whole group of islands. The center for such trading originally was in Kohala on the island of Hawaii, as Kamakau tells us in figurative approximation to Hawaiian text. In the following passage, various plays on words give the text an amusing range of double meanings: "The grandparents of these things are at the outer part of Kohala, Hawaii; the father, Hikapoloa and Lanihopo the mother."[4] Here *Hikapoloa* combines *hika* (to stagger)] with *poloa* (all night), while *Lani* (chief) is paired with *hopo* (fool).

Trade in liquor was carried on mainly by English and American vessels, and it flourished not only in the Hawaiian chain but also in the Society Islands, Friendly Islands (Tonga), Bay of Islands, New Zealand, and to a lesser extent the Cook Islands. The Marquesas, Tuamotus, Gambiers, and Australs saw less of this trade because ships infrequently visited them in the early contact period. Trading liquor was largely a monopoly of royalty or chiefs or was otherwise controlled by them.[5] A kind of informal licensing prevailed in which the sale or exchange of liquor was carried on with the permission of island rulers either by traders or by runaway sailors who set up grog shops.[6]

Members of royalty and chiefs in both Tahiti and Hawaii held stores of foreign liquor in reserve and when it grew short in supply put a taboo on its use by their native followers. Chiefs in some instances were drawn directly into the trade, aided by foreign traders who encouraged them to take goods on credit and then used their indebtedness to gain concessions or freedom to trade. Boki, governor of Oahu, is described by Bingham[7] as one such chief who sought to liquidate his debts and enrich himself by setting up a tavern in Honolulu around 1827, then issuing licenses to others to do the same.

In 1825, the native governor of Maui and his wife both owned grog shops. The scope of the local liquor trade at this time is indicated by the presence of twenty-three grog shops within the distance of one mile at the port of Lahaina. Liquor sellers tended to be either sailor deserters or natives, the latter often in the secret employ of a chief. In 1836, fourteen of the thirty-five ships that landed at Honolulu carried liquor, and while somewhat less flourishing than Lahaina, nevertheless the town there had twelve grog shops and six wholesale liquor stores.[8]

THE *KAVA* PROTOTYPE

The widespread use of *kava* meant that Polynesians had experience with not only an "intoxicant" but also a cultural form that served in part, at least, as a prototype to follow in their subsequent adoption of alcoholic beverages. This is apparent in the continuity of linguistic terms in the Society Islands where *ava* became the generic term for "liquors." There the native drinks were called *ava maohi* (indigenous), while imported alcoholic drinks were given the name *ava popaa* (foreign); specific types of native alcoholic beverages were distinguished by the names of the fruits used in their preparation, such as *ava panaipo* (pineapple liquor).[9]

Other evidence of syncretism between the use of *kava* and liquor are to be seen in the practice of reserving spirituous liquors for the chiefly class (*alii*), especially in Hawaii, and of designating as sacred certain liquors, such as brandy (*palani*) and gin (*kini*), and their use by medicine men (*kahunas*) when the sacred species of the *kava* plant was not available. Other indications of their functional equivalence was the repetition of *awa* prayers when liquor was drunk, offerings of liquor to the gods, and the propitiation of Pele, the Hawaiian volcano goddess, by pouring liquor into lava streams.[10] Finally, the separate consumption of liquor by men and women in Hawaii and the Cook Islands bears a similarity to early *kava* drinking patterns.

The most conspicuous sign of persistence of a *kava* cult pattern is found in the kava circle, which became the characteristic arrangement of clandestine drinking groups in the Cook Islands, Society Islands, Tonga, Hawaii, and Samoa. The seating of drinkers in a circle, rotation serving by a person from a fixed point in the circle, the use of coconut cups, and serving from native receptacles such as *kumetes* (Cook Islands) all token the importance of *kava* culture in shaping or providing a learning base for early Polynesian drinking practices. A kind of negative indication of its importance as a prototype of liquor drinking is seen in the Maori of New Zealand, who did not drink *kava* and who also failed to develop any distinctive ways of drinking alcoholic beverages after they became available to them.

FESTIVE DRINKING

The earliest forms of drinking in Polynesia can best be described as festive in nature;[11] that is, liquor became an item added to feasts, which expressed dominant cultural values, especially in Eastern and Central Polynesia (Cook Islands). Feasts were primarily occasions for the free and extensive consumption of accumulated food supplies, water pageantry, choral singing (chants), dancing, dramatic entertainment, and warlike athletic contests or demonstrations.

In Tahiti, feasts could be family affairs or embrace neighboring villages or an entire district. In other instances, the population of an entire island convened for festivities or even groups of islands. Some feasts were adventful, such as those held for visiting chiefs or royalty; others occurred at definite times or during certain periods of the year.

Festive drinking, along with eating, generally was on a come-one, come-all basis, with many people taking part. While the occasion was one of informality, religious rituals involving the use of liquor sometimes served to initiate activities. This might be a brief prayer by the medicine man (or missionary at a later day), as apparently happened in Tahiti[12] and also in Hawaii.

Age, sex, and social rank affected the extent and form of participation in feasts associated with drinking. Informants in all Polynesian Islands save Samoa spoke of strict rules against allowing youth below the age of eighteen years to drink, which were enforced in earlier historical periods largely through community pressure on parents. Participation by women was variable. In Tahiti, married women apparently drank freely with men. During the reign of Kamehameha in Hawaii, men and women while convened together nevertheless drank from separate receptacles and had separate supplies of liquor.[13] The same seems to have been true of early orange beer feasts in the Cook Islands. Later women were excluded from bush beer schools. Consistent with older *kava* drinking traditions, in Hawaii, the *alii* (royalty) and chiefs drank apart from commoners and usually drank spirituous liquors, while the latter drank brews or wines.

Kamakau's observations speak generally of the rules governing the use of liquor at feasts in Hawaii:

> When the manufacture of liquor became general in Hawaii, the chiefs and chiefesses began to become very fond of liquor; and it was made in two kinds of liquor. First, the tabu liquor which was used by the men exclusively; the women not being allowed to use it. Second, the free liquor, which was for women, but not to be taken together with men. Those who used it as being free, that is, both sexes drinking together, must do so without offering any to the gods, and these men and women were those who served food and drink to the chiefesses. Liquor at this time also became general at feasts where chiefs would drink their liquor and the chiefesses would drink theirs; then, too, the commoners would drink theirs.[14]

In the case of the commoners, the liquor drunk not only was "free" but also had a lower alcoholic content.[15] Those who made use of distilled spirits were the chiefs and those who followed in their numerous trains; the lower classes used fermented juices of sugar cane, *ti* root (a woody plant of the Lily family), or fermented potatoes.

Feasts in eastern Polynesian culture coincided with seasons or cycles of productive work, coming, for example, at the end of a fishing season and with the completion of work projects. Other commonly held feasts were those that marked births, anniversaries, and deaths. In Hawaii today, feasts are called *lu'aus,* but they are more appropriately termed *aha'aina* (group eat). A feast that included drinking was called *inu-lama ui-ui* (to drink rum and brew).

In Hawaii, a family made lengthy preparations for a feast, accumulating food, borrowing calabashes from neighbors to make *ui-ui,* and, if they could afford it, purchasing cases of liquor or barrels of wine. At one such feast, given on the birthday of the grandson of a *kahuna* on Maui in 1889, a dozen barrels of wine and "numerous" cases of whiskey, gin, brandy, and sake were served. Strong liquor was given to the *haoles* (Caucasians) and to ranking Hawaiians who were seated at a special table; sake was given to the Japanese present and wine to the Hawaiians. Liquor was dispensed by a *ku'ene* (waiter or steward), who had two assistants. Careful attention was given to placement of tables under a *halau* (temporary shelter) to allow control of the dispensing of the liquor.

When royalty was present, a *kahuna* either from the local village or accompanying the royal party gave thanks to Hawaiian gods, then dipped a stripped branch with *ti* leaves (*lai ti*) into a calabash of *ui ui* on the table before him and sprinkled droplets onto the tables. A name chant for the royal persons might follow; then the host gave a speech urging all to avoid trouble and to be *hau oli* (have a good time). This signaled the beginning of eating and drinking and entertainment, which included hula dancing. However, it was considered dangerous to perform sacred hulas at these gatherings; only the secular *hula'auwana* were performed.

The *ku'ene* served guests individually from pitchers (putting bottles on the mats or tables in the "white man's way"), and if a man became unpleasantly drunk he was given no more drink. Husky guests were designated to intimidate or expel potential troublemakers forcibly if necessary. Such persons might thereafter be excluded from other feasts. Children ate apart at a feast of their own, where they were permitted to drink *uala-awa-awa* (sweet potato beer).

Protestant missionaries in Hawaii never attended feasts such as these, but Catholic priests might, which may in part explain the emphasis the former gave to the disorderly aspects of early Hawaiian drinking in their historical accounts. There is little doubt that away from centers where drinking practices of Europeans and Americans prevailed, in situations where it was under native auspices, festive drinking by Polynesians had a pattern of its own, with a modicum of discipline and control. While it had a spreelike quality, so did their feasts, all in consonance with their cultural values. In the interims between their feasts, Hawaiians and Society Islanders alike were capable of and even showed a preference for sobriety. This is attested to by the commentary of a missionary stationed on Maui around 1836: "They [Hawaiians] never took a dram and went to their work, but uniformly made preparation beforehand, and when ready, gave themselves up to festivity and myth, sometimes for a number of days in succession."[16]

Much the same impression is gained from observations of drinking by natives of Rai'atea (Society Islands) in 1835: "The systematic way in which the natives intoxicate themselves is not the least curious feature in their character. They will refrain long from spirits, or very abruptly relinquish their use . . . many amongst them consider that a moderate use of ardent spirits is tantalizing and disagreeable and will often refuse to partake of any unless they can obtain enough to produce the 'happiest effects.' "[17]

It needs to be said that not all natives attended feasts where drinking took place. And not all Hawaiians become drinkers; as Kamakau indicated, there were exceptions: "Some did not touch liquor because it was bitter to their tastes, some because it caused idleness. Some because their wives had been taken away from them, and others for other reasons."[18]

Festive drinking probably centered around beverages of low rather than high alcoholic content, orange beer in Tahiti and the Cook Islands, and various types of brewed fruits and plants in Hawaii. During the nineteenth century, Tahitians changed over to wine and later to beer, and study of their drinking in the 1960s revealed a common dislike on their part for high-proof alcoholic drinks. They seemed to prefer beer drunk to achieve a slow, persistent high, which elsewhere I have called "plateau drinking." This had every appearance of an adaptation to the continuing high value Tahitians place on the spaced-out pleasures and dancing that are central features of "*la vie tahitienne*."[19]

Cook Islanders continued their liking for orange beer, roughly 10 to 12 percent alcoholic content, and brews of comparable strength made from store-bought ingredients up through the present time. Beer school drinking was not aimed at achieving any particular state of intoxication, and drunkenness was not uncommon. Its distinctive features, most pronounced in outer islands away from Rarotonga, were its ritual nature: drinking rounds and a rough system of control to eliminate troublesome drinkers from the groups, plus periods of probation before allowing their reentry into the groups.

It is difficult to generalize about the more specific drinking patterns of Hawaiians with reference to the amounts drunk, rapidity of drinking, and degrees of intoxication. Accounts by missionaries and others emphasize their propensity for drunkenness, but some informants indicated that Hawaiians had a graded series of terms for various stages of intoxication, probably derived from the lore of *kava* use, with some notion of the desirability of stopping after two glasses. An ideal state of intoxication was described as *noe noe,* which was likened to "love feelings," in sharp contrast to *ona,* meaning drunk. Final stages of drunkenness were compared to the groveling of a pig.

How much of the latter may reflect missionary attitudes is difficult to say, but most of the information points to heavy intoxication as a common practice. The downing of coconut shells or water glasses filled with liquor prevailed. Furthermore, intoxication or drunkenness was not disapproved in the myths and legends of Hawaiians; to the contrary, it was apotheosized in the antics of their gods. Finally, it must be said that Hawaiians themselves admitted to their inability to control their drinking once started and to its undesirable consequences as well as describing more pleasant associations it had for them.

BREAKDOWN OF THE TABOO SYSTEM

The diffusion of alcohol consumption among Hawaiians at the beginning of the nineteenth century, when their social system was still intact, lends some credence to the proposition that basic incompatibility exists between intoxication from alcohol and religion. This generalization may apply especially to societies having highly ritualized religious practices, for the obvious reason that intoxication "spoils" ritual by destroying its precision and dissipating requisite attitudes of awe and reverence that give it meaning.[20] In any case, intoxication seems to have contributed to the breakdown of the Hawaiian taboo system, which was an elaborate network of avoidances and sumptuary rules having to do with food, eating, drinking, travel, locales, and interpersonal contacts, as well as ceremonies for getting rid of spiritual pollution.

Around 1809, the reigning monarch, Kamehameha I, who united most of the Hawaiian islands under his control, turned into a dangerous drinker, liberally consuming both trade liquor and that made in his special distillery. On the advice of his two expatriate counselors, John Young and Isaac Davis, he successfully cut down to moderate drinking by using a marked water glass.[21] In the meantime, heavy drinking, especially in the chiefly class, spread and became commonplace. On one occasion, Kamehameha's favorite wife, Kaahumanu, committed adultery while intoxicated. In 1818, he decided that the abuse of liquor threatened the well-being of his kingdom, so he called a Council of Chiefs and commanded that all stills be destroyed and drinking ended.[22]

This order was carried out, but Kamehameha died the next year, and his successor was too weak to deal with the interregnum disorders that followed. The death of a king normally created a period of freedom from all taboos, leaving it to the new king to reestablish them by appropriate ceremonies. A priest seeking to determine whether the queen had caused Kamehameha's death by sorcery had his taboo flags knocked down and his wand broken by a drunken chief. Later, in an involved sequence of events, the new king failed in an effort to consecrate a *heiau* (shrine) due to the drunkenness and disorder of those present.[23] Finally, in response to importunities of his mother and the queen regent, he acquiesced in "free" eating and drinking between men and women.

Hiram Bingham, one of the first of the missionaries to Hawaii, claimed that drinking by the chiefs lessened their fears of the taboos and that they wanted them abolished so that they could indulge without risks of violating their religious ceremonies.[24] But this is a one-sided explanation. It ignores other forces that were at work undermining the legitimacy of the taboos.[25] Drunkenness is best seen as a catalyst or as instrumental in the acts of more aggressive chiefs, women prominent among them, who sought to overthrow the system.

No evidence indicates that anything comparable to the Hawaiian events occurred in the Cook Islands. Rather, it seems that chiefs in that area more or less turned away from their indigenous religion to Christianity or perhaps to the leadership of the missionaries, because they had grown weary of lengthy and exhausting internecine warfare. However, in Tahiti, Pomare II sometime after his conversion in 1812 used deliberate intoxication of his people to initiate attacks on the appurtenances of the old religion: "He encouraged his followers to intoxicate themselves and when sufficiently drunk they were sent out to wreck the *maraes* (temples) and destroy the images. Great fires were lit and the principal images thrown in. The image of Oro . . . had musket balls fired through it before it was burned. . . . Food which previously had been sacred, was publicly eaten by the reforming priests."[26]

INFLUENCE OF THE MISSIONARIES

Any consideration of attempts to bring the use of alcohol in Polynesia under some kind of control necessarily recognizes the roles of the missionaries. Protestant missionaries dispatched by the London Missionary Society (LMS) first entered Polynesia at Tahiti in 1797, followed by their theological cousins of the American Board of Foreign Missions in Hawaii in 1820. LMS workers settled at Rarotonga in the Cook Islands in 1824 and in Samoa and Tonga in 1828–30. During its early formative period, the Protestant mission movement in the Pacific was by no means identified with the establishment of prohibition or temperance. In New England, whence came the American missionaries, many ministers had reputations as heavy drinkers, if not drunkards. The first group of missionaries to Hawaii carried liquor in their stores and made liberal use of it during their voyage and for considerable time thereafter in Hawaii.[27] In Tahiti, missionaries distilled liquor for purposes of trade as early as 1806, although they sought to keep this a secret from the natives. It is also true that drunkenness among them figured as one of their more serious problems.[28]

The American missionaries in Hawaii were the first to propound the necessity for general prohibition. In 1830, they formulated and discussed a series of proposals whose essence was to bind themselves and their followers to abstinence from alcoholic beverages.[29] These were implemented by a native temperance society organized in Honolulu in 1831, which listed resolutions for members that included promoting abstinence and refraining from trafficking in spirits, distilling, "treating," and using spirits as payment for work.

While the emerging temperance movement in the mainland United States and elsewhere had an influence among missionaries in the Pacific area, it must be understood there as an indigenous growth. Hawaiian missionaries took pride in the fact that their temperance organizations saw action before the first temperance conventions in the United States.[30] Notable, too, in this connection, was the publication of the first newspaper devoted to liquor control, *The Temperance Advocate and Seamen's Friend.* Later called simply the *Friend,* it was first published in Honolulu in 1843.

In 1829, prohibitory laws were enacted in Hawaii by the queen regent and the chiefs forbidding the manufacture and retailing of liquor to white residents and natives alike. The former, however, denied the jurisdiction of the Hawaiian rulers over their drinking prerogatives, and it is probably correct to say that foreigners never were successfully prevented by legal means from selling and using liquor. In 1839, the French government intervened in Hawaiian affairs by gunboat to ensure free entry of Catholic priests and wines and brandy as a specified import duty. Somewhat later, Britain brought pressure to guard the import of English and Scotch liquor,[31] although the United States explicitly avoided this kind of power politics. Despite these imperialist intrusions, a form of prohibition against selling or giving liquor to Hawaiians held for differing times and places until 1882, having been formalized into laws between 1840 and 1852. Licensing of liquor outlets was permitted in Honolulu during this period but not on the other islands. In 1882, this practice was abandoned, and prohibition for native Hawaiians came to an end largely in response to the changed ethnic composition of the island population and decline in the power of missionary groups. By this time, it made little sense to deny liquor to Hawaiians, many of whom were of mixed ancestry, and at the same time allow it to Japanese, Chinese, and other minorities. Rising nationalism and ambitions of Kin Kalakuaua also contributed to the end of prohibition for Hawaiians.

English missionaries in Tahiti were less favorably disposed toward total prohibition than the Americans in Hawaii, whom they regarded as strange if not fanatical on the subject. Their views were complicated by the problems of excessive drinking among themselves and divergent ideas of missionaries in the leeward islands who had some notion that natives could be taught to drink like gentlemen. Between 1815 and 1819, a code of laws was drawn up by Pomare II with the assistance of missionaries in Tahiti, which prescribed penalties for drunkenness. Around 1829 manufacture of fermented brews was made illegal, but success in enforcement of the laws thereafter was ephemeral. During wars between different island groups circa 1830, controls over illegal distilling broke down, and it is doubtful if prohibition even took hold at all on Bora Bora.

Meantime, particularly after 1830, an increase in shipping augmented the inflow of spirits and floating population in Papeete of seamen, deserters, and malcontents from South America and Australia. Queen Pomare and her chiefs with the advice of the missionaries imposed curfews and authorized house searches and confiscation of liquor stores. Constables, who were paid from fines, put suspects as well as the guilty in stocks. Special laws were passed to regulate the conduct of foreigners, including provisions that spirits and wines be secured on ships in port or transferred to the sovereign's bonded store ashore. No more than two gallons of spirits could be withdrawn at one time, and resale was punished by fines.[32]

But foreigners and traders opposed enforcement of the missionary-inspired laws, some with knives, guns, and bulldogs. Moreover, the missionaries themselves were split by political differences.[33] Whatever was gained by the measures against traffic in spirits was more than countered by growing drunkenness from orange brew, now a main source of convict labor for road building in Tahiti.[34]

Unstable conditions, weakness of the native government, and discrimination against Catholic priests, as it had earlier in Hawaii, caused the French military to take forceful action between 1843 and 1845, with ultimate assumption of sovereignty over Tahiti and other islands. Protestant missionary influence predictably declined and with it any hope of achieving the prohibition they had come to believe was necessary.

In 1845, a conference of chiefs and others debated the subject of distillation and brewing, during which commoners complained of the class distinction that denied them the right to orange beer while chiefs and foreigners could purchase imported liquors. The conference voted to abrogate the taboo on distilling, and the captain of the commissary of Tahiti felt bound by the decision.[35] Later, distilling was again made illegal and there followed a lengthy history of inconsistent and often contradictory regulation of the manufacture, import, and use of alcoholic beverages, by means peculiar to the French colonial administration.

Missionaries in the Cook Islands, as in Hawaii and Tahiti, prevailed on the natives to set up a code of laws under which the use of liquor was forbidden. But, as elsewhere, enforcement proved to be difficult, particularly in the case of the ruling *ariki* (chiefs). Success and failure fluctuated with ups and downs of Christianization. On the island of Atiu, which became a center of orange beer culture, progress was notably slow. In time, however, the missionary church evolved into a native institution (in contrast to Hawaii), with its deacons directly involved in the problems of liquor control.

Distilling never seems to have gotten started in the Cook Islands, but the orange beer culture introduced from Tahiti in 1851 for a while threatened to disrupt what in effect had become a theocratic state. During the later part of the nineteenth century, a curious and unparalleled symbiosis grew up in Rarotonga between the church and bush beer-drinking groups, taking shape in a patterned evasion of the law. Reformed drinkers were co-opted as a special group within the church. Alternately, prayers and hymns became part of the beer school rituals.

The system of control headed by the deacons of the church employed espionage and even torture to achieve its ends; native police were especially motivated to hunt down brewers and drinkers by the division of fines between the district and the church. Such repressive measures were countered by those taken by the drinkers, leading to a clandestine pattern of bush drinking within an internal discipline of its own.

Stores selling liquor began to appear in the Cook Islands after 1860, whose operations caused the so-called Mission Party to designate French and German traders as "corrupting liquor salesmen," in contrast to the British, who enjoyed a reputation as "honest traders." Saloons were flourishing in Rarotonga by 1890, and concern over the liquor traffic plus fear of a French invasion impelled the chiefs to ask Britain to make the islands a protectorate. The British commissioner installed prohibition for the Maori, but chiefs complained that this was discriminatory, so a licensing system was activated. The resident missionary in Rarotonga, aided by distant New Zealand groups, fought the commissioner on this, but it remained in effect until 1898, when it lapsed.[36]

A makeshift, extralegal arrangement for dispensing liquor was put into effect, lasting until 1915. New Zealand, which had exercised administrative control over the islands since 1901, then made prohibition part of the organic act incorporating the Cook Islands as part of its Island Territories. Under this legislation, a medical permit system was instituted that made liquor available to foreigners and the chiefs; this system continued until the early 1960s.

While liquor from foreign sources made its way into the Samoan and Tonga Islands about the same time as elsewhere in Polynesia, consumption was limited and did not become a matter for public controversy until well into the present century. An important reason was that illegal brewing of the sort found in other Polynesian areas did not take hold in Tonga or Samoa until after 1920. In New Zealand, however, as early as 1832 missionaries were actively seeking prohibition of ardent spirits to the Maori population.[37] The influence of temperance-minded church groups there remained strong until present times not only affecting the local natives but also becoming a force in liquor controversies in the Cook Islands and Samoa after they came under the sway of administrators in and from New Zealand.

RESISTANCE AND REACTION

A commonly held stereotype of the nineteenth-century foreign missionary in the Pacific is that of a stern uncompromising Puritan bent on the destruction of native ways and pursuing religious and moral purposes at all costs. If valid, this conception is more applicable to Hawaii than elsewhere. But even there, native informants spoke charitably of the missionaries as "not so bad" and in the same breath condemned native church members as the real agents of missionary repression. This was even more conspicuous in the ruthless methods of the church deacons in the Cook Islands and equally harsh policing methods employed earlier in Tahiti. But repressive measures worked only sporadically, and prohibition on the whole proved to be no more successful than in other parts of the world where it has been tried.

The most effective sanctions for missionary control over making and using liquor were excommunication and removal from church offices. These were given special meaning by the deprivation of status and power, which church membership conferred, and in Hawaii it sometimes meant deprivation of lands of chiefs. Such measures created understandable ambivalence of chiefs toward the missionary church as well as conflict among themselves, which in turn affected their willingness to observe rules and laws about drinking.

Drinking by chiefs was a sore problem for the missionaries in Hawaii, Tahiti, the Marquesas, and the Cook Islands. They tended to explain this psychologically—that is, that chiefs developed strong desires or weaknesses for liquor and were loath to give it up. But from another view, it can be laid to traditional cultural conceptions that rulers and chiefs were exempt from secular morality. Thus, although they might join in placing taboos on drinking by commoners, they felt themselves free from such restraints. The missionary James Chalmers voiced his misgivings about the chiefs on Rarotonga in these words:

> My experience is that the native chiefs and policemen are not fit in themselves to carry out the laws [of prohibition]. . . . During Makea's time we succeeded in putting it [drink] down to a considerable extent; but he was a great hindrance, being himself much addicted to drink, both foreign and native. . . . I remember once getting some of the inferior chiefs together and going on a deputation to Makea and Manarangi, who was chief justice, and had lapsed from church membership, and from his social position through drink. . . . One of the *mataipos* spoke very seriously to Makea Abela, and Manarangi pulled him up by asking in a bit of song, "Whence is Makea?" and the old *mataipo* replied in song, "Who, then speak?" And we returned, forced thus to remember that Makea was beyond and above all law and human beings.[38]

Missionary demands for prohibition also interfered with feudal prerogatives of chiefs to exact levies of consumable goods from their subjects for the periodic indulgence of themselves and their followers. This was one of the underlying issues in the conflict between them and missionaries over the growth of trade. The involvement of Hawaiian chiefs in liquor trade prior to the arrival of the missionaries has already been noted. This practice persisted, particularly in the case of Boki, governor of Oahu, who became an adviser to the second Kamehameha. Other chiefs also engaged in secret liquor trading.

The Tahitian monarch Pomare II is stated to have seen in Christianity a means to expand his political and economic power to other islands. He carried on an energetic trade with his ships in pork, pearl shell, and sandalwood, at times in competition with the missionaries.[39] On Atiu and Mangaia in the Cook Islands, chiefs gained control of the church in the second quarter of the nineteenth century and used it for their own purposes. They became middlemen in the trade of arrowroot, coconut oil, and fresh food to sailing ships, and they also encouraged trade through European and Chinese traders.[40] Paramount as well as other chiefs were drawn into liquor trade and smuggling, if for no other reason than the need to use alcohol as an inducement to recruit labor and promote native industry.

The strongest feeling of the missionaries about native drinking centered on traders, whom they regarded as corrupting influences. At the same time, traders saw missionaries as competitors using their position to secure an unfair advantage, such as exemption from taxes. Furthermore, there were times when natives would not work for traders or planters for wages and could be motivated only by payment with rum.[41] Small wonder that traders felt little compunction about selling or trading liquor to natives or even took satisfaction in defeating the purposes of the missionaries. These were circumstances in which liquor took on symbolic meaning of a political as well as economic or moral nature.

Drinking as a symbolic act of protest figured importantly in the collective reactions of Polynesians to the rapid and superimposed cultural changes that complicated their lives. This appeared in sectarian and cultlike movements quite early in Tahiti, Hawaii, and Marquesas and among the Maori in New Zealand. One cult striking openly and definitely at the missionaries flourished in Hawaii around 1832: "There were numbers possessing influence, yet loved indulgence . . . and regarded the restraints of Christianity as irksome. Several young men, belonging to a class attached to the King, and distinguished from the rest of their countrymen by the term *Julu Manu* [feather or birdfeather] were among the advocates of loose morals and vile sports."[42] An entry from a missionary journal leaves no doubt that drinking was an integral part of the cult: "The King has the girl Kalama. He insists that his attendants drink rum. He holds out a glass for each of his *hulumanu* [court favorite] and forces them to drink, saying that those who drink are his *mea make make* [stout fellows]."[43]

Another passage tells how the king (Kamehameha III) put strong pressure on converted church members to drink rum, concluding that, "he probably adopted this course because he thinks his cause will be promoted by it."[44]

A similar kind of resistance and subversion of missionary endeavors was practiced by King Pomare in Tahiti during the second decade of the nineteenth century:

> The King's conduct has been the greatest check to civilization of the people as well as to their consistent conduct. He himself has taken not one step towards civilized life, and he has taught the natives to disregard everything the missionaries say to him on that head. He has also by his drunken and abominable manner of life drawn aside the people and even members of the church, who when they are cast out of the church are received into great intimacy with him and so hardened in their sins.[45]

Reaction to missionary domination also emerged at a grass-roots level among Tahitian commoners beginning in 1826 with the appearance of the *mamai* cult. This was a visionary, millenarian movement fed by the disillusionment of Tahitians with the new religion, which failed to bring them the wealth and prosperity they anticipated. Inspired by the dreams of its leaders, the cult insisted that the commencement of the millennium allowed them to do as they pleased, including making spirits, becoming intoxicated, and returning to the "old practices" interdicted by the missionaries. One account referred to "wild young people . . . who go into the forest at night, that they may commit lewdness and intoxicate themselves when they please, and that the laws and scriptures may be set aside and the missionaries banished."[46]

Although Catholic missionaries were more accommodative than Protestants, resistance to their efforts in the Marquesas during the mid-nineteenth century was of even sterner stuff. Violent attacks on mission property occurred, preceded in nearly all instances by distilling of *eau de vie de coco* (*naume*) and drunkenness. Chapels were stripped of their contents and numerous churches desecrated and burned, followed by resurrection of so-called "forbidden practices," such as nude dancing and cannibalism.[47]

In such contexts, the manufacture and consumption of alcoholic beverages had at least two significant consequences: first, they openly debased or degraded the temperance-oriented morality of the missions; second, intoxication freed natives to revive or improvise some version of their older culture in an effort to make their lives more meaningful or satisfying, or perhaps bearable.

It is tempting to say that native drunkenness functioned to integrate missionary efforts and promote their solidarity by articulating their values and placing them in contrast to the corrupting secular values of traders and the beach people. Likewise, the behavior associated with native intoxication, especially dancing and sexual promiscuity, can be seen functionally as reaffirmation of the evils for which the missions were organized and funded to banish.

But missionaries varied in their ideological commitments and their choice of means to their ends, as well as the success or failure of their ministries. In the Cook Islands, missionaries objected more to the form of native drinking than to the use of alcohol per se—drinking that not infrequently ended in drunken sleep, with bodies strewn about on the ground where the revel took place. One missionary on Rarotonga proposed to the chiefs that natives be allowed to drink orange beer with their meals as a measure to avoid bush beer-drinking fests. The paramount chief at the time, however, vetoed this measure, saying that it would never do: "there would be no rejoicing then at all."[48]

This may well signify how importantly intoxication had become enmeshed or indispensable in activating traditional patterns such as singing, recitation of genealogies, dancing, and sex indulgence that expressed deeper values in native cultures. However, it would be wrong to compute some common cultural motivation at work to subvert attempts at prohibition, for chiefs differed in their support for controls, even when the ruler took a strong positive stand on the side of prohibition.

Prohibition tended to succeed in areas where chiefs were won over to the temperance cause and where unanimity could be maintained among them. Whenever rifts appeared in the fabric of authority, through dissension or open war, outbreaks of illegal distilling, brewing, and drunkenness followed in their wake. Added to this is the probability that Polynesian chiefs were likely to treat prohibition as a taboo that could be lifted on important occasions, rather than as an enduring or unexceptionable law in a European or American sense.

CONCLUSION

While some generalizations can be made about the consequences of introducing intoxicating liquors into primitive societies, they are nonetheless subject in all cases to serious qualification based on recognition of the effects of unique or intrusive factors and their interaction with the culture and environment of the society in question. One tenable conclusion is that the prior existence of some form of patterned use of intoxicants other than alcohol directs or shapes subsequent development of patterns of alcohol consumption. *Kava* drinking provided a prototype for alcohol use in all Polynesian societies save for the Maori in New Zealand, where the plant did not grow. Significantly, Maori drinking there, while extensive, never emerged in any distinctive patterned form.

There is also some reason to believe that persistence of *kava* drinking where it occurred may have slowed or perhaps modified the degree and manner in which Polynesians took over foreign liquors and drinking practices. Decisions by missionaries in Hawaii, Tahiti, and the Cook Islands to forbid *kava* drinking may have speeded the shift to alcohol consumption, in contrast to Tonga and Samoa, where no such repression was attempted. But this is too simplistic and ignores that probability that *kava* drinking was (and still is) more profoundly integrated into cultures of the latter two societies, where it has served as ritual to demarcate and reinforce differences in status, rank, and authority among chiefs and nobles.

Resistance to the spread of brewing, distilling, and consuming foreign liquor also may have been related to the "greater conservatism or toughness" of the social systems in Tonga and Samoa. The absence of good ship anchorages in Western Samoa and the reputation of its people as untrustworthy may have impeded the influx of beach people and traders. In both societies, foreign missionaries never achieved the commanding position of influence they had in Tahiti, Hawaii, and the Cook Islands. Moreover, Tongan and Samoan missions were more readily absorbed and converted into native churches. Finally, Tonga escaped foreign domination, which occurred in the other Polynesian areas.

Yet while foreign occupation may explain how drinking and illegal brewing got introduced among the Western Samoans, it doesn't account for their rapid spread and the greater difficulties experienced in their control. Indeed, the situation was something of a paradox considering the strong disapproval expressed by Samoans of *kava* drunkenness practiced by the Tongans (also Fijians) and the relatively powerful system of social control at hand in their village councils. One possible source of the more extensive illegal drinking in Western Samoa may have lain in the need to express tensions, which accumulated during the troublous time between 1920 and 1936. A more specific factor may have been the greater difficulty of expelling deviants from the villages after New Zealand administrators took control over Western Samoa. But even more significant was the growth of drinking and in some cases brewing by ranking *matai,* who could be disciplined only under very unusual circumstances. Action against young untitled men involved in drinking tended to lose its legitimation when chiefs sitting on the council were known to be doing the same. Finally, the divisiveness and conflict never far below the surface of Samoan society at times disrupted the process of social control, which fits rather well with observations made by some perceptive chiefs that outbreaks of drinking in the villages usually occurred where disagreements appeared among the *matai*.

As overall assessment of the effects of alcohol on Polynesian societies is complicated by the tendency for the American or European observer to assume that problems inevitably accompany the introduction of intoxicating liquor into native societies, ignoring the fact that natives may not perceive the consequences of drinking and drunkenness in the same light as the observer. Many of the same difficulties with alcohol intoxication found elsewhere also characterize drinking in Polynesian societies: quarrels, jealousy, fighting, and damage to property. But these vary in form, degree and the ways in which they are socially perceived. In another essay, I have concluded that intoxication appeared to be well integrated with Tahitian values and reasonably well reconciled with the culture and social organization of the Cook Islanders. In neither area did the native males see drinking as a major problem, save for the occasional Tahitian who developed health problems with drinking or a few ranking chiefs in the Cook Islands who complained that drinking interfered with the work of some of their people.[49]

On the other hand, Hawaiians more often expressed ambivalence about their drinking, although this was entangled with their general bitterness about the way in which their islands had been taken over by the *Haoles* and then the Japanese, in the course of which their culture had been debased and grossly commercialized.

The strongest ambivalence about alcohol and clearest expression of native opinion against its use emerged in Western Samoa. A real contradiction was seen between alcoholic intoxication and the central elements of the Samoan way of living, which stressed decorum, ritual, and implicit acceptance of the chiefs' authority. While the *matai* system of social control through family chiefs and village councils was being eroded by other factors following World War II, the most visible and concrete expression of this came when drunken young men disrupted the quiet of the villages to invade sacred areas, to curse and even physically attack the *matai* in some instances. Samoans are comparatively more combative and destructive when they are drunk and hence are a more serious police problem than other Polynesians. Unlike Tahitians, they carry grudges, and they are more likely to use weapons in drunken fights and cause serious injuries or death, something absent in Tahiti and relatively infrequent in the Cook Islands.

Drinking and drunkenness in Marquesan society most nearly approximate symptoms of social disorganization or *anomie,* depending on how valid the reader may regard the application of such Durkheimian concepts to Polynesian societies. In the 1950s on Nuku Hiva, in the Marquesas, in areas removed from the main port settlement, Suggs found that drunken parties featuring sexual promiscuity were commonplace. Drinking at these parties, "orgies," as Suggs termed them, ordinarily became a contest between adult males, each trying to outlast his chosen competitor so that he could take his wife sexually. Younger men skulked about during these drinkfests waiting for sexual opportunities, at times engaging in sex relations with persons of their mother's generation or even in incest. Suggs concluded that such behavior, while similar to older patterns, had long since lost whatever cultural meaning it may have had as well as any restraints from chiefly control.

> Now native social and political organization is gone and with it the elaborate and colorful religion. There is no longer any propitiatory significance to drunkenness and sexuality, for the Gods of Polynesia have withdrawn to their home in the sunset. . . . These festivities are hardly of value now for society; they cause continual animosity, friction, and heap loads of guilt upon the shoulders of the nominally Christian natives who have managed to absorb only the negative aspects of Christianity. . . . The purpose [of this endless debauchery] is one that perhaps the Marquesans themselves would have trouble articulating; it is to resist with the only weapons left the white tide that has very nearly engulfed their way of life.[50]

Such data caution against too easily accepting a stereotype of the Polynesians as happy, friendly natives capable of integrating the whites' liquor with their older cultural values. Even the mild-mannered Tahitians, who have adapted their drinking to still functioning song and dance rituals, on some drunken occasions expressed otherwise well-concealed hostility toward their French rulers. However, granting the seeming degeneracy or meaninglessness of Marquesan drinking behavior is scarcely reason to deny or even qualify what has been said about drinking among the Tahitians and Cook Islanders.

The question of the degree to which alcoholic intoxication is or can be culturally integrated is not one for simple answers. It is complicated in studies of Polynesians by the highly metaphorical, equivocal nature of their language; their peculiar skills and arts of evasiveness and deception; and their facility for clandestine manipulation of those possessing authority over them.

NOTES

1. This passage roughly translates as "I spoke to them of their drinks; they know nothing other than water: the foul odor of wine and eau-de-vie is repugnant to them." Comte Louis Antoine de Bougainville, *Voyage Autour du Monde: Par la Fregate du Roi, la Boudeuse et la Flute, l'Etoile en 1766, 1767, 1768 & 1769* (Paris: Le Breton, 1771), 214.

2. Sir Joseph D. Hooker, ed., *Journal of the Right Hon. Sir Joseph Banks . . . during Captain Cook's First Voyage in H. M. S. Endeavour in 1768–71 to Terra del Fuego, Otahite, New Zealand, Australia, the Dutch East Indies, etc.* (London: Macmillan, 1896), 139. See also observations by James Cook on his first voyage, in Robert Kerr, *A General History and Collection of Voyages and Travels,* vol. 12 (London: Cadell, 1824), 18. The Maori of New Zealand also are stated to have been repelled by liquor when they first tasted

it, calling it *waipiro* or "stinking water." *Report of Government Departments,* vol. 3. (Wellington, New Zealand: Government Printer, n.d.).

3. Papers of S. M. Kamakau, Hawaiian Collection, University of Hawaii, Typewritten, No. 35. Historical Commission, Territory of Hawaii, 40–43.

4. Papers of S. M. Kamakau, 40–43.

5. Daniel Wheeler, "Effects of the Introduction of Ardent Spirits and Implements of War," extracts from the letters and journal of Daniel Wheeler, *Now Engaged in a Religious Visit to the Inhabitants of Some of the Islands of the Pacific Ocean, Van Dieman's Land, and New South Wales,* 2d ed. (London: Harvey & Darton, 1843). See also *Tracts Relative to the Aborigines,* published by direction of the Meeting for Sufferings, from 1838 to 1842, no. 2, 2–21 (London: Marsh, 1843); John Turnbull, *A Voyage Round the World, in the Years 1800, 1801, 1802, 1803, and 1804: In Which the Author Visited Madeira, the Brazils, Cape of Good Hope, the English Settlements of Botany Bay and Norfolk Island* (London: Maxwell, 1813), 227; and Archibald Campbell, *A Voyage around the World, from 1806 to 1812: In Which Japan, Kamschatka, the Aleutian Islands, and the Sandwich Islands Were Visited* (Edinburgh: Constable, 1816), 45.

6. Louis B. Wright and Mary I. Fry, *Puritans in the South Seas* (New York: Holt, 1936), 176*ff.*

7. Hiram Bingham, *A Residence of Twenty-One Years in the Sandwich Islands* (New York: Sherman Converse, 1847), 328.

8. Letter by Ephraim Spaulding and William Richards, in *Missionary Letters, American Board Archives* 106 (June 10, 1836); *Sailors Magazine* 10, no. 2 (October 1837).

9. Gilbert Henry Cuzent, *Iles de la Société Tahiti: Considérations Geologiques, Météorologiques et Botaniques sur l'Ile: Etat Moral Actuel des Tahitiens, Traits Caractéristiques de Leurs Moeurs* (Rochefort: Theze, 1860).

10. Eugene Burns, *The Last King of Paradise* (New York: Pellegrin & Cudahy, 1952), 202*ff.*

11. Edwin Lemert, "The Forms and Pathology of Drinking in Three Polynesian Societies," *American Anthropologist* 66 (April 1964): 361–74.

12. Frederick O'Brien, *Mystic Isles of the South Pacific* (New York: Garden City, 1921), 416.

13. Papers of Kamakau, 40–43.

14. Papers of Kamakau, 40–43. It should be noted that liquor could be made "free" by the *alii.* Possibly it was made free for male and female stewards because they had access to it anyway.

15. Papers of Kamakau, 40–43.

16. Letter by Ephraim Spaulding and William Richards.

17. Frederick Debell Bennett, *Narrative of a Whaling Voyage Round the Globe, From the Year 1833 to 1836,* vol. 1 (London: Bentley, 1840), 124–26.

18. Papers of Kamakau, Paper 27, p. 25.

19. Lemert, "Forms and Pathology of Drinking," p. 368; Robert Levey, "*Ma'ohi* Drinking Patterns in the Society Islands," *Journal of the Polynesian Society* 75, no. 3 (1966): 304–20.

20. Edwin Lemert, "Alcohol, Values and Social Control," in *Society, Culture and Drinking Patterns,* ed. David Pittman and Charles Snyder (New York: Wiley, 1962), 55*ff.*

21. Archibald Campbell, *Voyage around the World, 1806–1812,* 131, 215.

22. W. D. Westerfelt, "Kamehameha's Method of Government," *30th Annual Report of the Hawaiian Historical Society* (1922): 24–38.

23. Bingham, *A Residence of Twenty-One Years in the Sandwich Islands,* 73.

24. Bingham, *A Residence of Twenty-One Years in the Sandwich Islands, 78ff.*

25. Stephenie Seto Levin, "The Overthrow of the *Kapu* System in Hawaii," *Journal of the Polynesian Society* 77, no. 4 (1968): 402–30; Malcolm C. Webb, "The Abolition of the Taboo System in Hawaii," *Journal of the Polynesian Society* 74, no. 1 (1965): 21–39; William Alexander, "Overthrow of the Ancient Taboo System in the Hawaiian Islands," *25th Annual Report of the Hawaiian Historical Society for the Year 1916* (1917): 37–45.

26. Niel Gunson, "An Account of the *Mamaia* or Visionary Heresy in Tahiti 1826–1841," *Journal of the Polynesian Society* 71, no. 2 (1962): 210.

27. "Minutes of the Prudential Meetings of the Mission," November 16, 1819, to July 22, 1920, *Archives of the Hawaiian Evangelical Association Board of Missions* (Honolulu, HI).

28. Niel Gunson, "On the Incidence of Alcoholism and Intemperance in Early Pacific Missions," *Journal of Pacific History* 1 (1966): 43–62.

29. *Minutes of General Meetings of the Sandwich Islands Mission 1830–1837,* vol. 1 (Honolulu: Mission Press, 1830).

30. Bingham, *A Residence of Twenty-One Years in the Sandwich Islands,* 411.

31. Bingham, *A Residence of Twenty-One Years in the Sandwich Islands,* 537–612.

32. *The Tahitian Laws Referring to Foreigners, Within the Dominions of Queen Pomare,* trans. S. Wilson, interpreter to the Tahitian government; enacted and revised by the Legislative Assembly of Tahiti, 1843 (Papeete, 1843).

33. John Davies, *The History of the Tahitian Mission, 1799–1830* (Cambridge: Published for the Hakluyt Society at the University Press, 1961), 355.

34. Edward Lucett, *Rovings in the Pacific: From 1837–1849; with a glance at California, by a Merchant* (London: Longman, Brown, Green & Longmans, 1851), 266.

35. "Important Discussion of the Distillery of Native Intoxicating Liquors at Tahiti," *The Friend* 3, no. 15 (August 1, 1845); *Reédition du Bulletin Officiel des Etablissment Francas de l'Oceanie* (1847), 146, 173, 176.

36. *New Zealand Papers Relating to Cook and Other Islands,* nos. 1, 2, 7, 10, 12, 20 (1887–1903). Also, Richard P. Gilson, "The Administration of the Cook Islands," master's thesis (University of London, 1952), 80–93, 122–24.

37. "The Missionary Register (for 1834)," *Proceedings of the Church Missionary Society* (London: Church Missionary House, 1834), 549–51.

38. Richard Lovett, *James Chalmers—His Autobiography and Letters* (London: Religious Tract Society, 1903), 79–80.

39. Niel Gunson, "Pomare II of Tahiti and Polynesian Imperialism," *Journal of Pacific History* 4 (1969): 65–82.

40. R. G. Crocombe, "From Ascendancy to Dependency—The Politics of Atiu," *Journal of Pacific History* 2 (1967): 97–111.

41. Frederick O'Brien, *White Shadows in South Seas* (Garden City, N.Y.: Garden City, 1920), 11, 54, 146, 201.

42. Bingham, *A Residence of Twenty-One Years in the Sandwich Islands,* 447.

43. *Levi Chamberlain Journals 1822–1849,* typed transcripts, vol. 16 (January 3, 1832).

44. *Levi Chamberlain Journals,* vol. 17 (February 11, 23, 1833).

45. Richard Lovett, *The History of the London Missionary Society, 1795–1895* (London: Frowde, 1899), 228.

46. Niel Gunson, "An Account of the *Mamaia,*" 215, 219, 227.

47. Simeon Delmas, *Essai d'Histoire de la Mission des Iles Marquises depuis les Origines Jusqu'en 1881*. (Paris: Bureau des "Annales des Sacres-Cours," 1929), 146–52.

48. Lovett, *James Chalmers, His Autobiography and Letters,* 79.

49. Lemert, "The Forms and Pathology of Drinking," 272.

50. Robert C. Suggs, *The Hidden Worlds of Polynesia* (New York: Harcourt, Brace & World, 1962), chap. 5.

Part III

Juvenile Justice, Law, and Social Control

Chapter 12

Dilemmas of Intervention

Roscoe Pound called the juvenile court one of the great social inventions of our time. But the enthusiasms heralding its birth and early history have dampened considerably with the slow stain of passing time. Its later years have been those of unmet promise and darkened with growing controversy. Evidence that it has prevented crime or lessened the recidivism of youthful offenders is missing, and dour sociological critics urge that it contributes to juvenile crime or inaugurates delinquent careers by imposition of the stigma of wardship, unwise detention, and incarceration of children in institutions which don't reform and often corrupt. The occasional early voice of the dissenting judge and of the frustrated lawyer has grown to a heavy swell of modern contention that the juvenile court under the noble guise of humanitarian concern and scientific treatment of the problems of children too often denies them the elements of justice and fair play.

Even more impressive than the mounting volume of polemic literature and responsible criticism arraigning the court are the concrete actions taken by a number of leading states, such as New York and California, Minnesota, and indeed, the state of its origin, Illinois, which in years immediately past have substantially or drastically revised their laws dealing with the form and operations of the juvenile court. Other states have seen the appointment of committees of inquiry and new legislation introduced to amend significant aspects of their juvenile or family courts. Events as well as the literature of protest compel thoughtful persons to a searching reconsideration of the makeup and purposes of the juvenile court in a society dominated by large-scale social organization, aggressive public welfare ideologies, and mass-produced justice.

Excerpts from "Juvenile Court: Quests and Realities." Task Force Report: Juvenile Delinquency and Youth Crime. A Report of the President's Commission on Law Enforcement and Administration of Justice. Washington, DC: U.S. Government Printing Office, 1967. Pp. 91–98.

THE PHILOSOPHY AND FUNCTION OF THE JUVENILE COURT

Much has been said of the philosophy of the juvenile court and little that is definitive can be added to it, other than to note that the very preoccupation with its philosophy sets it apart from other courts. In general, American courts created for children were given broad grants of power by legislatures to protect and help children, depart from strict rules of legal procedure, and utilize kinds of evidence ordinarily excluded from criminal and civil adjudication. There have been attempts by some writers to discover historical continuity between the juvenile court and courts of equity or chancery following guardianship proceedings. But these have been held to be dubious exercises at best, and in the words of a wry English judge, little more than spurious justifications for the sometimes "highhanded methods of American judges." As he and others have noted, equity procedure clearly requires evidentiary findings within specifiable limits conspicuously lacking in our early juvenile court statutes.

It is less profitable to speculate on the philosophy of the juvenile court than to examine its historical development and the variety of its adaptations will benefit by heuristically distinguishing the official goals of the court from its functions, particularly those which sociologists call unintended or unanticipated consequences of purposeful action. In so doing it becomes apparent that the functions of the juvenile court in reality are several, dictated by its peculiar sociolegal characteristics. Thus while it is well known to sociologists of law that regular courts may serve a number of extralegal or nonlegal ends, such as, for example, an action for damages brought solely to embarass a business competitor, the anomalous design of the juvenile court has made its extraneous, nonlegal functions paramount.

In historical retrospect the juvenile court has the look of an agency of social control directed to raising and maintaining standards of child care, protection, and family morals, a purpose currently reinforced by its close association with social welfare organizations. At the same time the juvenile court by virtue of its inescapable identity as a court of law is an agency of law enforcement seeking to reduce and prevent crime, but also protecting legal rights. Finally, it serves purposes derived from its essentially local nature as an arena of conflict resolution, in which conflicts within and between families, between individuals, and between organizations (not excluding those within the court itself) are aired, dramatized, and sometimes turned into cold war compromises.

Despite their insular character and the cloak of independence given juvenile courts by their connection with the regular courts, they tend to reflect patterns of values and power alignments within the community or areas they service. When this is joined with the fact that there are fifty federated states, these states having from five to fifty-eight more or less autonomous juvenile courts each, it is painfully clear that efforts to outline the distinctive philosophy and function of the juvenile court are feckless. It is, however, possible to state that juvenile courts in action generally reveal variations in the order in which values falling within the three areas of function of the court are satisfied. This permits questions to be raised as to whether and how the juvenile court should be restructured so that certain value orders do not occur, or further, so that some of the values currently satisfied will be excluded from its decisions and patterns of action.

There are some social science propositions which can serve well enough as guides for those seeking to install new forms and methods in the juvenile court. A salient one is that the family, even though badly attenuated or disturbed by conflict, morally questionable, or broken by divorce or death, continues to be the institution of choice for the socialization of children. Neither the Spartan gymnasium, nor the Russian creches, nor the Israeli Kibutz nurseries, nor scientifically run childrens' homes have been found to successfully duplicate the sociopsychological mystique which nurtures children into stable adults. Explicit recognition of this might very well preface the juvenile court codes and statutes of the land. At the same time it would be well to delete entirely from such laws pious injunctions that "care, custody and discipline of children under the control of the juvenile court shall approximate that which they would receive from their parents," which taken literally becomes meaningless either as ideal or reality. Neither the modern state nor an harassed juvenile court judge is a father; a halfway house is not a home; a reformatory cell is not a teenager's bedroom; a juvenile hall counselor is not a dutch uncle; and a cottage matron is not a mother. This does not mean that the people referred to should not be or are not kindly and dedicated, but rather that they are first and foremost members of organizations, bound by institution controls and subject to its exigencies; they are enforcers of superimposed rules. Where conflicts arise between the interests of a youth and those of the organization to which these functionaries are bureaucratically responsible there is no pattern of action which can predict that they will observe an order of value satisfaction favorable to the youth's interest.

STIGMA

Social scientists familiar with the juvenile court and its problems in the main agree that one of the great unwanted consequences of wardship, placement, or commitment to a correctional institution is the imposition of stigma. Such stigma, represented in modern society by a "record," gets translated into effective handicaps by heightened police surveillance, neighborhood isolation, lowered receptivity and tolerance by school officials, and rejections of youth by prospective employers. Large numbers of youth appearing in juvenile court have lower class status or that of disadvantaged minorities, whose limited commitments to education already puts them in difficulties in a society where education increasingly provides access to economic opportunity. Given this, the net effect of juvenile court wardship too often is to add to their handicaps or to multiply problems confronting them and their families.

Lest these seem like animadiversions or imprecise charges, consider the hard facts that social welfare agencies can be identified which, as a matter of policy, without delving into the facts of the case, arbitrarily refuse to accept as clients youth who have been wards of the juvenile court. The reality of stigma due to wardship is also borne home by the firmed policy of the Armed Forces, which may make it the grounds for rejection, or most certainly the bar to officer candidacy. The paradoxical expression of stigma often colors the statements of probation and correctional officers, even judges, who at certain stages of a youth's progress through juvenile court and beyond, openly label him as a type destined for failure.

Proposals, laws, and administrative action to preserve the anonymity of juvenile court proceedings through closed hearings, sealing case records, and expunging records are probably worthy moves, but it is vain to expect them to eliminate the stigma of wardship and contacts with the juvenile court. In smaller communities, as one judge observed, "Everyone knows about juvenile court cases anyway." In larger communities strongly organized police departments can be expected to resist rigorous controls over delinquency records detrimental to their efficiency, and will search for ways to circumvent them. Employers denied information from juvenile courts often get the desired facts from the police.

Expunging records is not the simple operation it may seem. In California it requires initiative from the party concerned and usually the assistance of an attorney; the procedure necessitates a hearing, and it may be complicated or impossible if a person has been a juvenile ward in more than one county. Private and public organizations can and do protect themselves by including questions about a juvenile record on application forms for employment or for occupational licenses, indicating that perjured replies will be grounds for rejection. The applicant has the unpleasant "damned if you do, damned if you don't" choice of lying or revealing damaging facts about himself. Finally, it is doubtful whether total anonymity of juvenile court hearings and records is in the public interest.

While the successful management of stigma by individuals is not impossible, the necessary insights and social skills are not given to many people, least of all immature youth or those struggling with other status handicaps. A number of social psychologists, including the author, believe that social rejections provoked by such stigma may reinforce a self-image held by the individual that he is no good or that he can't make it on the outside. They may feed a brooding sense of injustice which finds expression in further delinquency, or they may support, strengthen, and perpetuate ideological aspects of delinquent subcultures. In this sense the juvenile court may become a connecting or intervening link of a vicious circle in which delinquency causes delinquency.

PREVENTING DELINQUENCY

The indiscriminate way in which stigma embraces juvenile court wards raises the most serious questions about an important part of the rationale for state intervention into the lives of youth and parents through the juvenile court. Reference here is to the idea that delinquency can be or will be thereby prevented. This belief rests upon uncritical conceptions that there are substantive behaviors, isometric in nature, which precede delinquency, much like prodromal signs of the onset of disease. The viability of these ideas probably can be traced to their lineal ties with older, repressive Puritan philosophy; they received new life from early twentieth-century propaganda of the mental hygiene movement, which helped to birth child guidance clinics, school social work, and establish juvenile courts in many areas. Quaint examples of these views were the nineteenth-century convictions that smoking or drinking by youth, shining shoes, selling newspapers, or frequenting poolrooms insidiously set them on a downward path toward a life of crime. Their contemporary survivals can be seen in unproved concepts like predelinquent personality, or delinquency prone, and in laws of a number of states which make truancy, running away from home, or refusal to obey parents or school officials jurisdictional bases for juvenile court control.

Social science research and current theory in social psychology refute the idea that there are fixed, inevitable sequences in delinquent or criminal careers. As yet no behavior patterns or personality tendencies have been isolated and shown to be the antecedents of delinquency, and it is unlikely that they will be. Furthermore, youthful actions conventionally regarded as delinquent tendencies in a number of jurisdictions, such as truancy, curfew violations, incorrigibility, and running away from home on close examination are found to correspond to no behavior entities, but rather to arbitrary definitions by school authorities, parents, and police. Truancy is defined variously, depending on the area, by anywhere from three to ten days of unexplained absences. An older New York investigation into a large number of cases of truancy disclosed little or no similarity in the contingencies associated with school absences. Indeed, to a degree they were simply a measure of the willingness or availability of parents to write excuses for their children. Runaways found in juvenile court cases cover departures from home ranging from a few hours to two months, and incorrigibility may mean anything from refusing a mother's order not to see a boyfriend to attacking a parent with a knife. While curfews are useful administrative devices for policing communities, there are attorneys who argue that the associated ordinances are questionable law because they leave violations incapable of definition.

The allegation of incorrigibility often is difficult to distinguish from that of parental neglect or unfitness, and both kinds of allegations at times arise in a welter of accusations and counteraccusations which are quieted by arbitrary fixing of the blame by a probation officer assigned to investigate the case.

The brave idea that the juvenile court can prevent delinquency is further deflated or even reduced to absurdity by sociological studies of unreported or hidden delinquency. These have brought to light that the majority of high school and college students at some time or another engage in delinquencies, not excluding serious law violations. The main difference which emerged from comparisons of delinquencies by college students and those by youths who had been made wards of juvenile courts was the greater recidivism of the latter group. While these data admit of several interpretations, on their face they demand explanation as to why the large population of youth committing delinquent acts and made court wards commit more rather than fewer delinquencies. The conclusion that the court processing rather than the behaviors in some way helps to fix and perpetuate delinquency in many cases is hard to escape.

There are other data which suggest that formal efforts by the juvenile court to shape the course of childhood and adolescent development away from hypothetically dire directions in the large may be gratuitous or self-defeating. The reference is to facts or common knowledge that most youth pass through epochs in their lives when they engage in activities definable in other than their contexts as delinquency. Children normally play hookey, help themselves to lumber from houses under construction, snitch lipstick or other items from ten-cent stores, swipe some beer, get a little drunk, borrow a car, hell around, learn about sex from an available female or prostitute, or give the old man a taste of his own medicine. Transitional deviance not only is ubiquitous in our society but universal to all societies, especially among boys turning into men—Margaret Mead's droll observations on adolescence in the south seas to the contrary notwithstanding.

Most youth phase out of their predelinquency, so-called, and their law flaunting; they put away childish things, ordinarily as they become established in society by a job, marriage, further education, or the slow growth of wisdom. Maturation out of the deviance of adolescence is facilitated by a process of normalization in which troublesome behavior, even petty crimes, are dealt with by parents, neighbors, and law people as manifestations of the inevitable diversity, perversity, and shortcomings of human beings—in other words, as problems of everyday living calling for tolerable solutions short of perfection. This means the avoidance whenever possible of specialized or categorical definitions which invidiously differentiate, degrade, or stigmatize persons involved in the problems. The costs of "muddling through" with children who become problems have multiplied with the rising plateau of mass conformities needed for a high-energy society but they must be absorbed in large part where the alternatives are even more costly.

THE THREE-MINUTE CHILDREN'S HOUR

The ideology of delinquency prevention is much more urban than rural. Handling problems of youthful disorders and petty crime in rural areas and small towns, characteristically by sheriffs' deputies, town police, the district attorney, and probation officers in the past and even yet today in many places has been largely informal. Sharp distinctions are drawn between less consequential moral and legal infractions—"mickey mouse stuff"—and serious delinquencies, with no implications that one conduces to the other. This is reflected in the reluctance of elective officials and those beholden to them to make records of their action, but at the same time for action in serious misdemeanors and crimes by youth to be swift and punitive. The juvenile court usually reserves formal action for real problems of families and the community; the functional context of youthful misconduct ordinarily can be realistically gauged and its consequences dealt with in a number of different situations.

A major difficulty in the large bureaucratic urban juvenile court is that the functional context of child problems directed to it easily gets lost; it has to be reconstructed by bits and pieces of information obtained through investigations and inquiries conducted under highly artificial circumstances, and communicated in written reports which easily become stereotyped as they pass from person to person. There is little or no direct community feedback of criticism and reaction which might put individual cases into a commonsense context which would encourage normalization. This plus the rapidity with which cases are heard in large courts (three minutes per case in Los Angeles circa 1959) explains why the distinction between mild and serious child problems breaks down or disappears. A notorious illustration of the tendency came to light in Orange County, California, in 1957 when a private attorney put his own investigator to work on a case of an eight- and nine-year-old boy and girl accused of a sex crime against a seven-year-old girl. It was discovered that the probation officer presenting the case in court had not even investigated, and the private investigator's report swiftly pared down the charge to an imputed incident witnessed by no one and reported two days after it supposedly occurred.

While it would push facts too far to insist that the ideology of preventing delinquency is used deliberately by juvenile courtworkers and judges to justify slipshod operations which bring cases of benign youthful misbehavior before them under the duress of formal allegations, nevertheless it has allowed them to change the basis of jurisdiction from one problem to another. The practice is baldly indicated in the statement of a California judge arguing for retention under juvenile court jurisdiction of simple traffic violations by juveniles:

> Moreover it seems to have been demonstrated that the broad powers of the juvenile court can be helpfully invoked on behalf of children whose maladjustment has been brought to light through juvenile traffic violations. A girl companion of a youthful speeder may be protected from further sexual experimentation. Boys whose only amusement seems to be joyriding in family cars can be directed to other more suitable forms of entertainment before they reach the stage of borrowing cars when the family car is unavailable.

POLICE AND COMMUNITY DELINQUENCY PREVENTION

The ideology of delinquency prevention and statutes incorporating special laws for regulating the conduct of children have not been ill adapted to the needs and problems of police in large cities, and to some extent have been their outgrowth. It needs to be emphasized, however, that police generally are less concerned with the prevention of delinquency in individual cases than in its prevention and control as a communitywide problem variously manifested in gang violence, disturbances of public order, a rise in crime rates, or mounting property losses. The special utility to police of specious legal categories describing delinquent tendencies is most obvious when they seek to break up youthful gang activity, quell public disturbances, such as occur at drive-ins or public parks, gain access to witnesses or sources of information to solve a crime series or to recover stolen property. While the arrest and detention of youth to clear up other crimes may be efficient police tactics, abuses may arise at the expense of individual youths if such methods can be pursued under diffuse charges. Unfortunately there have been and are judges willing to allow juvenile detention to be used for these purposes. It was for reasons such as these that the Juvenile Justice Commission of California, following a statewide survey, in 1960 recommended legislation to encourage the use of citations for minor offenses by juveniles, and to require that detention hearings be held within specified time limits to act as a check on overzealous police action.

Lest a picture be left of police as ruthless manipulators of juveniles of law enforcement ends, be it noted that in a number of areas they have sought to aid juveniles avoid clashes with the law through setting up recreation programs, Big Brother assignments, informal probation, and even police social work. However, such undertakings have declined in recent years and tend to be looked upon as too widely divergent from essential police functions. This also may point to growing disillusionment with more generalized or communitywide delinquency prevention programs. Police in some cities sharply disagree with community organizers of such projects over the issue of maintaining the autonomy of neighborhood gangs; they tend to take a jaundiced view of proposals and attempts to divert such groups from law breaking into more compliant pursuits.

Research assessments of community programs to prevent delinquency, such as the Chicago area project, the Harlem project, and the Cambridge-Somerville youth study, have been disappointing; results either have been negative or inconclusive. Possible exceptions are community coordinating councils, especially in the Western United States where they originated. However, they seem to work best in towns with populations of between 2,000 and 15,000; it remains unclear whether they can be adapted successfully to large urban areas. Significantly, they work chiefly by exchanging agency information and referrals of cases to community agencies, with full support and cooperation of the police. In effect they represent concerted action to bypass the juvenile court, and it might be said that their purpose if not function is prevention of delinquency by preventing, wherever possible, the adjudication of cases in the court.

TREATMENT OF CHILD PROBLEMS AND DELINQUENCY

Much of what has already been said about preventing delinquency by means of juvenile court intervention is equally applicable as criticism of intervention by the court to treat youth problems and delinquency by therapeutic means. The idea of therapeutic treatment found its way into juvenile court philosophy from social work and psychiatry, its pervasiveness measurable by the extent to which persons educated and trained in social work have indirectly influenced the juvenile court or moved into probation and correctional officer positions. An underlying premise of therapeutic treatment of children is that scientific knowledge and techniques exist, making possible specific solutions to individual and family problems. It seeks to impose the positivism of hard science upon individual behavior.

Scientific social work, whose tenets were originally laid down by Mary Richmond in her early work, "Social Diagnosis," eventually came to lean heavily upon theories of Freudian psychiatry, taking over its psychobiological orientation and the medicinal idea that childhood problems and delinquency are symptoms of unresolved Oedipal conflicts. Updated versions of socially applied psychoanalysis conceive of delinquency as an acting out of repressed conflicts in irrational, disguised forms. Accent in treatment is laid upon the internal emotional life rather than upon external acts; the social worker or the psychiatrist is a specialist who understands the problems while the client does not; the specialist knows best, studies, analyzes, and treats, much in the manner of the authoritative medical practitioner.

A divergent, competing line of thought in social work repudiates scientific treatment in favor of a more simple conception of its task as essentially a helping process, in which problems are confronted in whatever terms the child or youth presents them; responsible involvement of the client is a sine qua non of success in this process. Needless to say, this conception of the nature of social work is much more compatible with a philosophy of democracy.

Generally speaking, social workers advocate a more curtailed dispositional function for the juvenile court and advocate assigning to other agencies many of the tasks it has assumed. Some social workers seriously doubt whether the helping process can be carried on in an authoritarian setting, and to emphasize their stand refuse as clients children who have been wards of the court. Other social workers believe that judges go beyond their competence, and should use their power solely for adjudication, after which determination of treatment should pass on to social work agencies. A smaller number of social workers hold to a more sanguine view of reconciling personal help and authority within the role of the probation officer. Finally, there are some social workers who are not beyond using juvenile court power as a tool for getting access to clients, or prolonging their contacts with them because they will benefit from treatment. Experience showed that this pattern became aggravated in Utah during the period when juvenile courts there were under the administrative control of the state department of welfare.

A long-standing, ubiquitous problem of social workers and psychiatrists of whatever theoretical persuasion has been that of the noninvolvement of their clients or patients. Clients are either disinclined to seek their services or they break off contacts after they have been established, or they respond superficially without showing interest in changing their personal values or life styles. Much of the difficulty stems from the identification of social workers with middle-class values and the invidious moralistic implications of imputing defective personalities to those they try to assist. As a result, barriers to communication often become insurmountable.

Actually, comparatively few juvenile court cases are referred to social workers for treatment and many juvenile court judges and probation officers are inhospitable toward social workers. According to a U.S. Children's Bureau study some years ago, the most frequent disposition of juvenile court cases was dismissal, followed by informal or formal supervision under a probation officer. Dismissals can scarcely be called treatment even though the associated court appearance before an admonitory judge may have a chastening effect upon some youths. At most, such cases have a brief exchange with an intake or investigating officer who asks some questions, issues a stern warning, and says he hopes he will not see the boy again.

The consequences of supervision of delinquents by probation officers either in parental homes or in foster homes have been little studied and the outcome, even when successful, little understood. Probation practices with juveniles have little in common if the nation is taken as a whole, and often they consist of a bare minimum of office interviews and phone or mail reports. The frequent claim of probation officers that they could give more help to their charges if they had more time for supervision must be scouted as an occupational complaint rather than an accurate prediction of treatment possibilities. What little research there is on the subject has shown that mere reduction of the size of caseloads of probation and parole officers does not in itself lower rates of recidivism of those supervised.

If the results of probation supervision of delinquents on the whole are disappointing or inconclusive, even less can be said on behalf of the treatment of juvenile offenders undertaken under institutional commitments. Sociological analysis and evaluations of correctional programs in institutional settings tend to be uniformly negative, with some writers taking a position that the goals of correctional programs in prisons and reformatories are inherently self-defeating. This follows from the very fact of incarceration, which by necessarily posing a series of problems of personal deprivation for inmates, generates a more or less antithetical subculture which negates and subverts formal programs of rehabilitation. The logistics of processing delinquents or criminal populations brings large numbers of recidivists to the institutions, where they control informal communication and face-to-face interaction which importantly shapes the course of inmate socialization.

The problems of correctional institutions for delinquents have been highlighted in the popular press and literature as those of poor physical plants, niggardly appropriations and underpaid, undereducated personnel, but to the social scientist they lie far deeper. At this writing it remains doubtful whether the generously funded and well-staffed California Youth Authority has neared its original purpose of providing individualized treatment for youthful offenders. This has not been due to a lack of dedication of its leadership, but rather has resulted from having to assume the task of institutional administration, in which sheer numbers of commitments, contingencies, conflicting values of staff and custody people, and organizational inertia daily conspire to defeat the purpose of treatment. The top people of CYA have not been unaware of its dilemmas, which accounts for recent moves to establish large-scale community treatment projects and a probation subsidy program devised to stimulate local innovations in the supervision or treatment of juveniles as alternatives to commitment.

The less-than-sanguine remarks here directed to the ideology of delinquency treatment do not exclude the possibility that clinically trained and humanly wise people cannot help youth solve problems which have brought them athwart the law. Rather the intent is to leaven professional contumely with humility, to place the notion of treatment into a more realistic perspective, and to point out denotative differences between dealing with problems of human relationships and treatment as it has evolved in the practice of medicine. The treatment of delinquency is best regarded as a kind of guidance, special education, and training, much more akin to midwifery than medicine, in which hopeful intervention into an ongoing process of maturation is undertaken. Objective criteria for the use of methods of intervening and controlled conditions necessary for predictable outcomes are neither present nor likely to bc. Hence the actions of a judge, probation officer, correctional counselor, or an institutional psychiatrist at most can be small influences brought to bear among many simultaneously affecting child development and emergence of youth into adulthood. Although the power and the authority of the juvenile court can determine that certain intervenings will take place in a prescribed order in the process of socialization they cannot control the meanings and values assigned to such occurrences.

JUDICIOUS NONINTERVENTION

The aims of preventing delinquency and the expectation of definitively treating a profusion of child and parental problems have laid an impossible burden upon the juvenile court, and they may be seriously considered to have no proper part in its philosophy. If there is a defensible philosophy for the juvenile court it is one of judicious nonintervention. It is properly an agency of last resort for children, holding to a doctrine analogous to that of appeal courts which require that all other remedies be exhausted before a case will be considered. This means that problems accepted for action by the juvenile court will be demonstrably serious by testable evidence ordinarily distinguished by a history of repeated failures at solutions by parents, relatives, schools, and community agencies. The model should be derived from the conservative English and Canadian juvenile courts, which in contrast to the American, receive relatively few cases.

This statement of juvenile court philosophy rests upon the following several propositions:

1. Since the powers of the juvenile court are extraordinary, properly it should deal with extraordinary cases.
2. Large numbers of cases defeat the purposes of the juvenile court by leading to bureaucratic procedures antithetical to individualized treatment (guidance).
3. The juvenile court is primarily a court of law and must accept limitations imposed by the inapplicability of rule and remedy to many important phases of human conduct and to some serious wrongs. Law operates by punishment, injunction against specific acts, specific redress, and substitutional redress. It cannot by such means make a father good, a mother moral, a child obedient, or a youth respectful of authority.
4. When the juvenile court goes beyond legal remedies it must resort to administrative agents, or itself become such an agency, which produces conflicts and confusion of values and objectives. Furthermore, it remains problematical whether child and parental problems can be solved by administrative means.

It may be protested that the conception of the juvenile court adumbrated here is so narrow as to emasculate it or take away any distinctive purpose. However, if it can be accepted that many acts termed delinquent in reality are not equatable with adult crimes, and that many situations called dangerous for youth on close examination turn out to be functions of moral indignation by persons and groups who, to paraphrase Maitland, "Screw up standards of reasonable ethical propriety to unreasonable heights," then organized nonintervention by the juvenile court assumes a definite protective function for youth. It has become equally or more important to protect children from unanticipated and unwanted consequences of organized movements, programs and services on their behalf than from the unorganized, adventitious "evils" which gave birth to the juvenile court. America no longer has any significant number of Fagans, exploiters of child labor, sweatshops, open saloons, houses of prostitution, street trades, an immoral servant class, cruel immigrant fathers, traveling carnivals and circuses, unregulated racetracks, open gambling, nor professional crime as it once existed. The battles for compulsory education have long since been won and technological change has eliminated child labor—perhaps too well. The forms of delinquency have changed as the nature of society has changed; social and personal problems of youth reflect the growth of affluence in one area of society and the growth of hostility and aggression in a nonaffluent sector. Current sociological theories of delinquency stress drift and risktaking as causes on one hand and on the other deprivation and dilapidated opportunity structures.

The basic life process today is one of adaptation to exigencies and pressures; individual morality has become functional rather than sacred or ethical in the older sense. To recognize this at the level of legislative and judicial policy is difficult because social action in America always has been heavily laden with moral purpose. However, if the juvenile court is to become effective, its function must be reduced to enforcement of the ethical minimum of youth conduct necessary to maintain social life in a high energy, pluralistic society. Given this lower level of function, it can then proceed to its secondary task of arranging the richest possible variety of assistance to those specially disadvantaged children and youth who come under its jurisdiction.

STRUCTURING THE JUVENILE COURT

A philosophy of judicious nonintervention demands more than verbal or written exhortation for implementation. Action is needed to research and redefine the jurisdiction of the court, the nature of the roles assigned to its personnel, and its procedures. Ideally it will be so structured that it will have built-in controls, feedback mechanisms, and social scanning devices which make it self-regulating and adaptive. This by no means signifies that the juvenile court should or will become inner directed; if anything, contacts and interaction with the community and its agencies will have more importance, if for no other reason than to guard its stance of nonintervention.

It follows that relationships between juvenile courts and policing agencies probably will become more critical with a shrinkage in juvenile court functions. However, it can be hoped that this will be an irritant means whereby more police departments develop juvenile bureaus and upgrade their competence for screening and adjusting cases within their own cognizance. Even now it is common practice for many police departments to dismiss large numbers of juvenile arrests or adjust them within the department. More and better trained juvenile officers and rationalizing of their procedures can greatly decrease referrals to juvenile courts. This does not mean that police should develop their own probation or social work service, but rather will parsimoniously utilize contacts with relatives and referrals to community agencies, or at most, engage in brief, policeman-like counseling with youths where they believe it may do some good. One way to answer the cry of American police for public support is to funnel grants of aid into juvenile officer training and police consultation services.

Since police probably always will to some extent seek to employ the juvenile court for their own special purposes of keeping law and order or preventing crime in the large, the second line of defense protecting jurisdictional boundaries of the juvenile court must be manned by intake workers of the juvenile court or the probation department serving it. These ideally should be organized into an intake, referral, and adjustment division, where the maximum effort of the court is made by its most competent personnel. Organizational considerations suggest that it should have a good deal of autonomy, assuming that a high caliber of staff is reached, and be oriented toward the social welfare agencies of the community. Denial of applications for petitions should be its clear-cut prerogative.

In some large probation departments it may be possible to erect a still higher level of screening by a special division of the workers who file petitions for assuming jurisdiction by the court. Again, some organizational independence would be needed to reject petition applications sent forward by intake people. To an extent such screening already exists in many probation departments but tends to be overshadowed by functional specialization due to the heavy volume of investigations and placements in overworked courts. If probation departments were so empowered that investigations of the factual basis of law violations were a mandatory police function, more time and energy could be allocated to screening, referrals, and dispositions work.

As Paul Tappan and others have noted, referral of cases from juvenile courts to social work agencies is complicated by unwillingness of the latter to expend their resources on hostile or uncooperative clients. Believing that contact with the juvenile court fosters uncooperativeness in youth, many agencies, as previously stated, refuse their referrals. Juvenile courts that take on the treatment of children with small difficulties, which often are indistinguishable from those daily being handled in large numbers by welfare agencies, forego their opportunities to make use of referrals at a later date. For this reason, it appears that referrals should be made immediately, prior to detention, minus confrontations with youth and parents, or without investigations which go beyond the reasons for their referral to the court. Intake interviews and citation hearings should not turn into fishing expeditions to uncover and record problems to justify further action by the court.

SOURCES

1. The California Juvenile Court. *Stanford Law Review,* 10, 1958, 471–524.

2. Richard Cloward. *Social Control in Prison,* "Theoretical Studies in Social Organization of the Prison." Social Science Research Council, New York, 1960, 20–48.

3. *Comparative Survey of Juvenile Delinquency*—Part I. North America. United Nations, N.Y., 1958.

4. Bernard Fisher, "Juvenile Court: Purpose, Promise, and Problems." *Social Service Review,* 34, 1960, 75–82.

5. Margaret Greenfield, *Juvenile Traffic Offenders and Court Jurisdiction.* Bureau of Public Administration, University of California, Berkeley, 1951.

6. Tadeuz Grygier, "The Concept of a State of Delinquency—an Obituary." *Journal of Legal Education,* 18, 1965, 131–141.

7. Joel Handler, "The Juvenile Court and the Adversary System: Problems of Function and Form." *Wisconsin Law Review,* 54, 1965, 7–51.

8. Jacob Isaacs, "The Role of the Lawyer in Representing Minors in the New Family Court." *Buffalo Law Review,* 12, 1962, 501–521.

9. Alfred Kahn, *A Court for Children,* Columbia University Press, 1953.

10. Orman Ketcham, "Legal Renaissance in the Juvenile Court," *Northwestern University Law Review,* 60, 1965, 585–598.

11. Edwin Lemert, "Legislating Change in the Juvenile Court, MNS." Center for the Study of Law and Society, Berkeley, Calif., 1966.

12. ———, "Revisionism and the Juvenile Court Law, MNS." Center for the Study of Law and Society, Berkeley, Calif., 1964.

13. David Matza, *Delinquency and Drift.* John Wiley & Sons, Inc., 1964.

14. Henry Nunberg, "Problems in the Structure of the Juvenile Court." *Journal of Criminal Law and Criminology,* 48, 1957, 500–515.

15. Lloyd Ohlin, *Conflicting Interests in Correctional Objectives,* "Theoretical Studies in Social Organization of the Prison." Social Science Research Council, New York, 1960, 111–129.

16. Maynard Pirsig, "Juvenile Delinquency and Crime: Achievements of the 1959 Minnesota Legislation." *Minnesota Law Review,* 44, 1959, 363–410.

17. Austin L. Porterfield, *Youth in Trouble.* The Leo Potishman Foundation, Fort Worth, 1946.

18. Roscoe Pound, "The Limits of Effective Legal Action, 22nd Annual Report of the Pennsylvania Bar Association," Bedford Springs, Pa., XXII, 1916, 221–239.

19. "Report of the Governor's Special Study Commission on Juvenile Justice," I, II. By I. J. Shain and Walter Burkhart, Sacramento, 1960.

20. "Report of the Minnesota Legislative Interim Commission on Public Welfare Laws," Minneapolis, 1959.

21. "Report of the New York Joint Legislative Committee on Court Reorganization," II, The Family Court Act, Albany, N.Y., 1962.

22. "Report of the Special Committee on Juvenile Courts of the Utah State Bar." Salt Lake City, May 1962.

23. "Report of the Wisconsin Legislative Council, Conclusions and Recommendations of the Child Welfare Committee," VI, part I. Madison, 1955.

24. Margaret Rosenheim (ed). *Justice for the Child,* Freepress of Glencoe, New York, 1962.

25. William H. Sheridan, "Juvenile Court Intake." *Journal of Family Law,* 2, 1962, 139–156.

26. James Short, Jr., and F. Ivan Nye, "Extent of Unrecorded Juvenile Delinquency." *Journal of Criminal Law and Criminology,* 49, 1958, 296–302.

27. Eugene E. Siler, Jr., "The Need for Defense Counsel in Juvenile Court," *Crime and Delinquency,* 2, 1965, 45–58.

28. Paul Tappan, *Delinquent Girls in Court.* Columbia University Press, New York, 1947.

29. R. Weiss, "The Illinois Family Court Act." *University of Illinois Law Forum,* 1962, 533–549.

30. Glenn Winters, "The Utah Juvenile Court Act of 1965." *Utah Law Review,* 9, 509–517.

Chapter 13

Children and the Law in Twentieth-Century America

What follows is an account and analysis of social action designed to reform procedures in the juvenile courts of California. In general, it deals with the social action that led to legislative reform, truculent resistance to the action, and the consequences of these. My twofold task is to describe the account for what amounted to a small-scale revolution in the laws regulating the juvenile courts of the state, and to inquire into the consequences this revolution had for practices in the courts and related agencies of law enforcement. At the same time, this study has a bearing on a theory of legal change. Accordingly, it is addressed to three questions: (*a*) a general query as to how law, particularly procedural law, develops on a long-term basis; (*b*) more specifically, under what conditions and by what processes revolutionary changes in law occur; and (*c*) to what extent social change can be directed or controlled by means of legislative enactments.

LEGAL CHANGE

The sociologist seeking to discover regularities in the process of legal change gets caught between the heavily theoretical bent of modern sociology and the critical, pragmatic themes present in much American legal philosophy and writing on the history of law. A close focus on historical factors by earlier writers tended to fix the idea that no generic theory of law is possible, and that "principles" at best are applicable only to discrete bodies of the law.[1] Similarly, early sociological jurisprudence and "legal realism" were not highly productive of theory, but rather ran heavily to negative criticism, even nihilism. Sociologists currently inquiring into the law run the risk of being overly concerned with its immediate problems

---

"Introduction." From *Social Action and Legal Change: Revolution within the Juvenile Court Chicago:* Aldine Press, 1970. Reprinted as originally published. Pp. 1–30.

or merely applying their methodology to studies in the well-trodden area of the judicial process.[2]

The abortive efforts in years past to develop a science of law and the confused state of legal theory today may well be the result of excessive preoccupation with case law and the search for principles that guarantee absolute certainty in predicting the outcomes of cases.[3] Hope for a broader theory of law also has been deferred by the older idea that legislative change is catastrophic, or at best a spurious intervention into an otherwise pragmatic process of legal growth. Thus codification of law has been more the subject of polemics than of research. Finally, the fast-welling growth of administrative law in the present century and the difficulty of integrating it with case law of the courts has clouded the horizons of those searching for recurrent uniformities in legal development.

An underlying problem may have been that researchers thus far have failed to address themselves fully to problems peculiar to interrelationships among judicial, administrative, and legislative processes. Furthermore, there has been a lack of recognition of the importance of distinguishing between procedural law and substantive law, with too much emphasis on the latter. It is very likely that a generic sociological theory of law, to be profitable, will have to be oriented to the study of procedures, and the formal and informal organization of administrative agencies and legislatures, as well as courts, rather than to substantive principles of law.[4]

PROCEDURAL REFORM

Procedure as a general topic of interest, of course, has not been neglected by legal historians and philosophers; concern with procedure has antecedents in primitive law, Roman law, and medieval law. Endeavors to reform legal procedure have a lengthy history in England and other civil-law countries, and numerous legal changes in nineteenth-century America justify calling it a century of procedural reform, notable for widespread legislative codification of court rules as well as of substantive law.[5] The twentieth century likewise has witnessed important reforms in legal procedure, the most impressive being those of Federal Rules of Civil Procedure, brought about by joint action of the U.S. Congress and the U.S. Supreme Court. These reforms in turn stimulated a number of states, including California, to follow the lead of the federal courts in simplifying their procedures.[6] Finally, beginning with the 1950s, there has been a rapid series of far-reaching and controversial appellate decisions in federal and state courts explicating rights of the accused in adult criminal proceedings.[7]

While nineteen-century legal reform movements appear to have sprung from humanitarian motives, or perhaps from the quest for a more universal form of justice, those of the twentieth century have been fathered by administrative concerns, technological and organizational complexities, and sheer population growth. The large absolute increase in law matters reaching the courts, intruding from many precincts of society, plus the multiplication of courts and judges, pose pressing questions as to how the judiciary should be organized, what policies it should follow, and what its relationship to the large-scale organization of the "administrative state" should be. The administration of a mounting body of public law, and the actions of numerous quasijudicial administrative agencies regulating the lives of corporations and associations, as well as licensing individuals to practice professions and occupations, have tremendously magnified the importance of legal procedure in modern society.

LEGAL REVOLUTION

A great deal of legal development is or has been evolutionary, in the sense of being a gradual, cumulative growth of rules, one building on another. Most pronounced in specific case decisions of the judicial process, this growth can nevertheless be observed in legislative amendments and codifications of existing laws, as well as in the daily decisions of administrative agents of government. To some extent even regulatory commissions and boards become bound by precedents of prior decisions and evolve systems of law.[8]

If, however, organic growth is a feature of legal development, so is revolution, taking form in discrete changes, discontinuities, or "new departures" in legal ideas and practices. This was clearly recognized by Holdsworth in his comments on legal theories:

> Some theories have not been ephemeral. They have provided an illuminating generalization of new facts, which has been generally accepted, and they have therefore shaped public opinion in the new age and made them accepted commonplaces which . . . are powerful agents in moulding a constitution. . . . They have opened up new points of view to which old rules and principles must be adapted.[9]

Frequently cited examples of revolutionary law are those that stirred reforms of the eighteenth and nineteenth centuries in England—above all, Jeremy Bentham's principle of utility.[10] Others to which revolutionary impact has been credited are the concepts of sovereignty, of incorporate persons and incorporate groups.

Revolutionary reforms in law, procedural reforms especially, that occurred in the nineteenth century in both England and the United States were mainly legislative. They were accomplished only in the face of extensive and powerful resistance from practitioners of the law, namely lawyers and judges, a fact all the more impressive when one considers their peripheral origin, being fomented by a few persons either marginally committed to the legal system or outside it completely.[11] Equally impressive was the dramatic publicity and public opinion marshaled to initiate legislation of these reforms, as seen in the activities of English and Scotch law societies at the time, and in Charles Dickens' legal caricatures.[12]

The ubiquity and stubbornness of resistance to radical legal change suggests that, as a system or systems of law mature, conditions are created that make anything beyond minor adaptive alterations in the systems unacceptable to those who are identified with them. This becomes manifestly clear when attention is extended beyond the law as a system of concepts to its concomitant practices and associated organization.

> So it is with reform in law. All the forces of tradition, of established habit, and in many cases of personal interest are united against reform, and the inertia of the busy men accustomed to existing methods and often too old to learn new ones—of men who are content to say "Let well enough alone" without inquiring too closely whether it is "well" or not.[13]

The conservatism of lawyers and judges confronted with proposed changes inheres in the reification of systems of rules by which courts operate. This in turn is reinforced by the existence of a highly specialized legal profession with an outlook made homogeneous by a common reporting system, the reduction of law to accepted textbook sources, and methods of legal education and teaching that transform concepts into precepts.[14]

LEGAL REVOLUTION AND SCIENTIFIC REVOLUTION

Assuming that there are broad similarities between law and science, it is possible that in the absence of any well-worked-out theory of legal change, a theory of scientific revolutions may be useful for determining the processes by which legal revolution comes about, as well as for organizing and interpreting the special data of this study.

Kuhn has argued cogently that the key to scientific revolutions is the appearance of new paradigms, which offer categorically different perspectives on facts and which make possible or cause a change of "world view" among scientists.[15] Paradigm innovation must be contrasted with *normal science,* which is essentially a form of puzzle-solving unattentive to facts without relevance to existing or accepted paradigms. Normal science, as the term suggests, has a moral or value base; it is a system demarcating classes of relevant facts worth study, a specially devised technology and material apparatus, together with empirical experiments designed to articulate a paradigm. As such, it carries multifarious commitments of a community of scientists to textbook ideas, methodology, research organization, colleagues, and rules and lines of activity. Paradigms thus are constitutive of the structure of science.

> They . . . prove to be constitutive of the research activity . . . in learning a paradigm the scientist acquires theory, methods, standards together, usually in an inextricable mixture. Therefore, when paradigms change, there are usually significant shifts in criteria determining the legitimacy both of problems and proposed solutions.[16]

According to Kuhn, new paradigms appear because of anomalies, which are facts left unexplained by extant paradigms. As these increase in number, doubts about old paradigms or awareness of their deficiencies spread, and a crisis arises. New paradigms promise to explain or reconcile the anomalies as well as the facts articulated by the old paradigms. Novel paradigms most often are created by youthful scientists, primarily because they are less committed by prior practice to the traditional rules of normal science; they are freer to conceive new images of the world, new sets of rules for problem-solving, and to sympathetically entertain new classes of facts. By the same reasoning, resistance to new paradigms is strongest among older scientists, who have long-standing practical commitments to the established ways of perceiving their worlds of study.

PERILS OF PARADIGMS

Transposing theoretical models from one discipline to another carries a temptation to try to account for too much, or to ignore important differences between subject matter or between classes of facts that may be relevant in one field but not in the other. Nevertheless, a distinction between *normal law* as a cumulative enterprise, and legal revolution as the transition to new legal principles, offers a provocative way of formulating hitherto known but unorganized facts about legal change. The notion of anomalies as facts or cases ill-fitting traditional principles of law, which augment to a crisis prerequisite for the generation of new legal concepts, is equally attractive for the purposes of this study. Locating the sources of resistance to change in the functioning claims of going systems, as well as in ideological loyalties, seems applicable to legal, as well as scientific, revolutions.

At this point, however, there is some divergence, since legal revolutions are consummated more slowly than scientific ones, owing to differences in the testing processes of different fields. For example:

> One can test the value of medicine in its practical effects on selected cases. The result of a few experiments closes debate. The effect of change in the law, or in legal procedure, cannot be tested as quickly, and hence must long remain a subject for discussion with subsequent delay.[17]

Another notable difference between legal and scientific revolutions lies in the obscuring effects of legal fictions on radical transformations in law. Words and phrases may be so interpreted or classes of facts so defined that a whole new pattern of law is furthered under the guise of precedent of *stare decisis*. Jerome Hall, for example, has well described how large and significant changes in informal procedures for mitigating criminal justice in nineteenth-century England were sanctioned and concealed through the application of administrative fictions.[18] However, it is intriguing here to recall Kuhn's assertion that scientific revolutions tend to be made invisible by a kind of falsification of scientific history through revisions of textbooks, which lend specious continuity to otherwise fundamental departures from traditional science.[19]

If there is a major weakness in Kuhn's analysis, it is his tendency to see the scientific world as made up primarily of interacting individuals, ignoring, for example, the obvious tremendous effects of the organized support and direction of science by government, corporations, universities, and foundations. Similarly, he fails to touch on the sectarian tendency of scientists, and the formation of "schools of scientific thought."[20]

In any event, it is plain that legal reform, especially that effected by legislation, frequently if not typically takes place through the interaction of groups. Hence, even if the general attributes of the revolutionary process in science described by Kuhn are tenable, they must be modified to allow for the importance of groups in the dynamics of legal reform. Groups are of central importance because they affect processes of evaluation and decision-making, as well as the form and course that resistance to reform takes. In societies in which individuals must seek fulfillment of their values through organized groups to which they give allegiance, a process of evaluation, as contrasted to simple value satisfaction, occurs. This means that values or aims tangential and even contrary to many individually held values must be supported when group decisions are made.[21]

SOCIAL ACTION AND PLURALISM

Social action differs from scientific activity in that it is much more concerned with direct action and ends sought than it is with facts, hypotheses, and the relevance of facts to hypotheses. Reform movements of the past often were directed toward changing people, which is to say, changing a whole pattern of values to which they putatively subscribed. Social action in modern-day Western society is less a movement to annihilate existing values and create widespread acceptance of new values than it is a form of planned intervention in an ongoing process to *influence the order in which values of different groups are to be satisfied. The objective is to modify sequences of overt action through influencing decisions at points of power, rather than to change the values of groups and individuals participating in the decisions*. Conversion to the abstract or moral rightness of programs is less important than change in action patterns in particular situations.

This is not to say that unorganized, irrational, expressive social movements born of individual "strain" and "deprivation" have disappeared or lost importance.[22] Nor can it be denied that there are social movements and countermovements best defined and analyzed as "symbolic crusades," dedicated to protecting or advancing whole "styles of life."[23] Nevertheless, the functional pluralism of modern society, and the diversification and complexity of value aggregations and individual value hierarchies, necessarily lead to a means orientation in social action. To survive or succeed, social action quickly takes organized form, utilizes professional staff, relies on research methods and findings, and operates within time and budgetary limitations. At the same time, there is a necessary subordination of expressive, moral, symbolic functions to calculational, strategic, and bargaining elements inherent in much if not most modern organizational interactions.[24]

Election of a pluralistic model for the analysis of social action in the present instance is advised, with recognition that some sociologists would favor "class," "status group," personality structure, or situated behavior models. Noted, too, is that pluralism has been subjected to criticism. A theoretical difficulty has been the specification of conditions under which interaction counterbalances the values of competing groups without carrying society down the path of confusion, decay, or self-destruction. Overemphasis on the mere facts of organization and the articulation of interests may underplay the importance of explicit and implicit rules that apart from such interests regulate group interaction. Furthermore, social action or organization of interests may be exclusively in terms of such rules. That social action can through law alter the rules and thereby alter the pattern of value satisfaction between groups and individuals is one of the happy possibilities of pluralism.[25]

LEGISLATIVE CHANGE AND SOCIAL CHANGE

American sociologists in some respects have traveled a full circle in their speculations about the efficacy of legal change as a means of directing the course of social change. In the early days of sociology, a conviction that social reforms could and should be brought about through legislation was widely held. "Attractive legislation," for example, was one of the chief means advocated by Lester F. Ward to achieve his vision of social telesis.[26] Others also believed that a "science of legislation" was possible.[27] However, in time the more conservative views of William G. Sumner came to prevail on this subject.[28] The monumental example of the failure of national Prohibition, and the rediscovery of the primary group in research on military and industrial organizations, strengthened the sociologists' conviction that informal, rather than formal, controls were decisive in shaping behavior. More recently, major trends and events have compelled sociologists to re-examine long-held conclusions about law and social change, and to consider again the possibilities of social reform through law.

As organizations and associations increase in size and power, it becomes less probable that patterns of action can be successfully changed or directed through interaction in locally based institutions. At the same time, it is more likely that groups in action will turn to the state as an agency of intervention to defend their own values or to promote values of groups that are favorable correlates of their own. Thus social action more frequently than in the past takes place in a context of power relations and coercive controls that are monopolies of the state. Legislation as well as litigation has become an important means by which groups seek to legitimize their claims and encapsulate their values in a favorable position in social structure. Whether in fact they succeed, or to what extent, or what untoward consequences may follow is at best an open question.

Some social scientists who became involved in legal action to obtain greater educational opportunity for American Negroes in the early 1950s argued from weak and uneven evidence that social change can be achieved through legal action if the law is unequivocally pronounced and consistently enforced.[29] Others have a more qualified view that law change may not directly produce desired social changes but nevertheless can initiate them.[30] In contrast to these positions, Honigman, an anthropologist, concluded from his study of the problem in a non-Western society that attempts to guarantee value dominance by projecting conflicting interests into the political arena or area of public law does not necessarily lead to conflict resolution, and that the result may be a continuation of conflict in different form.[31] Finally, there are more dismal research conclusions that legislation or judicial orders may have consequences opposite to changes intended, or may precipitate conditions less desirable than those existing prior to change.[32]

It is significant that much of the recent research and speculative writing on the subject of inducing social change through law has formulated the problems within a context of pluralism. Unfortunately, there is no agreement on how pluralism operates; several writers have made it a condition of successful social change by means of legal action,[33] while another has stressed the inconclusiveness of legal action in pluralistic situations.[34] Further research, however, requires emphasis on the pluralistic basis of goals as well as of resistance.

PLURALISM AND THE GOALS OF SOCIAL ACTION

Social action also can be viewed from its point of impact, and if impact is defined as that which follows intervention into an ongoing process, then it generally describes the perspective of this study. Some impact research by sociologists has taken the shape of "evaluation studies," designed to estimate or measure changes in attitudes or behavior in relation to the aims of newly instituted programs or policies. The practical difficulties of organizing and carrying out this kind of research are considerable and have received comment.[35] Here only two things need to be said about them: (1) the goals of programs being evaluated often are obscure or they change during the course of evaluation; (2) many of the programs have originated and are pursued in an atmosphere of conflict and controversy.

These observations suggest that programs of action arising from situations characterized by value dissensus may have consequences different from those in which there is consensus, for the reason that the chosen goals have generic differences. In such instances clarity of goals cannot simply be assumed; their nature must be ascertained in some effective or "real" sense, as through investigation of the group interaction that produced the goals.

For purposes of research the social scientist must identify with the goals of social action, but in so doing, he must be able to locate the basis of these goals in the diverse values of particular groups. Through inquiry into past interaction, he can best determine how these values are distributed in social structures or positioned with reference to power or access to power. This allows him not only to explain how the legal action occurred but also to say things about the means likely to be available for implementation of legislated goals, and the likelihood of their amendment or even ultimate repeal. The mere fact that goals of action become law does not *ipso facto* guarantee full, uniform, or consistent recourse to the power of the state for their support. Powers of the state wend their way back in intricate ways to the powers of groups.

A significant point seldom heeded in efforts to sharply separate social action and its effects is that interaction changes the pattern or action of individuals or populations subject to law prior to its enactment or change.[36] Group conflict often crystallizes values in the form of enduring issues; group cleavages are created, and new forms of defensive organization may appear, along with intransigence and interpersonal hostilities. Taken together, these forms of opposition often get forged into a part of the larger phenomena of resistance to social action.

RESISTANCE TO SOCIAL ACTION

The argument pursued here is that social action in value-conflict situations, when "successful," alters the position of certain values by upgrading them in a public pattern of action, meaning that henceforth they will be satisfied before others in a variety of group and individual contexts. Whether this occurs, whether "target"-value orders remain unchanged, or whether unsought values are upgraded and change the pattern of action to one of resistance must be discovered through research.

Resistance, of course, is not necessarily fatal to social action. However, a science of social action, if applicable, must facilitate predictions of the probable occurrence, extent, and form of resistance. Thus are those planning the strategy of intervention equipped to face further crucial questions as to the available power and means of overcoming resistance, and estimate whether attendant losses offset goal gains. Knowledge of the latter in turn permits the social scientist to make more comprehensive assessments of the worth of the goals themselves. It also strikes directly at the heart of a more fundamental question, namely, the merits and demerits of legal action in contrast to other forms of social action to achieve the same goals.

THE BASES OF RESISTANCE

There is scant sociological knowledge about the phenomena of resistance to induced social change; discussions of the subject must be found in scattered contexts in other fields. In jurisprudence the issue gets phrased as one of enforceability of law, and traditionally, American legal scholars have paid it little attention.[37] Public administrators and those who write about them have been more sensitive to problems of resistance, but seem to limit their concern to the question of authority. Applied anthropologists tend to see resistance mainly in terms of patterned values and attitudes.[38] In those few instances in which sociologists have considered resistance to change, it has been likewise from the viewpoint of attitudes.[39] Attitudinal studies or personality-structure studies admittedly are helpful in determining the intensity with which values are held and in making estimates of the degree of "moral indignation" likely to be provoked by social action. Their effectiveness is limited, however, because many people pay only lip service to values and norm and because it is difficult to reproduce in questionnaires or interview schedules the situational and ecological realities of individual choice-making. More important is the fact that in pluralistic societies persons who are subjects of legal change respond to issues as they perceive them in relation to their own value hierarchies, rather than to the public intent of social action. These issues get created or defined at points of interactions where the demands for change are made.

While issues can be ephemeral or spurious, nevertheless an evolutionary-revolutionary perspective on legal change requires that issues that prevail, recur, and accumulate be deemed to have identifiable connections with *interests* of individuals or groups. Interests are specialized values, or *claims* that persons or groups have on others or on material things for service, time, attention, use, and enjoyment. Interests connote immediacy and valuing of something as a means to an end. People thus may assign value to a procedure because it is instrumental in satisfying diverse interests. A deputy sheriff may value a legal procedure because it is a means to increase his salary through fees; a prosecutor because it enables him to successfully prosecute cases; a judge because it saves time and helps keep his docket clear.

Issues are definable as value conflicts in which interests are present in varying degrees and are articulated with varying amounts of clarity. The underlying processes of valuation in which interests are aggregated and polarized into issues are not always or necessarily accurate or rational; individuals and groups may misjudge their interests, or time may be required to sort out and order their interests in a prospectively changing situation. Some people are defensively oriented, which causes them to perceive threats to their interests that are minimal or even nonexistent. Finally, some, such as children, only vaguely understand their interests, or are incapable of knowing them, leaving the task of their expression to others.

Rights may be thought of as interests sanctioned in varying degrees and ways by the coercive power of the state, or interests consensually recognized, so that they are unquestioned parts of an established pattern of action. One of the outstanding characteristics of the administrative or welfare state is the extent to which it positively or politically articulates interests of classes of its population and seeks through legislation, adjudication, and administration to raise them to the level of rights.[40]

THE NATURE OF ISSUES

No ready-made scheme for classifying issues is at hand. However, they can be sorted out in a very rough way according to the *kinds* of values at stake, the *costs* of any change in their order, and the perceived *legitimacy* of the change. Several distinctions in kinds of values are useful in predicting the rise of issues and resistance. One is between implicit and explicit values, and here it can be said that issues are more likely to arise when threatened values are well defined (converted into interests?) in relation to other values than when they are only vaguely held. The familiar differences between sacred and secular values obviously suggests the greater probability of resistance when the former are under attack. Finally, a line can be drawn between substantive and procedural values. While procedures commonly are thought of as means to the fulfillment of values, it is also true that they become values in themselves under certain circumstances. Norms of organizational procedure may be informal as well as formal, and in some cases they are regarded as unwritten but well-understood "rules of the game." While some changes can be accommodated within existing rules of procedure, others cannot. Change in the basic rules of interaction or the threat of such often arouses resistance because it represents sacred values, taken as self-evidently right and unquestionable.

"Rules of the game" tend to result from past accommodations of individuals and groups in terms of status and power. They are reinforced in the daily interaction of concerned parties and are likely to be instrumental means to ends other than those sought by social action. Changing rules of the game may or may not threaten directly these other values, but it does make their continued satisfaction doubtful and thus puts them in issue. Those subject to change may see their choice as changing or not changing the "system," rather than acquiescing to changes in part of the system to preserve the rest.[41]

In other situations resistance is compounded from the aggregation of values neither exclusively sacred nor of an "either-or" nature critical to the preservation of a system. In these settings resistance may take form in bargaining or transactional behavior: individuals and group representatives make choices on a give-and-take basis, sacrificing something of lesser value to gain or protect something of higher value. In this process it is often the *costs* of means of following proposed lines of action, apart from values *per se,* which become deciding factors in resistance. Generally these costs are anticipated in terms of time, money, effort, and psychic stress necessary to implement a contemplated action.

The impact of social action in a highly differentiated society tends to be segmental and unevenly distributed; hence costs do not fall equally on affected groups and individuals. For this reason the issues they raise often reduce to questions of who will have to bear the burden of the proposed changes, rather than of the substantive worth of the changes. In sorting out issues, people view changes in the light of their probable effects upon means already allocated to satisfying other values.

Changes may be resisted if they call for greater expenditures of time, money, or energy to maintain these commitments. Thus a board of supervisors in a county with a low tax base may oppose a law creating local mental health clinics on a contributing basis, not because it opposes help for mentally disturbed people, but because it is already committed to a heavy program of road-building from which it can't retreat. In another county the board may resist or be indifferent because it already has cheaper or even superior means to the same end through the use of facilities of a nearby outpatient clinic. It is from a kind of sociography of costs particularizing which groups and individuals are asked to make value or cost sacrifices that predictions of resistance can most reliably be made.

When the costs of change fall more heavily on some groups than others, those affected may come to resist through a sense of injustice, believing that the demands of the program or law are unfair, or that they are being denied "equal protection of the laws." There are situations, however, in which resistance must be traced to other than substantive values or more tangible cost factors. This kind of resistance has an incomprehensible quality in that the proposed action may have no adverse effects or may even carry benefits for the recalcitrants. Indeed, in some instances the latter appear to be unaware of the particular kinds of demands being made upon them. Here resistance can be comprehended only in terms of the perceived legitimacy of the legal action.

Legitimacy derives from the notion, especially strong in Anglo Saxon legal institutions, that an action is valid only if it proceeds from the consent of those subject to it. Judgments like these are commonly made from the way policy is formed, laws enacted, or court decisions reached. They are also formed from ideas defining those precincts of human life that the law or the state may or may not invade, or from ideas as to what penalities may be applied. Finally, resistance may be ideologically founded when changes are brought about by groups regarded as "not having the right," or by those deemed unqualified to make the related decisions for change.

UNANTICIPATED CONSEQUENCES OF CHANGE

Theoretically, resistance can be interpreted broadly to mean apathy, superficial compliance, and diversionary action amounting to sabotage or subversion, as well as open defiance and opposition or organized conflict. In addition to these immediate consequences of social action, others may be far less foreseeable because they are second- or third-order results. Thus social action changes law, which in turn sets other changes into motion, and so on, in a chain of actions or interactions. The end products may include new and unwanted forms of human action.

Where procedural rules reflect some sort of balance of values reached through past interactions, as seems to be true in systems of justice within law courts, or in a stabilized administrative organization, it is not always possible to say that changes sought by laws or new rules will end at prescribed points. A whole new pattern, paradigm, or order of value satisfaction may eventually appear.

ISSUES, ANOMALIES, AND CRISES

If legal issues by and large are traceable to conflicts of values and interests, then it follows that law may be adaptive or maladaptive, depending on whether it safeguards values, interests, or rights. When the law fails to provide procedures, remedies, or positive orders for this purpose, it falls short of meeting human demands and is maladaptive. This is felt most keenly when other means of safeguarding interests are unavailable or are too costly to use. The individual cases in which recognizable interests through petition or trial are left unsatisfied or are frustrated are anomalies. If there are enough anomalies, they become fertile ground for the rise of issues, depending on the nature of social communication. When issues accumulate and draw in a wide spectrum of diversified interests, a crisis in law exists.

Common to legal crises is the more generic issue of the fairness or justice of law or procedure. The ubiquitous concern with justice and fairness can be ascribed to universal values inherent in natural law, but it may be more realistic to regard them as acquired through childhood socialization in primary groups, particularly in play and games. It is here that "rules of the game" are learned, together with pragmatic respect for the fundamental presuppositions of human interaction.[42] Adult experience reinforces this learning and engenders the idea that without rules and procedures, fairness and justice in social life is unlikely. But, at the same time, adults also learn that particular procedures and rules are problematical in their efficacy.

The common law of England is apotheosized as the source of the doctrine of supremacy of law, or justice through law, but in operation it left something to be desired, as where the award of damages was an insufficient remedy, or where a suit against a powerful adversary was difficult to win. The revolutionary concept of equity and the creation of separate equity courts came from anomalies like these. Over several centuries, however, equity procedure became so tangled and costly that it too became anomalous law. Crisis again generated a radical new concept of utilitarian law, to be implemented by means of legislative reforms in court organization and procedure. Anomalies of both law and equity came to light as societies turned to mass production and distribution of goods by corporations, and as it became necessary to protect the interests of classes of workers, consumers, clients, and unemployables. With mass production came the great level development of the twentieth century—rule-making by regulatory agencies, and administrative justice. Some have called this a return to "executive justice," whose evils the rule of law was designed to prevent; but it is also recognized that its rapid growth must be laid to maladaptation of traditional legal machinery.

> The present popularity of executive justice . . . is attributed to defects in our legal system, to an inadequacy of our legal tradition to the demands of a new idea of justice. The problem of adjusting the law, shaped by the individualism of the past three centuries . . . in the United States is aggravated by . . . a bad adjustment between law and administration.[43]

In the early part of the twentieth century, the American judiciary was content to relinquish broad areas of work to commissions, boards, and administrators. In recent decades there has been strong feeling that administrative justice in the modern age may recapitulate many of the ancient evils identified with courts of all-powerful monarchs, namely arbitrariness, prejudice, political control, and denial of simple elements of procedural fairness. The extent to which this is true may be debated, but the anomalous existence of dual systems for adjudicating conflicts of interests in our society cannot. A supervening issue is whether conflicts of interests meeting jurisdictional criteria for hearing in regular courts will be adjudicated under law, while those adjudicated by administrative means are independent of law or at best tenuously subservient to it. The issue reflects the need, not only for courts to reorganize and simplify procedure toward the greater administration of justice, but for regulatory agencies and administrators to evolve procedures or an "ethos of adjudication" that give the rule of law a higher position in the order of values they satisfy.[44] Whether "the twain shall never meet," or whether a creative synthesis is possible in the midlands of law and administration, is one of the central concerns this study seeks in part to clarify.

JUVENILE JUSTICE

Generally, executive justice has moved along a one-way street, with administrators assuming or being clothed with judicial prerogatives. This has been most obvious in regulatory activities and welfare administration, but executive justice also has invaded the criminal law, detectable in powers of probation commissions, parole boards, and boards of corrections, grand examples being the Adult Authority and the Youth Authority of California. Only incidentally and exceptionally have courts metamorphized into something like administrative agencies. Traffic courts and other informally specialized courts, such as those handling drunkenness cases, or perhaps divorce and small-claims courts, have taken on many of the qualities of administrative agencies. Their distinctive features are the large numbers of cases handled, the swiftness with which they are dispatched, and the implicit presumptions of guilt or liability. The quality of the justice they administer, however, remains questionable.

The juvenile court, in contrast to the above developments, stands almost alone as a deliberate effort to innovate a special form of executive justice within the existing framework of American court systems. Its creation has been termed the "great social invention of the twentieth century," and a revolutionary idea in defining and handling problems of children.[45] But the origins of the juvenile court in the United States are less well described as legal reform than as a revolt against legal procedure for coping with juvenile problems affecting the community. The origins are found in the convergence of certain social movements aimed at removing children from criminal court jurisdiction and effecting their more humane treatment by agents of the state. Overriding goals were the protection of children from exploitation and the corrupting influences of urban environments, and the provision of welfare assistance. These were to be achieved through informal proceedings and individualized treatment. Seen in this light, the juvenile court was antiprocedural or, at the very least, aprocedural. Procedures were to be dictated by fatherly concern of a judge, humanitarian philosophy and clinical considerations.

The diverse origins of the juvenile court in many jurisdictions, coupled with the tendency of early partisans to describe the court in ideal terms, make generalizations about the legal rationale for its intended organization and procedure difficult. Some advocates held that the juvenile court descended from the English Chancery and that it utilized equity proceedings under the doctrine of *parens patriae,* which in literal terms means that the state through the court acts in the capacity of a substitute father. This interpretation, however, is better regarded as a rationalization than as a realistic description of practices as they actually come into play in the court.[46] The court became different things in different places, and even today, varies with the type of cases or problems coming before it.

The absence of a legally definitive procedure in the early juvenile courts cannot be attributed entirely to desires of its advocates to vest it with an atmosphere of informality. There was little guidance or procedural directives in statutes establishing the courts in various states, because legislators saw them primarily as child-welfare agencies.[47] Other kinds of factors militated against the evolution of generic legal procedure within the courts themselves. Among these: (1) The line of continuity between traditional courts of law and the juvenile court proved to be very tenuous, owing to the use of lay judges and the low level of commitment and interest among legally trained judges assigned to it. (2) Relatively few appeals were taken from juvenile court decisions, and when they were, higher court decisions sustained wide limits of discretion for the lower court; hence an important source of clarification necessary for the growth of law was absent. (3) Early probation officers and welfare workers connected with the court were nonprofessional and had little conception of procedure or its importance. (4) Clients of the court tended to be powerless people, often ethnic minorities, little equipped to make articulate demands on the court. (5) Legal counsel was seldom present to initiate adversary or other action that might have generated continuity with criminal or other legal procedure.

The failure of juvenile courts as a whole to evolve a generic legal procedure does not mean that distributively they failed to develop procedures of their own. In the earlier history of these courts, procedures evolved rather freely from the interaction of participating individuals and groups with a direct interest in the proceedings, among whom, depending on the community, were police, judges, probation officers, welfare workers, church workers, and law enforcement people. This interaction for the most part was localized and mainly reflected the interests and order of values prevailing in the local community.[48] Interpersonal relations had much direct and indirect effect on procedures, and the court characteristically was identified with the personality of the judge. One of his unique problems was to preserve the autonomy of the court in the midst of strong pressures continually exerted on it.

LATER EVOLUTION OF THE JUVENILE COURT

The evolution of organization and procedures of juvenile courts for more than a half a century was so uneven and diversified as to defy common characterization. Development was slow, almost glacial, and fulfillment fell far short of the ideal. It required twenty-five years, until 1925, before a majority of states had fallen in line behind Illinois in passing juvenile court legislation. A study in 1920 disclosed that only 16 percent of juvenile courts then in existence (2,034) had achieved the bare minimum of requirements to justify the name.[49] Rural areas lagged far behind the urban, so much so that many had purely nominal juvenile courts. The critical missing elements were adequate probation service, use of social information in adjudication and dispositions, methods of detention other than jail, and informed judges educated to the purposes of the court.[50]

The spirit of positivism that flowered during the hectic Depression years of the 1930s, the upgrading of social work, psychiatry, and psychology, plus the professionalization of probation officers, inaugurated the "age of treatment" in the juvenile court, causing its image as an arena of fatherly intercession into children's lives to fade—a diminution at times thrown into sharp relief by conflict between judge and social worker. With the accelerated urbanization of American society following World War II, many juvenile courts were transformed by voluminous case loads and specialization into bureaucratic organizations. Complex organization of the court, rotating judges, community pressures, and the development of "policies" by probation departments made it less and less possible to say who was protecting the special interests of the child. No longer could it be assumed that the interests of the judge or the probation officers were identifiable with the child's. Confusion mounted over the purposes of the court.

CHANGING VIEWS OF THE JUVENILE COURT

A certain amount of public dissatisfaction with the juvenile court institution has been more or less endemic in American society, evidenced by early attacks on its constitutionality and by the continuing struggles to upgrade its standards of treatment. As time wore on, the great enthusiasms heralding the birth and early years of the court began to dampen. What had been called the "great social invention" [see p. 190—eds.] lost some of its sacred aura as the occasional lone voice of a dissenting judge or frustrated lawyer began to be joined by others. It began to be perceived that the high expectations for the court were not fulfilled; proof that it had helped to prevent crime or lessen recidivism was difficult to discover. By 1950, dour sociological critics had begun to wonder if the juvenile court did not actually contribute to crime or inaugurate delinquent careers by the imposition of the stigma of wardship, by unwise detention and the incarceration of youth in institutions more likely to corrupt than reform.

The first strong blows at the later-day juvenile court were struck by the sociologist-lawyer Paul Tappan, who was well armed with first-hand knowledge of New York youth courts, as well as being fully acquainted with relevant literature. It is both revealing and significant that an unpracticed lawyer with a sociological background should be the one to attack the juvenile court for its denial of due process of law to youth taken under its jurisdiction. This accusation gained force as an integral part of sociological criticism, which exposed the gross confusion of purposes in the juvenile court together with the fallacy of assuming welfare functions for which it was unfitted.[51]

Tappan's charges had a solid empirical basis in his research on the court for wayward girls in New York City. He demonstrated clearly how the loose administrative application of legal classifications to girls in this court led to their effective stigmatization in the network of metropolitan welfare agencies, thus explicating what George H. Mead once called the "modern elaborate organization of taboo." In a larger way Tappan sharply illuminated the dubious consequences of the largess of court power to treat the "whole child," when it operated through group-made policy decisions in a milieu of functionally organized child-welfare services.[52]

Tappan's strong interest in reform and his contentious presentation of materials caused his work to fall short of a full theoretical analysis of the juvenile court. In the same way, much of the criticism subsequently levied against the juvenile court was couched in legal or ideological terms. Questions about the structure of the juvenile court were little discussed in the context of the changing nature of the larger society. A completely neglected aspect of the problem was the changes taking place in social categories of youth, and their implications for the great powers exercised by juvenile courts and related correctional agencies.

IN LOCO PARENTIS

In a less obvious way the changing perspectives on the juvenile court were portents of challenges to the rising level of authority imposed on youth in American society. This was implicit in the history of the juvenile court, which coincided closely with the shift of the socialization process away from the family. The necessity for prolonged education, compulsory education laws, and the growth of an identifying "teen-age" culture differentiated a category of *youth* from *children*, both of whom, however, remained under the legally undifferentiated categories of "juvenile" and "minor."[53] In essence the juvenile court, along with schools, police, and correctional agencies, extended control for a longer and longer period of time over "children," and expanded control in more and more areas outside the home, all under the aegis of paternalism.

While the juvenile court became part of the nexus of pyramiding controls serving positive intervention to raise and maintain social and technological standards, the legal illusion preserved was that the court intervened only on evidence of family failure. Also kept alive was the illusion that the juvenile court acted as a family surrogate and had primary-group characteristics, despite its having become functional and associational. An added incongruity was the perpetuation of a family model for the court to exert controls over youth at ages (fourteen to twenty-one) where the family never had been influential.

NOTES

1. See W. S. Holdsworth, *Some Lessons from Our Legal History* (New York: Macmillan, 1928), p. 110.

2. See Harry Jones, "A View from the Bridge," *Law and Society*, special supplement to *Social Problems* (summer 1955), especially 44*ff*; also Jerome Skolnick, "The Sociology of Law in America," *ibid.*, pp. 34–9.

3. For example: Frederick Pollock, "The Science of Case Law," in *Essays in Jurisprudence and Ethics* (London: Macmillan, 1882), Chap. IX. Llewellyn, in seeking to correct the nihilism of early legal realism, insisted that the behavior of judges was not adventitious, and the need was to look for patterns and tendencies in case series, rather than for conformity to rules and principles. However, he, like others, concentrated on cases. (Karl Llewellyn, *The Common Law Tradition* [Boston: Little-Brown], 1960).

4. This is closely akin to Llewellyn's view that research should start with "remedies," conceived in a modern sense of behavior. Karl Llewellyn, "A Realistic Jurisprudence: The Next Step," in *Essays on Jurisprudence From the Columbia Law Review* (New York: Columbia University Press, 1963), pp. 149–83.

5. Edwin W. Field, *Recent and Future Law Reforms* (London, Pamphlet in University of California Berkeley Library, 1843); Max Rheinstein (ed.). *Max Weber on Law in Economy and Society,* (Cambridge: Harvard University Press, 1954).

6. Peter Freund, "The Essentials of Modern Reform in the Litigative Process," *Annals of the American Academy of Political and Social Science,* Vol. 287 (May 1953); Arthur T. Vanderbilt, *The Challenge of Law Reform* (Princeton: Princeton University Press, 1955), Chaps. I, III.

7. Edward Barret, "Police Practices and the Law," *California Law Review* 50 (1962), 11–55.

8. For an example, see Philippe Nonet's study, "Administrative Justice: A Sociological Study of the California Industrial Accident Commission," Ph.D. dissertation, Center for Study of Law and Society, University of California, Berkeley, 1966.

9. Holdsworth, *Some Lessons from Our Early History,* p. 111.

10. *Ibid.,* p. 192; see also Jeremy Bentham, *A Fragment on Government* (London, 1776); also his *Principles of Morals and Legislation* (New York: Hafner, 1948).

11. Vanderbilt, *loc. cit.;* Field, *loc. cit.,* 25f; David D. Field, "Law Reform in the United States and Its Influence Abroad," *American Law Review* (1891), pp. 518, 521; Caleb P. Patterson, *The Administration of Justice in Great Britain* (Austin: University of Texas Press, 1936), Chap. IV. Arthur E. Sutherland, "The Machinery of Procedural Reform," *Michigan Law Review* 22 (1922), 295.

12. *Bleakhouse* (London: Bradbury and Evans, 1853); William Holdsworth, *Charles Dickens as a Legal Historian* (New Haven: Yale University Press, 1928); Robert Neely, *The Lawyers of Dickens and Their Clerks* (Boston: The Christopher Publishing House, 1938).

13. Moorfield Storey, *The Reform of Legal Procedure* (New Haven: Yale University Press, 1921), p. 16.

14. Holdsworth, *Some Lessons from Our Legal History,* p. 16; Sutherland, "The Machinery of Procedural Reform," *loc. cit.;* Lord Chorley, "Procedural Reform in England," *David Dudley Field Centenary Essays,* ed. Alison Reppy (New York: School of Law, New York University, 1949), 99f; Henry Fowler, "A Psychological Approach to Procedural Reform," *Yale Law Journal,* Vol. 43 (1954).

15. Thomas S. Kuhn, *The Structure of Scientific Revolutions* (Chicago: University of Chicago Press, 1962).

16. *Ibid.,* p. 108.

17. Storey, *The Reform of Legal Procedure.*

18. Jerome Hall, *Theft, Law and Society,* rev. ed. (Indianapolis: Bobbs-Merrill, 1952), Chap. IV.

19. Kuhn, *The Structure of Scientific Revolutions,* Chap. XI.

20. Leslie White, *The Social Organization of Ethnological Theory* (Houston: Rice University Studies, 1966), p. 52.

21. See W. F. Cottrell, "Men Cry Peace," in *Research for Peace* (Oslo Institute in Social Research, 1954), pp. 112–25; also Earl Latham, *The Group Basis of Politics* (Ithaca, N.Y.: Cornell University Press, 1952).

22. For this type of analysis see Neil J. Smelser, *Collective Behavior* (New York: Free Press, 1963), p. 8.

23. Joseph Gusfield, *Symbolic Crusade: Status Politics and the American Temperance Movement* (Urbana: University of Illinois Press, 1963).

24. The distinction between means-oriented social action and irrational action was first made in the little-noted report some years ago. See J. Stewart Burgess, "The Study of Modern Social Movements as a Means for Clarifying the Process of Social Action," *Social Forces* 22 (1943–44), 269–75.

25. For discussions of pluralism see: David Truman, *The Governmental Process* (New York: Knopf, 1951); H. M. Magid, *English Political Pluralism* (New York: Columbia University Press, 1941); Leicester Webb, *Legal Personality and Political Pluralism* (Melbourne: Melbourne University Press, 1958), esp. 178–97.

26. *Applied Sociology* (Boston: Atheneum Press, 1896), pp. 337–39.

27. Ernst Freund, *Legislative Regulation* (New York: Commonwealth Fund, 1932);

Ernst Freund, "Prolegomena to a Science of Legislation," *Illinois Law Review* 13 (1918), 264–92; Robert Sorensen, "Sociology's Potential Contribution to Legislative Policy Determination," *American Socio. Review* 16 (1951), 239–48.

28. *Folkways* (Boston: Ginn, 1907), p. 87. More recently it has been argued that Sumner was not as pessimistic about social reform by law as he is generally believed to have been. Harry Ball, and George and Ikeda Keyoshi, "Law and Social Change: Sumner Reconsidered," *American Journal of Sociology* LXII (1962), 537–40. Writers sharing a conservative view on reform through legislation, but with qualifications are: Frank Parson, *Legal Doctrines and Social Progress* (New York: Viking, 1911); L. L. Bernard, *Social Control* (New York: Macmillan, 1939), Chap. XX. Albert Dicey, *Law and Public Opinion in England* (London: Macmillan, 1952); Theodore Roosevelt, *American Ideals* (New York: Putnam 1897); Roscoe Pound, "The Limits of Effective Legal Action," *22nd Annual Report of the Pennsylvania Bar Association* (1916), pp. 221–39; R. M. MacIver and Charles Page, *Society: An Introductory Analysis* (New York: Rinehart, 1949), pp. 175–81; R. La Piere, *A Theory of Social Control* (New York: McGraw-Hill, 1954), pp. 316–22.

29. "The Effects of Segregation and Consequences of Desegregation," Appendix to Appellant's Brief at pp. 13–14, Brown v. Board of Education, 347 U.S. 483 (1954); Kenneth Clark, "Desegregation: An Appraisal of the Evidence," *Journal of Social Issues* 9 (1953), 2–76.

30. Arnold Rose, "The Use of Law to Induce Social Change," *Transactions of the Third World Congress of Sociology* VI (1956), 52–63.

31. John J. Honigman, "Value Conflict and Legislation," *Social Problems* 7 (1959), 34–39.

32. See, for example, Harold and Florence Goldblatt, "The Effective Social Reach of the Fair Housing Practices Law," *Social Problems* 9 (1962), 365–70; Don Hager, "Housing Discrimination, Social Conflict and the Law," *Social Problems* 8 (1960), 80–87; for discussion of studies showing unanticipated and questionable consequences of changes in court procedure, see Maurice Rosenburg, "Court Congestion: Status, Causes, and Proposed Remedies," in *The Courts, the Public and the Law Explosion,* ed. Harry Jones (New York: Prentice-Hall, 1965), pp. 46–59.

33. Arnold Rose, *op. cit.*, Warren Breed, "Group Structure and Resistance to Desegregation in the Deep South," *Social Problems* 10 (1962), 85–93.

34. Honigman, *op. cit.*

35. Howard Freeman, "Conceptual Approaches to Assessing Impact of Large Scale Intervention Programs," *Proceedings of the American Statistical Association Social Statistics Section* (1964); 192–98. Robert Morris (ed.), "Centrally Planned Change: Prospects and Concepts," *National Association of Social Workers* (1964); Ernest M. Jones, "Impact Research and Sociology of Law: Some Tentative Proposals," *Wisconsin Law Review* (spring 1966), pp. 1–9.

36. Steward Macaulay, "Changing a Continuing Relationship Between a Large Corporation and Those Who Deal With It"; "Automobile Manufacturers, Their Dealers and the Legal System," *Wisconsin Law Review,* (summer and fall, 1965), pp. 483–575; 740–858.

37. Roscoe Pound, "The Limits of Effective Legal Action," p. 230; Karl Llewellyn, "A Realistic Jurisprudence: The Next Steps," in *Essays on Jurisprudence From the Columbia Law Review,* (New York: Columbia University Press, 1963), pp. 148–83.

38. See George Foster, *Traditional Cultures and the Impact of Technological Change* (New York: Harper, 1962).

39. Reinhard Bendix, "Compliance Behavior and Individual Personality," *American Journal of Sociology* 58 (1952), 292–302; L. D. Eron and R. S. Redmount, "The Effect of Legal Education on Attitudes," *Journal of Legal Education* 9 (1957), 431–43; Richard Schwartz, "The Effectiveness of Legal Controls," manuscript, Northwestern University; Richard La Piere, *op. cit.*, p. 369; W. F. Cottrell, *Energy and Society* (New York: McGraw-Hill, 1955), pp. 271–75. Sumner is perhaps the only older sociologist who outlined and discussed a set of concepts for estimating "probable support" or resistance to proposed legislation. See Harry Ball and George and Ikeda Keyoshi, *op. cit.*, 538 ff.

40. The distinction between values and interests may be gratuitous, indicating no more than difference between ends-values and means-values. However, the term "interest" will be used largely because of its common usage in the literature of law and politics.

Legal realism appears to reject ends-means analysis in favor of purely behavioral analysis. See Jerome Frank, *Law and the Modern Mind* (New York: Anchor Books, 1963); also his *Courts on Trial* (New York: Atheneum, 1963).

However, Llewellyn, who is ordinarily regarded as a legal realist, makes it clear that such concepts as rules, rights, and interests, and presumably ends-means schemes, are tenable if they are inferred from overt action, rather than subjectively intuited as being discoverable "in the mind of the judge." Karl Llewellyn, "A Realistic Jurisprudence," *loc. cit.;* this is pretty much W. F. Cottrell's general point of view on social action, which I have attempted to follow here. See his "Men Cry Peace," *loc. cit.*

41. W. F. Cottrell, *Energy and Society,* p. 273.

42. For discussions of this problem: Edmund N. Cahn, *The Sense of Injustice* (New York: New York University Press, 1949); David Matza, *Delinquency and Drift* (New York: John Wiley, 1964), Chap. IV; Edmund Bergler and Joost Meerloo, *Justice and Injustice* (New York: Grune and Stratton, 1963); Allen Barton and Saul Mandlovitz, "The Experience of Injustice as a Research Problem," *Journal of Legal Education* 13 (1960), 24–9. Garfinkel's demonstrations of effects of deliberately deviating from presumed rules of routine activities and games are instructive here. He seems to be arguing that such rules should be studied by a kind of Gestalt sociology, as implied by the title of one of his core articles. Harold Garfinkel, "The Routine Grounds of Everyday Activities," *Social Problems* 11 (1964), 225–50.

43. Roscoe Pound, "Justice According to Law," *loc. cit.*, p. 255.

44. The phrase is Pound's. Roscoe Pound, "The Rule of Law and the Modern Welfare State," *Vanderbilt Law Review* I (1953), 31; Harry W. Jones, "The Rule of Law and the Welfare State," in *Essays in Jurisprudence From the Columbia Law Review,* pp. 410–13.

45. Roscoe Pound, "The Juvenile Court and the Law," *National Probation and Parole Association Yearbook,* 1944 (New York, 1945), pp. 1–22; Alfred Kahn, *A Court for Children* (New York: Columbia University Press, 1953), Chap. X.

46. Paul Tappan, "Juridical and Administrative Approaches to Children with Problems," in *Justice for the Child,* ed. Margaret Rosenheim (New York: Free Press, 1962), Chap. VII.

47. F. J. Davis, "The Iowa Juvenile Court Judge," *Journal of Criminal Law, Criminology, and Political Science* 42 (1951–52), 338–50.

48. The best available documentation on the early history of a particular juvenile court probably is in Ben Lindsey and Rube Burrough, *The Dangerous Life* (London: Harold Shalor, 1931); considerable historical data on the diverse origins of early juvenile courts

can be found in Hastings Hart, *Preventive Treatment of Neglected Children* (New York: Russell Sage Foundation, 1910), especially Chaps. XII, XVII, and XXIII.

49. Evelina Belden, *Courts in the United States Hearing Children's Cases,* U.S. Children's Bureau, Publication No. 65 (1920).

50. *Ibid.*

51. Paul Tappan, "Treatment without Trial," *Social Forces* 24 (1946), 306–12.

52. Paul Tappan, *Delinquent Girls in Court* (New York: Columbia University Press, 1947).

53. For a discussion of changing statuses of youth, see Hans Sebald, *Adolescence* (New York: Appleton-Century-Crofts, 1968), pp. 38–9, 95–118.

Chapter 14

Why Children Should Be Kept Out of Court

This monograph is an effort to develop a series of models for diverting children and youth away from juvenile courts, so that their problems which otherwise would be dealt with in a context of delinquency and official action will be defined and handled by other means. It is premised on the idea that an excessive number of children are being processed by juvenile courts, that children are unnecessarily referred to juvenile courts, and that in many cases the harm done to children and youth by contacts with these courts outweighs any benefits thereby gained. Moreover, the interaction between child and court and unanticipated consequences of the processing of a child in many instances contributes to or exacerbates the problem of delinquency.

The reasons for this undertaking grow out of major shifts which have taken place in thinking and public policy in regard to the preeminent position of the juvenile court as an agency for dealing with the problems of children and youth. Vast changes have taken place in American society since the birth of the juvenile court at the beginning of the twentieth century—changes which make reexamination of the court long overdue, both as an institution and as a working organization in a community context. One of the most striking developments in the picture of child and youth problems has been the great increase in contacts between youth, law enforcement bodies, and the juvenile court. For example, in 1966 between a million and a million and a half arrests were made of persons under eighteen years of age, and it was estimated that 27 percent of all male youths can expect to have been arrested before they have reached age eighteen.[1] The proportion of those who actually become known to police by this age will be much greater because large numbers of youthful "offenders" are disposed of by police without record or formal action.

Excerpts from *Instead of Court: Diversion in Juvenile Justice*. Chevy Chase, MD: National Institute of Mental Health. Center for Studies of Crime and Delinquency. Washington, D.C.: U.S. Government Printing Office, 1971. Pp. 1–18, 94–95.

Approximately one-half of police arrests of juveniles result in their referrals to juvenile courts. According to several community studies, about one-fifth of the male population will have been referred to juvenile courts by age eighteen.[2]

If these are valid measures of serious youth problems, then American society is in a critical if not moribund state. A preferred explanation is that the difficulties in reality lie elsewhere, that there is something badly wrong with the agencies which apprehend, receive, define, and process problems of children and youth. And indeed, this largely has been the tenor of the social criticism which has been directed toward police activities and juvenile procedures in recent decades. Mounting dissatisfaction and concern have been captioned by the far-reaching decision in the Gault case, in which the United States Supreme Court felt it necessary for the first time to review the work of juvenile courts. In paraphrase, the decision held that the wide powers of the juvenile court have not appreciably diminished youthful crime, that inconsistencies in its philosophy can have adverse effects upon youth under its control, and that gross injustices may result from its procedures in which youth are punished more severely than adults for comparable offenses.[3]

CRITICISM OF THE JUVENILE COURTS AS AN INSTITUTION

It is unfortunate that the Supreme Court's opinion in the Gault case was reached in an atmosphere more political than scholarly, leaving a suspicion that its purpose was to invite elimination of the juvenile court. At best, the decision was a synthetic justification for extending a number of rights of criminally accused persons to juveniles. Justice Harlan, whose opinion both concurred and dissented, decried the absence of a rationale for the decision, at the same time emphasizing the need to determine the requirements of due process of law, not by criminal or civil criteria, but rather by criteria "consistent with the traditions and conscience of our people":

> The central issue here . . . is the method by which procedural requirements of due process should be measured. . . . the protections necessary cannot be determined by . . . classification of juvenile proceedings either as criminal or as civil. Both formulas are too imprecise. . . . The court should instead measure the requirements of due process by reference both to the problems which confront the state and to the actual character of the procedural system which the state has created.[4]

Justice Harlan missed the fact that the juvenile court is more of a local than a state agency, but his insistence on the need to examine it as an institutional system responding to variable problems in a geographical setting reflects a sociological view: in essence that decisionmaking and judicial outcomes in juvenile courts are phenomena of social organization rather than law *per se*.[5] The variation in such organization is considerable; indeed, this is one of the core difficulties in trying to understand the juvenile court. How to comprehend the protean local adaptations of the many juvenile courts and yet capture those features which make it distinctive as an institution is no mean task. Perhaps this can best be done by combining several loosely linked perspectives on the court—its institutional differentiation, its efficacy as a working organization, also as a treatment agency, its bureaucratization, the overreach of law by the court, and its consequences as a deviance designating agency.

INSTITUTIONAL DIFFERENTIATION

A perennial problem of juvenile courts, particularly as they are seen by national, standard-conscious agencies, has been their failure to differentiate according to the early model. Much of this has been blamed on the character of juvenile court judges, many of whom took conservative views of the court or else lacked the background and special education to appreciate and fulfill its ideal goals. Many courts had no probation officers, while others had to do with untrained and poorly educated personnel; social investigation and written reports were conspicuously absent, and access to specialized services was limited or nonexistent. Years ago, Carr called attention to these facts as evidence that "most courts have to be substandard."[6] The persistent failure of courts to differentiate is born out by a 1963 study which revealed that only 71 percent of juvenile court judges had law degrees; and of "full time" juvenile court judges, 72 percent spent a quarter or less of their time on juvenile matters. One-third of the judges had no probation officers to carry out work of the court, and but a small portion could call on psychological or psychiatric consultation services.[7]

Undifferentiated juvenile courts are much more numerous than others, but overall they serve a smaller proportion of the population. Their substandard quality appears to be directly related to the low population density of the areas they serve, where sheer economics or high per capita costs of servicing cases makes specialization difficult or impossible.

THE COURT AS A WORKING ORGANIZATION

In looking at juvenile courts serving large population areas which have reasonably adequate resources to differentiate along specialized, professional lines, different kinds of problems come to light, the most important of which is an overburden. As a juvenile court differentiates, it develops a number of interdependent relations with local and state agencies—police, sheriffs departments, boards of supervisors, welfare departments, schools, hospitals, clinics, correctional institutions, and professional associations. While such agencies serve the court, they also make claims on it, one of the main consequences being that it receives far more referrals than it has resources to handle. Attempts are made to meet this problem by concentrating on screening cases at intake, but nevertheless their volume means that much if not most of the manpower of the court has to go into investigations and court hearings.

It has been argued that the court's case-processing methods are ill adapted to its tasks. For one thing a great deal of information often is collected which either is not used or cannot be related in any specifiable way to the kinds of decisions the courts make in particular cases. Storage and retrieval of information by hand-filing methods frequently is inadequate to the magnitude of its work. There is an absence of methods for monitoring and assessing the work of the court, nor can it forecast the direction of its movement with any accuracy. One result is that cases are not disposed in line with a continuous or clear policy; policy of the juvenile court often is a reflection of inconsistent demands being made upon it at a particular time by particular agencies. Salient among these is the effort of police to coopt the court in their jobs of maintaining public order. A comparison of the working of the juvenile court with that of the modern business corporation makes it appear poorly managed, inconsistent, duplicative, and costly in effort.[8]

THE COURT AS BUREAUCRACY

The necessity of processing large numbers of cases with diversified problems transforms the juvenile courts into hierarchical organizations with divisions, departments, specialists, and routinized procedures. As such, they take on the qualities and problems of bureaucracy. Cases are passed from functionary to functionary and from one department to another, hence, decisions often are reached in piecemeal fashion or in consultations between various levels of authority. While there is a strain towards rationalized procedures, nevertheless responsibility tends to be diffused, and conflicts between individual workers or between divisions are endemic. Group interaction within the court, routines, contingencies, and organizational requirements profoundly affect the fate of cases.

What in the early days of the juvenile court was envisioned as a quasi-personal relationship between a child and a judge or between a youth and a probation officer turns into a relationship between a child or youth and a large, complex organization. Given the overburden of cases born of external demands on the court, the exigencies of its internal operations make it extremely difficult or impossible to predict that the interests of the child will be those of any particular member of the organization or of the court as a whole. Until recently, juvenile courts failed to make any adaptations to this crucial problem, in part because ideal aspects of the original model of the court as a protectorate of children obscured its significance and in part because recognition of this kind of problem would compel fundamental changes in the design of the court itself. The problem has further ramifications, best seen in questions about the inherent limits of law as a means of social control.

THE COURT AS THE OVERREACH OF LAW

Many of the difficulties of the juvenile court revolve around its character as an enterprise originally designed to use the power and authority of law to achieve ends not amenable to legal means. These strictures were anticipated years ago by Roscoe Pound in his classic paper on the limits of effective legal action. In it he noted that this kind of question comes to the fore in epochs when efforts are made to cause law to coincide with morals. When this happens the individual becomes the unit of law and wide discretion is given to magistrates (judges). The limits of legal sanctions inhere in the intangibleness of moral duties, which although of great public concern, defy public enforcement. As cases in point, Pound observed how obligations for the care of health, morals, and education of children—even truancy and incorrigibility—were coming under the jurisdiction of juvenile courts. When these matters are committed to courts they necessarily delegate the work of enforcement to administrative agents, such as probation officers, whose capacity to achieve these ends is questionable.[9]

Although Pound remained favorable to the juvenile court idea throughout his career, he was aware of its inherent shortcomings. In his estimation there were two main threats to the juvenile court, both inherently forms of the overreach of law:

> It remains to speak of two movements in current thinking which may threaten the continued development of the juvenile court. One is the movement to reach the causes of all delinquency and so particularly of juvenile delinquency through programs of official national agencies and local welfare agencies subordinate to or allied with them. . . .
>
> Another aspect of current thinking is the move towards absolutism the world over. The subject . . . affects every agency of government which involves the exercise of discretion with reference to the interests of individuals. Especially the movement for a wide administrative criminal jurisdiction may easily be carried so far with mistaken zeal that administrative criminal tribunals and the juvenile courts may be pushed back or fall back into ordinary criminal courts of the old type.[10]

A critical retrospective on the establishment of the first juvenile courts reveals them to have been less a carefully planned innovation than the climax of a nineteenth century reform movement to rescue children from "depravity and immorality" of lower class urban environments. Another part of its impetus came from reformers who turned to the juvenile court idea as an oblique way of attacking the evil of child labor through using the court to enforce compulsory education laws. In its early history it was not unusual for the court to be pressured to take custody of children as a device to coerce parental conformity in matters of divorce, adultery, and insobriety. Some of the early controversies between judges and welfare workers revolved around these issues, with conservative judges in some instances using their considerable discretionary power to resist the zeal of reformers.[11]

The juvenile court's emergence in Illinois solved a major problem for private charity organizations there, which had seen statutes giving them control over delinquent children declared unconstitutional, while those allowing control over dependent and neglected children were sustained on appeal.[12] Combining jurisdiction over all three classes of children in a "socialized court" theoretically civil in nature provided the much sought legitimation of the values of the moral reformers. Unfortunately the envisioned ideal that delinquent children would thereafter be defined and treated as "neglected" proved false; in practice the reverse often was true, i.e., dependent and neglected children fell under the pall of delinquency and in many cases were subjected to the same kinds of sanctions.

THE OMNIBUS NATURE OF DELINQUENCY

Designations of delinquency in the first juvenile court laws were radical departures from traditional principles of Anglo-Saxon criminal law which parsimoniously applied sanctions to conduct manifestly violating narrowly defined laws and leaves but small scope for preventive law. Early statutes describing juvenile delinquency were omnibus in nature, drawn with the intent of bringing the widest possible gamut of child and youth problems under the bind of law. They embraced juvenile law violators, but "predelinquents" as well; later statutes added those with "delinquent tendencies." While the statutory phrasing under which juvenile courts assumed their almost unlimited jurisdiction has varied widely, delinquency is generally described as: (1) actions which if committed by adults would be punishable as crimes; (2) actions or states of being applicable only to minors—special children's offenses such as idleness, begging, junking, smoking, using alcohol, loitering or sleeping in alleys, curfew violations, presence in a gambling place or house of prostitution, playing ball in the street, engaging in street trades, and associating with adult criminals; (3) very generalized unspecified acts or states such as truancy, incorrigibility, immorality, and being in danger of leading a lewd and lascivious life.

The passage of time has seen the elimination of long lists of outmoded acts and morally hazardous conditions from juvenile court laws in some states, but reliance on nonspecific jurisdictional categories has continued, including "runaways," "beyond control" of parents and school authorities, and actions "endangering morals and welfare." In eight states delinquency is not defined, but is left to the discretion of the juvenile courts themselves.[13]

SUBSTANCE AND SHADOW OF DELINQUENCY

Nationwide the substantive meaning of delinquency has to be restricted to the body of similar findings between jurisdictions as to what constitute law violations by minors. Otherwise, definitions are artificial, arbitrary, and conventional.[14] The meaning of delinquency is relative, and peculiar to time and place. It must be discerned in the routine perceptions and practices within the court as effected by external claims of agencies and individuals making up its overburden.

In courts where social work philosophy and psychiatric ideologies prevail, the shadowy nature of delinquency determinations is furthered, or perhaps validated, by the idea that wrongdoing is a symptom of underlying pathology of the person or of his family situation. This "pathology" is inferred not so much from conduct as from "patterns" or "tendencies," judged to exist or intuited by probation officers, social workers, or clinical consultants. From their view, it may be more urgent to take or retain official control over a youth who has committed a benign offense than one guilty of a law violation.

THE COURT AS A TREATMENT AGENCY

In actuality juvenile courts as a whole have not been receptive to psychiatric ideology and social work methods. Pressures on the courts to mete out punishment to delinquents and the inclination of probation officers to see themselves as surrogates of law and community interests have determined otherwise. Conceptions of treatment held by probation officers are much more likely to be correctional in nature and communicated from within their own field. The desire to do "treatment" and enthusiasm for novel ideas of therapy are often met with among probation officers, but then countered in the same breath by the occupational complaint that caseloads are too overwhelmingly large to allow time for treatment. When pushed for justification of what they do, judges and probation officers are likely to describe the working dispositions of their cases as treatment or in more candid moments recognize them as expedients for disciplining unruly youth.

About one-half of all cases received by juvenile courts are dismissed or continued without a formal disposition—in other words, little more occurs than processing itself. One long-accepted justification for what otherwise might seem a meaningless spinning of its wheels by the court is that errant youth are thereby given an experience with supervening authority hitherto missing from their lives. Commonly this means a confrontation with a probation officer in the presence of parents or a stern lecture from a judge in a courtroom, and warnings of dire consequences of further misconduct.

A more painful accompaniment of these proceedings in a certain number of cases is a stay in detention. This often is a pragmatic move so that the youth can "cool off" or "think things over"; not infrequently it is a type of punishment decreed in lieu of other forms of incarceration. At still other times detention is a direct accommodation to needs of police who are trying to solve a crime series or recover property; no pretense of treatment is made.

Next to continuances the most frequent disposition in juvenile court cases is placement on probation. But probation often is a nominal type of control which adds up to relatively few contacts between probation officers and their wards, their average number being about one or less per month.[15] In defense of this procedure it has been argued that merely placing a youth on probation, regardless of what else happens, is in itself a form of treatment. Seen more realistically it is a form of attenuated surveillance.

Leaving aside the question of commitments to schools and institutions, what the juvenile court does by way of treatment is so intertwined with its other purposes as to defy specification and evaluation. Undoubtedly there are cases in which encounters with juvenile court personnel, stays in detention, and probationary status suffice to make youth more law abiding or at least more cautious and careful about actions likely to result in arrest or referral to the court. Those so responding are probably fortunately situated or culturally and psychologically endowed to profit from their experiences. In contrast, there are those for whom juvenile court appearances and their consequences simply add new problems to old, redefine old problems in more ominous and fateful terms, or become episodes in delinquent careers.

THE COURT AS AN AGENCY FOR DEFINING DEVIANCE

A final way of perceiving the juvenile court illuminates the way in which it designates deviance, shapes its expression, and helps to perpetuate it in secondary form.[16] It does so by redefining normal problems of children and youth as special problems requiring legal action and restraining controls. In a real sense it "causes" delinquency by processing cases of children and youth whose problems might be ignored, normalized in their original settings, or dealt with as family, educational, or welfare problems. Prima facie supporting evidence for this conclusion comes from studies of so-called "hidden" or "unofficial" delinquency, which show that a high percentage of college students and high school students have committed acts similar to those of boys who were wards of juvenile courts or inmates of correctional schools.[17]

One difference between college students and juvenile court boys, also between high school boys and those in correctional schools, was that the officially processed boys had committed *more* actions definable as delinquent than their counterparts. This fact might allow the conclusion that the processed youths represented cases in which normalization of their actions had been tried and failed. However, close examination of these studies indicates that when both frequency and seriousness of infractions are considered, there is a good deal of overlap in the distributions of cases of official and "unofficial" delinquency. This is most seen in the Cambridge-Somerville study in which a comparison is possible between youth who became juvenile court cases and those who did not. The former, the "official" cases, disclosed a frequency range of from five cases per youth to over 323, with a median of 79 for a five-year period. During this same time the range for the frequencies of unofficial cases was from zero to 266, with a median of 30. Twelve and a half percent of the official cases fell below the median of the unofficial cases, while 21.3 percent of the unofficial cases were above the median of the officially processed offenders.[18]

The areas of overlap between official and unofficial delinquency can be assumed to embrace primarily the special children's offenses and those in non-specific categories of "delinquent tendencies." It is in these areas that the process of redefining normal child and youth problems into those requiring court intervention meets with the least resistance. However, as will be shown, criminal statutes also may be stretched or so interpreted to accomplish the same end. The difference between official and normal delinquencies lies in their context, primarily in the values, motivations, and policy decisions of complainants seeking to define the problems whose solution lies in juvenile court intervention. The more immediate meanings behind such allegations as incorrigibility, truancy, curfew violations, and moral danger are distributive aspects of the extraneous group and individual demands which make up the overburden of the court.

For example, incorrigibility when put into its social context is a term which many times connotes little more than conflict between a teen-age youth and parents, in which unreasonable demands are made by the latter and in which a probation officer becomes a partisan. Sometimes the application of this term is merely a convenient vehicle for abdicating parental responsibility for a child. Outside the family it may mean that a teacher or vice principal has concluded that a child is a troublemaker whom he will not tolerate further in the school. Truancy, which usually is arbitrarily defined by school policies, reflects a wide variety of situations other than willful absence by the child. A study conducted in 1960 found that among other things the label of truancy was sometimes simply applied as a result of failure of parents to send written excuses to school.[19] Curfew violations may mean many things, but typically they flow from crude police action seeking to maintain order in public places. The allegation of moral danger tends to arise out of behavior or situations, real or fancied, which arouse sufficient sexual anxieties in others to demand court action. Normal sex play of children witnessed by neighbors may suffice.

The overreach of law in converting normal problems into delinquency is even more striking when allegations of law violations are made. These range from adventitious overblown charges arising from domestic quarrels to routine use of maximum charges in ways comparable to practices in regular criminal courts. Usually these stem from strong personal involvements or from the vested interests of organizations. Consider the following, witnessed in a Northern California county juvenile court:

> Naomi, age 13, was charged with assault on her grandmother, the case against her aggressively presented by the probation officer. Under his questioning, the grandmother angrily stated that the girl had pushed her and struck her without provocation in the early morning hours in her own house. This had badly upset the grandfather who came downstairs on the scene shortly thereafter. He verified his wife's version of the events.
>
> But slowly under cross examination by the defense attorney it became clear that the girl had done no more than push her grandmother down into a chair to compel her

to listen to her. This was a reaction to events of the previous evening when the grandmother in the girl's presence had called her mother a whore, mainly because she was associating with an Indian, the two having gone to San Francisco the night in question. The girl was badly disturbed, brooded about the remark, finally phoned her grandmother to demand a face-to-face explanation in her house, where the alleged "assault" occured. Further questioning made it fairly clear that the court action was one of a long series of harassments to remove the mother and girl from a small house owned by the grandmother.

The importance of vested interests in routine exaggeration of crime charges involving youths is best seen in auto thefts, which in many cities make up the lion's share of court cases involving boys. Most of these are "joy riding" offenses rather than taking with the intent of converting the property of others to personal use. The vehicles usually are abandoned after a short period, and recovery rates are quite high. Yet because of the crucial importance of automobiles and because of the special interests of insurance companies in these matters, probation officers in many jurisdictions charge the maximum statutory offense.[20] Here law typically goes beyond its province to make maximum findings because juvenile courts are not constrained by strict rules of criminal evidence.

STIGMATIZATION

Juvenile court proceedings originally were held to be civil in nature, confidential, and to be concluded without creation of a record. Events proved them to be punitive, correctional, and stigmatizing in effect if not in intent. This came about from persistent opinion and pressures from groups that saw the court as a means of repressing crime. The location of juvenile courts within the regular system of courts, their close relations with police departments, use of jails for detention, and dispositions depriving children of their freedom all sustained the punitive and stigmatizing features of these courts.

Stigmatization is a process which assigns marks of moral inferiority to deviants; more simply it is a form of degradation which transforms identities and status for the worse. It is both implicit and explicit in formal procedures in the court. Intake interviews, and those in subsequent investigations, often are inquisitions seeking admissions of guilt or of complicity in offenses necessary to meet legal requirements of petitions, or to obtain evidence in other cases. Detention means loss of freedom, removal of personal possessions, subjugation to arbitrary security rules, and surveillance—in some juvenile halls by microphones and closed circuit television. Girls, on admission to detention, may have to submit to routine pelvic examinations, with the implications of possible pregnancy or venereal disease.

Court hearings on many occasions are equivalents of degradation rituals in which probation officers recite in detail the moral failings or "unfitness" of children, youth, and parents. Hostile witnesses add to the condemnations, and judges often deliver sermon-like lectures, larded with threats, which confront children and parents with choices of reform or dire consequences. For emphasis, judges have been known to read incriminating facts or opinions from the probation record.

While such dramatized insults to identity and integrity cut deep for some, their impact varies and is absorbed or discounted by others. Less easy to cope with are the objective consequences of stigmatization resulting from the creation of a court and police record. While not open public records, nevertheless their contents get known. This can and does act as a handicap in seeking certain types of employment, professional schooling, and acceptance in the armed forces. A paradoxical handicap, one of special importance in the larger discussion of this report, is that once a child becomes a ward of a juvenile court, many welfare agencies will not accept him as their client.[21] Henceforth, he loses his chances of having his problems treated as welfare matters.

THE ESCALATION OF STIGMA

Probation officers, welfare workers, and others are familiar with cases of children who have come into juvenile court as dependent wards, later were classed as incorrigible, and at last typed as law violator delinquents. Court workers are very apt to look on this sequence as a kind of unfolding process in which the potential for delinquency becomes overt. Omitted from their thinking, and that which impresses many sociologists, is the influence of court experiences themselves in the generation of such sequences or careers.

A certain portion of the escalation of delinquent careers is almost purely arbitrary or results from bureaucratic responses to court overload. For example, in 1966 juvenile courts in California sent eighty minors to the Youth Authority, by reclassifying them from code section 600 (dependency, unfit homes) to 602 (law violations) without bringing them back to court for rehearings.[22] A common problem cloaked by such actions is the inability to find foster home placements or lack of other resources. This leads to the administrative expedient of legally redefining the child's problems so that he or she may be turned over to the state agency. There is no way of knowing how widespread this kind of circumvention is, but results of a 1966 survey of fifteen to twenty correctional institutions showed that about 30 percent of their inmates were children committed for conduct that would not have been judged criminal for adults. Similar studies brought out the fact that 48 percent of 9,500 children in state and local detention programs had no record of criminal acts.[23]

SECONDARY DEVIANCE

One of the great paradoxes of organized society is that agencies of social control may exacerbate or perpetuate the very problems they seek to ameliorate. In so doing they foster conditions of secondary deviance. Such deviance evolves out of adaptations and attempted adaptations to the problems created by official reactions to original deviance.[24] From this point of view the sanctions, dispositions, or "treatment" imposed by the juvenile court personnel too often simply add another series of problems to original problems of parents and children, then further stigmatize the failures to cope with the new problems. The specifics of this process lie in the reactions made to special status which sets wards apart and special conduct standards which hold them accountable in ways not expected of other children. Probation exemplifies this process, wherein a youth is forbidden to associate with persons he regards as his friends, a girl is barred from seeing her boyfriend, or a child is ordered not to see an "unfit" parent.

A teenager placed in a foster home is expected to obey orders of people who are strangers; the boy placed in a ranch school must tread a narrow path hedged with rules, many of which are drawn up with his potential deviance in mind. A youth may violate rules with perfectly good motive—to show loyalty to friends, to visit with a parent, or to look for employment. In other cases a boy may take leave from a ranch school because of problems beyond his power to solve. Yet the court typically defines such action as "failures" or disobedience of its orders, which become legal justification for more severe measures whose effect is to move a minor farther along the road to correctional school. Probation officers or judges sometimes are aware at the time of a disposition that it is destined to "fail," yet they will say that they have no choice when it comes to the more fateful dispositions which follow such failures.

DELINQUENCY AS A PROCESS

Becoming delinquent is not a simple aggregation of the effects of juvenile court experiences, but rather a process in which parents, neighbors, teachers, school officials, and police as well play significant roles. No less important is the subjective response of "self reaction" which children and youths make to these significant others. While becoming delinquent is by no means a unilinear process, frequently it discloses a cumulative reinforcement of problems confronting a child in different social contexts. Parents may be loveless, punitive, or rejecting toward a child, or they may place him prematurely on his own resources. The child may be labeled as the "bad one" or black sheep of the family; neighbors may focus hostility on such a child and make him a scapegoat. Teachers may add another facet to the child's disrepute with the designation of troublemaker, or a vice principal may insist that the child be removed from his school. Finally, the police, who are the main source of juvenile court referrals, form stereotyped judgments of the child based upon fragmentary information of his family or his school record.

While there is no agreement on the precise way a child becomes delinquent, much indicates that the process consists of predominant interactions in which the child's sense of integrity and moral worth are placed in question. This is most likely to happen when relationships of trust vital to personal growth are attenuated or changed to those of distrust. When this occurs, wariness, cognizance, and surveillance replace the easy mutual acceptance of trust. There is little effort to normalize deviance or to see it as a problem amenable to ordinary solutions.

Deviance which subsequently gets defined as delinquency represents efforts by children and youth to defend their autonomy and somehow preserve character in the face of degrading interaction. For children this includes a lot of testing and retaliative behavior, often idiosyncratic in nature, which invites problematic definitions. For the adolescent, deviance is more apt to be shaped in peer group audiences which serve to validate character claims or "rep." It is not unusual for this to turn into character contests involving both police and juvenile court officials. The subjective aspects of this process have been analyzed well by Werthman elsewhere.[25] Here the main concern is with the special attributes of the institutional context which pose character problems for the child.

The place of the juvenile court and that of the police differ in several fundamental ways from the family, neighborhood, school, and welfare agencies. Whereas the latter are organized primarily around presumptions of trust, the reverse is true of the police; they institutionalize distrust, suspicion, and inquisitorial methods. Distrust is problematical for primary groups but, conversely, trust is problematical in police and court organizations. When police and probation officers cultivate trust, it is likely to be for instrumental reasons, and it easily deteriorates into exploitation. This is in contrast with the family, where parent-child relations fluctuate, get repaired, and leave room for forgiveness and mutual sharing of blame. In the school the nonconforming child may still find a basis for accommodation and trust with teachers. To a very limited degree this is even possible between police and street youth. Not so, however, for the juvenile court, whose formal decisions and actions are clothed with finality, and whose errors must be laboriously proved by appeal. There are no procedures by which a juvenile court can admit openly that it has been wrong, nor does its charter allow it to make reparations.

Awareness of the fateful nature of juvenile court processing on the part of judges and probation officers helps explain the large proportion of cases that are dismissed, continued, or assigned to informal supervision. From what has been said it seems plain that the bulk of such cases should have been previously normalized or defined as problems other than delinquency. However, their presence and processing through to disposition reflect efforts of court personnel to solve their own dilemmas. They provide means to satisfy the extraneous claims making up the overburden of the court, to validate its presumptions of treatment, and to quiet public demands for repressing delinquency. At the same time some protection and individualized consideration are given children and parents.

IMPLICATIONS FOR PUBLIC POLICY

Examination of the juvenile court from several perspectives leaves it painfully clear that too often it seeks to do things best not done; it undertakes ambitious tasks without available means and it fails to apply means at hand to clearly defined ends. Moreover, the juvenile court aggravates many problems it tries to ameliorate, and, in an undetermined number of cases, it furthers delinquent careers.

Questions of public policy raised by these criticisms are twofold: (1) whether some of the actions of children and parents now subject to definition as delinquency or unfitness should not be conceived as nonproblematical and either ignored or written off simply as part of the inevitable, everyday problems of living and growing up; (2) whether many of the problems now considered as delinquency or preludes to delinquency should not be defined as family, educational, or welfare problems, and diverted away from the juvenile court into other community agencies.

The first question resolves itself into other questions, mainly relating to what kinds of youthful actions and family situations should be used to make such determinations. The diversity of American culture and shifting public opinion makes substantive answers to these questions difficult. In general terms, however, it appears that the emphasis should be on *conduct* and its *manifest consequences*. Other criteria obviously applicable are those of *recurrency* and *injury to self and others*. The stance of the juvenile court should be nonintervention; the standards of proof should be high; the burden of proof should rest on those seeking intervention.

The second question comes with cases in which a serious problem is demonstrably present, but there is good reason to believe that it can be worked out in other than the authoritative setting of the court. Here the special laws applicable only to children should be closely reexamined, with a view primarily to their abolition or substantial revision in that direction. Leaving aside the emotionally charged topic of drug use by minors, the time is past due for overhauling laws governing the use of alcohol by minors. The same is true for laws dealing with the curfew, the possession of knives, and some forms of theft. Truancy, runaways, incorrigibility, beyond control, and lewd or immoral conduct all refer to problems which according to our line of thinking are best amenable to control by law and the most likely candidates for other kinds of social control.[26] For these problems are almost always matters of arbitrary definition; in a wide range of instances they reflect normal reactions of maturing youth to arbitrary authority or other intolerable conditions. Finally, in an equally impressive number of cases they are simply a guise for transferring or "dumping" problems from one institutional setting to another, concealing reasons which are unclear, indefensible, or both.

Changes in public policy aimed at narrowing the jurisdiction of the juvenile court and limiting the range of problems definable as delinquency can be formed by appellate rulings, legislation, and finding new ways of administering the law. In the past, appeals from juvenile court decisions have not been influential in constraining unwise action by juvenile courts, and it remains to be seen what the full effects of the U.S. Supreme Court ruling in the Gault case will be. It is more likely that relevant changes will have to come from state legislation and local administration. Yet there is risk that passage of statutes to restrict the volume of cases reaching juvenile courts may miss their targets if they do no more than describe new substantive bases for jurisdiction, for the reason that complainants as well as juvenile court personnel are likely to rationalize or define their problems in whatever terms the new statutes state. More effective constraints lie in new procedural or adjective law.

Such procedural requirements include intake screening, detention hearings, bifurcated hearings, sharp separation of findings of fact and information related to dispositions, official records advice as to right to counsel, provision of counsel, and limitations on dispositions according to the type of jurisdiction assumed by the court. Many changes along this line have already been made in various states.

Probably the most revolutionary change under way in the present day juvenile courts is the entree and presence of counsel in a growing number of cases. Increasingly aggressive advocacy has had direct effects on procedures, among them delays, complications, and increased costs. In areas where this has been occurring—California juvenile courts, for example—a general result is to move the courts closer to a kind of negotiated, plea-bargaining justice similar to that which has evolved in adult criminal courts.[27]

Two important changes in our larger society are encouraging the exercise by juveniles and parents of their rights to counsel and vigorous defense in juvenile court, changes which combine to push the courts towards a more narrowly conceived agency, dealing primarily with serious law violations. One of these is the heightened sensitivity of minority populations to real or fancied abuses of police power and to civil rights issues. The other is the swelling numbers of youth apprehended for violating narcotics laws, many of whom have middle class status. Among the consequences of the first change is a greater likelihood—particularly of Negroes in ghetto areas—of resistance to arrest, or even attacks on police. This means that arrests for minor offenses lead to secondary charges of interfering with police or assault. Protracted hearings follow, necessitating evaluation of conflicting testimony and extensive arguments over the law of arrest.

The situation regarding the enforcement of narcotics laws is one of imbalance, in which the stringency of penalties has outstripped the social harm of the offenses. The threat of prison makes engaging or assignment of counsel commonplace. Defense, at times helped by a sympathetic judge or prosecutor, tends to exploit technicalities of the law as a means of rebalancing the scales of justice. Hence, the excesses of legislators seeking to stamp out the "drug evil" may well have the unanticipated effects of making the juvenile courts more legalistic, more like a criminal court.

However, this seems unlikely to happen solely through changes in law and increased use of counsel. Such a view overplays the influence of law in producing changes, particularly more positive and constructive changes needed to lessen the overburden of the juvenile court. It is doubtful that problems of overload and the overreach of law can be solved unilaterally so long as juvenile courts are part of a reciprocating system of community and state agencies and so long as parents and individuals can freely initiate court action. It is also questionable whether public opinion will be favorable to withdrawal of juvenile courts from many problem areas without some new forms of control coming into being.

In sociological terms it can be said that if something is removed from a reciprocating system of groups, something must be put back. Hence if the problem domain of the juvenile court is to be made smaller and more specialized, other definitions of youth problems need to be developed and new means invented to deal with them. This can be accomplished by reorganizing existing agency resources or by inventing new types of organization, or both. In both instances the organizational principle or objective will be that of bypassing the juvenile court process.

IS THERE A BETTER IDEA?

Social scientists probably are at their best as institutional critics; they are more likely to know what does not work and what is unlikely to work, than what will. When social invention is essayed, their productions are no less apt to be follies than those of others who struggle to solve the riddles of human problems. Hence it is with a proper measure of humility advised by what has or has not been learned from materials examined in this volume that the following are proposed as minimal considerations for the construction of a diversion model:

1. Diversion should be closely articulated with the workings of the juvenile justice system because that's what it is about.
2. Police should become the chief sources of referrals to diversion agencies because that's where most official processing starts.
3. There should be positive gains to police from their making referrals.
4. Diversion agencies in large cities probably are best located near schools but not in them.
5. Serious truancy and cases of aggravated disciplinary problems should be referred routinely to diversion agencies. No school should be allowed to dismiss or suspend a child without finding that provision has been made for his continuing education or employment.
6. In unfit home cases, absence of home care, incorrigibility complaints by parents or school authorities, and moral danger cases, the police, sheriff's departments, district attorneys, and probation departments should be compelled to find that no agency exists or none is willing to accept the cases before referring them to juvenile court or filing petitions.

7. Diversion agencies should reserve the right to reject cases but should not refer cases to the police or juvenile court.

Stated in more positive terms the purpose of a diversion agency should be to preempt problems which otherwise would enter the juvenile justice system. Its purpose should *not* be case finding; nor should it be the coordination of services. Rather it should be problem solving, conflict resolution, or the provision of services germane to the specific nature of the deviance and the imminence of official action. Special attention should be given to "making the victim whole" or satisfying complainants that "something is being done" about the problem. Mediation, arbitration, and restitution should be freely used. Finally, public relations techniques are recommended to dissipate spurious moral indignation which often complicates nonofficial handling of delinquents.

Much of what has been suggested here pertains to jurisdictional matters and procedures and neglects to say what kind of an organization design is necessary for diversion. Yet this is a logical consequence of the kinds of questions asked throughout this monograph: what kinds of problems of children and youth should be officially recognized and what happens when they are. These are operational questions, not questions as to what can be done for or to minors. Therefore the form of diversion agencies may not be too important so long as they are operationally oriented.

It may be most profitable to conceive of diversion as an integral part of a system—in this case, of the juvenile justice system. This poses a question as to what the juvenile justice system is and how cases flow into and out of it. Some believe that it can be defined by research:

> there is need for a large scale program of action research involving personnel at all levels focusing on connections between agencies, developing common information sources and data banks, predicting and testing ultimate goal oriented changes in each component as it affects the others.[28]

There are others who are less sanguine about the possibilities of "systems research" or who believe it is a snare or delusion. The debate is unsettled.

Meanwhile, it seems safest to hold that diversion of children and youth from the official court system is a state of mind; once it is established as a predominant social value, the question of adaptation of means to the end should be more easily answered.

NOTES

1. Alfred Blumstein, Systems analysis and the criminal justice system, *American Academy of Political and Social Science,* 1967, 375, 92–100.
2. *Op. cit.,* p. 99.
3. *In re Gault,* 387 U.S. I (1967), pp. 1–81.
4. *Op. cit.*

5. Aaron Cicourel, *The Social Organization of Juvenile Justice,* New York: John Wiley and Sons, 1968, Chapters I, II.

6. Lowell Carr, Most courts have to be substandard, *Federal Probation,* XIII, 1949, 22–23.

7. Shirley McCune and Daniel S. Skoler, Juvenile court judges in the United States, Part I, *Crime and Delinquency,* 1965, 11, 121–131.

8. Robert Vinter, The juvenile court as an institution, *Task Force Report: Juvenile Delinquency and Youth Crime,* President's Commission on Law Enforcement and the Administration of Justice, 1967, Washington, D.C., pp. 84–90.

9. Roscoe Pound, The limits of effective legal action, *Twenty-Second Annual Report of the Pennsylvania Bar Association,* XXII, 1916, 221–239; ———, The juvenile court and the law, reprinted in *Crime and Delinquency,* 10, 1964, 490–504.

10. Roscoe Pound, The juvenile court and the law, p. 503.

11. Edwin M. Lemert, *Social Action and Legal Change,* Chicago: Aldine Publishing Co., 1970, Chapters I, II.

12. Anthony Platt, *The Child Savers,* Chicago: Aldine Publishing Co., 1969, Chapter 5.

13. *Comparative Survey of Juvenile Delinquency, Part I, North America,* UNESCO, No. 58, IV, 2–4.

14. Manuel Lopez-Rey, Juvenile delinquency, maladjustment and maturity; *Journal of Criminal Law and Criminology,* 1960, 51, 31.

15. Lewis Dana, What is probation? *Journal of Criminal Law and Criminology,* 1960, 51, 189–204.

16. Edwin M. Lemert, *Human Deviance, Social Problems and Social Control,* Englewood Cliffs, N.J.: Prentice Hall, Inc., 1967, Chapter 3.

17. Austin Porterfield, *Youth in Trouble,* Fort Worth, Texas: Leo Potishman Foundation, 1946, Chapter 2; Mary Shirley and Helen Witmer, The incidence of hidden delinquency, *American Journal of Orthopsychiatry,* 1946, 16, 686–696; James F. Short and F. Ivan Nye, Extent of unrecorded delinquency, *Journal of Criminal Law and Criminology,* 1958, 49, 296–302.

18. Edwin Powers and Helen Witmer, *An Experiment in the Prevention of Delinquency—the Cambridge Somerville Youth Study,* New York: Columbia University Press, 1951, Chapter XVIII.

19. Sophia Robison, *Juvenile Delinquency,* New York: Holt, Rinehart and Winston, 1960, pp. 148–155.

20. Jerome Hall, *Theft, Law and Society,* 2nd ed. Indianapolis: Bobbs-Merrill Co. Inc., 1952, Chapter 6.

21. Alfred J. Kahn, *A Court For Children,* New York: Columbia University Press, 1953, pp. 59–60.

22. *Proceedings of the 1966 Institute for Juvenile Court Judges and Referees,* 1966, Long Beach, California, Judicial Council of California, p. 22.

23. William H. Sheridan, Juveniles who commit non-criminal acts: Why treat in a correctional system? *Federal Probation,* 1967, XXXI, 26–30.

24. Edwin M. Lemert, *op. cit.*

25. Carl Werthman, The function of social definitions in the development of delinquent careers, Task Force Report: Juvenile Delinquency and Youth Crime, *op. cit.,* Appendix J., 155–170.

26. See Sol Rubin, Legal definitions of offenses by children and youths, *Illinois Law*

Forum, 1960, Winter, 512–523; Alfred Kahn, Sociology and social work—challenge and invitation, *Social Problems,* 1957, 4, 220–228.

27. See Edwin M. Lemert, *op. cit.*

28. A. W. McEachern, A systems approach to juvenile delinquency, April 1969, Public Systems Research Institute, University of Southern California, manuscript.

Chapter 15

Children and the Law in Italy

The juvenile court in Italy was established many years after those in the United States and other European countries. Even after its creation problems of differentiation and staffing remained, and delays plus ineffective services continue to complicate day-to-day operations of the juvenile courts. I propose that the juvenile court in Italy has been a spurious development, reflecting contradictions between the culture of legal certainty and familism, and the adoption of a pattern of discretionary justice based on the positivism of Ferri. Operations of the juvenile court resemble rituals aimed to satisfy conflicting values. Signs are that its legitimacy has been weakened and that other forms of social control have emerged or reemerged.

This article deals with the development of juvenile justice as it has been influenced by culture and social organization in Italy. Put most generally, I examine the way in which a society responds to the strain between formal law and newly introduced means of achieving substantive or distributive justice, or what Max Weber (1967: 226) called the "inevitable conflict" authorities in different legal systems confront between an abstract formalism of legal certainty and the desire to realize substantive goals. More specifically I will describe and analyze adaptations made in a social system with an unusually high degree of emphasis on legal certainty when those with power to do so seek to institutionalize discretion as a means of dealing with juvenile crime. The inevitable conflict in this instance concerns whether, to what extent, and how children and youth should be held responsible for their misdeeds and crime.

In the United States, where the juvenile court was born in 1899, conflict arose between the tenuous jurisprudence of *parens patriae* and the views of judges loath to abandon notions of legality in processing cases of juvenile delinquency (Lemert, 1970: 73). For a number of years, however, this conflict was muted and sub rosa due largely to the decentralized nature of the juvenile courts, their low

Excerpts from "Juvenile Justice Italian Style." *Law & Society Review* 20, 4 (Winter 1986): 509–44. Pp. 509–11, 538–42. Reprinted by permission of the Law and Society Association.

visibility, the scarcity of appeals, and the lack of accountability of judges involved. Beginning in the 1950s, controversy over the issue of fairness, juvenile "rights," and the fallacies of "treatment" of juvenile delinquents ultimately led to increased legalization of juvenile court procedures through a variety of appellate court decisions and legislation. A dual result of this development was increased decriminalization of status offenses and greater criminalization of procedures in cases of juveniles held to have committed crimes (Rubin, 1979: chap. 12).

In contrast to the United States, the government in Great Britain was originally unwilling to make broad grants of discretionary power to its magistrates when it established juvenile courts. In trying children and youths for crimes, British courts were constrained to follow procedures similar to those used in adult courts. It was only after a finding of guilt that discretion entered by provision that the court could then consider the welfare of the child. Since the 1960s legislation in England, Wales, and Scotland has moved in a direction opposite to that in the United States and toward more rather than less discretionary handling of juvenile offenders under the aegis of generic social work, children's panels, and police cautionary schemes (Lemert, 1976: 66).

In the case of Italy it is difficult to designate a consistent trend in the changes that have taken place in its juvenile justice system. That which is most conspicuous in its history is the delay in establishing the juvenile court long after the recognition of its need, plus an equally long period required to implement the original legislation. Italy (along with Switzerland) was among the last of the Western European nations to set up a juvenile court and thereafter needed nearly forty years to completely differentiate and fully staff its operations (Baviera, 1976: chap. 16). But even with this the court in most aspects achieved only the form but not the substance of juvenile justice. While the same can be said about juvenile courts in other countries, in Italy the explanation for such a development lies in a much more profound and articulated sensitivity to the inconsistencies and ambiguities of law and in the religio-familistic values that influence its expression and administration. I will try to show that from the time of its inception the Italian juvenile court has been a spurious[1] development, or a precariously institutionalized form of justice likely to disappear or be replaced by other types of social control. This is apparent in the account of its labored history and in the depiction of its ongoing operations. In exploring this idea first historically then concurrently several factors emerge as more significant than others in producing differences between juvenile justice in Italy and that in the United States and Britain. Among these factors are doctrinal conflict, organizational stress, the power of the Catholic church, the ascendancy of the family, and the Italian ethos. I will show how these factors influenced, in varying degrees, the antecedents, the official actions, the ultimate creation, and the differentiation of the juvenile court. Likewise I will show their relative importance in vitiating the current working of the court by its denial of discretion, need to extract minors from the system, delay, and persisting institutionalization.

CONCLUSION

At the beginning of this article it was proposed that the Italian juvenile court may be a spurious or paradoxical development in which efforts were made to reconcile a form of discretionary justice with a system of law that apotheosizes legal certainty. Evidence for this idea came from sociohistorical materials emphasizing the long delay in establishing such a court and the equally long period needed to evolve an adequate organization with sufficient judicial personnel and social services.

Further testimony that the Italian juvenile court is more of a symbolic demonstration or a set of rituals than a vehicle of substantial justice is the relatively small number of minors who are actually sanctioned. While in the past the numbers who were sanctioned by incarceration was larger, the meaning of such incarceration must be sought rather than assumed. There is a real question whether in retrospect incarceration was not in essence the aggregated use or exploitation of available government and church institutional care in the interests of abandoned children and impoverished families rather than an expression of widespread punitive impulses toward minors or of a collective desire to "treat" them.

While falling short of being the product of purely symbolic legislation and law in the sense argued by Arnold (1955) and Aubert (1966), Italian juvenile justice nevertheless clearly reflects compromises between salient values of Italian culture. Formal arrest and processing of offending minors, with careful attention to the selection of lawful dispositions and careful consideration of questions of imputability and immaturity (on which there is an extensive literature), satisfy the values of legal certainty. The priority of these values is insured by the presence of a prosecutor committed to a career in the Ministry of Justice and subject to its control. The values that motivate judges within the legal constraints are less easy to fathom, but they undoubtedly express in different ways the familism that is central to Italian culture and guarded by the church. Thus Barzini has called the family the first source of power in Italian society, "the fundamental institution in the country, a spontaneous creation of the national genius . . . the real foundation on which the social order rests" (1980: 190).

The place of familism in the legal culture is attested by the fact that the Italian Constitution recognizes the family as a "natural society" (art. 29). It also recognizes the rights of individuals to pursue self-help through private organizations to assist those in need. According to di Gennaro and Bonomo (1980: 7), the law asserts that the rights of minors are to be enjoyed within the family and presumes that the family will minister to their needs. In this view the role of public officials is one of nonintervention, positive only in the sense of providing the minimal means to meet the needs of children, particularly when no adversarial issues exist between parents and child.

This is not to say that Italian judges are unaware of the necessity for public authority to assume a more positive role in protecting the rights of minors and to take jurisdictional control when no effective head of a family exists. They do recognize that the traditional authority of the *padre-padrone* peasant family has been either attenuated or has disappeared under the stresses of urbanism and industrialism. Moreover, they also recognize the rights of individuals apart from families, as, for example, the rights of women in the areas of property, divorce, and abortion (Pocar and Ronfani, 1978: 619, 623, 633). But given the limitations of available services and facilities, it is still likely to be true that juvenile court intervention works best when residual resources within the family or extended family can be used to solve the problems of minors. This was illustrated for the author by one appellate case in which the judges spent the best part of an entire morning working out a divided custody arrangement that satisfied the various relatives involved.

It must be remembered that Italy is a relatively poor country and that life there is hard, even pitiless, for most people and that the hold of detached humanitarianism and dedication to specific reformist causes is weak at best. Survivalism comes closest to describing the national ethic, which usually means contriving arrangements through interpersonal networks that advance the cause of the individual and his family and protect them against precipitous misfortunes.[2] The motivation and commitment, or lack of commitment, of juvenile court panels must be understood in the context of values that expect little from law and public institutions in the solution of everyday problems. When paternalism is exercised by judges it is likely to be in the form of routine indulgence or leniency or acquiescence with arrangements made by families and private organizations.

A final commentary on the burden of this article *in re* the anomalous nature of the Italian juvenile court can be taken from an interpretation of changes in Italian juvenile justice offered by de Leo (1983). Noting the decline in both denunciations and the number of minors jailed or imprisoned from 1970 to 1979, he asserts that this, along with other signs, indicates a decline in the criminalization of the behavior of minors due to a basic change in the social conception of delinquency as justification for their social control. By this he means that the creation of the juvenile court extended social control over children and youth by defining or redefining problems of their schooling, supervision, parental discipline, poverty, and comportment that come under their jurisdiction. He attributes this change in conceptions to the salient problems of terrorism and drug dependence, which have modified patterns of social control. De Leo further notes that adolescence in Italy is now prolonged to the age of twenty-eight or even thirty, with more instability found in the eighteen to twenty-eight age group than among those from fourteen to eighteen years old.

De Leo finds that juvenile justice in Italy has lost both its credibility and its legitimation and that the social prestige of juvenile court judges has diminished markedly, with the result that fewer judges seek the role as a career and are migrating to other sectors of the justice system. The loss of credibility of juvenile justice owes much to the fact that its purported objective—reeducation—has produced results contrary to this goal, yet the paternalism dominant in institutions established for this purpose prevents their being redefined in punitive terms. Hence a belief has grown that they and related social services cannot produce consistent results of any kind.

The countertrends, according to de Leo, are seen in a renewed social definition and legitimation of the family, church, school, mass culture, and sport as forms of social control. Confirmation of this can be seen in the increase in numbers of members of marginal groups—in-migrants, Asians, Africans, Palestinians, and Gypsies—entering the justice system.

The data on which de Leo's statements rest are rather limited, and the ten-year trend in arrest and incarceration rates of minors may very well reverse itself. Still, his interpretation is plausible and certainly consistent with the line of thought if not the facts presented here. However, another interpretation of the anomalous nature of the Italian system of juvenile justice, not entirely at odds with the thesis of this article, is that its flaws, imperfections, and often seemingly perfunctory operation are an expression of Italian values that favor weak public agencies of social control and that are based on the distrust and alienation that Italians feel toward the institutions that govern them. Two writers have called Italians "natural Jeffersonians" from long experience preferring weak rather than strong and effective government (Spotts and Wieser, 1986). A similar view is expressed by Barzini (1980: 191), who asserts that Italians, by historically relying on the family in times of crisis, have actually promoted anarchy and fomented chaos that rendered useless the development of strong political institutions.

NOTES

The Center on Administration of Justice, University of California at Davis, and the Ford Foundation supported the research for this article. Professor Floyd Feeney, University of California at Davis, did much to make it all possible. Professor Franco Ferracuti, University of Rome, provided invaluable assistance for the author's research in Italy. Others providing valuable help were Gilda Scardaccione, Researcher, University of Rome, and Gaetano de Leo, Professor, University of Rome.

1. The term "spurious" derives in part from the older anthropological distinction between genuine and spurious cultures (Sapir, 1924: Tumin, 1945).

2. Barzini has commented on the strange absence of literature on the informal workings of Italian society, which he describes as "infinite manoeuvres and labryinthine intrigues, the conspiracies, the plots and counterplots necessary to prosper even modestly in Italian life" (1980: 229).

REFERENCES

Arnold, Thurman. *The Symbols of Government*. New Haven: Yale University Press. 1955.

Aubert, Vilhelm. "Some Social Functions of Legislation." *Acta Sociologica* 10, 1–2 (1966): 98–120.

Barzini, Luigi. *The Italians*. New York: Atheneum, 1980.

Baviera, Ignazio. *Il Diritto Minorile*. Milano: A. Giuffre Editore, 1976.

Di Gennaro, Giuseppe and Luisa Bonomo. "Italy." In *Justice and Troubled Children Around the World,* ed. V. L. Stewart. Vol. 3. New York: New York University Press, 1980.

Lemert, Edwin M. "Choice and Change in Juvenile Justice." *British Journal of Law and Society,* 3, 1 (Summer 1976):59–75.

———. *Social Action and Legal Change*. Chicago: Aldine, 1970.

de Leo, Gaetano. "Tramonto o Eclisse della Delinquenza Minorile?" *Rassegna di Criminologia* 14 (1983).

Pocar, Valerio and Paola Ronfani. "Family Law in Italy: Legislative Innovations and Social Change." *Law and Society Review* 12,4 (Summer 1978): 607–43.

Rubin, H. Ted. *Juvenile Justice: Policy, Practice, and Law*. Santa Monica, CA: Goodyear Publishing Co., 1979.

Sapir, Edward. "Culture: Genuine and Spurious." *American Journal of Sociology* 29,4 (January 1924): 401–29.

Spotts, Frederick and Theodor Wiser. *A Difficult Democracy: A Survey of Italian Politics*. Cambridge: Cambridge University Press, 1986.

Tumin, Melvin. "Culture, Genuine and Spurious: A Re-Evaluation." *American Sociological Review* 10,2 (April 1945): 199–207.

Weber, Max. *On Law and Economy and Society,* ed. Max Rheinstein. Tr. Edward E. Shils and Max Rheinstein. New York: Simon and Schuster, 1967.

Part IV

Law, Society, and Jurisprudence

Chapter 16

The Origins of American Sociological Jurisprudence

In the earliest period of American law, which we refer to here only for contrast, a young republic borne aloft by revolution adapted Enlightenment views of inalienable human rights to a set of unusual, if not unique, social and economic conditions, to say nothing of unprecedented room for geographic expansion. These conditions encouraged a "rugged individualism" that bore a theoretical resemblance to the Jeffersonian idea of a politically self-determined yeoman peasantry but that in fact bordered on anarchy. In time, as the United States changed from a nation of small farmers to one of industries and cities, individualism and the sacredness of private rights, in social life as well as in law, began to be questioned. This because individuals in their roles as workers, customers, renters, home owners, passengers on street cars and railroads, and visitors of banks and insurance companies increasingly became subject to the power of associations, organized groups, and corporations not only through which they sought to satisfy their needs but at times against which they fought to protect their deepest interests.

MECHANICAL JURISPRUDENCE: LEGAL FORMALISM

Early sociological jurisprudence is best understood by reference to the antithetical development of a legal doctrine referred to by Roscoe Pound (1906 [1963], 1908) as *mechanical jurisprudence.* Also called *legal formalism,* this doctrine can be thought of as a jurisprudence of conceptions in which law becomes increasingly authoritative, technical, deductive, amoral, and narrow in application, obedient to broad principles illustrated by precedent. From one point of view, this sort of jurisprudence may be seen as a kind of ossification or ritualization of law, but in America it appeared as a particular historical development following an earlier

Previously unpublished.

period when law was modified to encourage its use for entrepreneurial and industrial growth.

According to Horwitz (1975, 1977: 259*ff.*), the movement toward legal formalism in the United States after 1850 was facilitated by three factors: (1) the rise in power of the legal profession, with separate and autonomous interests, seeking validation of its status by representing law as a neutral, objective, apolitical system; (2) convergence of the interests between the elite of the legal profession and newly powerful mercantile groups; and (3) efforts of mercantile groups to reify legal doctrine, once it had been transformed in their own interests, into a system of fixed and inexorable rules.

Legal historians differ as to how far economic factors shaped American law. The difficulty of proving assertions such as those of Horwitz with hard evidence, the regional differences in American law, and the fact that legal conflict often existed between parties with similar class status caution against making unqualified generalizations on this question. Certainly, other than economic influences contributed to the growth of American law during the period in question. Prominent among these is the powerful influence of science.

In the second half of the nineteenth century, the rise of science includes the emergence of the social sciences but was perhaps epitomized by the spread of the theory of evolution. Science was founded on the philosophy of positivism, which sought to exclude subjective judgments from human thought in favor of rigorous reasoning from facts to general conclusions. Once reached, these conclusions, generalizations, or scientific laws became the basis for explaining new facts. This nineteenth-century science closely patterned itself on the methods of the physical sciences, which followed a mechanistic model of causation, assuming fixed relationships between causes and effects.

It was precisely this conception that inspired efforts to convert the study and application of law into a formal legal science. One notable result was the introduction of the case method into legal education by C. C. Langdell at Harvard University. Accordingly, law was to be made into an academic science by breaking it into component parts, collecting all the relevant adjudicated cases, sorting them out, classifying them and discovering their underlying principles. In this light, cases were thought of as equivalents of specimens studied by geologists. The law library furnished the laboratory where the specimens, derived from the legal literature, might be found.

FORMALIZED LAW IN APPLICATION

Appellate court decisions of the second half of the nineteenth century brought significant changes in such legal concepts as eminent domain, contract, collection of debt, bankruptcy, property law, insurance, torts, and the criminal law as well. Their net effects were to diminish or narrow the scope of public law, as, for example, in eminent domain, and to free commercial and industrial organizations from ethical and moral restraints (Horowitz 1977: 73*ff.*). The abstract form of contracts (i.e., whether there was a "meeting of minds" and whether "wills" were present when agreements were reached) took precedence over considerations of substance and consequences for the parties involved, such as whether there was a fair price or whether duress was present.

Another means for converting law into statements of abstract relationships and avoiding particularized equitable—read "fair" or "just"—inquiries into the circumstances of individual cases was through the segregation of legal issues. Thus, purchase of insurance, once a main type of contract, was first distinguished from sales contracts, then finally treated as a completely separate and autonomous area of the law, giving insurance companies an anonymity and privilege enjoyed well into recent times. In a similar fashion, equitable protections in foreclosures of mortgages—for example, rights to redeem property after foreclosure—were attenuated by redefining them as conditional sales contracts.

THE DEATH OF EQUITY

Nineteenth-century legal practice eroded and finally eliminated equity, which traditionally had been the means by which the values of fairness and justice were invoked to mitigate the harshness of formal law. The discrete changes in separate areas of law became the subject of a more comprehensive movement for codification of law in the United States. This was conceived as a major effort to achieve scientific precision in law and remove its political and moral elements. One consequence of the first American codification of law, in New York state in 1848, was to merge equity with law. Thereafter, equity lost its distinctive place in relation to law and became a matter of procedure rather than of the substance of natural justice. Prevailing thought of the time caused this to be regarded as a triumph of the scientific development of law.

LAW AND THE SOCIOLOGY OF GROUPS

It is tempting to say that as equity disappeared as a standard for the application of law, sociological jurisprudence emerged to take its place. But the issues that arose were more complex, calling for specific adaptations of the existing atomistic, subjectivist conception of law to the realities of groups and associations, which appeared with the new economic and social life of an industrializing society. In this new kind of society, when individuals combined in groups for narrowly defined, specific ends, such as labor unions, questions arose in litigation as to what these groups actually were in regard to the property they held, the contracts they negotiated, their liability and accountability, and whether their individual members or officers might be subject to criminal prosecution.

The conception of rights of individuals as natural and inalienable had, and has, a fixed, formal quality not easily squared with the growing complexity of socioeconomic problems in industrial societies. This was particularly apparent in the practice of treating associations as individuals in legal decisions. Nor was the conception of society as having absolute sovereignty with power to command individuals who are bound to obey particularly meaningful in a society in which the power of corporations at times rivaled that of the state. As Pound noted in his classic discussion of mechanical jurisprudence, quoting from an older source (Figgis 1907: 206), what was needed was recognition of "the innumerable bonds of association and the naturalness of social authority . . . as against an abstract and unreal theory of State omnipotence on the one hand, and an atomistic and artificial view of individual independence on the other" (Pound, 1908: 609).

THE FIRST REVOLT

Among the first American jurists to rebel against formal, mechanical jurisprudence was Oliver Wendell Holmes (1841–1935), known for his long career on the U.S. Supreme Court and the epigrams enlivening his writing style. Some of his most quoted ideas appeared in a paper entitled "The Path of the Law" (1897 [1992]), the published version of an address at Boston University, presumably a criticism of Langdell's logical system of scientific case law. Generally speaking, Holmes took issue with prevailing views as to the sources and consequence of law. "The life of the law," he wrote in an even more famous earlier passage, "has not been logic: it has been experience" (1881: 7) He went on later in the same passage to clarify what he meant by "experience": (1) felt necessities of the age, (2) prevalent moral and political theories, (3) intuitions of public policy and community opinion, and (4) prejudices that judges share with their fellow creatures.

The skepticism in Holmes's ideas stands out clearly in his characterization of law as a set of prophecies that if a man does or omits certain things, he will be made to suffer in this or that way by judgment of the court. A right or a duty, he claimed, cannot be considered apart from the consequences of its breach, to which certain sanctions are added afterward. Like other American philosophers, Holmes was a pragmatist who saw law as a means to various ends. Thus, the reason that law was a profession and people were willing to pay lawyers was to provide themselves with some sense of how to avoid or prepare for the possible use of public force against them through the instrumentality of the courts.

Holmes saw jurisprudence of his own time as the beginning of a philosophical reaction in which the worth of legal doctrines, descended often without question over centuries, was being reconsidered by deliberate, conscious, and systematic questioning of their grounds. He was familiar with the work of sociologists of his time and drew from the French sociologist Gabriel Tarde's *Laws of Imitation* to explain the tendency of jurists to receive a heritage of law from prior generations through unthinking imitation (1897 [1992]: 468). However, he rejected any idea that this should keep the jurist from using thought and choice to set at least part of the law in better order.

To illustrate, Holmes showed how the ancient requirement of a trespass as an essential legal element of theft was made ambiguous by historical accretions of judicial decisions and statutes, so much so that embezzlers still were able in some cases to exploit the confusion and escape prosecution altogether. Holmes accepted sociological ideas in the same tentative, pragmatic way he accepted or rejected legal rules. Thus, he wrote:

> What have we better than a blind guess to show that the criminal law in its present form does more good than harm? I do not stop to refer to the effect which it has had in degrading prisoners and in plunging them further into crime. I have in mind more far reaching questions. . . . [A] modern school of continental criminalists . . . suggested that we must consider the criminal rather than the crime. The formula does not carry us very far. . . . [I]f the typical criminal is a degenerate, bound to swindle or to murder by deep-seated organic necessity . . . it is idle to talk of deterring him by the classical method of imprisonment. He must be got rid of. . . . [I]f on the other hand crime, like normal human conduct, is mainly a matter of imitation, punishment may fairly be expected to keep it out of fashion. (1897 [1992]: 470)

Holmes's skepticism gave rise to questions that foreshadowed legal realism, some of which are viable today. He doubted whether, in effect, any real distinction could be maintained between civil and criminal law or, more particularly, among a personal injury, failure to keep a contract, and certain misdemeanors. In all instances, the net effect may be that the wrongdoer must pay out money, in the form of either fines or damages.

Roscoe Pound

While Holmes recognized factors outside the law that influenced judicial and legislative actions, his views of jurisprudence were never formulated systematically. It remained for Roscoe Pound (1870–1964) to introduce a number of ideas that became the core of sociological jurisprudence, chief among them his conception of law as a form of social control. This came from his acceptance of the functional proposition that law or rules are means to ends, rather than ends in themselves. The overall end of law for Pound was to order activities so as to enable them to satisfy as much of the "whole scheme of demands" as possible with the least friction and waste. The term Pound used to refer to the demands and claims people make on one another was "interests," and he insisted that the legal order was concerned with interests, not rights; rights were merely one way law seeks to secure interests.

The reconciliation of the authority of the state or social control and interests of the individual lay in a process Pound called "social engineering." This was one of balancing various interests that he classified as individual, public, and social, corresponding to persons, associations, and society. Social engineering involved discovering the principle for determining interests and selecting the means by which the law can secure them, taking into account the limits on effective legal action. It was this last conception he outlined in a speech to the American Bar Association (1906 [1963]), which first attracted the attention of the legal world to his talents. The limits of effective legal action more or less inhered in the nature of social control by rules, as indicated in the following: (1) the difficulty of ascertaining facts and applying them to rules, as in the case of a claim of "mental suffering"; (2) the intangibility of moral duties, such as "obedience" and "care" for children's health and welfare, issues that here can only be addressed by administrative means; (3) the subtlety of modes of infringement of important interests and rights, such as alienation of affection and intrusions of privacy; (4) the inapplicability of legal machinery of rules and remedy to many phases of human conduct, especially in the area of sex and marital behavior (the law can work only through punishment, specific redress, and preventive orders); and, finally, (5) the law is reactive—it depends on an individual complaint to set it in motion.

Given these limits, Pound proceeded to trace the evolution of law from a primitive state in which morals and law were not differentiated and law was relatively unimportant as a means of social control to its modern status. He later identified periods of history in which law varied from a narrow and fixed form, relying on a few rigid rules—the *jus strictum* of early Roman times—to a broadened conception in which there were attempts to convert moral obligation into legal duty, such as honoring one's father. The nineteenth-century legal system for Pound represented a period of mature law, directed to achieving equality and certainty, emphasizing legal reasoning from rules, property, and contract. The turn of the century in which Pound wrote saw a reaction to nineteenth-century law in which the neglect of the moral worth of the individual and his claim to a complete social and moral life was leading to a revolution marked by the incursion of social science into the law.

The influence of sociology on Pound's ideas is not easy to assess. A good deal has been made of the effects of his personal association with Edward Alsworth Ross while at the University of Nebraska, but it may be that Ross influenced him much more than the other way around (Geis 1964). He was familiar with the works of other American social scientists, such as Lester Frank Ward, who was also Ross's uncle by marriage, and Albion Small, from whom he is said to have taken his ideas about the role of interests in the law (Geis 1964: 274). However, Pound actually derived this idea from the nineteenth-century German jurist Rudolph von Jhering (1924: 408*ff.*). There is as much and perhaps more evidence that his ideas came from the writings of German and French jurists, whom he read extensively, as from American writers (Geis 1964: 281, n. 54).

Pound lived during the period when evolutionary progressivism was an American political movement, and his writing reflects a conviction that social evolution could be affected by law in the direction of progress, which he saw as the change from culture to civilization. This he defined as "the social development of human powers towards their highest possible unfolding" (1923: 143). In all of this, Pound spoke for a kind of sociological positivism, although, as already pointed out, he vigorously rejected positivism as it developed in law. In actuality, Pound's jurisprudence was more psychological than sociological, for it rested on the concept of interests: individual interests and interests imputed to a reified society. He drew from a psychological tradition, which pitted the individual against society, while at the same time searching for methods to synthesize the two, and cherished the idea of the discovery of individual interests that furthered social interests.

Benjamin Cardozo

Further indication of the strong psychological bent in early sociological jurisprudence can be found in the writings of Benjamin Cardozo (1870–1938), which contain numerous references to the social scientists of his time. Cardozo followed Pound in the shift from an analytical to a functional attitude toward law. As he himself put it, "The rule that functions well produces a title deed to recognition" (1960: 103). This essentially pragmatic view was born out by Cardozo's willingness to consider "logic, history, custom, utility and standards of right conduct" as forces shaping the law, but with the proviso that deciding which of these govern a juristic decision must depend on the value of social interests that will be promoted or impaired (110*ff.*).

Imputing the existence of social interests necessarily required a conception of society or community, and here Cardozo (1960: 110) sought for some objective measure of its presence but admitted the available concepts were shadowy ones. Hence, he, like Pound, was compelled to rely on a psychological method (i.e., study and reflection on experience to solve a problem). Cardozo (1928: 88) tried to explain groups by saying that they re-create individuals, that under certain circumstances their wills are transformed by the will of others. This he called "the social mind," a "tissue of operative psychological forces which in their higher development crystallize into unity within unity" (89). Cardozo in the manner of Pound drew a hard line between individual and society, between the "social" and the "antisocial," and assumed the legal task of reconciling the two through producing a combination of atomistic individuals, a "union of disunions" or a "harmony of disharmonies" (8). This conception was consistent with the interests of sociologists in social processes that, on one hand, brought the individual into association with others and, on the other, produced dissociation, conflict, or noninteraction.

Neither Holmes, nor Pound, nor Cardozo, while serving as spokesmen for the reaction against the unquestioning acceptance of rules in law and reliance on logic for their application, was radical in outlook. In a sense, psychological sociology merely enlightened their views or added another dimension to their pragmatic juristic methods. This is clear in Pound's identification of certain areas of the law where strict application of rules was valid: "In matters of property and commercial law, where the economic forms of the social interest in general security—security of acquisitions and security of transaction—are controlling, mechanical application of fixed, detailed rules or rigid deductions from fixed conceptions is a wise engineering procedure" (1923: 154). Thus, for Pound, one promissory note was like any other.

THE SECOND REVOLT: THE RISE OF LEGAL REALISM

A more radical school of sociological jurisprudence, that of the legal realists, emerged a little before 1920 and came into sharp prominence about 1930. It got its start among scholars at the Yale Law School, which held to text-and-lecture teaching of law in contrast to the scientifically orthodox case method Langdell instituted at Harvard. Generally, those who were classed as realists believed that early sociological jurisprudence did not go far enough in its revolt against analytically derived law, and they refused to exempt any areas of the law from bold and searching criticism. Rather than beginning with prior rules and testing their relevance to legal problems according to social and other criteria, the realists challenged assumptions made about the existence of rules and their influence on judicial decisions. They looked elsewhere for grounds of legal decisions and considered how the psychological process of rationalization affected the invocation of rules. The skepticism of the realists covered fact finding, rule finding, and opinion giving, and so strong was their sense of mission that some advocated abandoning or replacing current legal terminology altogether because it was too ambiguous and imprecise to describe problems of law in twentieth-century America. Realists had no easy generalizations to take the place of the jurisprudence they questioned as outmoded; rather, they tried by adopting a special perspective and method to discover the patterns of behavior, which underlay the law in action.

Jerome Frank

While the first realist ideas appeared in scattered law journals, they got ushered forcefully before the legal world in 1930 with the publication of *Law and the Modern Mind* by Jerome Frank (1889–1957). This book unmistakably helped set the form and tone of the new school of jurisprudence. It more or less accused people involved with the law of perpetuating a basic myth of certainty and consistency. The myth was portrayed as a paradox in which popular denigration of lawyers as liars, pettifoggers, practitioners of duplicity, evasion, and systematic deception of clients was coupled with the great respect laypersons had for the law itself. The accepted explanation of the paradox was that the law is clear and definitive but that lawyers and court officials unnecessarily complicate it.

The reality, said Frank, is that legal rules never can be comprehensive, universal, and eternal because everything changes, in the course of which new problems continually arise having no precedents. This constant flux in the state of society requires a legal system with fluidity and pliancy, and thus the very uncertainty of the law is a measure of its social value. Lawyers, said Frank, conceal these facts because they must satisfy clients who pay them to win cases. They explain failures by claiming the case would have been won if all the facts had been brought out or that where the facts were clear the law had become "unsettled" due to a bad statute.

Judges, too, contribute to the illusion of a certain, objectively discoverable law by their air of finality conveyed with their decisions as well as their writing style and courtroom manner. In actuality, or so Frank believed, the judge dispensed a form of *khadi* justice, in which his decisions were conditioned by hunches, intuition, prejudice, irascibility, and various other emotional and unpredictable factors. (For a background discussion and definition of *khadi* justice, see Weber 1958: 219, 221.) The guise of certainty given to such decisions was no more than a concession to the need for a father image felt by those dealing with the law. Here Frank turned to Freudian psychology to account for the judge's behavior. A similar Freudian theme colored his contention that the modern mind (i.e., a mature mind) will recognize the uncertainty of law and the fact that every judicial decision results from a unique combination of elements.

Later, after he became a federal appellate judge, Frank took a more conservative view of rules and precedents, which he conceded had their value. However, he continued to believe that the central problem in law was ascertainment of facts, and he sought diligently to find ways of improving the quality of justice at this level. While he believed that the idiosyncrasies of judges played havoc with systems of rules, nevertheless, as a solution for the problem, he favored maximum discretion for trial judges.

Putting Frank in the school of sociological jurisprudence may be a misnomer, especially since he explicitly dissociated himself from the school in its radical form (1951: 574*ff*.). Yet his analysis of the basic myth was sound sociology, or at least good social psychology, and certainly he was an informed social ethnographer of the lower courts. His insistence on maintaining maximum discretion for judges on the surface was inconsistent with his criticism of judges as unpredictable or motivated by hidden impulses. However, this is understandable from his belief that the solution for problems of the lower courts was cultivation of the mature mind that could accept and deal with law as it is.

Karl Llewellyn

Karl Llewellyn (1893–1962) can best claim eminence as one who gave depth as well as breadth to realistic sociological jurisprudence. He was marked by Yale, where he was both an undergraduate and later a law student under certain teachers whose approach to the law showed the influence of earlier legal realists.

Llewellyn's initial works were in German, but in 1929 he delivered a series of lectures for law students that were later published as a stirring book, *The Bramble Bush,* followed in 1930 by a casebook on the law of sales. These established him, along with Jerome Frank, as an outstanding critic of traditional jurisprudence and with passing time a central figure in the realist movement. Llewellyn's work defies exact characterization, for he labored variously as a craftsman to adapt law to economic realities, sought to appreciate its aesthetic qualities, and tried to clarify theoretical aspects of the relation of law to society.

Like Pound, Llewellyn took the law in action as his starting point, but unlike Pound, he treated the influence of rules as problematic, in the area of economic transactions no less than in other areas. Llewellyn was unsatisfied with Pound's large generalizations about law, the broad categories prevailing in formal jurisprudence, and sociological notions such as Max Weber's ideal types. He insisted on narrowing the scope of study of traditional legal terms and putting them in an extralegal sociohistorical context whenever possible. This approach is illustrated in his distinction between the primitive model of a sale in the present and a sale as a contract for future delivery, a difference between selling materials in the face-to-face situations of local markets where buyers and sellers were known to one another and purchase at a distance of materials yet to be fabricated and transported through intermediaries. A whole new set of legal issues came to light as the latter kind of transaction became more common: there is a shift to buyer protection, warranties, the right to inspect goods, transference of title, and various conditions affecting the time and place of payment.

A unique contribution of Llewellyn was the idea of "type situations," not the Weberian ideal types but rather those of limited empirically identifiable recurrent situations, especially applicable to business and commerce. Somewhat more sweeping was his notion of judicial styles in appellate decisions culled from numerous cases and explicated in *The Common Law Tradition* (1960). From his research, Llewellyn proposed two theoretical models: the grand style and the formal style, which he contended provided a basis for foretelling judicial decisions, then largely thought by the legal world to have become unpredictable. Among the predictors were the legal rule, principles, diagnosis of the legal problem, the court's conception of its role, sources of justification, including "situation sense," interpretive techniques, and aesthetic desires for "functional beauty" in legal reasoning.

Llewellyn's early unqualified skepticism about the influence of rules and precedents in law became more moderate and particularized over time. While obviously regarding rules as no more than means to ends, he allowed that there was a broad range of possibilities in their actual use: officials might pay no heed to rules at all, they might partially heed them but construe them all out of recognition, they might pay lip service to rules then do something else, and, finally, officials might listen carefully and act accordingly. In the formal style of adjudicating, rules were the premises for legal reasoning; in contrast, the grand style was open to the influence of principles, policy, situation sense, wisdom, justice, and social research findings as well as "authoritative sources" (statutes and cases).

Llewellyn's Sociology

Llewellyn had been a student of William Graham Sumner at Yale and presumably was conversant with the latter's strong conviction that social reform must await the creation of a science of society. In any case, Llewellyn argued strongly for a working separation of law as it is from law as it ought to be, a distinction whose grasp is essential to understanding Llewellyn's work as a whole. Thus, the "as is" of law in society was primarily the descriptive sociology of legal institutions. These he chose to call "law government," organized to carry out "law jobs." Law jobs called for the meeting of needs, necessary for a human group to survive and fulfill its purposes. These have to do with adjustment of "trouble cases," adaptation to changing needs, allocation of authority, and achievement of a juristic method.

One of Llewellyn's more important and novel contributions to ethnographic research in law, shared with E. Adamson Hoebel, was the use of "trouble cases," or points of conflict, as sources of data, a method happily chosen to study the law ways of the Cheyenne Indians. This departed from the conventional field method of anthropological interrogation of selected informants as a way of reconstructing prior social organization of "memory cultures" of nonliterate societies. But it was consistent with Llewellyn's focus on law in action, for the research began with recollection of trouble in particular instances and then proceeded to inferences from what was done to individuals and groups to solve the difficulties. This method, which appeared first in the jointly authored *Cheyenne Way* (1941), subsequently became standard in the anthropology of law.

While Llewellyn stressed the study of the "as is" of law, he was not opposed to critical evaluation of law in terms of ideals. However, he rejected any notion of ultimate values or universal ethical principles as criteria for this purpose and insisted that any such analysis be grounded in the context of a particular society. In effect, therefore, he was a strong ethical relativist.

Llewellyn's separation of is and ought in law seems to place him with the positivists, but he recognized the importance of teleology and choice in lawmaking, as well as "instinctive" functional responses of human beings to their situations or positions in society. Llewellyn's outlook shows an equally cautious or qualified attitude toward legal science, which he accepted as one of the behavioral sciences, arguing that the study of behavior was at the center of all systematic legal scholarship, just as it was in economics, psychology, and sociology. However, it was to him fruitless to expect any high degree of precision in any aspect of the study of human behavior, legal or otherwise. Expectation of emulating the natural sciences in law involved risks and problems: setting impossibly high standards, falling victim to the snobbery of scientism, studying trivial topics because they are susceptible to quantification, and attempting to quantify material not amenable to such methods, producing much research of extremely dubious utility and value.

REFERENCES

Cardozo, Benjamin. *The Nature of the Judicial Process*. New Haven, Conn.: Yale University Press, 1960.

———. *Paradoxes of Legal Science*. New York: Columbia University Press, 1928.

Figgis, John Neville. *Studies in Political Thought from Gerson to Grotius*. Cambridge: Cambridge University Press, 1907.

Frank, Jerome. *Law and the Modern Mind*. New York: Brentano's, 1930.

———. "'Short of Sickness and Death': A Study of Moral Responsibility in Legal Criticism." *New York University Law Review* 26, no. 4 (October 1951): 545–633.

Geis, Gilbert. "Sociology and Sociological Jurisprudence: Admixture of Lore and Law." *Kentucky Law Journal* 52, no. 2 (Winter 1964): 267–93.

Holmes, Oliver Wendell. *The Common Law*. Boston: Little, Brown, 1881.

———. "The Path of the Law." *Harvard Law Review* 10, no. 8 (March 25, 1897): 457–78. Reprinted in *The Essential Holmes: Selections from the Letters, Speeches, Judicial Opinions, and Other Writings of Oliver Wendell Holmes, Jr.*, ed. Richard A. Posner. Chicago: University of Chicago Press, 1992.

Horwitz, Morton. *The Transformation of American Law, 1780–1860*. Cambridge, Mass.: Harvard University Press, 1977.

———. "The Rise of Legal Formalism." *American Journal of Legal History* 19 (October 1975): 251–64.

Llewellyn, Karl. *The Bramble Bush*. New York: Columbia School of Law, 1929.

———. *Cases and Materials on the Law of Sales*. Chicago: Callaghan, 1930.

———. *The Common Law Tradition: Deciding Appeals*. Boston: Little, Brown, 1960.

Llewellyn, Karl, and E. Adamson Hoebel. *The Cheyenne Way: Conflict and Case Law in Primitive Jurisprudence*. Norman: University of Oklahoma Press, 1941.

Pound, Roscoe. "Causes of the Popular Dissatisfaction with the Administration of Justice." *Speech to the American Bar Association*. Chicago: American Judicature Society, 1906 [1963].

———. *Interpretations of Legal History*. New York: Macmillan, 1923.

———. "Mechanical Jurisprudence." *Columbia Law Review* 8 (1908): 605–23.

Von Jhering, Rudolph. *Law as a Means to an End*. Eng. trans. Issac Husik. New York: Macmillan, 1924.

Weber, Max. *From Max Weber: Essays in Sociology*. Ed. and trans. H. H. Gerth and C. Wright Mills. New York: Oxford University Press, 1958.

Chapter 17

The Changing Foundations of Sociological Jurisprudence

The temptation was strong to entitle this essay "The School That Never Was: Sociological Jurisprudence," largely because close scrutiny from the perspective of present-day sociology makes it doubtful that sociological jurisprudence ever incorporated more than a few very general ideas that merit designation as sociological. This school of jurisprudence in origin appears to have been largely an in-house, intramural development to which sociologists made no more than incidental or casual contributions. One can even say that the school—in America, at least—more or less sprang full blown from the brow of Roscoe Pound, barely admitting some sideline assistance from the esteemed Benjamin Cardozo and deferential allusions to the epigrams of Oliver Wendell Holmes.

The compendious writings of Pound, embracing a vast erudition from many sources and spanning half again a normal human lifetime, make specification of direct influence from sociology on his work a difficult task. To the difficulty must be added a pronounced change in his views during the latter part of his life, a period during which the legal realists preempted much of the field of jurisprudence. Evidence of ties between sociology and jurisprudence in their early days is thin indeed, resting on scattered footnotes, a few acknowledgments, in some cases hearsay in letters, and inferences from Pound's social encounters. Small wonder that Geis (1964) subtitled his discussion of sociological jurisprudence "An Admixture of Lore and Law" or that Selznick (1959: 116) referred to the early merger of law and sociology as a quick and easy victory without much substance.

But granting the foregoing, nonetheless a school of jurisprudence widely known as sociological did exist and may be said to persist or perhaps subsist today. What in fact it was and has become may be said to be problematic, reflecting the growth and promulgation of ideas whose foundations have changed substantially with time. Here I will examine these changes with a view to mitigating the considerable

---

Previously unpublished.

estrangement of the disciplines of law and sociology, whose union has been apotheosized as a way to rescue the former from its plight as a dismal science.

THE PAPER BRIDGE: JURISPRUDENCE AND SOCIOLOGY, OLD AND NEW

It is of more than casual interest that, with the exception of Selznick, no American sociologist has written about jurisprudence. Consequently, sociological jurisprudence has taken its meaning either from European writers schooled in the continental tradition of law or from American jurists and law school faculty. If Bodenheimer (1962: 116) is correct in saying that the most radical expression of sociological jurisprudence was legal realism, then it may be justifiable to call it a preeminently American product, a point emphasized by the absence of its development in the British Isles.

Sociological jurisprudence on close examination in any case betrays only the most tenuous of formal ties with American sociology, these to be found primarily in Pound's writings. Under close scrutiny they appear as allusions to writings of social science contemporaries such as Lester Frank Ward, Charles Ellwood, William McDougall, E. C. Hayes, and E. A. Ross rather than any substantial borrowing from them or any systematic building on their ideas. One of Pound's (1942) major contributions to sociological jurisprudence, *Social Control through Law,* contains only incidental references to Auguste Comte and Emile Durkheim and none to others.

In contrast, Pound's (1911a, 1911b, 1912) most comprehensive statement, "The Scope and Purpose of Sociological Jurisprudence," contains a number of references to American sociologists, primarily Lester Frank Ward and Albion Small. But generally these men are cited to support Pound's criticisms of individualistic, mechanical, and formal jurisprudence. Although Pound and Ross were on the same campus, the University of Nebraska, from 1903 to 1906, Pound took little heed of his work, which culminated in an influential book on social control (Ross 1922 [1901]). Despite his plea for the unity of law and social science and some reservations, Pound's (1912: 509) real conviction about sociology surfaces in his one comment on Ross: "Such a book as Professor Ross' *Social Psychology* (1908) *written by a lawyer* [emphasis added] would be worth many volumes of the conventional analytical and historical jurisprudence."

It is likewise true that although Pound drew quotations from Small's writings—even using the latter's definition of culture in one passage (1912: 493)—when he constructed his theory of interests, he completely ignored Small's own theory of interests, drawn from many of the same German sources. It is probably correct to say that Pound invoked a limited number of statements from the writings of American sociologists mainly to validate or authenticate core ideas that he derived from sources in European jurisprudence—for example, Rudolph von Jhering, Rudolph Stammler, Josef Kohler, Eugen Erlich, and Leon Dugiut. The preferred interpretation of the antecedents of the main thrust of Pound's thought is that they lie in the pragmatism of William James, a psychologist and philosopher. On the other hand, it seems clear that Ward's concepts also strongly influenced his thinking. The most important of these was "social telesis": "We must study and thus come to know the efficient social forces . . . not to know beforehand . . . their inexorable working . . . but to be able to apply them consciously to social ends" (Pound 1912: 506–7). The other influence traceable to Ward was more of a perspective that insisted that the "true causes" of all social phenomena are psychic forces. This view definitely identifies Pound's outlook with psychology or, if preferred, the social psychology of his day; this point he makes quite explicit:

> While juristic thought was developing a psychological tendency from within, a psychological movement was going on without, which was presently to develop this tendency still further and to give it a new direction. . . . Not only does social psychology occupy a chief place in recent sociological jurisprudence, but modes of juristic thought, the world view of judges and doctrinal writers and the psychology of juristic methods are coming to be the subjects of special study. (1912: 509; see also Pound 1921: 30)

In retrospect, it is eminently clear that Pound's "sociological" jurisprudence in reality was a psychological one, although the play of social influences was nevertheless centripetally oriented toward the individual. Of course, one may argue that this was the cast of sociology during the efflorescence of Pound's thought and that he scarcely could be expected to rise above its limitations even if he were so moved. This point cannot be denied, especially if we take as representative Small's (1905) definition that sociology is "a science of human interests and their workings under all conditions" (cited in Pound 1912: 491).

Granted that Pound's early seminal ideas turned jurisprudence in new directions, nevertheless he did little more than adumbrate a sociological jurisprudence. No one saw this more clearly or stated it more trenchantly than Karl Llewellyn (1962: 7–8, n. 3):

> Sociological jurisprudence remains bare of most that is significant in sociology. "Law in action" is left as a suggestion, while further discussion of the law centers on precept. The limits of effective legal action—a formulation that fairly shrieks for study of the habit and control set-up of society (that complex, industrialized, urban, indirect cooperation society he has given us words for) is left without study of the society to which law is supposed to have relation. . . .
>
> What would one not give for the actual appearance of the long-awaited Sociological Jurisprudence, if its author would integrate it in terms of those pioneering thoughts of his which thus far have been waiting to be called together in a Constituent Assembly.

But if Llewellyn faulted Pound for not drawing on significant sociology, close scrutiny leaves the work of the former vulnerable to a like criticism. He never revealed in any detail what he deemed to be significant sociology, and he rejected the sociology of his day as unsuited to his purposes; its concepts, he charged, were too vague to be of great use (Llewellyn 1962: 365). Others linked with Llewellyn as legal realists took much the same arrogating view of sociology. Thurman Arnold (1935: 8, 88, 106) saw sociology as a spurious field that emerged or was created to give expression to humanitarian ideas not readily accommodated in economics and law. Jerome Frank (1949: 147) spoke of "so-called sociological jurisprudence" and insisted that in reality it was psychology, specifically the psychology of judges, its advocates were talking about—and not very good psychology at that. This sociological jurisprudence was, in any case, "too frock-coated, too preoccupied with judicial statesmanship in the so-called 'higher courts' " (149*ff.*).

While Frank was described as an omnivorous, wide-ranging reader (due to insomnia, it is said), evidence that he had absorbed much extant sociology is scant. Only three sociologists' names can be found in the index of *Courts on Trial:* W. F. Ogburn, William Graham Sumner, and Dorothy Swain Thomas. The first two are cited in an adversely critical light, the latter to demonstrate the fallacy of using social statistics to establish social laws. To Frank (1949: 210), the efforts of sociologists to create a social science, as well as of his fellow realists to build a legal science, were pretentious and dubious enterprises:

> The subject matter of . . . social studies permits so little exactitude that a science of society seems never likely to be invented. Certainly none is on the horizon. . . .The basic trouble is that all the so-called social sciences are but phases of anthropology. Their attempted generalizations relate to the customs and group beliefs (the mores, the folkways), matters which, especially in a changing modern society, are not readily predictable, because of the numerous elusive and accidental factors, including the fortuitous effects of forceful ("earthquake") personalities.

Frank pushed farther than any of the realist school toward an atomistic, personalistic psychology of law, giving prominence to unconscious motivations in assessments of credibility of witnesses and facts by judges and juries in trial courts. The affinities of his work with sociology are barely discernible, perhaps no more than an insistence that studies of law be turned to "where the action is," to the trial courts rather than to the more formalized arena of appeals. However, in a perverse way, by attacking mysticism, myth, and magic in law, he was addressing questions of how legal control is validated in secular society and the relation of monopoly of information and skills as the basis of power by a particular occupational group.

FUNCTIONALISM

The common theme that permits conjoining the otherwise disparate ideas of legal realists, whether "first revolt" or "second revolt" vintage, and their alignment with older but by no means extinct sociology is functionalism. (On the two revolts, see chapter 16, "The Origins of American Sociological Jurisprudence.") This theme conceives law as means to ends, functionally necessary for the satisfaction of individual needs and the preservation or maintenance of society itself. The functional theme of the realists had Hobbesian overtones, most clearly put by Frank (1949: 7), who held that the primary function of the courts was to "prevent brawls which might cause social disruption." Llewellyn (1962: 357), with his poetic workaday style, referred to the fundamental job of law and government as producing and manufacturing the "groupness of a group" or the existence of society. Specifically, this meant cleaning up trouble, which otherwise in some groups is "dealt with by tommyguns and tear gas" (1962: 359). Arnold stresses the unintended function of law, which contributes to social stability primarily by its palliative effects. He writes that "the function of law is not so much to guide society, as to comfort it. . . . [I]t operates to induce acceptance of things as they are . . . by creating a realm somewhere within the mystical haze beyond the courts where all our dreams of justice in an unjust world come true" (1935: 34*ff.*). Pound had perhaps the broadest conception of the function of law as a means of social control and cohesion to be achieved through balancing competing interests, guided by ideals.

Pound's functionalism at first blush seems to coincide with the inclusive, architectonic formulations of sociologists and anthropologists seeking to show how a social institution contributes to the operation and survival of a whole social system. But in his view of the limits of effective legal action, Pound (1916) had a built-in constraint against overgeneralization. However, he never developed these or most of his other ideas beyond their original statement, perhaps because he never tried to test them against a delimitable body of data. Moreover, although Pound lived and wrote well into the epoch of functional analysis in sociology and anthropology, he never borrowed from it and remained pretty much the grand synthesizer of law as a reflection of turn-of-the-century progressivism.

In contrast, Llewellyn at least appeared to be familiar with system builders in sociology and rejected them in favor of conceptual systems on a less ambitious scale. He and his fellow realists were content with smaller game; indeed, Llewellyn questioned whether anything like "society" existed (see, e.g., 1962: 3–41), which, while sacrilegious to present sociology, was nevertheless a fair question in his day. Translated into current terminology, the legal realists sought to nurture a middle-range sociological jurisprudence, neither a grand system nor mere empirical description.

INSTITUTIONAL ANALYSIS

The legal realists, in turning away from the large purposes of achieving social progress through the instrumentality of the law, invoked the sociological concept of institution as their unit of analysis. As Llewellyn (1962: 355) notes in trying to preserve some continuity with Pound's thought, "[A]nybody can suspect that the 'legal order' is meant to include . . . such going enterprises as courts, legislatures, law publishers, and police. All you have to do is borrow a concept from sociology: institution, and make explicit therein the relevant going practices and relevant specialists and relevant physical equipment and the manner of organization of the whole."

By focusing on the institution, legal realists more or less marched in step with sociologists of their era, who by 1930 had rejected evolution and the concomitant faith in progressive social change. The nineteenth-century battle over ascendancy of the corporation and the city in American society had been fought and more or less won; the period of consolidation was at hand, and the motion of the necessity of conflict in evolutionism could only be discomfiting or threatening. As W. F. Cottrell (1972: 4) well describes the shift, "Evolution was relegated into the background while less dangerous ideas, largely involving static models, became popular. . . . Adaptation became the mode; each little segment was treated as a world in itself, developing local equilibrium through countervailing power."

So it was with the empirical studies of the realists, dealing mostly with interrelationships between law and economics or government and business (see Llewellyn's extensive bibliography in 1962: 74–76), with some marginal interest in the control of crime. Perhaps the best exemplar is Llewellyn's (1925: 677) lucid summary of the effects of legal institutions on economics, which he characterizes as "guaranteeing the presuppositions of the economic order" and "affording machinery for working out of competition and the flow of capital" through an "untold host of legal adaptations." While he allows for reverse effects of economics on law, Llewellyn patently regarded law as among the conservative institutions in society: "In law, on the other hand, the focus of study is not change but regulation, not flux but constancy" (1962: 88). In another context, Frank (1949 [1930]: 108) echoes this sentiment: "Law's precise office is not change, but to prevent change; or when that will not do, then to adjust with the least possible rearrangement to the new conditions."

The preference for institutional analysis found among the legal realists may indicate its special utility in contrasting the old with the new in settings in which the new is taken as given and means sought to reformulate or shape the old. Thus, Walton H. Hamilton (1932: 87), whom Llewellyn (1962: 366) cites approvingly in one of his discussions of institutions, asserts that institutional symbols arise from the stress and strain of change:

> As long as it [institution] remains vital, men accommodate their actions to its detailed arrangements with little bother about its inherent nature or purpose. As it begins to give way or is seriously challenged, compelling arguments for its existence are set forth. The picture as it is painted is likely to be rather a work of art than a representation of fact . . . institutional development drives a fault line between current fact and prevailing opinion.

THE CHANGED PSYCHOLOGICAL BASE OF SOCIAL JURISPRUDENCE

While the latter-day realists gave little allegiance to grand purposes of social control through law and narrowed their perspective from society to institutional components, they also sought standing ground on a new kind of psychology. Whereas Pound saw the "psychological movement" as posing a problem of how given individual interests were transmitted or combined with social interests to achieve progress, realists of the so-called second revolt were concerned with explaining how or why individuals, government officials, or judges failed or succeeded in adapting laggard institutions of the law to twentieth-century economic realities, above all in specific empirical contexts.

Both groups of realists converged in their refusal to accept at face value the reasons given for judicial determinations and perhaps in acceptance of the ubiquitous occurrence of rationalization (Llewellyn) over and against logic, reason, or deduction. Beyond this, their theories diverged widely, ranging from psychoanalysis through behaviorism, Gestalt psychology, and group psychology, to a kind of culture-personality analysis, seeking to account for mental action in terms of behavior, inhibitions, personal impulses, emotive urges, hunches, impact of facts, or institutional compulsion (Kennedy, 1938, 1939). While Llewellyn (1962: 16–18) was willing to retain Pound's concept of interests, he nevertheless insisted that it be given objective referents in behavior and be restated as groupings of behavior to make interests compatible with his concept of institution.

The change in psychological emphasis in jurisprudence emerging in the 1920s had its analogue in sociology, as critics there took issue with the turn-of-the-century social psychology of Edward Alsworth Ross (Bodenhafer 1921; Karpf 1932): "Ross . . . for all practical purposes . . . assumes the self as given, the individual as already given. His problem is then the rather futile one of attempting to mould and shape the complete individual into social conformity, to bend the individual will into some sort of social order" (Bodenhafer 1921: 442).

In his mellow years, Ross (1977 [1936]: 114) himself summarized without malice the eclipse of his own views: "What has come to be called 'social psychology' in this country now deals with the psyche, not so much groups or collectivities as of individuals developing in social settings and interacting constantly with others. . . . I am content. I lift my hat to Dewey, Mead, Cooley, Veblen, and Thomas."

But it is difficult to discover much direct influence running from the newer social psychology acquiring recognition in sociology to realistic jurisprudence during its epoch of dominance. This is conspicuously true with respect to Mead's social behaviorism and Cooley's organicism, from which symbolic interactionism ultimately grew. This took strong hold among University of Chicago sociologists, giving rise to a school of thought at least as destructive of realism in jurisprudence, which persists even today in a generation of so-called neo-Chicagoans. Yet one looks in vain for evidence of the diffusion of its ideas across the evanescent bridge between law and sociology; such concepts as "self," "other," "role," "socialization," and the idea that meanings assigned to experience are derived from social interaction nowhere graced the law journal literature, nor do they yet in any great degree.

Basically, then, the psychology of the legal realists remained a psychology of institutions, seeking to show either how individuals affected institutions or how variously formulated aspects of institutions affected individuals. These encompassed such concepts as "practices" (Llewellyn 1962: 12), folklore and myth (Arnold 1935), "behavior sequences" (Moore and Sussman 1932), and "type situations" allegedly invoked by judges (Radin 1930). In all cases, the realists searched for the significant determiners of judicial behavior behind, under, beyond, or below the manifest or apparent rules of law. (Radin's little-noted idea that judges base decisions on a store of type situations acquired from prior experience anticipated in general by several decades a frequently cited ethnomethodological conception in modern sociology, namely that of "normal crimes" [Sudnow 1965].)

Probably the term *instrumentalism* more aptly captures the form and content of the psychology of legal realism. It was far more functionalist psychology than functionalist sociology, perhaps best represented by John Dewey's conception of mind as an instrument of adaptation to a changing environment, brought to awareness by conflict and shaped by learn-by-doing projects (Llewellyn 1962: 284–85, 508–9). Insofar as the psychology of the realists sought to generalize from behavior alone, it led into the trap of solipsism from which Mead tried to rescue Watsonian behaviorism; and insofar as it tried to explicate the complexities of law in terms of psychic states, it was reductionistic.

REFERENCES

Arnold, Thurman. *The Symbols of Government*. New Haven, Conn.: Yale University Press, 1935.

Bodenhafer, Walter B. "Comparative Role of the Group Concept in Ward's Dynamic Sociology and Contemporary American Sociology: The Group Concept as Used by Some Contemporary Sociologists." *American Journal of Sociology* 26, no. 4 (January 1921): 425–74.

Bodenheimer, Edgar. *Jurisprudence: The Philosophy and Method of the Law*. Cambridge, Mass.: Harvard University Press, 1962.

Cottrell, William F. *Technology, Man, and Progress*. Columbus, Ohio: Bobbs-Merrill, 1972.

Frank, Jerome. *Courts on Trial: Myth and Reality in American Justice*. Princeton, N.J.: Princeton University Press, 1949.

———. *Law and the Modern Mind*. New York: Coward-McCann, 1949 [1930].

Geis, Gilbert. "Sociology and Sociological Jurisprudence: Admixture of Lore and Law." *Kentucky Law Journal* 52, no. 2 (Winter 1964): 267–93.

Hamilton, Walton H. "Institution." *Encyclopaedia of the Social Sciences,* ed. Alvin H. Johnson. New York: Macmillan, 1932.

Karpf, Fay B. *American Social Psychology: Origins, Development, and European Background.* New York: McGraw-Hill, 1932.

Kennedy, Walter B. "Realism, What Next?" *Fordham Law Review* 7, no. 2 (May 1938): 203–15.

———. "Realism, What Next? II" *Fordham Law Review* 8, no. 1 (January 1939): 45–78.

Llewellyn, Karl. "The Effect of Legal Institutions upon Economics." *American Economic Review* 15, no. 4 (December 1925): 665–83.

———. *Jurisprudence: Realism in Theory and Practice*. Chicago: University of Chicago, Press, 1962.

Moore, Underhill C., and Gilbert Sussman. "The Current Account and Setoffs between a Bank and Its Customer." *Yale Law Journal* 41 (June 1932): 1109–33.

Pound, Roscoe. "Limits of Effective Legal Action." *Twenty-Second Annual Report of the Pennsylvania Bar Association* (1916): 221–39.

———. "Scope and Purpose of Sociological Jurisprudence: Schools of Jurists and Methods of Jurisprudence." *Harvard Law Review* 24, no. 8 (June 1911a): 591–619.

———. "Scope and Purpose of Sociological Jurisprudence: Social Utilitarians, Neo-Kantians, and Neo-Hegelians." *Harvard Law Review* 25, no. 2 (December 1911b): 140–68.

———. "Scope and Purpose of Sociological Jurisprudence: Sociological Jurisprudence." *Harvard Law Review* 25, no. 6 (April 1912): 489–516.

———. *Social Control through Law*. New Haven, Conn.: Yale University Press, 1942.

———. *A Theory of Social Interests*. Chicago: University of Chicago Press, 1921.

Radin, Max. "Statutory Interpretation." *Harvard Law Review* 43 (1930): 863–85.

Ross, Edward Alsworth. *Seventy Years of It: An Autobiography*. New York: Arno, 1977 [1936].

———. *Social Control: A Survey of the Foundations of Order*. New York: Macmillan, 1922 [1901].

———. *Social Psychology: An Outline and a Source Book*. New York: Macmillan, 1908.

Selznick, Philip. "The Sociology of Law." In *Sociology Today: Problems and Prospects,* ed. Robert K. Merton et al. New York: Basic Books, 1959.

Small, Albion W. *General Sociology: An Exposition of the Main Development of Sociological Theory from Spencer to Ratzenhofer*. Chicago: University of Chicago Press, 1905.

Sudnow, David. "Normal Crimes: Sociological Features of the Penal Code in a Public Defender Office." *Social Problems* 12, no. 3 (Winter 1965): 255–76.

Chapter 18

Jurisprudence, Law, and Sociology

The systematic study of law by sociologists and its establishment as a specialty is a comparatively recent development, and as a field, it is not as clearly defined as some might desire. Moreover, it would be pretentious to claim the existence of an agreed-on body of knowledge exclusively meriting the term *sociology of law*. Such a claim is complicated by the fact that political scientists, psychologists, and anthropologists, as well as philosophers, also study law. Yet the influence of sociological ideas and perspectives on thinking and research on law has been unmistakably present, and it is the purpose of this essay to examine and critically evaluate this influence.

One way to begin this exploration is with a backward, historical look at the body of writings called jurisprudence, with a view to seeing how sociological jurisprudence emerged. *Jurisprudence* is likely to be a strange and intimidating term on first acquaintance, but with a little factoring it can be rendered into simple dictionary meanings of *juris-*, or "law," plus *prudence*, or, more expansively, "wisdom shown in the exercise of reason, forethought and self-control." But however verbally simplified, this is still a difficult combination to grasp. In general usage—that is, by those who write and teach about the topic—*jurisprudence* has meant "philosophy or science of law." Other more specialized meanings have identified it variously with the "comparative form of developed or codified systems of law" or the "course of decisions in the courts" (in contrast to *legislation* or *legal doctrine*). In still more specialized usage, it may refer to decisions in special classes of cases, such as "equity jurisprudence," "medical jurisprudence," "dental jurisprudence," and "engineering jurisprudence."

But to make *jurisprudence* one with different kinds of law makes the term redundant and misses much of the meaning it has acquired from the thought of those who have written about the subject. It is something more than law or even the underlying principles of law; it is the larger ideational context of law, considered as either the philosophy of law or the science of law, keeping in mind that law

---

Previously unpublished.

cannot be a science in the sense of validated generalizations found in chemistry, physics, or biology. However, there is an accumulation of knowledge about law consisting of different perspectives, underlying assumptions, and methods for criticism and research, which justifiably can be called jurisprudence.

The earlier stated intention to begin with a historical view of jurisprudence indicates that an identifiable continuity can be found in its development in that new ideas about law have built on or from the old. Many of the formulations of jurisprudence have arisen as reactions to traditional or established ways of thinking about law found unacceptable or inapplicable to newly emerging social and cultural conditions in particular societies. Thus, in a very general sense, the growth of jurisprudence has been dialectical in that one set of legal ideas has in time generated another set tending to oppose or contradict the first. This tendency was conspicuous in the early speculations of Greek philosophers about natural law; thus, Plato attacked the ideas of the Sophists on the subject, only to have his ideas criticized in turn by Aristotle. Later the analytical jurists reacted against natural law philosophy, which was then heavily weighted with the theology of medieval Christianity. Finally, sociological jurisprudence came to the fore initially in protest against the formal analytical jurisprudence of nineteenth-century America.

SCHOOLS OF JURISPRUDENCE

Discussions of jurisprudence often organize their subject matter into "schools," implying that there are or have been groups of scholars in close proximity and interaction with one another and committed to one fairly homogeneous system of ideas about law, usually dominated by one or two outstanding thinkers. Something like this did exist in Greece and in European universities but much less so in America. Any designation of a school of thought about law or indeed any area is of necessity an arbitrary procedure and often tends to slight or ignore the differences among writers who have been grouped as members of a particular school. This usually comes from some person's interpretation of what dominant theme or underlying assumptions figure in their writings.

Lon Fuller (1960) some years ago employed a clever hypothetical exercise he called "The Case of the Speluncean Explorers" to personify different kinds of jurisprudence. These were inferable from the decisions of judges in a mythical Supreme Court of Newgarth in the year 4300. The "facts of the case" were given by the chief justice with a Dickensian name, C. J. Truepenny, and are summarized here.

A party of five cave explorers was entombed in a cavern by a landslide whose proportions were so great and of such a nature that the likelihood of their rescue before they starved to death was slim. The difficulties in the rescue effort were emphasized by the death of ten workmen at the rescue site. After twenty days of excavating, communication with the entrapped men was established by a two-way radio they happened to have with them. Conversations followed in regard to how long they could live without food and whether consuming the flesh of one of the trapped men would keep them alive long enough to be rescued. A physician at the site confirmed this proposal, but when inquiries came over the radio as to see who should be eaten, no person in authority was willing to advise the trapped men. At a subsequent trial following the killing and eating of one of their party, the four survivors of the ordeal were found guilty of murder as charged. But both the judge and the trial jury recommended executive clemency in the case, with commutation of the sentence of death by hanging to six months' imprisonment. On appeal to the Supreme Court, Chief Justice Truepenny concurred with the lower court recommendation on grounds that although the statute covering the case was clear and permitted no exception, nevertheless it was an extraordinary case. The "tragic situation in which the men found themselves" (62) was sufficient reason for mitigating the penalty.

Associate Justice Foster was deeply shocked at the "sordid expedient" urged by the chief justice, which risked denial of fundamental justice by leaving the ultimate decision to a "whim of the executive" (62). His reasons for proposing a finding of innocence were put as follows:

> I take the view that the enacted law or positive law of this Commonwealth, including all of its statutes and precedents, is inapplicable to this case, and that the case is governed instead by what the ancient writers in Europe and America called the "law of nature.". . . When a situation arises in which the coexistence of men becomes impossible, the conditions that underlie our precedents and statutes has ceased to exist . . . and the force of our positive law disappears. (63)

Judge Foster concluded that the men were both morally and geographically removed from the legal order of civil society and in a state of nature justifying action on principles appropriate to their situation, hence innocent. To strengthen his views, he further stated that even if the statute applied, the defendants were simply exercising their right to self-defense.

A third judge, Tatting, upheld the established law and its principles and denied the self-defense analogy. However, "beset by equivocation on all sides," he decided to withdraw from the case, a move without precedent (70–71).

Justice Keen favored a complete pardon for the defendants but in its absence felt compelled to adhere to the statute and recognize the doctrine of legislative supremacy. For these reasons, he stated that the convictions must be affirmed (76).

A final judge, Handy, saw the problem as one of practical wisdom and human realities. Laws should be seen as means to ends or instruments to be adapted flexibly to the interests of the citizenry. He stated that the defendants already had been punished enough, and polls showed that public opinion was on their side; furthermore, the likelihood of executive clemency was remote. Therefore, this judge concluded that the men were innocent and that the sentence should be set aside (81).

Since the court was evenly divided and since Judge Tatting refused to reconsider his withdrawal, the decision of the lower court was affirmed. The defendants were executed.

"The Case of the Speluncean Explorers" speaks of several things: the respective powers and responsibilities of the three branches of government—executive, legislative, and judicial; the influence of feelings on judicial decisions; the range of differences in the way judges view law; and the extent to which facts outside the law are or should be considered. For purposes here, the case is valuable to cast light on the premises, philosophies, or assumptions that give law or legal decisions a larger ideological meaning. The sharp contrast and interplay of appellate opinions in the case serve to dramatize several kinds of jurisprudence, among them analytical jurisprudence, natural law, and legal realism.

These do not, however, exhaust the full scope of thought and writing making up the field of jurisprudence, to which at the very least would have to be added the historical and cultural schools, utilitarianism, and, of course, sociological jurisprudence. Coverage of the vast literature dealing with the various schools of jurisprudence, an accumulation of centuries, is not possible. Consequently, their themes and tenets at most can be summarized in barest outline here, particularly since my purpose is to trace the forerunners and emergence of sociological jurisprudence.

NATURAL LAW

The assertion by Judge Foster that the Speluncean explorers could not be held accountable to human-enacted law because they were in a state of nature has ancient antecedents, first coming to light in the speculations of classical Greek philosophers (Barker 1951). These appeared in the fifth century B.C. among the Sophists, who led an intellectual revolt against the religion-dominated societies of their day, especially attacking beliefs in the divine source of law (Bodenheimer 1962: 5*ff.*). For the Sophists, "man is the measure of all things," and laws are artificial rules for social living, reflecting human arbitrariness and changing with time and circumstances. As human creations, laws may run contrary to nature, whose demands are rigorous and exacting. Man may disobey the laws he makes and suffer no penalties, but not so for violators of the laws of nature. One intrusive law of nature is that of inequality, which rests on the innate superiority of the strong over the weak. Much human lawmaking, according to the Sophists, was an attempt by the weak to reverse this tendency and to make men equal. That which in our language has come to mean sophistry (sophistication) played a part in this by using rhetoric to convert weak arguments into strong ones. Needless to say, relativism and skepticism figured considerably in the natural law ideas of the Sophists.

Socrates is said to have regarded the thinking of the Sophists as perverse and dangerous to the welfare of society (Bodenheimer 1962: 6*ff.*). He and his pupil Plato turned speculation about law toward the conditions for the achievement of justice. Plato (429–348 B.C.) accepted the generic or natural inequality that existed among people and proposed an ideal society, highly stratified, in which each and all were placed according to their capacities and abilities, described in some detail in his *Republic*. The most exceptional men—“philosopher kings”—were designated to be rulers, and judges were designated with wide discretion to settle disputes. Plato’s utopian vision counseled a rule of the wise rather than rule by law (Pound 1951).

Aristotle (384–322 B.C.) represented an opposing point of view that a good and just society was possible only under the rule of law. He conceded that if a man possessed outstanding virtues and political wisdom, he should be the permanent ruler, but his role should be that of a lawgiver who contributes to the body of laws guiding the course of the state.

For Aristotle, the state and law were inherent in the necessities of nature, and although men made the laws, there was an element of natural law in this positive law that was derived from the nature of man, who is a social animal. From this came his distinction between contingent law and natural law. Finally, Aristotle apparently was first to speak of the necessity of equity in law, a type of remedial procedure that permits the modification of generalized rules to attain a just outcome under unusual circumstances (Bodenheimer 1962: 11*ff.*).

THE STOIC LAW OF NATURE

The Stoic philosophers (340–265 B.C.) deserve attention not only because of their place in Greek thinking but also because of their influence on the later natural law of the Romans and the Christian Church. Stoic ideas were all-embracing, placing humans in a universe of nature that included plants and animals and that was the embodiment of a divine mind. Reason was the expression of this force in the individual and was the source of all law and justice. Stoics believed in a cosmopolitan world in which all were citizens, without cultural barriers between peoples, such as the line Greeks drew between themselves and barbarians (from a Greek word meaning babblers, people who couldn’t speak Greek). But the Stoics were scarcely democratic revolutionaries inasmuch as they accepted that people, though equal according to natural logic (*logos*), could in fact be unequal. The inner source of this passivity lay in the identification of failure to control the passions with evil.

JURISPRUDENCE OF THE ROMANS: “THESE BORN JURISTS”

The Romans were first to articulate and promulgate a system of law not only in Rome but throughout the Near East and much of Europe. While there had been statutes, codes, and constitutions in societies before those of Rome, its rulers and intellectual class clearly differentiated law as a distinct institution with specialized officials and detailed procedures. They described, classified, and analyzed their laws, ultimately compiling them into a comprehensive code under the emperor Justinian (529 A.D.).

Law for the Romans was the art of the just and the good, intended as a system of rules for the guidance of human conduct or, more precisely, for men of honor. These were discovered in nature through the use of reason based on experience. In early centuries, a simple distinction was drawn between *jus natural* and *jus civile,* the latter being laws derived to regulate the status and relationships of Roman citizens. With the growth of the empire and the incorporation into it of a great number of conquered peoples differing in race, language, and culture, a third class of law was recognized: *jus gentium,* which served to resolve conflicts between noncitizens and between them and the Romans. There was also a kind of equity called *jus honorarium* (Bodenheimer 1962: 15–17).

The earliest Roman law evolved out of official sanction or support given by magistrates to the self-help actions (remedies) of aggrieved parties. Over the course of six hundred years, a body of law accumulated based on such customs, plus statutes, plebiscites, advice from the Senate, imperial constitutional provisions, edicts of magistrates, and lawyers' opinions. The most creative contributions to law came from lawyers, who were known as jurisconsultants or *jurisprudentes,* who generally were nobles educated in the law and licensed to send sealed opinions to the magistrates. These were binding on the latter's decisions unless some disagreement existed among the jurists themselves.

Roman law reflected rulers' concern with problems of the administration and organization of a far-reaching empire, and it had a strong pragmatic cast. At the same time, it came to be influenced by Stoic philosophy. This was prominent in the writings of Cicero (104–43 B.C.), who conceived law to rest on a universalistic, timeless sense of justice found in all men, educed and refined by the powers of reason. The Stoic ideas of the equality of all men coupled with their repudiation of force or political action to redress social inequality may have had a special utility for the thinking of the Roman ruling classes. Diffusion of the humanitarianism of Stoic thought is said to have improved the status of slaves with passing time, raised the status of women and children, and, by the third century A.D., led to the granting of citizenship to provincial subjects of Rome (Bodenheimer 1962: 17*ff.*, 19; Watson 1966).

Apart from larger philosophical ideas and administrative necessities that produced a three-way jurisdictional partition in Roman law, we have little firm knowledge about social and cultural values that may have affected it. However, there is no doubt that a conception of civil honor held central importance in the lives of Romans and was reflected in their private and public law, including the punishment for crimes. Gradations of status and honor set Romans apart, ranging from the highly placed senators down to plebeians and slaves. Discrimination in the administration of justice was explicit, taking shape in differing access to privileges as well as differential punishments for the commission of crimes. Dishonorable acts and crimes could degrade those involved to the status of infamy (*infamia*). (For a distinction between two types of infamy, *infamia juris* and *infamia facti,* which do not concern us further here, see *Black's Law Dictionary* 1979.) Among other things, pursuing a dishonorable profession, engaging in trade, or having a criminal record barred one from membership in orders such as that of the Decurions and also from public offices and denied the person the right of testifying in legal proceedings.

CHRISTIANITY AND NATURAL LAW

Natural law was further proliferated and given new form in the writings of Catholic theologians beginning with the thirteenth century, a century that saw the translation and revival of Aristotle's philosophical works. Church writers of the era, like the Roman jurists, extolled reason as the necessary means for discovering natural law, but they believed that the source of such law lay in a person's innate moral sense rather than in experience: it was located in the heart but recognized by the head. For the theologians of this period, there was also a higher natural law that ruled the divine cosmos and was an expression of God's will. This was revealed through the Scriptures as interpreted by the hierarchy of the church, particularly by the pope, whose spiritual descent from Peter, founder of the church, presumably clothed his pronouncements with infallibility.

There are similarities between the story of Adam and Eve and Stoic philosophy, both of which conceived of a pristine state of goodness in which humans lived. The subsequent appearance of evil in the world and the necessity of its control were reasons for the acceptance by the church of secular law. However, should the dictates of positive law come into conflict with divine law then, Christians could ignore the former.

SECULAR NATURAL LAW

A significant change in the conception of natural law took place in the seventeenth and eighteenth centuries, by which time the political power of the Catholic Church and the intellectual influence of religion had declined in Western Europe and Britain. This period saw the rise of rationalism and "pure reason" in law plus the glorification of the "rights of man." Among the first to formulate the new worldly natural law were Hugo Grotius (1583–1645) and Thomas Hobbes (1588–1679), followed by John Locke (1632–1704) and Jean-Jacques Rousseau (1712–1778). Best known are the so-called social contract theories of Hobbes, Locke, and Rousseau that postulated a pristine, rational act of contractual agreement among isolated individuals (or families) as the basis for establishing the first political societies, law, and social control (Strauss 1953).

All of these writers were concerned with the problem of legitimacy and limits of sovereign power of newly emerging nation-states, but they differed sharply in their conclusions. Hobbes believed that individuals renounced their natural rights in return for government-insured order, while Locke, who was much admired by American revolutionary thinkers, insisted that people retained their natural rights to "life, liberty, and the pursuit of happiness" even though they delegated to others the power to rule them. This allowed for civil resistance to unjust laws. Rousseau went farthest of all in insisting that no act of government was valid unless it expressed the complete will (*la volonté générale*) of all. Needless to say, there was and is a strong theme of individualism in American and French beliefs about the natural rights of man, amounting to what some regard as philosophical anarchism. This has been reflected in the continuing struggles in the two nations over the nature of political authority.

While natural law of the eighteenth century became an ideological rationale for revolution, by the nineteenth century it was being cited to justify the economics and politics of emerging capitalistic society that sought to narrow the scope of government and expand freedom for individual enterprise. A kind of self-regulating society was envisioned, brought into being by individuals' economic motives and the freedom to compete with one another. Just as there was an "economic man," so there was a "litigious man" theoretically motivated to resort to law when his natural rights were encroached, with the aggregate result that rights as well as the forces of economic production were kept in an automatic equilibrium.

NATURAL LAW IN SOCIOLOGICAL PERSPECTIVE

Those familiar with sociology may well wonder whether natural law is not the antithesis of sociological jurisprudence, which emphasizes the importance of variable and contingent sociocultural factors at work in the emergence and administration of law. Closer scrutiny of natural law reveals that it, too, has been variable, having appeared throughout history as an ideal basis for criticizing, accepting, or rejecting positive law. Since the social conditions giving rise to criticism of existing law have varied greatly in different epochs, so, too, has the substance of natural law speculations. Thus, the Sophists held that humans are unequal in nature, whereas the Stoics believed that all humans are equal in the scheme of the universe. Greek, Roman, and early Christian natural law condoned slavery, but not so the secular natural law of the eighteenth century.

On balance, the philosophies of natural law raise two sociological issues: (1) whether universal ethical principles or values exist that condition or limit the variation in cultures and law and (2) whether there are functional prerequisites of social organization and law. The universality of ethical principles is a complex question. The study of preliterate societies by anthropologists has led them to answer the question affirmatively; all such societies, for example, prohibit and punish incest within the immediate family; frown on sexual promiscuity; and recognize marriage, the compulsory care of children, personal property, and stratification. Theft is also widely recognized as a crime, along with murder and psychic aggression such as sorcery.

However, as Linton (1952: 659) says, ethical similarities among world cultures are primarily conceptual in nature, and variation is rampant as to details of the behaviors, persons involved, and the situations to which they apply. This leaves a considerable unanswered question as to whether processes of social control are affected by abstract values as opposed to the effect of specific values in immediate situations. Selznick (1968: 50; 1969: 11, 24), a sociologist seemingly sympathetic to a modern version of natural law, states that the prior existence of a legal order implies that it should serve social needs and aspirations and must not deprive individuals of what is essential to their dignity and status.

While some may agree with this position, disagreement is likely to come with any attempt to specify what legal procedures are consistent with human dignity and whether they are found by logical analysis of empirical research into social facts. Whether, for instance, court procedures that deny rights of nonincrimination, jury trial, and confrontation of witnesses allow criminal suspects more or less dignity is not easy to decide. Both the Soviet and American constitutions guarantee citizens certain "rights," but the substance of the respective rights has little or nothing in common.

Another difficulty with the question discussed here is that while universal values may exist, this says nothing about the order in which they are recognized and aggregated in the application of law or how conflicts between them are resolved. Justice may be a universal value, but it always exists in relation to other values, often in opposition to it. Abraham Lincoln was a wise and just man, but during his presidency, he clearly placed preservation of the union above freedom for slaves. Likewise, he was willing to suspend the right of habeas corpus in dealing with the problem of political opposition to his war policies.

A final difficulty with assuming the existence of universal values implied by natural law is that all societies tend to restrict the application of their ethical principles to members of the in-group. Those belonging to the out-group—foreigners, strangers, slaves, and enemies—do not enjoy equal protection of the in-group ethics and law. This is most apparent among primitive peoples but is also found among modern societies, especially during periods of revolution. Thus, few procedural guarantees were given to those who were tried and guillotined during the French Revolution of the followers of the rights-of-man philosophy. The treatment of Tories during the American Revolution was equally arbitrary and cruel.

FUNCTIONAL NECESSITY AND LAW

From another sociological viewpoint, natural law can be considered as inferences or deductions about the functional necessities for the working of society and its very survival. The idea that some form of sovereignty and law itself are required to live in human groups and society is one such inference coming from the secular natural law of the social contract theorists. But the only valid test of this idea of the indispensability of law in general or specific forms of law is whether people can get along without them, and history has not yet provided a sufficient test for this kind of theory.

Fuller (1968), an exponent of modern natural law, rejects the existence of universal "higher-law axioms" or an external unchanging code of nature. In its place, he proposes that there is a kind of procedural natural law that he incorporates under six propositions about rules: they should be known to all, be nonretroactive, be clear, have the possibility of compliance, be stable, and be faithfully executed. Fuller (1968: 6–8) in essence articulates what he regards as prerequisites of a "good" legal system, a departure from which represents "pathology of law." Yet however much one may be committed to the idea of rule by law, one still must ask whether societies not observing such legal rules will fail to survive and be less just, less productive, or less considerate of public welfare than those societies that do.

At least two of Fuller's requirements for ideal law—the possibility of compliance and faithful execution of law—are in reality substantive rather than procedural qualities. Hence, compliance with law most often depends on the choices and will of its subjects rather than on their physical ability to do so. Child support and alimony laws meet most of Fuller's requirements, but many men do not comply with them for a variety of reasons understandable only in terms of their values, evaluations of situations confronting them, and interactions with other people. In the same vein, the faithful execution of laws must no less reflect particular values and choices of those administering them and consideration by them of what effect satisfying one value has on others. In the last analysis, procedures or rules simply represent someone's values that are subject to ordering among other values. There will be circumstances in all societies in which faithful execution of laws will do more harm than good, which indicates the weakness, if not fallacy, of treating any form of law as an abstract good.

UTILITARIANISM

Utilitarianism is best understood as a movement for the reform of law and courts that was most influential in England in the early and middle parts of the nineteenth century. The intellectual progenitor of the movement, Jeremy Bentham (1748–1832), was a precocious youth who entered Oxford University at age twelve and studied law at Lincoln's Inn while still in his teens. However, he was repelled by what he saw of the law in practice and chose a writing career, beginning with an uncompromising item-by-item attack on William Blackstone's *Commentaries on the Laws of England* (Bentham 1776; Monro 1967: 281). Bentham sought to discredit the natural law philosophy of Blackstone but more so the impression Blackstone created of the common law of England as monolithic and consistent. He directed pointed criticisms at the confusions, contradictions, equivocations, and illogicalities as well as erroneous citations he found in the great man's work.

Bentham explicitly repudiated many prevailing legal ideas as intuitionism—a belief in intuitively apprehended absolute principles of law, one unhappy effect of which was the legislating of imaginary crimes and stigmatizing actions that offend no one. He had little respect for such concepts as "common reason" and legal fictions that were widely accepted as intrinsic elements of law. Common reason, for example, on close examination usually turned out to be the reason of a particular judge. Bentham believed that judge-made law confused rather than clarified the law, and he wanted legislators to recognize that there are no absolute principles of law and that legal obligations rest on the single aim of increasing happiness and reducing suffering.

The rejection of a search for absolute law and seeing it as a means to an overarching end, plus Bentham's insistence on taking the consequences of acts as the criteria for formulating laws, gave a sociological color to his thought. He was no empirical social scientist, however, but rather an armchair analyst who tried to explain human reactions to law in terms of hedonism. Laws for him could be tested beforehand by a moral arithmetic he devised in which the relative amounts of pain and pleasure anticipated from conforming to or violating law determined what course of action individuals would follow. Bentham used this conception extensively to criticize and propose reforms of the criminal law; he gave finely detailed attention to the fit between punishments and crimes on the assumption that given the right balance and dramatic qualities of punishment, reason would deter those contemplating illicit pleasures.

The utilitarian movement and Bentham's ideas, some stemming from those of Beccaria and other eighteenth-century writers (Postema 1986: 307), are associated with the classical school of penology. Those identified with this movement and school sought to mitigate the severity and arbitrary nature of punishments that prevailed in prerevolutionary Europe and in England, where in the eighteenth century, for example, the number of capital crimes had risen to several hundred. One result of this was that criminal law often was unenforceable and crime flourished. The civil courts of England were equally in need of reform due to exorbitant costs of litigation and interminable delays, a state of affairs dramatized by Dickens in his novel *Bleak House* (see also Holdsworth 1928; Neely 1938).

Solutions to these difficulties for the utilitarian appeared to lie in centralizing the source of lawmaking and systematizing the law in written form. The supremacy of Parliament ultimately made such reforms possible in England, and the discretion of judges was diminished in many continental countries when they became career officials in ministries of justice subject to administrative control. Systematization of law was sought by means of codification, which had antecedents in Roman law but which acquired its modern meaning from the forces and ideology of the French Revolution. The Napoleonic Code and the codes of other European countries showed considerable influence of Bentham's ideas and the utilitarian movement.

HISTORICAL AND CULTURAL JURISPRUDENCE

While codification may have been well suited to the social and legal needs of France and other societies, it never caught hold in England or the United States and met with formidable resistance in Germany. There, an anti-Napoleonic counterjurisprudence emerged with contentions that law generates spontaneously from the traditions and the "silent inner life of the people" (Bodenheimer 1962: 71). Closely associated was a belief that codification creates rather than solves problems of clarifying law. The most articulate spokesman (1975 [1831]) for this school of thought was Friedrich Karl von Savigny (1779–1862), who stated that "law will be found since an early age to have acquired a fixed character peculiar to the people, like their manners, language and constitution. . . . [L]aw is a spontaneous emanation from the life and spirit (*Volksgeist*) of the people" (Cohen and Cohen 1951: 387).

In opposing codification, Savigny insisted that it was ill adapted to the German language and that the uneven development of law in the different states in Germany made it premature. Distrusting codifiers, he assigned a limited role to jurists and legal scholars, calling them no more than "trustees of the people" and "representatives of the spirit of the community" (Cohen and Cohen 1951: 388).

Cultural or historical jurisprudence in many ways was rooted in a sociopolitical reaction to the excesses of the French Revolution, whose forces were consolidated by defensive alliances of the post-Napoleonic period. Savigny's views were no less than those that might be expected from a conservative nobleman of his time who was disdainful of the rationalistic egalitarianism of the French. An intriguing paradox is that while nationalism encouraged codification in France, it discouraged its development in Germany—perhaps because there nationalism was more romantic and mystical.

EVOLUTIONARY JURISPRUDENCE

An English variant of nineteenth-century conservative jurisprudence came to the fore in the work of Sir Henry Maine (1822–1888), which put the history of legal growth into a framework of evolutionary theory. This postulated the gradual, unilinear development of law through a series of identifiable stages, progressive in nature. Maine denied the existence of primitive anarchy and said that the social contract theorists, while familiar with their own societies, merely guessed at the state of existence in archaic societies. He believed that the state evolved out of families (*gens*), first passing through a tribal stage. General stages of law included royal judgments, custom as expounded by aristocracies of a small class of lawgivers, then codified customs. Finally came law in modern progressive societies, which reformulated older law by means of equity, legal fictions, and legislation. Like Savigny, Maine distrusted codification.

Maine's (1963 [1861]: 100) most frequently cited contribution was his conception of the evolution of sociolegal relationships from status to contract—that is, from an early stage of societies when privileges and responsibilities were ascribed by age, sex, and kinship to a modern stage in which they were more or less created by voluntary agreements or by contract. This was illustrated with historical materials showing the shift from fixed inheritance from father to son down to modern testamentary inheritance. Another sequence of development indicated by Maine was that from torts (private wrongs) to that of crimes defined and punished by the state (218).

Historical and evolutionary jurisprudence had little influence on Anglo-American law, and Pound (1951: 25–26) regarded it as a jurisprudence of conceptions. Llewellyn and Hoebel (1941: 52*ff.*) faulted it for a failure to distinguish between law and other forms of social control. Another difficulty with this jurisprudence is that terms like "spirit of the people" are mystical and lack referents needed for empirical research. The theory of unilinear evolution of human societies and their movement through identifiable stages in different cultures has been abandoned by social scientists, except possibly in the most generalized sense. Nor do they any longer accept the idea of progressive development held by nineteenth-century evolutionary anthropology.

Nevertheless, historical and evolutionary jurisprudence was a large move toward sociology, for it located law in the culture, language, and traditions of people. While law obviously is more than an indigenous growth, questions about legitimacy, the popular uses of law, and its limitations as a form of social control all gain understanding from the study of its historical background and its cultural context. Despite Pound's (1916) objections, one of his most significant articles dealing with the limits of effective legal action was no less than a contribution to historical jurisprudence, as was much of his other writing.

POSITIVISM AND LAW

Positivism is a philosophical view of the world, a method for its study, and a rationale for its control. The term used in this larger sense is attributed to Auguste Comte (1798–1857), sometimes credited with being the father of sociology. Like other thinkers of this time, he was taken with the idea of unilinear change, especially as it applied to the evolution of thought. This process, he believed, passed through several stages: the first characterized by the belief in the operation of supernatural causes, which corresponded roughly with the period from the Middle Ages up to the time of St. Thomas Aquinas (1226–1274). The second stage of human thought Comte called metaphysical, during which thinkers searched for ultimate principles or causes behind phenomena, covering the time from the Renaissance up to 1850. Positivism emerged at this time and was thought prevailing in the contemporary age of science. In precise terms, it starts with the assumption that the only valid knowledge is that derived from sense-observable data, and it is concerned with effective rather than with final causes. Positivists reject a priori any questions about the divine influence in law because there is no way to test its empirical existence and because it cannot be dealt with as an effective or proximate cause.

A more modern type of positivism, known as logical positivism, was formulated after 1920 by German and American philosophers. This field of thought rejects most prior philosophy, and its followers endeavor to restrict its scope to that of the clarification of ideas, statements, and propositions through the use of symbolic logic, a form of reasoning falling between language and mathematics. Logical positivists disdain ethical statements as being no more than expressions of feeling and emotions without cognitive significance. They also reject values as tools for analysis because they believe that they cannot be demonstrated empirically and because they add nothing to the explanation of human actions. As will be shown later, this question cannot be dismissed in such an arbitrary fashion.

ANALYTICAL POSITIVISM

In a narrower sense, analytical positivism is applied to the work of legal scholars who emphasize the use of logical analysis to discover, classify, and systematize law. In the process, law is sharply separated from morality. Law is seen as it is rather than as it ought to be and is looked upon as autonomous and internally self-consistent. The source of law for this school is sovereign authority.

The writer most closely associated with the formulation of analytical jurisprudence is John Austin (1790–1858), who was a professor at University College in London, founded by Jeremy Bentham to further the utilitarian movement. He was the first thinker in England to deal with the fundamental ideas and forms implicit in mature (closed) systems of law. He is said to have applied Germanic logic to study intensively both Roman law and the common law. Austin adopted Hobbes's definition of law as the sovereign's command conceived in general terms (e.g., "Thieves shall be hanged"). From this assumption, he reasoned that if there was a command, then it was the duty of subjects to obey—an obligation objectively reinforced by the evil (sanctions) coming to those who refuse.

Although Austin adhered to Bentham's principle of utility, more generally he sought to extricate law from older ideas of natural law that confused the dictates of conscience, personal morality, and customary practices with the legal imperatives of the state.

While the legislature tends to be the sovereign source of lawmaking for the analytical positivists, Austin had some difficulty reconciling this view with unmistakable evidence of lawmaking by judges in common law countries. He tried to solve this problem by saying that the sovereign might implicitly delegate power to make laws to the judiciary, recognizing that the state may reverse the rules that judges make. This was probably truer in England than in the United States, where legislatures are conceived as being an autonomous branch of government on a par with the judiciary.

One of the chief partisans of analytical positivism in the United States was John C. Gray (1931: 1–5, 144*ff.*). Significantly, he viewed law as rules laid down by the courts in the course of determining legal rights and duties. For him, judges did indeed create law, thus stating a distinctive American opinion that statutes passed by legislatures do not become law until they are tried and tested in concrete cases at the hands of judges. Gray went so far as to insist on the hegemony of judges in civil law countries as well as in those of the common law world (94).

PURE LAW

As noted, Austin did not entirely emancipate his thinking from the premises of morals and ethics. It remained for a modern thinker, Hans Kelsen (1881–1973), to devise a scheme of law in which he sought to exclude all values and ideological elements; this he called the "pure theory of law." Law in this theory consists of a special class of norms or "oughts" to which sanctions are attached, in essence a coercive body of norms to regulate human behavior. This class was a hierarchical order ascending from norms of lower to higher rank: a legal ruling gets validity from a statute, and a statute from a constitution. And behind or beyond all of these lies the "grand norm" derived from the "first constitution."

Kelsen's theory represents the ultimate quest by positivists for completely autonomous law answerable only to its own inner logic. However, even Kelsen was unable to banish entirely the question of the social legitimation of law. He had to recognize the obvious fact that however accurately they were deduced, laws still might be ineffective or unenforceable; something besides the norm and its associated coercion determined its validity. Recognition of this point also compromises Kelsen's sharp separation of law as it is and law as it ought to be, since it accepts ineffectiveness as a criterion of what is law and what is not. In other words, subjects of law make judgments of what law ought to be, a fact that the analyst must take note of.

The concept of the basic norm as used by Kelsen also has raised a question as to whether his system does not rest in a natural law assumption. This is because one must ask what led people to accept the first constitution (1949: 261). There is more than an overtone of eighteenth-century social contract theory in his thinking.

A tough-minded sociologist has difficulty taking Kelsen's theory seriously and may be tempted to join with those who regard it as a myth or as an exercise in pure ratiocination. But the widespread interest in his theory is not easily dismissed. Perhaps it has to be understood as part of the same forces making for the modern revival of natural law, an intensified search for ways of validating law during an epoch of rapid social change marked by a "legitimation crisis." Some might even interpret this retreat to formalism in law as a reaction to more extreme kinds of sociological jurisprudence untempered by awareness of the limits of law as means of social control. Full appreciation of this problem, which is central to the macrocosmic study of law, will be enlightened by an in-depth examination of sociological jurisprudence itself, along with its more extreme expression in legal realism.

REFERENCES

Barker, Ernest, Sir. *Greek Political Theory: Plato and His Predecessors*. 4th ed. London: Methuen, 1951.

Bentham, Jeremy. *A Fragment on Government*. London: Payne, 1776.

Black's Law Dictionary. 5th ed. St. Paul, Minn.: West, 1979.

Bodenheimer, Edgar. *Jurisprudence: The Philosophy and Method of the Law*. Cambridge, Mass.: Harvard University Press, 1962.

Cohen, Morris, and Felix S. Cohen, eds. *Readings in Jurisprudence and Legal Philosophy*. Boston: Little, Brown, 1951.

Fuller, Lon. *Anatomy of the Law*. New York: Praeger, 1968.

———. "The Case of the Speluncean Explorers." In *Landmarks of Law: Highlights of Legal Opinion,* ed. Ray D. Henson. New York: Harper, 1960.

Gray, John C. *The Nature and Sources of the Law*. New York: Macmillan, 1931.

Holdsworth, William. *Charles Dickens as a Legal Historian*. New Haven, Conn.: Yale University Press, 1928.

Kelsen, Hans. *General Theory of Law and the State*. Cambridge, Mass.: Harvard University Press, 1949.

Linton, Ralph. "Universal Ethical Principles." In *Moral Principles of Action: Man's Ethical Imperative,* ed. Ruth N. Anshen. New York: Harper, 1952.

Llewellyn, Karl, and E. Adamson Hoebel. *The Cheyenne Way: Conflict and Case Law in Primitive Jurisprudence*. Norman: University of Oklahoma Press, 1941.

Maine, Henry Sumner, Sir. *Ancient Law: Its Connection with the Early History of Society, and Its Relation to Modern Ideas*. Boston: Beacon, 1963 [1861].

Monro, D. H. "Bentham, Jeremy." *Encyclopedia of Philosophy,* ed. Paul Edwards. New York: Macmillan, 1967.

Neely, Robert. *The Lawyers of Dickens and Their Clerks*. Boston: Christopher, 1938.

Postema, Gerald J. *Jeremy Bentham and the Common Law Tradition*. Oxford: Clarendon, 1986.

Pound, Roscoe. *Justice According to Law*. New Haven, Conn.: Yale University Press, 1951.

———. "The Limits of Effective Legal Action." *Twenty-Second Annual Report of the Pennsylvania Bar Association* (1916): 221–39.

Savigny, Friedrich Karl von. *Of the Vocation of Our Age for Legislation and Jurisprudence*. English trans. Abraham Hayward of *Vom Beruf Unserer Zeit für Gesetzgebung und Rechtswissenschaft* [1831]. New York: Arno, 1975.

Selznick, Philip. *Law, Society, and Industrial Justice*. New York: Russell Sage Foundation, 1969.

———. "Law: The Sociology of Law." *International Encyclopedia of the Social Sciences*, vol. 9, ed. David Sills. New York: Macmillan, 1968.

Strauss, Leo. *Natural Right and History*. Chicago: University of Chicago Press, 1953.

Watson, Alan. *The Law of Persons in the Later Roman Republic*. Oxford: Clarendon, 1966.

Chapter 19

Criminalization and Historical Context

Librarians concerned with indexing sources and citation research sometimes refer to the language of the social sciences as "dirty," meaning that it is ambiguous when compared with that of the natural sciences. A major instance of this is the confusion between *criminalization* as a term taken to mean the socialization of individuals into crime and the legislative/administrative process by which human actions are defined as criminal and those committing them subjected to social control. Further blurring of the term as I have phrased it here occurs in discussions of overcriminalization, decriminalization, legalization, and deregulation. These indicate something of the wide variety of perspectives from which changes in criminal law have been studied and also resulting problems in data collection and analysis (Galliher and Cross 1983: 29–30).

A further difficulty, noted by Hagan (1980: 624), is the confusion between description and explanation, which here I take to mean the description of a process and identification of the influences that enter into the process. Many, perhaps most, studies of criminalization are of the latter kind, which cite historical data consistent with a preconceived theory but omit discussion of the process of criminalization. In short, they are neither critical nor historical in the accepted sense. Hagan also notes the lack of understanding of connections between groups involved in making legislation (622).

My own perspective is not historical in a strict sense, nor is it an exercise in the formulation of theory. Rather, it proceeds by examining several of the more prominent theories of criminalization within the context of bodies of data that have been cited or can be cited to test their validity. An underlying question is whether, given the complexities and permutations of the criminalizing process, any supervening theory is at all possible. If this be so, then we are left to say how criminalization can be studied, from what viewpoint, and with what method.

Originally presented as a talk at the International Society for Law and Society, Amsterdam, the Netherlands, June 1991. Not previously published.

GENERIC ASPECTS OF CRIMINAL LAW

Partial light can be shed on criminalization by reference to ideas about its origin. Some of these are speculations that I gingerly acknowledge as sociobiological. These draw on studies of animal behavior that propose that crime is a form of territorial invasion or predation. Social control or punishment comes, at least in some species, such as chimpanzees, from the tendencies of group members to combine under the leadership of dominant animals against disruptive individuals (Gruter 1979; Gruter and Bohannon 1983).

While the very notion of sociobiology raises the hackles of many sociologists, nevertheless the idea that some sort of infracultural impulses power the criminal justice process among human beings is difficult to set aside. Thus, Oliver Wendell Holmes (1963: 35) long ago stated that no law can be complete that ignores the natural sense of justice. However, it is more current and precise to say that it is a natural sense of injustice that drives the social control of crime (Cahn 1964). Donald Black's (1983) richly documented article on crime as social control tells us that the analogue of primitive redress lurks not far below the surface of contemporary criminal justice.

A substantial anthropological research literature attests to the existence of vengeance, its collective expression, and the process of emendation, which are the essence of law in preliterate societies (Goebel 1976: 341*ff.*). But whether primitive social control features justice and fairness in the contemporary sense of these terms is doubtful. Rather, social control in primitive social settings worked to preserve harmony or social balance (Nader 1969), often at the expense of individual welfare, influenced, if not determined, by contingencies of day-to-day survival in hostile or ecologically marginal environments (see, e.g., Hoebel 1954: 67*ff.*).

Older speculative theories with a Marxian cast, such as those of Gumplowicz (1883) and Ratzenhofer (1893), posited the conquest of one group by another and their merger as a source of political organization and law (for secondary discussions, see Sorokin 1928: 480–83). But Lowie (1962: 151*ff.*), using comparative data, found only qualified support for these ideas. A dramatic exception was the emergence of coercive rules for the communal buffalo hunt, which were enforced by tribal police among American Indians of the plains.

Although anthropologists as well as historians generally have abandoned the search for cultural origins and reject old-style evolutionary theories of law, it is worth noting an older study by A. C. Hall (1902) that viewed both the emergence of crime and criminal law as benchmarks of progressive social evolution. Converting morality into law for Hall was a means of punishing rebellious social laggards (i.e., criminals) who resisted the social movement for improvement of themselves and social institutions.

Although Hall wrote with evolutionary theory in mind, he tested it with detailed references to the growth of the criminal law in Anglo-Saxon and Norman Britain, recognizing contrary instances as well as those that supported his theory. More important, he saw a variety of influences on emerging law—by the church, military organization, and the central government, especially through the role of the monarch seeking to exploit local justice needs to strengthen kingly jurisdiction at the expense of manorial courts (Hall 1902: 134, 195, 227, 239).

Unfortunately, theories covering the sweep of centuries and even the descriptive chronicles of those who avoid theory often raise more questions than they answer. History does not always record the critical facts necessary to test ideas, and the researchers may be confronted with archaic terms, obscure texts, uncertainty of dating, plus gaps and forgeries that sorely complicate their tasks. Little wonder that the highly praised *Felony and Misdemeanor* by the aforementioned Goebel (1976) was written by someone skilled in etymology and semantics.

What can be drawn from studies of the early history of law is the very tentative and partial nature of the patterns of political intervention that later became the basis of criminal jurisdiction. These seem to have been little more than giving sanction to self-help or cautious specifications of procedures to be followed in negotiated settlement of trouble cases [see p. 235 for a brief background on "trouble cases"—eds.]. The historic importance of process suggests that substantive criminal law followed rather than preceded its administration.

All of this confirms my belief that criminalization can best be studied through focusing on bodies of data having specified or delimited provenience (Merton 1957). One such study, inspired no doubt by his association with E. H. Sutherland at Indiana University, is Jerome Hall's (1952: 3–33) account of "The Carrier's Case." In this essay, he skillfully drew together a variety of social, economic, and political factors to show how English judges beholden to a king and with the freedom of star chamber procedure constructed a felony out of the conversion of property not otherwise fitting the existing conception of such crime. Less well known but equally enlightening is Hall's account of the growth of the law of theft in eighteenth-century England as a response to the changed nature of property (100–102). He was among the very first scholars to provide an empirically grounded analysis of criminalization as it derived from the interplay of legislation and judicial decisions and from the consequences of judicial style for the administration of the criminal law (34*ff.*).

The period of Hall's work from 1935 to the 1950s produced relatively little research on the development of the criminal law on the American side of the Atlantic despite the perennial urging found in Sutherland's (1924, 1934) textbooks. Sutherland's (1950) own study of sexual psychopath laws in the United States more or less stood alone during this period. Beyond Sutherland in this era one must look to England, where Radzinowicz published the first of his four volumes on the history of English criminal law in 1948.

Much of the law and society literature during and after the 1950s in the United States revolved around questions as to whether legal change can produce social change, with considerable attention given to whether morality can be legislated. Insofar as such queries applied to racial discrimination, criminalization was only of marginal interest. Law enforcement and civil rights of the accused, including those of juveniles, were only beginning to attract the interests of social scientists as issues for research.

LABELING THEORY AND BEYOND

The advent of labeling theory in the 1960s brought into prominence the generation and application of legal rules that define deviance. Much of the interest of social scientists centered on Howard Becker's theory that new rules stem from the activities of "moral entrepreneurs." The term was readily taken up but later criticized. While Becker (1963: 149) cited Gusfield's (1955) early article on moral reform, it was never made clear whether these crusaders were individual leaders or representatives of groups or of a social class. Nevertheless, he applied the idea to an analysis of the origin of laws controlling marijuana sale and use, in the course of which he unabashedly asserted that it can serve as a model for the study of legislation in general as well as for understanding informal rule making (Becker 1963: 145).

It is true that outstanding personalities figured prominently in legal reforms of the Progressive era in the United States; it is also true that the history of marijuana legislation with which Becker documented his theory was largely the work of the Federal Narcotics Bureau and its director. But whether it involved their moral crusading as opposed to mundane striving for sheer bureaucratic power has been questioned (Dickson 1968). At best, this is a very simplistic conception of criminalization not too far removed from what used to be called the "great man theory of history."

In any case, the history of the criminalization of opiate use and traffic in the United States reveals a far more complex picture in which organized interests and interacting groups predominated. Problems having to do with the occupation of the Philippine Islands and the interests of Great Britain, India, and China became significant influences on drug policy and law, made felt through the U.S. State Department. Organized groups—of medical doctors, as well as patent medicine manufacturers, wholesalers and retailers, makers of Coca-Cola and Pepsi, hospital operators, church and missionary groups, plus different federal departments, such as the Bureau of Chemistry in the U.S. Department of Agriculture—took part in the interaction leading to the passage of the Harrison Narcotics Act of 1914. While some conspicuous leaders emerged in the battles over opiate control in the United States, they didn't fare well. Some were discredited, and one was removed by the president of the United States himself (Musto 1987: 12).

In Britain, where the main issue of drugs at the turn of the twentieth century was that of the opium trade, some reform leaders changed sides during the controversies. Leadership was mainly governmental. As was generally true, Victorian pressure groups could do little but confirm a course of action already decided on by the government. The reform movement directed at international opium trade was never broad based; rather, it tended to be elitist, with support from the Liberal Party and nonconformist clergy. The debate over opium in general was confused, and some antiopium tradespeople defended certain forms of personal opium use. Opium consumption by the working class never became an important issue, as did its use by middle-class persons, especially women and literary notables such as Thomas De Quincey, Samuel Coleridge, John Keats, and Elizabeth Barrett Browning. Ultimately, of course, the domestic opiate problem was medicalized rather than criminalized. Yet in some ways the treatment of opiate addiction under medical supervision was more moralistic than in the United States (Berridge and Edwards 1981: 173*ff.*).

STATUS GROUPS AND CRIMINALIZATION

The fact that moral reformers and those who were the object of their reform were of the same social class in Britain gives us pause when attention is directed to writers favoring a status group theory of criminalization. In this connection, as already noted, Becker cited Gusfield's (1955) early work on the temperance movement to support a status group theory of the origin of rules. Chambliss (1964), who claimed that the origin and transformation of vagrancy laws in Britain were attributable to the efforts of a dominant group to impose controls on migrants, also cited Gusfield. Homage given to the status group theory likewise is found in Platt's (1969: 8, 77) *The Child Savers,* which attributes the emergence of the juvenile court law in Illinois to the work of middle-class women reformers. Clearly, the seminal ideas planted by Gusfield took root in a small but conspicuous literature on reform movements appearing in the 1960s.

Gusfield applied Weber's concept of status politics to the explanation of the temperance movement and associated criminalization of alcohol use by emphasizing the motivation of its supporters to acquire prestige or to defend their existing status from attack or erosion—hence the title of his book *Symbolic Crusade* (1963, revised edition 1989). Parts of the book still resonate with a provocative and highly original interpretation, but the sources of the data have bothered me in a different way. Most of them came from midwestern states and only one from the South—namely, Maryland. Oklahoma and Kansas, the bastions of legal abstinence for many years, are strangely missing. More significant, there is little reference to the multifaceted nature of groups supporting temperance in different areas, such as anti-Negro and anti-Catholic groups in the South and antilabor, anti-German, and anti-Irish organizations in northern cities and elsewhere (see Lee 1944).

Whether anything like status groups in the Weberian style ever emerged in the United States is doubtful. The Junkers, a frontier group in East Prussia analyzed by Weber (1946: 386–96), had an internal system of social controls, such as the officers' corps rules on marriage, designed to preserve their homogeneity. The prime example, to my mind, however, is found in the legal culture of Italy, which

Merryman (1965: 39) called *la dottrina*. It was maintained among Italian judges by social controls exercised through the Ministry of Justice, affecting personal behavior as well as judicial—a pattern without parallel in American society. (Actually, Weber [1967: 268*ff*.] did not hold that the content of new law was imposed by status groups but rather could be one outcome of compromise between them or, alternately, the product of a "conscious universal reorientation of legal life.")

In a revised statement added to a new printing of *Symbolic Crusade,* Gusfield (1989) seemed to give more weight to a dramatistic theory of status politics, going well beyond Weber's ideas. In this connection, I note that the ideas of law as drama and legislation as symbolic has antecedents in the work of Thurman Arnold (1955) and Vilhelm Aubert (1966). More recently, the invocation of drama as part of a process of the superindoctrination of law can be found in the provocative work of a group of Marxist historians at the University of Warwick, who studied the growth of criminal law in eighteenth-century England. Their thesis was that with the decline of religion and monarchical prerogatives, the English gentry of the period sought in various ways to establish criminal law primarily as ideology in order to ensure deference of commoners toward themselves and their property. An important aspect of this movement involved majestic pageantry, especially at the assize courts and quarter sessions, including parades of legal notables, captioned by funereal speeches and enactments by terror-inspiring judges. Judges and others also collaborated to dramatize the fine details of legal procedure and thus lend a transcendent aura to law as justice. A final element of this law was the quality of mercy through clemency, which mitigated the draconian impact of death sentences (Hay 1975: 269).

Unhappily for the Marxian interpretation of law as merely instrumental or an epiphenomenon of class structure, one of the group, E. P. Thompson (1975), concluded from his part of the study that law had its own dynamic and that the English gentry, if not hoisted on its own petard, was at least caught up in an institutional net of its own making. This because law by its nature seeks to transcend inequalities of class power and reconcile the interests of all degrees of men. To use Thompson's (1975: 269) own language: "The oligarchs and the great gentry were content to be subject to the rule of law because law was serviceable and afforded their hegemony the rhetoric of legitimacy."

To say that status groups or social classes strive to impose their morality through law on others is to say too much and too little. Apart from the questionable existence of status groups themselves, the interaction between them and the people subordinated is scarcely unilateral. The so-called exploited classes are not characteristically helpless or without means to assert their values and frustrate or, indeed, at times direct the course of social control. This is demonstrated by Jerome Hall's (1952: 262*ff*.) discussion of the administration of the criminal law in eighteenth-century England, for some unfathomable reason ignored by the Warwick historians.

During this time, jurors during criminal trials often reconstrued, blatantly reinterpreted, or consciously falsified factual evidence to avoid a finding of guilt in capital crimes largely because punishments were so far out of line with the seriousness of the crimes charged, such as theft of a duck or a pair of shoes. The intermediating factor here, I conclude, was some natural sense of justice or current public opinion or perhaps both.

The effects of public opinion on the process of criminalization are easier to see in the late eighteenth-century prosecutions for the forgery of bank notes, a more urban phenomenon beyond the ken of the English landed gentry. Death had been decreed for the forgery of a one-pound note at a time when the Bank of England, "the old lady of Threadneedle Street," periodically repudiated its own banknotes and made them worthless paper. Antibanker feeling ran strong at this time, a current most certainly felt in jury deliberations of the era.

These facts point to an influence on the administration of the criminal law given relatively little heed by the Warwick historians—namely, that of public opinion. It was not just the jurors who spared defendants by bringing in fictitious verdicts. Complainants themselves and prosecutors also collaborated in the "pious perjury" mitigating the law's impact, and not all judges were the fearsome exponents of judicial terror highlighted by the Warwickians. Jerome Hall enumerates a number of ways in which they conspired to save defendants from death: narrow interpretation of statutes, recommendations to juries and counsel, and failure to apply statutes when they clearly governed cases. Public opinion and the beginnings of classical penology clearly had begun to modify criminal justice in the eighteenth century. Thus, more than one strand of thought and sentiment were at work to shape the criminal justice process of the era (Hall 1952: 118, 137–39).

CONCLUSIONS

I offer several conclusions from my brief critical review of the theories and studies of criminalization by social scientists. First, the process stands badly in need of study and research in its legal as well as sociological aspects, particularly if we concede that the administration of the law as well as legislation are integral parts of a process having their own dynamics. Merely to study social movements aimed at criminalizing aspects of human behavior is insufficient because many criminal laws, especially those affecting procedures, have no such antecedents. Moreover, many such movements have failed their purposes; this is especially true in cases in which the legislative body is elitist, as California's has been in the past.

While some proposed changes in criminal law are preceded by popular agitation, legislative division, and conflict, others no less important are simply introduced and uneventfully given a pass. My guess is that something like this happened when capital crimes were rapidly multiplying in eighteenth-century

England, at a time when gentlemanly patronage prevailed to acknowledge and pass private bills of the gentry.

The dramatistic metaphor is certainly useful to describe a good deal of all-embracing legislative conflict and the turgid interaction between pressure groups and legislators, as well we know from congressional hearings during the Watergate crisis and those during the Reagan administration in the United States. Aubert's (1966: 98*ff.*) study of the Norwegian housemaid law stands out as an example of dramatistic analysis and resultant symbolic legislation. I myself have described how the critical impetus needed to pass changes in the California juvenile court law in 1960 came from the unanticipated dramatization of evils of the court by the naive testimony of an anachronistic judge from one of the northern California "cow counties" (Lemert 1970: 151–55). Yet the subsequent passage of the probation subsidy law, which had both criminalizing and decriminalizing effects for juveniles, sailed through the legislature without a dissenting voice and little discussion. The dramatistic theory certainly explains how issues are clarified, but it doesn't account for success in one case and failure in another.

The nature of the modern legislative process in changing criminal law is so variable, so readily affected by contingencies, by internal interaction of groups and individuals, by time pressures, and by structural constraints as to defy any generalization other than that the nature of the issue is likely to determine the outcome of the process (Berk, Brockman, and Lesser 1977: 207).

Given the abortive starts, stops, and restarts; accelerations; success and failures; drama and no drama characterizing the legislative process, I am inclined to believe that Cooley's old idea of social life as a tentative process serves us best in studying criminalization. This idea can be updated and informed by W. F. Cottrell's (1972: 14, 27, 30, 39) heuristic conception that gives a place to human choices made in the context of group interaction. Consequences of such choices are made known through feedback of "social intelligence" (Cooley 1966 [1918]: 351–62), which in turn, by reason of structured access to information, influences further choices to continue, discontinue, or mindlessly ignore a particular line of legal change.

While my prescription for studying criminalization is atheoretical, it is not aconceptual. It is middle-range research beginning with data rather than with theory, data around which or from which concepts can be derived or applied.

REFERENCES

Arnold, Thurman. *The Symbols of Government*. New Haven, Conn.: Yale University Press, 1955.

Aubert, Vilhelm. "Some Social Functions of Legislation." *Acta Sociologica* 10, nos. 1–2 (1966): 98–120.

Becker, Howard. *Outsiders: Studies in the Sociology of Deviance*. New York: Free Press, 1963.

Berk, R. A., H. Brockman, and Selma Lesser. *A Measure of Justice: An Empirical Study of Changes in the California Penal Code, 1955–71*. New York: Academic Press, 1977.

Berridge, Virginia, and Giffar Edwards. *Opium and the People*. New York: St. Martin's, 1981.

Black, Donald. "Crime as Social Control." *American Sociological Review* 48, no. 1 (February 1983): 34–45.

Cahn, Edmond. *The Sense of Injustice*. Bloomington: Indiana University Press, 1964.

Chambliss, William H. "A Sociological Analysis of the Law of Vagrancy." *Social Problems* 12, no. 1 (Summer 1964): 67–77.

Cooley, Charles Horton. *The Social Process*. Carbondale: Southern Illinois University Press, 1966 [1918].

Cottrell, William F. *Technology, Man and Progress*. Columbus, Ohio: Charles Merrill, 1972.

Dickson, Donald. "Bureaucracy and Morality: An Organizational Perspective on a Moral Crusade." *Social Problems* 16, no. 2 (Fall 1968): 143–56.

Galliher, John F., and John F. Cross. *Morals Legislation without Morality: The Case of Nevada*. New Brunswick, N.J.: Rutgers University Press, 1983.

Goebel, Julius, Jr. *Felony and Misdemeanor: A Study of the History of Criminal Law*. Philadelphia: University of Pennsylvania Press, 1976.

Gruter, Margaret. "The Origins of Legal Behavior." *Journal of Social and Biological Structures* 2 (1979): 43–51.

Gruter, Margaret, and Paul Bohannan, eds. *Law, Biology and Culture: The Evolution of Law*. Santa Barbara, Calif.: Ross-Erikson, 1983.

Gumplowicz, Ludwig. *Der Rassenkampf: Sociologische Untersuchungen*. Innsbruck: Wagnerisch Universitäts Buchhandlung, 1883.

Gusfield, Joseph. "Social Structure and Moral Reform: A Study of the Women's Christian Temperance Union." *American Journal of Sociology* 61, no. 3 (November 1955): 221–32.

———. *Symbolic Crusade: Status Politics and the American Temperance Movement*. Urbana: University of Illinois Press, 1963.

———. *Symbolic Crusade: Status Politics and the American Temperance Movement*. Rev. ed. Urbana: University of Illinois Press, 1989.

Hagan, John. "The Legislation of Crime and Delinquency: A Review of Theory, Method and Research." *Law and Society Review* 14, no. 3 (Spring 1980): 603–28.

Hall, Arthur Cleveland. *Crime in Its Relations to Social Progress*. New York: Columbia University Press, 1902.

Hall, Jerome. *Theft, Law and Society*. 2d ed. Indianapolis: Bobbs-Merrill, 1952.

Hay, Douglas. "Property, Authority and Criminal Law." In *Albion's Fatal Tree: Crime and Society in Eighteenth Century England,* ed. Douglas Hay, E. P. Thompson, and Peter Linebaugh. New York: Pantheon, 1975.

Hoebel, E. Adamson. *The Law of Primitive Man: A Study in Comparative Legal Dynamics*. Cambridge, Mass.: Harvard University Press, 1954.

Holmes, Oliver Wendell. *The Common Law*. Boston: Little, Brown, 1963.

Lee, A. M. "Techniques of Reform: An Analysis of the New Prohibition Drive." *American Sociological Review* 9, no. 1 (February 1944): 60–69.

Lemert, Edwin. *Social Action and Legal Change: Revolution within the Juvenile Court*. Chicago: Aldine, 1970.

Lowie, Robert. *The Origin of the State*. New York: Russell & Russell, 1962.

Merryman, John H. "The Italian Style: The Doctrine, the Law, the Interpretation." *Stanford Law Review* 18, no. 1 (November 1965): 39–65.

Merton, Robert. "The Bearing of Empirical Research on Sociological Theory." In Robert Merton, *Social Theory and Social Structure*. 2d ed. Glencoe, Ill.: Free Press, 1957.

Musto, David F. *The American Disease: Origins of Narcotics Control*. Oxford: Oxford University Press, 1987.

Nader, Laura. "Styles of Court Procedure: To Make Balance." In *Law in Culture and Society,* ed. Laura Nader. Chicago: Aldine, 1969.

Platt, Anthony. *The Child Savers: The Invention of Delinquency*. Chicago: University of Chicago Press, 1969.

Radzinowicz, Leon. *A History of English Criminal Law and Its Administration from 1750*. London: Stevens, 1948.

Ratzenhofer, Gustav. *Wesen und Zweck der Politik*. Leipzig: Brockhaus, 1893.

Sorokin, Pitirim. *Contemporary Sociological Theories*. New York: Harper, 1928.

Sutherland, Edwin H. *Criminology*. Philadelphia: Lippincott, 1924.

———. "Diffusion of Sexual Psychopath Laws." *American Journal of Sociology* 56, no. 2 (September 1950): 142–48.

———. *Principles of Criminology*. Chicago: Lippincott, 1934.

Thompson, E. P. *Whigs and Hunters: The Origin of the Black Act*. New York: Pantheon, 1975.

Weber, Max. *From Max Weber: Essays in Sociology,* trans., ed., and with an introduction by H. H. Gerth and C. Wright Mills. New York: Oxford University Press, 1946.

———. *Max Weber on Law in Economy and Society,* ed. and with an introduction and annotations by Max Rheinstein. Trans. Edward Shils and Max Rheinstein of Max Weber, *Wirtschaft und Gesellschaft,* 2d ed. (1925). New York: Simon & Schuster, 1967.

Afterword

Edwin M. Lemert: An Intellectual Portrait

Michael F. Winter

The study of social control is an old subject; it can arguably be traced to the classic religious concern with doing good and preventing evil, which loomed large in the late medieval and early modern periods, or even further to the ancient Greco-Roman preoccupation with the study of politics as the search for the ideal form of government. But the subject as known today is much more closely related to the seventeenth- and eighteenth-century concern with the idea of a social contract, an idea traceable largely to Hobbes, Locke, and Rousseau and exercising a powerful and continuing influence: individuals surrender the absolute liberty of nature in exchange for the more secure life of "civilized" society, an organized form of group life in which the combined authority of government and social norms comes to be recognized as the legitimate foundation of everyday life.[1] One of the key differentiating factors is the modern concern with the fates of individuals; ancient and medieval thought was more focused on the needs of the whole.

More recently, twentieth-century sociologists, who tend to assume the existence of socialized individuals living in groups, focus more specifically on the ways in which human behavior is molded by a range of social forces that attempt to ensure compliance with central goals and values. Inevitably, not all behavior can be controlled, and some considerable part falls outside the sphere of what is considered acceptable. Alcoholism, drug abuse, prostitution, uncontrolled aggression, and crime, as different as they seem and indeed are from one another, have a common thread uniting them: they are all unacceptable or intolerable

---

A revised and abridged version of Michael F. Winter, "Societal Reaction, Labeling and Social Control: The Contribution of Edwin M. Lemert," *History of the Human Sciences* 9, no. 2 (May 1996): 53–77.

forms of conduct that elicit a wide range of negative reactions. They are, in a word, deviant. It is important to note that none of these need be actually or statistically deviant, even though that may be the case; it suffices that they be perceived as undesirable.

In the nineteenth and well into the twentieth century, American sociologists often accepted a quasi-medical notion of deviant behavior as pathological, requiring treatment to normalize the individual. But this "medical model" of social problems, as it came to be called, became increasingly ill fitted for understanding the social problems of an era bounded by two world wars and rocked by a great economic depression. Social problems became harder to explain as aberrations of individual behavior, since they appeared to be rooted in chronic conditions of systemic social crisis. Moving beyond the nineteenth-century preoccupation with the biology of human nature, sociology came to see prostitution, alcoholism, crime, and aggression as rooted in widespread movements of social and cultural disorganization.

At the same time, as sociology became more sophisticated, and to that extent more critical of these and other assumptions, the model increasingly fell under intellectual suspicion. This is part of the story of the gradual emancipation of the study of social problems—one of the parent stems from which the modern study of social control originally grew—from the loose coalition of social reformers, lawyers, ministers, philanthropists, journalists, politicians, and others who originally dominated its development (Lemert 1972: 4–5; Lasch 1977).

This bare sketch serves only to illustrate that, historically speaking, there were two major postwar reactions to these early approaches, only one of which directly concerns us here. The other—the structural–functional approach of Talcott Parsons and his student Robert Merton—figures here only tangentially. Edwin Lemert, beginning in the 1940s, was one of the first sociologists to write about deviance, social control, and social problems from a social–psychological standpoint. With Parsons and Merton, the background figures are Emile Durkheim, Sigmund Freud, and Max Weber; with the social–psychological approach, the main figure is George Herbert Mead. At once theoretically sophisticated and empirically based, Lemert's sociology of social control is emblematic of the Meadean approach. Once the notion of deviance as disease is shed, the path is clear to seeing it in social terms, the result of a set of complex social processes operating in a social and historical context. If this seems relatively unproblematic today, it is in part because Lemert and a few other writers made it part of the common—or perhaps one should say preferred—stock of sociological knowledge. In this Lemert was not alone: anticipatory contributions were made by L. Guy Brown (Laub 1983b: 121*ff.*); and, somewhat later, an intellectual movement formed around the work of Lemert and John Kitsuse, Aaron V. Cicourel, Howard S. Becker, Erving Goffman, Fred Davis, Alfred Lindesmith, and others (Petrunik 1991). But this group was not particularly close-knit or cohesive, and contact among its members was sporadic and intermittent at best.[2]

COLLEGE AND GRADUATE SCHOOL

Edwin McCarty Lemert was born in Cincinnati, Ohio, to middle-class parents.[3] Lemert's father, who did not complete high school, became a successful insurance agent and was, in Lemert's words, "a self-made businessman" (Laub 1983b: 119); his mother was a housewife. (Lemert's paternal grandfather had been an attorney and the president of a provincial law school.) The couple had one other child, a boy, when Lemert was born in 1912. The lives of the two brothers were to be marked by an intense sibling rivalry. The competition between them was keen enough to cause both parents some dismay, but it may well have had a positive function, since the need to emulate the achievements and exploits of the older may account for some of Lemert's own drive to succeed. Themselves only modestly educated, the parents had the notion that one should head for medicine and one for the law. Lemert's eventual choice of sociology as an occupation left his father bemused and disappointed (Laub 1983b: 119).

As a student at Miami University of Ohio, Lemert had planned originally to prepare for the law, but he found the intellectual variety of undergraduate life beguiling and tried several courses of study, including political science and Spanish. Those familiar with the elegant restraint of his mature writings will already have guessed that he was fond of literature, even though he did not pursue it as a specialty. Indeed, one of his first serious productions was an unpublished novel that his strait-laced father discovered and destroyed, deeming it morally objectionable.[4]

The lures of literature, politics, and foreign languages notwithstanding, Lemert reached a turning point in his third year at college when he encountered two influential teachers, both sociologists. The first was department head Read Bain, an early positivist and admirer of George Lundberg, who saw the scientific method in sociology as a force for good, contra William Graham Sumner and others who dismissed progressivism.[5] But it was William F. Cottrell's broad-ranging social problems course that fundamentally redirected Lemert's energies and led to his changing his major to sociology. This early contact had a lifelong effect, providing Lemert with what he came later to refer to as the "feedback and choice" side of his orientation to the study of social problems and social control (Lemert 1974, 1976; Laub 1983b: 119–20).

Other early influences include a year as a social case worker in Cincinnati after graduation from college, where he also took a course from University of Cincinnati sociologist Earle Eubank, before heading to the Ohio State University for graduate work in sociology in 1935. One of the Ohio State department's more dynamic faculty was an anthropologist named John Gillin, who led Lemert to alter his program of study from sociology to a joint program of work in sociology and anthropology. He earned the Ph.D. in sociology and anthropology from Ohio State, with a dissertation, written under the supervision of F. E. Lumley, on "Technology and Social Controls in Soviet Russia," awarded in 1939. Though Lumley supervised his dissertation work, the end product very much reflected the continuing influence of Cottrell, who had introduced Lemert as an undergraduate to the importance of technology and its influence on society (Laub 1983b: 120).

EARLY CAREER: 1940–44

After leaving Ohio State but before coming to the University of California at Los Angeles in 1944, where he was to remain until 1953, Lemert taught for two years at Kent State University in Ohio (1939–41) and then at Western Michigan University (1941–43). These early experiences were notable for the opportunity to teach courses in social problems, or "social and personal disorganization," as it was often then called, and thus to become thoroughly familiar with the existing literature on the subject. There was also the fortunate necessity of teaching courses in neighboring disciplines such as history and politics, which, while not in any narrow sense advancing Lemert's position as a specialist, made teaching a broadening and much more interesting experience. He recalls, in particular, learning a fair amount about modern European history and early modern political philosophy. (Though not explicitly acknowledged in his published work, seventeenth-century political thought produced the influential notion of the social contract, one of the intellectual underpinnings of the sociological concept of social control.)

Two early contacts at Kent State blossomed into friendships and were to have lifelong effects. Leonard Broom, with a similarly combined sociology–anthropology Ph.D. from Duke University, had done research on Cherokee acculturation and was interested in ethnic and minority issues. Charles Van Riper, who also subsequently taught (and remained for many years) at Western Michigan University, was a speech pathologist with an eye and an ear for cross-cultural detail. Each of these, in contrasting ways, provided stimulating intellectual and personal contacts. It was largely because of Broom that Lemert was invited to teach at UCLA, where the research and writing of a number of early articles occurred and, more important, Lemert's major work, *Social Pathology: Systematic Approaches to the Study of Sociopathic Behavior,* was completed in 1951. (See chapter 2 in this volume for key excerpts.) Van Riper, who brought to the study of speech pathology an appreciation for the ethnographic record and the relation between language and culture, suggested the idea of aberrant language behavior as case material for use in the study of deviance. Lemert's subsequent investigations of stuttering are rooted in this early contact. In fact, the case of stuttering is particularly important for the distinction between primary and secondary deviation that Lemert drew explicitly in his later work (1951b, 1967a, 1972), perhaps because it offers such an extraordinarily clear example of this phenomenon. The young child who has trouble with certain speech sounds, for a number of reasons, hardly even notices the problem, and stuttering in this primary phase is barely noticeable. But in time, with the help of the reactions of parents and teachers, and the negative attention of peers, the problem becomes so magnified that the child hesitates, stammers, gets red in the face, and produces a whole new set of secondary characteristics, complicating the original problem beyond recognition.[6]

When mobility and coincidence combined to bring both men to Western Michigan University in the period just after they had known each other at Kent State, the two enjoyed opportunities for additional contact. Lemert capitalized on this to learn more from Van Riper about clinical psychology and speech correction. At about the same time, the proximity of a state mental hospital provided access to patients and records and thus provided a basis for the development of Lemert's first "sociopsychological and empirically based interests" (Laub 1983b: 121).

THE GOLDEN AGE OF UCLA: 1944–53

The situation at UCLA in 1944 was very far indeed from what it is today, and Lemert arrived there as the third of only three sociologists. Graduate study was only in the planning stages, and there were no graduate students until several years later. The two others were Constantine Panunzio (1939), who had written on European immigration to the United States and recruited Leonard Broom, who in turn urged Panunzio to recruit Lemert to the then young and struggling department of sociology and anthropology. (The department had been formed only a few years before, in 1940.) In anthropology, however, matters were somewhat different, since there were already two distinguished scholars: Ralph Beals and Harry Hoijer, both well known in their respective fields. (Beals, a specialist in acculturation, made major contributions to the study of Latin America; Hoijer was a specialist in anthropological linguistics focusing on the Indians of the western United States.)

There is no direct evidence, but one assumes that, given the stature of Beals and Hoijer, the university intended to recruit Lemert to help build the department as a center of graduate study and research and to supply promise in sociology to match existing strength in anthropology. In the years that followed, a number of promising, and later quite distinguished, scholars joined Lemert at UCLA: Ralph Turner, Donald Cressey, and Philip Selznick in sociology and Robert Heizer and William Lessa in anthropology, to name only a few. Though a comparatively new institution, UCLA was already well on its way to national distinction, and it demonstrated at least comparable strength in areas outside the social sciences as well. Chess games with philosopher Abraham Kaplan—later famous for his book *The Conduct of Inquiry* (1964)—provided opportunities to discuss epistemological issues and brought a welcome exposure to the philosophy of the social sciences, perhaps at least partly accounting for some of the theoretical sophistication of Lemert's work in a field largely dominated by very plain empirical methods.

As mentioned, there were no graduate students at first, but the undergraduates were highly committed and rewarding to teach. UCLA was at that time still a relatively new campus, many students were the first of their families to attend college, and several were new arrivals in California. With a department committed to the study of acculturation, assimilation, urbanization, immigration, and social problems, students and faculty found much to talk about. The atmosphere was thick with politics, and the seminar room was intense and lively, for many of these students—sons and daughters of garment workers recently arrived from New York—were flirting with left-wing causes. So were many of the faculty: from Lemert's department, Beals, Hoijer, and Broom and, from political science, Dean McHenry were all in some way involved in lecturing at the People's Educational Center in Los Angeles (Barrett 1951: 150*ff.*). They soon fell afoul of a right-wing countermovement.

A West Coast McCarthyite group, spearheaded by State Senator Jack B. Tenney of California and others, had sprung up to deal with these perceived threats to the social order; a loyalty oath was developed (December 1945) and administered, presumably in hopes of controlling the spread of left-wing radicals and communists in the university. Even Clarence J. Dykstra, the provost of the UCLA campus, was interrogated at length and repeatedly accused of fronting for Hollywood communists such as John Howard Lawson and Alvah Bessie. Though not himself summoned, Lemert was photographed with Ralph Beals, Harry Hoijer, and Leonard Broom when they were called in for questioning by the Tenney Committee.[7] An accompanying Hearst newspaper headline read "Are Some Professors Red, Pink, Red, White, and Blue?" More than one undergraduate in Lemert's classes wrote and did research related to political persecution, and given this volatile political climate, the idea of societal reaction to problematic behavior must have seemed quite natural to both them and their instructor.

In some of his earlier work, Lemert had already written on the roles of law and politics in social control (1945, 1946), but by the time this wave of McCarthyism hit the West Coast, his teaching and research had carried him into a much broader range of concerns. Until Lemert arrived, Broom had taught the social problems course, which he entitled "Social Disorganization," following the custom of the time. Both agreed that the best text of the many then available was L. Guy Brown's (1942) *Social Pathology: Personal and Social Disorganization,* which Lemert recalled as "an interesting, rather strange book in many ways." It was strange because while rooted in an older understanding of deviant behavior, at the same time it clearly anticipated something else, with its "central thesis of a process or an interaction." In fact, Brown's book was the only textbook Lemert felt comfortable using, and his dissatisfaction with other texts—along with some persistent attention from an agent at McGraw-Hill—formed a major motivation for working on his own.

THE COMBINED INFLUENCE OF SOCIOLOGY AND ANTHROPOLOGY

It is clear from the character of the department at UCLA that the connection between sociology and anthropology was for Lemert, as it was for many of the more important sociologists of the time, a critical and fruitful one. For his own research, certainly, and for much of his teaching for many years, this was a very happy alliance, even though some of his students came to regard it as an obstacle to their professional development. Some years later, Lemert recalled, the combination became unpopular with some of the graduate students at UCLA, who wanted to be known as one or the other, and not some combination of both, and thus came to feel the connection should be abandoned.[8]

From our vantage point, with all of the specialization that the intervening years has brought, the combination seems almost quaint, and yet without it the critical turn that Lemert and others made in reorienting the study of deviance and social control would scarcely have been possible, for that reorientation is partly based on the use of historical and ethnographic methods that were much more common in anthropology than in sociology. Anthropological method, as is clear from the case of Erving Goffman, brought a new kind of rigor to the use of case materials, transforming the anecdotal into the material of systematic interpretation.

The chance to work directly with anthropologists bore fruit in an early collaboration with UCLA colleague Robert Heizer, a short monograph on artifacts found in the Topanga Canyon area near Los Angeles, heralding the discovery of "Topanga Man" (Heizer and Lemert 1947). And it is directly visible in *Alcohol and the Northwest Coast Indians* (1954), a longer monograph published a few years later and excerpted here in chapter 7, as well as in many later papers. (For a sense of the ethnographic variety of Lemert's work, see particularly the papers published in the two editions of *Human Deviance, Social Problems, and Social Control* [1967a, 1972], which touch on a wide variety of human groups and cultures.) But the influence of anthropology actually extends through almost everything Lemert eventually wrote and is much deeper than these obvious examples indicate, for it reflects his discomfort with theoretical work that is not grounded in empirical method. His definition of "empirical," however, is not narrowly positivistic and rests more on the norms of ethnographic and even historical description than on commonly used quantitative methods, although he has generally been eclectic in regard to method and hospitable to a variety of usable orientations.

GRADUATE STUDENTS AT UCLA

If there is truth in the adage that good children make good parents, one of the secrets of success of the department that Lemert joined was a remarkable and very promising group of graduate students, who began to enroll about 1950. Indeed, in recalling the time at UCLA as a kind of golden age, he attributes this not only to the inevitable haze of hindsight and to the distinction of his faculty colleagues but perhaps even more to a brilliant cohort of graduate students. Many became highly distinguished sociologists of the postwar period: Sheldon Messinger, Aaron V. Cicourel, John Kitsuse, Scott Greer, and Wendell Bell.

At that time, Lemert recalled that all of the younger people were reading Talcott Parsons, particularly *The Social System,* which had appeared in 1950. Their interest was keen enough for them to ask Philip Selznick to offer a seminar on Parsons; and when Sheldon Messinger found himself the only student enrolled in a seminar with Lemert, the two decided, by mutual agreement, to discuss Parsons in depth (Messinger 1994a). But the students were more interested in Parsons than was Lemert, who read Parsons carefully on deviance but found it less useful than Robert Merton's approach and much less applicable to his course material and research than Brown's text.

Already showing some dissatisfaction with the available textbooks, Lemert produced some mimeographed versions of the essays that would eventually grow into *Social Pathology* and used these for his classes. Cicourel remembers reading these in connection with Lemert's social problems course in the fall of 1950. He also recalls that Lemert placed a heavy emphasis on the social–psychological processes that could be observed in the materials. In the lectures for this class, for example, Lemert spun out in some detail the illustration of the waitress who, in changing jobs, costumes, and clienteles, discovers that there are whole new sets of social expectations to be dealt with in these situations, as "this person began to internalize . . . the reactions of other people, even if they didn't perceive what they were doing as being necessarily unusual or different." Cicourel also confirms that Mead (more specifically, the pragmatist idea that the self is not a substantial entity given in advance of social interaction but is negotiated in the course of social interaction) was perhaps the most important theoretical influence in understanding these self-transformations (*Sociologists on the Labeling Perspective* 1982, transcript pp. 4*ff.*, 14–16).

The collegial and generally supportive atmosphere that the faculty enjoyed fortunately included these promising graduate students. Kitsuse eventually collaborated with Leonard Broom in a study of the Japanese–American family (Broom and Kitsuse 1956); and Cicourel, through a personal connection, was useful in Lemert's interest in check forgers. Cicourel and Kitsuse (1963) also collaborated on an educational study in which they developed a perspective anticipating what would later be called "labeling theory," published some years later; they also coauthored an influential study on the problem of using officially produced statistics in research, a critical essay aimed at both positivism and the standard structural–functional deviance approaches of Parsons and Merton (Kitsuse and Cicourel 1963).

Lemert himself did not use the term *labeling,* at least not to describe his own work, though he was obviously friendly to the idea. A more characteristic term for him is *societal reaction,* directing attention to the social response to the original act and thus drawing it away from the activity or its conditions. *Societal reaction,* clearly, is broader than *labeling,* which is one kind of societal reaction among many possible ones; the broader term stands to the narrower as type to token. Lemert attributed labeling theory per se to the Chicago-trained sociologist Howard

S. Becker (Laub 1983b: 124); he traced the term *societal reaction* as far back as Earle Eubank (1932), a sociologist at the University of Cincinnati with whom he studied briefly in the 1930s, though he did not credit Eubank with any analysis or development of the idea. Also, some of the general sense of the concept was present in L. Guy Brown's aforementioned text, if not the term itself. One writer argues that "societal reaction" is also attributable to Frank Tannenbaum's (1938) *Crime and the Community* (Gove 1975b: 3); but even if this is accurate, Lemert was unaware of Tannenbaum's book until considerably later (Petrunik 1991: 18).

In any event, the genesis of societal reaction in Lemert's work was independent of the rise of labeling theory and originated in discussions between Lemert and the faculty and graduate students at UCLA "and somewhat later among associates at the University of California at Berkeley" (Laub 1983b: 124–25). This group at Berkeley, Lemert stated, included a number of people affiliated with the Berkeley campus's Center for the Study of Law and Society: Sheldon Messinger, Erving Goffman, David Matza, the visiting Becker, and Philip Selznick.

According to Messinger, the group was loosely organized around the Delinquency Studies Project, funded by the University of California and some outside agencies, from 1962 to 1966, though the stream of its publication activity extended far beyond this period. In addition to those already mentioned, Irving Piliavin, Scott Briar, Ruth Kornhauser, Carl Werthman, Sally Davis, Herbert Mills, Anthony Platt, Jerome Skolnick, Elliot Studt, and Nils Christie were also associated with the project. "Discussion," Messinger (1994b) recalls, "was often heated, particularly over how one should conceptualize deviance, with Selznick and Kornhauser, in particular, resisting the view (which they imputed to others) that whatever society treated as deviance was, in effect, deviance."

The Delinquency Studies Project may have been more influential than many of the participants at the time realized; they were attracting attention, Lemert said, from as far away as Great Britain, where the circle came to be known as the "Pacific Seminar." By this time, according to Messinger (1994b), Berkeley was beginning to feel the additional influence of UCLA sociologist Harold Garfinkel, the founder of ethnomethodology, whom Messinger had known toward the end of his time at UCLA.

UNIVERSITY OF CALIFORNIA, DAVIS: 1953–70

The UCLA decade was obviously a very good one. By this time, Lemert had published a substantial number of articles, two shorter monographs, and the imposing *Social Pathology,* which appeared in 1951. This was clearly a major work, but it is unlikely that anyone at that time realized just how influential it would become over the next forty years. Now, of course, it has always been notoriously difficult to measure influence, and it perhaps cannot be done with any real precision. Certain indications nonetheless can be readily found. To begin with, it stayed in print for forty years, extremely unusual in a world in which books typically go out of print in three or four.

It is, of course, not possible to know exactly how many times the book has been cited, but the citation services, even with their known limitations, reveal over five hundred instances between 1956—the lower limit on publicly available citation data—and the present, which does not count any citations received between 1951 and 1956. It is still cited today, and the machine-readable version of the citation data, which begins only in 1972, shows a pattern of activity lasting nearly two decades.

Lemert had tenure and was about to be named the chair of a very distinguished department. Yet he chose precisely this time to leave. Lemert had been in contact for some time with Herbert F. Young, a chemist who was then the dean of the College of Letters and Sciences at Davis; Young was trying to change what had originally been the University of California's College of Agriculture into a new general campus of the university. Transforming the "University Farm," as many people called it at the time, into a diverse collection of colleges offering instruction in all fields presented many challenges, and recruitment was one of the more difficult. Young originally wrote to ask whether Lemert could recommend anyone to teach sociology and then, in a subsequent letter, whether Lemert himself might be interested in chairing a new combined department. This inquiry was by itself an exciting prospect. There were also personal reasons for the move. Despite the attractions of UCLA, life in Los Angeles, even forty years ago, was becoming difficult. In an event that may have been one of those proverbial decision points, one of his sons was hurt in a traffic accident. All this seemed to argue for a change, and he moved to Davis in the summer of 1953.

If the department of UCLA was small by today's standards, the department at UC Davis existed only tenuously. When Lemert arrived, it contained only one faculty member, an economist, who had taught the sociology courses. The campus already had agricultural economists, to be expected in a world-famous college of agriculture, but the situation was similarly benighted for the other social sciences fields, except for psychology: there was only one geographer, and there were no anthropologists. The whole College of Letters and Sciences contained at this point no more than two or three hundred students. Classes of four to six students were common. This situation of very small departments of one, two, or at most three people continued for the 1950s and even into the 1960s, when a much more significant expansion occurred.

In this early period at Davis, Lemert continued to rely on his established mix of sociology and anthropology, which had served him so well at UCLA. He recalled using texts that had large infusions of ethnographic material. In his course "Law and Society," for example, he drew on E. Adamson Hoebel and Karl Llewellyn; at that time the sociology of law was a relatively new field, even though criminology had been established for some time. The problem with criminological literature was similar to the problem with the literature of social problems—theoretically thin and methodologically somewhat dubious, it was too much of a practitioner literature to provide the kind of scholarly approach that the field called for. As in the case of social problems, anthropological approaches offered some of this.

Unfortunately (yet perhaps fortunately, as it turned out), the anthropological approach to crime was tainted by an unresolved biological determinism inherited from the nineteenth-century Italian criminologist Cesare Lombroso and (rather unsuccessfully) applied to the American situation by Earnest A. Hooton, a physical anthropologist at Harvard. Thus, while social and cultural anthropology made many useful contributions that the societal reaction viewpoint could make good use of, the physical anthropology of crime had to be held at arm's length (see Laub 1983a: 136, where Donald Cressey recalls Sutherland's abrupt dismissal of Hooton's geneticism), and this may have stimulated a new growth of properly sociological criminology that focused on criminal activity as a range of behaviors formed at least partly in response to social interaction.

By the end of the 1950s, Lemert had already produced some central work in sociological criminology—his articles on the grand jury as an agent of social control and on check forgers are probably the most notable of these—but his major contributions to the study of crime do not appear until somewhat later. (One of Lemert's classic essays on check forgery is reprinted here in chapter 8). In any event, the promise of social and cultural anthropology for his growing interest in alcohol studies was considerable, and thus his research activity at this point shows the familiar reliance on a combination of sociology and anthropology. In 1961–62, he received what was then a rather large grant from the U.S. Department of Health, Education, and Welfare to study alcohol problems in the Pacific Basin, primarily among Polynesian peoples.

This funding enabled Lemert to capitalize further on his early combined training in sociology and anthropology and, at the same time, to indulge his self-described "yen for rustic islands" (Lemert 1972: ix). In looking at his research activity during this period, one sees a gap of some thirteen years between the publication of *Alcohol and the Northwest Coast Indians,* in 1954, and the appearance in 1967 of the first edition of *Human Deviance, Social Problems, and Social Control,* the book that brought together many of the periodical articles that eventually issued from this period of federally funded alcohol research in the early 1960s. Building on the earlier historical and ethnographic study of alcoholism in the peoples of British Columbia, and also on still earlier research on American alcoholics (Lemert 1951a), Lemert did field studies of drinking in Hawaiian plantation society, Tonga, and the Cook Islands. The results sometimes assumed the form of cross-cultural comparisons and at other times a more generalized understanding of the interaction between alcohol use and culture patterns. This led to his joining the U.S. National Advisory Commission on Alcohol in 1968 and also in the same year to accept an invitation to join the editorial board of the *Quarterly Journal of Studies on Alcohol.*

Despite the problems of new campuses, UC Davis proved to be an environment in which Lemert continued to produce a remarkable flow of important articles and books, even more than one might have expected given his early promise and success at UCLA. Perhaps something about young departments and new ventures appealed to him. In any case, many of his publications were produced after the move from UCLA to Davis. Lemert remained as chair for a number of years, until 1967, when an administrative decision was made to move to a rotating chairmanship.

The most notable of his publications are the two editions of *Human Deviance, Social Problems, and Social Control,* both selections of previously published papers (appearing in 1967 and 1972), and a most remarkable essay on the social reaction to paranoia, reprinted here in chapter 9. "Paranoia and the Dynamics of Exclusion" (Lemert 1962) was translated into French and Italian, and, along with *Human Deviance,* whose second edition was also translated into Italian, it brought him a more international readership. The two editions of *Human Deviance* have been cited, in the citation services alone, close to five hundred times and show activity curves similar to those for *Social Pathology.* "Paranoia and the Dynamics of Exclusion," a journal article, is in a different category and much more difficult to track, since citing authors sometimes refer to the journal instead of the actual paper as the work cited, and thus estimates here are inherently conservative. Even with this methodological limitation and the limitations of citation services already mentioned, this paper has been and continues to be cited heavily. The appearance of these works signals the end of Lemert's most active period as a sociologist of deviance, for at this point—the time period is the mid-1960s—he shifted toward the study of law.

There are some interesting asides on the development of the paranoia article. Though meticulously and exhaustively researched, the idea for the paper came from a chance encounter some years before, as far back as the early 1950s. At that time Lemert was still at UCLA and was studying the way mental health officials recommended hospitalization. In looking over some preliminary findings, Lemert got the distinct impression that, at least in certain cases, "the symptoms of these individuals were far less important than the social situation and the relation of the behavior to a certain situation in determining whether they got recommended for hospitalization." Then a seemingly unrelated event provided unexpected illumination. One day in the lunch room at UCLA, two professors were talking about a problem they were having with a difficult student. One of the professors began to fidget and eventually got up and walked over to the door and closed it. "Suddenly," Lemert recalls, "I realized that people who have mental problems . . . in effect live in a different psychic environment than most people." A decade later, in the early 1960s, Lemert remembered an older study based on the idea that paranoids create a false community of suspicion around them, as a result of their disease (Cameron 1943–44). According to this view, paranoids imagine that everyone is against them. What Lemert had observed in the research at UCLA on hospitalization and saw enacted in the discussion of the student, however, was quite different: "what I was seeing was that the community . . . was real. That people did conspire at certain points in the interaction with these difficult people, they did conspire against them to exclude them from the interaction." This is not so much because paranoids are in fact sick but because they are extremely difficult to deal with. At about this time, Lemert presented a paper at California's Napa State Hospital, which "had quite an impact on the psychiatrists."

Some time after reading the paper, Lemert wrote up the research more formally and submitted it to *Sociometry*. The journal's referees were, in Lemert's recollection, somewhat hesitant, partly because it was at that time somewhat unusual for a researcher to take the viewpoint of the patient. But the editor, John Clausen, was very much in favor of publication (Winter 1995). After it appeared, it was much reprinted and cited and generated a great deal of controversy; it may well be the most famous article ever published by that periodical. Eventually it got translated into Italian and French, and there is a curious sequel relating to the article's influence in European circles. Visiting a young academic couple in Rome some years after, Lemert learned that the Italian scholar who had published the Italian version was a Communist Party official. At that time Italian communists were very interested in the American movement to deinstitutionalize mental patients. The paranoia article provided a scholarly review and discussion of the treatment of the mentally ill that suggested that their condition was partly a creation of their surroundings and provided support for the policy of deinstitutionalization, a policy the Italian communists very much wanted to pursue.

UNIVERSITY OF CALIFORNIA, DAVIS: 1970–93

The period of the early 1970s is pivotal. One reason is that Lemert no longer felt comfortable identifying with the more subjectivist wing of the movement he had played some considerable part in launching. Thus, he surprised and perhaps startled some, adherents and critics alike, by repudiating the narrower versions of societal reaction theory in the presidential address to the Society for the Study of Social Problems that followed his 1972–73 term of office (reprinted here as chapter 3; for the original, see Lemert 1974). Arguing for a Cottrellian approach, he suggested that both labeling theory and societal reaction theory had become excessively psychological and thus that the "macro aspects of deviance" had been neglected (Laub 1983b: 125–26; see also Lemert 1973, where he anticipates the theme of the presidential address in a discussion of the relevance of Cottrell's approach for social problems).[9]

Lemert was not alone in having reservations about the general approach to deviance found in the societal reaction and labeling theory schools. In the 1970s, a group of positivist sociologists, spearheaded by Walter Gove and others, paid Lemert and others the compliment of criticism by expressing their frustrations with the subjectivism of the Pacific Seminar approach and holding a counterrevolutionary "Vanderbilt Seminar." But their critique was fundamentally unfriendly and certainly not open to the creative development of the societal reaction theory. They called, in essence, for a return to a positivistic approach, arguing that deviance existed and should be studied quite independently of societal reaction or labeling (Gove 1975b). And even those strongly committed to some version of societal reaction theory, such as John Kitsuse, were prepared to admit that the theory could use some clarification, even if the critique did not address the issues Lemert himself had raised in his own thinking (Kitsuse 1975: 275). (The societal reaction approach to deviance has actually been subjected to an enormous volume of criticism, aside from the work of the group associated with Walter Gove and the Vanderbilt Seminar of the 1970s. One writer has unearthed a hundred critical treatments, distributed among several dozen authors, which he has in turn reduced to eight major types of criticisms. For a useful overview and summary, see Conover 1976.) Lemert's reservations about societal reaction theory are couched in theoretical terms, but this period is crucial for another reason, and that is the shift of interest from deviance and social problems toward crime and justice, particularly juvenile justice. Lemert had been writing about crime since the 1940s, but the concern with alcohol use and the conceptual development of the theory of deviant behavior occupied him for much of the 1950s and the 1960s. The shift may well be related to his own and others' criticisms, for it is more than a change of subject matter; it represents a change to many of the typical concerns of macrosociology.

Lemert's contributions to the study of crime, which became more frequent, also began to loom larger in the mid-1960s, as they attracted recognition in high political circles. In 1967, he was invited by President Johnson to join the National Commission on Law Enforcement and the Administration of Justice. His contribution to the Report of the Task Force on Juvenile Delinquency and Youth Crime, profiling and criticizing the juvenile court system, was widely cited and reprinted; it appears here as chapter 12. Other recognitions came as well: in addition to the presidency of Society for the Study of Social Problems, he was also elected, in 1973, president of the Pacific Sociological Society and received the E. H. Sutherland Award from the American Society of Criminology in recognition of lifetime achievement in 1974.

The change of focus is quite evident from 1970 forward. For example, the opening pages of *Social Action and Legal Change* (1970: 1), reprinted here as chapter 13, announce a threefold theme: how the law develops on a long-term basis; how revolutionary changes in the law occur; and whether or not social change can be controlled by legislative means. With support, once again, from the U.S. Department of Health, Education and Welfare, he presents the results of a historical study of a major paradigmatic shift in the concept of juvenile justice that was marked in California beginning about 1960.[10] Some years later, with support from the National Institute of Law Enforcement and Criminal Justice and the Ford Foundation (and with help from previous research by Professor Floyd Feeney at UC Davis's Center on Administration of Criminal Justice), Lemert and Forrest Dill studied the attempt to reduce incarcerations by providing counties with economic incentives to "divert" offenders into probationary and other types of programs (Lemert and Dill 1978). There is little reference to the social–psychological process orientation so noticeable in the work on deviance, and there is no argument to suggest that the burgeoning bureaucratic industry of criminal justice transforms primary criminal behavior into a deviant career, though these potential connections are too obvious to miss. Instead, the concerns are the typical structural problems of the sociology of law. Yet the powerful social–psychological notion of the construction of a secondary deviant identity seems presupposed by these later investigations, as many of the policy-oriented discussions suggest.

The work of his graduate students at Davis in the 1980s reflects this turn to the study of criminal justice: James F. Austin, Patrick G. Jackson, and Robert Tillman all worked in this area. Somewhat later, from a similar base, his last students explored newer areas like gender and crime (Jean Boettcher), missing children, gangs, and illicit drug use (Karen Joe Laidler).

The series of works on juvenile justice influenced sociologists and practitioners alike and brought Lemert a certain notoriety. Probation officers, for example, had mixed feelings about his liberal approach, which he referred to as "judicious nonintervention" (1967b: 96). In a general way, the overriding policy message of societal reaction and labeling theory was that leaving deviants and criminals alone was more likely to reduce their participation in undesirable activities, while interventionism, on the other hand, was likely only to perpetuate the problems everyone was supposedly trying to solve. But the message was not always welcome in agencies of social control, which were reluctant to adopt noninterventionism as a creed.

In policy circles, conservatism eventually won this particular battle, at least in the short run (David Matza points out that this conservatism appeared in academia as well as outside it; *Sociologists on the Labeling Perspective* 1982, transcript pp. 49 ff.). The idea of diverting juvenile offenders into probation or rehabilitation programs, instead of hearing their cases in court and then institutionalizing them, became a kind of negative litmus test for California conservatives in the 1970s and a decade later for the conservatives bent on dismantling President Johnson's Great Society. (The diversion theme was originally explored in a 1971 monograph published under the auspices of the National Institute of Mental Health, *Instead of Court: Diversion in Juvenile Justice,* whose first chapter and conclusion are reprinted here as chapter 14; perhaps something of the change in political weather that was brewing was indicated by the fact that it went out of print quickly. For a later retrospective summary, see Lemert 1981.) In the late 1970s, Lemert participated in a comparative study of juvenile justice in several countries, including Japan, Mexico, Italy, and the United States. While the diversity of methods, goals, and personalities prevented the larger aims of this project from being realized, it did not prevent him from publishing a study drawing on the Italian data from the project, excerpted here in chapter 15 (Lemert 1986).

The findings on the Italian juvenile justice system are quite interesting from a historical point of view; they suggest that the whole idea of juvenile justice is really foreign to the Italian legal system and of very recent adoption. But the biographical survey that began with the early exposure to Cottrell's social problems classes and the early papers submitted to Read Bain's *American Sociological Review* should end by noting that the most important feature of this latest period of Lemert's work—the period beginning in about 1965 with the Presidential Task Force and lasting into the 1990s—is the attempt to reconcile the social–psychological material on deviance with the macro work on juvenile justice. In understanding deviance, social psychology was invoked to explore the formation of a secondary self; in the study of juvenile justice, a different but clearly related kind of societal reaction occurs that situates the offender in a complex, highly organized world of surveillance and incarceration. In attempting to meet the criticism that interactionism tended to construct the individual as passive (Gouldner 1970: 381–82), Lemert returned, once again, to Cottrell, and constructed a feedback loop style model that emphasizes the role of value and choice on the part of the deviant or the criminal (chapter 4 in this volume presents a key statement of this issue). Thus, the result, in the final analysis, is a kind of circular model: it begins with primary deviance, which is followed by societal reaction, which in turn leads to secondary deviance. It is at this point that values and choices become critical in understanding the further evolution of the self: the self emphasizes some reactions over others, differentially prioritizing them before incorporating them into the material of an emerging identity (1973, 1974, 1976, 1978, 1981).

CONCLUSION: SOME LEADING CHARACTERISTICS OF THE WORK

In looking at the body of the work as a whole, the overriding theme is social control. Yet this is never made the specific focus of an integrative treatment, and so for the most part the theme is underlying and implicit. Surprisingly, none of Lemert's many critics seem to have noticed this. Perhaps this is because the range of specialized topics covered is so impressive and wide-ranging. (For a more detailed presentation on topics, methods, and populations studied, see Winter 1996: 70–72). The range of social groups studied is equally remarkable and includes many different populations in many different types of societies. Methodologically, there is a strong preference for empirical investigation, especially ethnographic, and the studies of mental illness reinforced this with much opportunity for collecting and analyzing cases. Nonetheless, Lemert was an unrelenting pluralist in gathering data, and one finds him relying on a wide range of techniques: primary historical sources, archival records, police department files, hospital records, and data from government agencies. He also used his own questionnaires on occasion to gather original data.

Despite this emphasis on empirical study, Lemert's most significant contributions are theoretical and centered on, generally speaking, societal reaction theory, along with the suggestion of the feedback and choice model. Also, despite Lemert's discomfort with ungrounded theorizing, societal reaction theory has been much used outside its original empirical contexts; it proved to be a highly exportable intellectual commodity. In any case, in the progressive elaboration of the theory, and in response to numerous critics, Lemert gradually clarified his own position, distinguishing it from Becker's labeling theory and other related developments, and ended by allying it closely with a Cottrellian view in which both subjective choice and objective reactions are given roughly equal weight.

The question of the range of the theoretical contribution actually calls for a separate treatment elsewhere, but for purposes of summary the following stages in its development are distinguishable: (1) the formulation of societal reaction theory in embryonic form in an article published in 1948 (25), reprinted here in chapter 1 and, of course, more fully throughout *Social Pathology;* (2) refinement of the theory with the casting of the distinction between primary and secondary deviation, which occurs first in the 1948 article mentioned earlier (27–28), then in *Social Pathology* (1951b: 54*ff.*), and which gets a later elaboration in the first edition of *Human Deviance, Social Problems, and Social Control* (1967a: 17*ff.*); (3) clarification of the distinction between the societal reaction approach and the labeling approach attributed to Becker (Laub 1983b: 124); (4) critique of structural–functionalist approaches to deviance (Lemert 1964); and (5) suggestion of the feedback and choice model of understanding deviance, at least partly in response to the many criticisms of the late 1960s and the early 1970s (Lemert 1974, 1976).

These five separable elements by themselves testify to the complexity of the theoretical contribution, and this complexity partly accounts for the critical attention that it has received. But this sprang from other sources as well. While Lemert is certainly not in any direct way responsible for the great variety of responses to societal reaction found in the literature, there is, and perhaps always was, some unresolved ambiguity in his own writings that may have stimulated some of the controversy. It seems fitting, given the centrality of this ambiguity, not only to recognize it here in this brief summary of Lemert's theoretical contribution but also to use it as a natural point of conclusion in the development of his work as a whole.

In this connection, Kitsuse (1975: 274) suggests that even in his later writings Lemert identified himself "as a spokesperson for the new perspective on deviance." This is clear from the preface to the second edition of *Human Deviance, Social Problems, and Social Control* (1972), where Lemert distances himself from the "older sociology," which tends to argue that deviance comes first, then social control follows; his own position, he avers, is the reverse: "I have come to believe the reverse idea (i.e. social control leads to deviance)" (1972: ix). Nonetheless, as Kitsuse (1975: 275) goes on to say, "the early statements by Lemert and Becker were importantly shaped by the conceptions that they opposed, so that they attempted to address old questions even as they sought to establish . . . a new perspective on deviance. If their critics . . . are less than appreciative of their efforts, it is in no small part a consequence of the ambiguities that are contained in them." Of course, the distinction between primary and secondary deviation itself is the recognition and partial resolution of the ambiguity. But Lemert went much further than this, for in his later work he took care to recognize the structural limits of individual choice, explicitly acknowledging that the subject's role in the formation of a deviant identity was indeed restricted to a range of given alternatives (Lemert 1981).

NOTES

I would like to thank Shields Library, University of California, Davis, and the Librarians Association of the University of California, Davis for financial support. My largest debt is to Edwin M. Lemert, who not only cheerfully endured the series of interviews that provided much of the intellectual biography but read and criticized several drafts of this essay as it was in the making. Sheldon Messinger of the University of California, Berkeley, also read and offered criticisms of a late draft and corrected some misinformation I had gathered along the way. Thanks are also owed to Professor Michael Petrunik (1980) of the University of Ottowa for a number of useful clarifications. I also very much appreciate the interest and support from a number of sociologists who worked with Professor Lemert as graduate students at the University of California, Davis, including Karen Joe Laidler and Patrick G. Jackson.

1. On this generally unacknowledged connection see Martindale (1966: 288 ff.) and Ross (1969 [1901]).

2. Because this essay focuses primarily on Lemert's contribution to American sociology, it cannot deal in detail with two important areas that deserve separate treatment elsewhere. The first is the story of the broader intellectual network of sociologists whose work both influenced and was influenced by Lemert; it includes but is not limited to those just mentioned (Petrunik 1991; Cole 1975). The second is the question of the impact of Lemert's work outside the United States. Aside from the French and Italian translations of two key works (Lemert 1962, 1972), Lemert's societal reaction theory has had significant impact in Great Britain (Winter 1992; Cohen 1972, 1985; Downes and Rock 1988; Plummer 1979), the Netherlands (Vincke and Versichalen 1981), Germany (Kloidt 1978), Switzerland (Malherbe 1977), and Sweden (Eriksson and Sundsvall 1979); and the idea of diversion in juvenile justice led to a featured speaking role at a conference in Germany, at the University of Wupperthal, in 1980 (Winter 1992). There is more to tell, for Lemert influenced as well the German criminologist Gunther Albrecht, the Italian sociologist of law Dario Melossi, and others in Belgium and the Scandinavian countries. But all this, however interesting, must wait for separate treatment elsewhere.

3. Unless otherwise noted, the biographical material and the direct quotes that follow are from a series of interviews conducted by the author with the subject in the summer of 1992 (Winter 1992).

4. Edwin M. Lemert, personal conversation with the author, January 14, 1986. I mention this here because the reaction to objectionable conduct became such a central theme in his mature work. He did not write about novelists as deviants, but it is hard to imagine that the experience did not influence him.

5. Lemert remembered Read Bain as highly unconventional, which at that time meant that he identified with the upstart positivist faction of the American Sociological Society and was intensely committed to a kind of Baconian vision of science as a force for human good. For these reformers of the late 1930s, whose number included F. Stuart Chapin at Minnesota and others anxious to see sociology develop as a science, one of the arch-enemies was William Graham Sumner. Bain's editorial involvement in the society's new flagship journal *The American Sociological Review* later provided opportunities for Lemert to publish a paper critical of Sumner in that journal. See Lemert (1942).

6. Edwin M. Lemert, personal conversation, July 21, 1994.

7. Some of the interchanges, which chart a narrow and eccentric course between the Scylla of power madness and the Charybdis of persecution mania, are reprinted in various annual volumes of the California State Senate's *Report of the Joint Fact-Finding Committee* (1945–53).

8. But this reservation was not shared by all, as a communication from Sheldon Messinger made clear. Letter to the author, September 4, 1994.

9. Reading about these turns over twenty-five years later, one may be tempted to argue with the rudimentary distinction between the "micro" and the "macro" that they seem to presuppose. But one must remember that in the 1970s American sociologists were only beginning to appreciate the subtleties of that issue. Much the same could be said of the idea that subjectivism—or what is now called social constructionism or social definitionism—is somehow blocked from tackling structural issues. In the late 1990s, everyone knows very well that many sophisticated variations of earlier approaches are flourishing, but our purpose here is to understand rather than to revise intellectual history.

10. More precisely, the research reported in *Social Action and Legal Change* was begun some years before its 1970 publication and was also supported by the President's Committee on Juvenile Delinquency and Youth Crime, in cooperation with the previously mentioned Delinquency Studies Project at the University of California, Berkeley. The American criminologist Lloyd Ohlin, a member of the President's Committee, contacted Berkeley sociologists David Matza and Sheldon Messinger. A number of projects were funded in addition to Lemert's. Sheldon Messinger, letter to the author, September 2, 1994.

REFERENCES

Barrett, Edward L. *The Tenney Committee: Legislative Investigation of Subversive Activities in California*. Ithaca, N.Y.: Cornell University Press, 1951.

Broom, Leonard, and John Kitsuse. *The Managed Casualty: The Japanese-American Family in World War II*. Berkeley: University of California Press, 1956.

Brown, L. Guy. *Social Pathology: Personal and Social Disorganization*. New York: Crofts, 1942.

Cameron, Norman. "The Paranoid Pseudocommunity." *American Journal of Sociology* 46, no. 1/6 (1943–44): 32–38.

Cicourel, Aaron V., and John Kitsuse. *The Educational Decision Makers*. Indianapolis: Bobbs-Merrill, 1963.

Cohen, Stanley. *Folk Devils and Moral Panics: The Creation of the Mods and Rockers*. London: MacGibbon & Kee, 1972.

———. *Visions of Social Control*. Cambridge: Polity, 1985.

Cole, Stephen. "The Growth of Scientific Knowledge: Theories of Deviance as a Case Study." In *The Idea of Social Structure: Papers in Honor of Robert K. Merton,* ed. Lewis A. Coser. New York: Harcourt, Brace, Jovanovich, 1975.

Conover, Patrick. "A Reassessment of Labeling Theory: A Constructive Response to Criticism." In *The Uses of Controversy in Sociology,* ed. L. A. Coser and O. N. Larsen. New York: Free Press, 1976.

Downes, David, and Paul Rock. *Understanding Deviance: A Guide to the Sociology of Crime and Rule-Breaking*. Oxford: Clarendon, 1988.

Eriksson, J., and H. Sundsvall. "Labeling Theory and Social Work." *Sociologisk Forskning* 16, no. 1 (1979): 39–49.

Eubank, Earle. *The Concepts of Sociology*. Boston: Heath, 1932.

Gouldner, Alvin W. *The Coming Crisis of Western Sociology*. New York: Basic Books, 1970.

Gove, Walter, ed. *The Labeling of Deviance: Evaluating a Perspective*. New York: Sage, 1975a.

Gove, Walter. "The Labeling Perspective: An Overview." In *The Labeling of Deviance: Evaluating a Perspective,* ed. Walter Gove. New York: Sage, 1975b.

Heizer, Robert M., and Edwin M. Lemert. *Observations on Archaeological Sites in Topanga Canyon, California*. University of California Publications in Archaeology and Ethnology, vol. 44, no. 2. Berkeley: University of California Press, 1947.

Kaplan, Abraham. *The Conduct of Inquiry*. San Francisco: Chandler, 1964.

Kitsuse, John. "The 'New Conception of Deviance' and Its Critics." In *The Labeling of Deviance: Evaluating a Perspective,* ed. Walter Gove. New York: Sage, 1975.

Kitsuse, John, and Aaron V. Cicourel. "A Note on the Uses of Official Statistics." *Social Problems* 11 (Fall 1963): 131–39.

Kloidt, G. "Der Soziologische Ansatz bei William I. Thomas in Licht der Soziologie Abweichenden Verhaltens." *Soziologenkorrespondenz* 5 (July 1978): 170–222.

Lasch, Christopher. *Haven in a Heartless World*. New York: Basic Books. 1977.

Laub, John. "Interview with Donald M. Cressey." In *Criminology in the Making: An Oral History,* ed. John Laub. Boston: Northeastern University Press, 1983a.

———. "Interview with Edwin M. Lemert." In *Criminology in the Making: An Oral History,* ed. John Laub. Boston: Northeastern University Press, 1983b.

Lemert, Edwin M. *Alcohol and the Northwest Coast Indians*. University of California Publications in Culture and Society, vol. 2, no. 6. Berkeley: University of California Press, 1954.

———. "Beyond Mead: The Societal Reaction to Deviance." *Social Problems* 21, no. 4 (April 1974): 457–68.

———. "Cottrell and Social Problems." *Sociological Focus* 6 (Fall 1973): 111–16.

———. "Educational Characteristics of Alcoholics: Some Critical Comments." *Quarterly Journal of Studies on Alcohol* 12 (September 1951a): 475–88.

———. "The Folkways and Social Control." *American Sociological Review* 7, no. 3 (June 1942): 394–99.

———. "The Grand Jury as an Agency of Social Control." *American Sociological Review* 10, no. 6 (December 1945): 751–58.

———. *Human Deviance, Social Problems, and Social Control*. Upper Saddle River, N.J.: Prentice Hall, 1967a.

———. *Human Deviance, Social Problems, and Social Control*. 2d ed. Upper Saddle River, N.J.: Prentice Hall, 1972. (Italian trans. C. Nazor and C. Soggia, *Devianza, Problemi Sociali, e Controllo Sociale*. Milan: Giuffre, 1981.)

———. *Instead of Court: Diversion in Juvenile Justice*. Chevy Chase, Md.: National Institute of Mental Health, Center for Studies of Crime and Delinquency; Washington, D.C.: U.S. Government Printing Office, 1971.

———. "Issues in the Study of Deviance." *Sociological Quarterly* 22, no. 2 (Spring 1981): 285–305.

———. "Juvenile Court: Quests and Realities." In *Task Force Report: Juvenile Delinquency and Youth Crime. Report of the President's Commission on Law Enforcement and the Administration of Justice*. Washington, D.C.: U.S. Government Printing Office, 1967b.

———. "Juvenile Justice Italian Style." *Law and Society Review* 20, no. 4 (Winter 1986): 509–44.

———. "Legal Commitment and Social Control." *Sociology and Social Research* 30, no. 5 (May–June 1946): 370–78.

———. "Paranoia and the Dynamics of Exclusion." *Sociometry* 25, no. 1 (March 1963): 2–20. (Italian trans. F. Basaglia and F. B. Ongaro, "La Paranoia e la Dinamica dell'Esclusione." In *La Maggioranza Deviante: L'Ideologia de Controllo Sociale Totale*. Turin: Einaudi, 1971. French trans. M. Makari, "La paranoia et le dynamisme de l'exclusion." In F. Basaglia and F. B. Ongaro, *La majorité deviante: ideologie du controle sociale total*. Paris: Union Générale d' Editions, 1976.)

———. "Response to Critics: Feedback and Choice." In *The Uses of Controversy In Sociology*, ed. L. A. Coser and O. N. Larsen. New York: Free Press, 1976.

———. *Social Action and Legal Change: Revolution within the Juvenile Court*. Chicago: Aldine, 1970.

———. *Social Pathology: Systematic Approaches to the Study of Sociopathic Behavior*. New York: McGraw-Hill, 1951b.

———. "Social Problems and the Sociology of Deviance." In *Human Deviance, Social Problems, and Social Control*. Upper Saddle River, N.J.: Prentice Hall, 1972.

———. "Social Structure, Social Control and Deviation." In *Anomie and Deviant Behavior*, ed. Marshall Clinard. New York: Free Press, 1964.

———. "Some Aspects of a General Theory of Sociopathic Behavior." *Proceedings of the Pacific Sociological Society* 16, no. 1 (1948): 23–29.

———. "Technology and Social Controls in Soviet Russia." Unpublished Ph.D. dissertation, Ohio State University, Columbus, 1939.

———. "Values, Valuation, and Choice." In *Sociology: Basic Concepts*, ed. Edward Sagarin. New York: Holt, Rinehart, 1978.

Lemert, Edwin M., and Forrest Dill. *Offenders in the Community: The Probation Subsidy in California*. Lexington, Mass.: Lexington Books, 1978.

Malherbe, Nelly. "Tendances recentes de la sociologie de la deviance aux Etats-Unis: origines et orientations générales." *Schweizerische Zeitschrift für Soziologie/Revue Suisse de Sociologie* 3, no. 2 (June 1977): 145–84.

Martindale, Don. *Institutions, Organizations, and Mass Society*. Boston: Houghton Mifflin, 1966.

Messinger, Sheldon. Letter to Michael F. Winter. September 2, 1994a.

———. Letter to Michael F. Winter. September 4, 1994b.

Panunzio, Constantine M. *Major Social Institutions*. New York: Macmillan, 1939.

Petrunik, Michael. "The Rise and Fall of 'Labeling Theory': The Construction and Destruction of a Sociological Straw Man." *Canadian Journal of Sociology* 5, no. 3 (Summer 1980): 213–33.

———. "Labeling's Maverick: Edwin Lemert and the Societal Reaction Perspective in the Sociology of Deviance, Social Problems, and Social Control." Paper presented at the Annual Meeting of the Society for the Study of Social Problems, Cincinnati, Ohio, August 1991.

Plummer, Ken. "Misunderstanding Labeling Perspectives." In *Deviant Interpretations,* ed. David Downes and Paul Rock. New York: Barnes & Noble, 1979.

Report of the Joint Fact-Finding Committee on Un-American Activities in California. Sacramento: Senate of the State of California, 1949–53.

Ross, Edward A. *Social Control: A Survey of the Foundations of Order*. Cleveland, Ohio: Case Western Reserve University Press, 1969 [1901].

Sociologists on the Labeling Perspective [1/2-inch videocassette]. Panel discussion with Edwin M. Lemert, Howard S. Becker, Aaron V. Cicourel, John Kitsuse, and David Matza. Moderated by Troy Duster. Sponsored by the Institute for the Study of Social Change, University of California, Berkeley, November 29, 1982.

Tannenbaum, Frank. *Crime and the Community*. Boston: Ginn, 1938.

Vincke, J., and Versichalen, M. "Het Etiketteerperspectif bij de Sociologische Studie van Afwijkend Gedrag." *Tijdschrift voor Sociale Wetenschapen* 26, no. 2 (June 1981): 137–54.

Winter, Michael. *Conversations with Edwin M. Lemert: Three Interviews*. June 8, July 9–10, and August 5, 1992.

———. *Interview with John Clausen*. March 8, 1995.

———. "Societal Reaction, Labeling and Social Control: The Contribution of Edwin M. Lemert." *History of The Human Sciences* 9, no. 2 (May 1996): 53–77.

Index

About the Author

Edwin M. Lemert (1912–1996), one of the foremost American sociologists of his generation, was the founder of the societal reaction theory of deviance. His many books include *Social Pathology* (1951) and two editions of *Human Deviance, Social Problems, and Social Control* (1967, 1972). In addition to his pathbreaking work in deviance and social control, he made major contributions to the study of criminology, alcoholism, law and society, and sociological jurisprudence, covering a wide and diverse range of human populations.

About the Editors

Charles Lemert is profesor of sociology at Wesleyan University in Connecticut. A prolific writer, he is the author of many books of note including, most recently, *Social Things: An Introduction to Sociological Life* (1997), and coeditor of *The Voice of Anna Julia Cooper: Including* A Voice from the South (1998).

Michael Winter is currently Behavioral Sciences Librarian, Shields Library, University of California, Davis. He is author of *The Culture and Control of Expertise: Towards a Sociological Understanding of Librarianship* (1988) and a number of articles in social theory and librarianship. His current interest is in the study of social control of knowledge and its dissemination.